The Empires of Persia: The History and Legacy of the Dynasties that Ruled Persia from Antiquity to Today

By Charles River Editors

Albor Zagros' picture of the ruins of the Gate of All Nations in Persepolis

About Charles River Editors

Charles River Editors is a boutique digital publishing company, specializing in bringing history back to life with educational and engaging books on a wide range of topics. Keep up to date with our new and free offerings with this 5 second sign up on our weekly mailing list, and visit Our Kindle Author Page to see other recently published Kindle titles.

We make these books for you and always want to know our readers' opinions, so we encourage you to leave reviews and look forward to publishing new and exciting titles each week.

Introduction

An ancient Parthian waterspout

The Empires of Ancient Persia

"By the favor of Ahuramazda these are the countries which I got into my possession along with this Persian people, which felt fear of me and bore me tribute : Elam, Media, Babylonia, Arabia, Assyria, Egypt, Armenia, Cappadocia, Lydia, the Greeks who are of the mainland and those who are by the sea, and countries which are across the sea, Sagartia, Parthia, Drangiana, Aria, Bactria, Sogdia, Chorasmia, Sattagydia, Arachosia, Hinduš, Gandara, Sacae, Maka." – An inscription on a terrace wall in Persepolis, circa 521 CE

"The Parthians in whose hands the empire of the east now is, having divided the world, as it were, with the Romans, were originally exiles from Scythia. This is apparent from their very name; for in the Scythian language exiles are called Parthi. During the time of the Assyrians and Medes, they were the most obscure of all the people of the east. Subsequently, too, when the empire of the east was transferred from the Medes to the Persians, they were but as a herd without a name, and fell under the power of the stronger. At last they became subject to the Macedonians, when they conquered the east; so that it must seem wonderful to every one, that they should have reached such a height of good fortune as to rule over those nations under whose sway they had been merely slaves. Being assailed by the Romans, also, in three wars, under the conduct of the greatest generals, and at the most flourishing period of the republic, they alone, of all nations, were not only a match for them, but came off victorious; though it may have been a greater glory to them, indeed, to have been able to rise amidst the Assyrian, Median, and Persian empires, so celebrated of o]d, and the most powerful dominion of Bactria, peopled with a thousand cities, than to have been victorious in war against a people that came from a distance; especially when they were continually harassed by severe wars with the Scythians and other neighboring nations, and pressed with various other formidable contests." – An ancient Roman account of the Parthians

Lying in the middle of a plain in modern day Iran is a forgotten ancient city: Persepolis. Built two and a half thousand years ago, it was known in its day as the richest city under the sun. Persepolis was the capital of Achaemenid Persian Empire, the largest empire the world had ever seen, but after its destruction, it was largely forgotten for nearly 2,000 years, and the lives and achievements of those who built it were almost entirely erased from history. Alexander the Great's troops razed the city to the ground in a drunken riot to celebrate the conquest of the capital, after which time and sand buried it for centuries.

It was not until the excavations of the 1930s that many of the relics, reliefs, and clay tablets that offer so much information about Persian life could be studied for the first time. Through archaeological remains, ancient texts, and work by a new generation of historians, a picture can today be built of this remarkable civilization and their capital city. Although the city had been destroyed, the legacy of the Persians survived, even as they mostly remain an enigma to the West and are not nearly as well understood as the Greeks, Romans, or Egyptians. In a sense, the Achaemenid Persian Empire holds some of the most enduring mysteries of ancient civilization.

The Parthian people created an empire that lasted almost 500 years, from the mid-3rd century BCE until 224 CE, and it stretched from the Euphrates River in the west to Central Asia and the borders of Bactria in the east (Brosius 2010, 83). In fact, the expansive empire challenged the Romans on numerous occasions for supremacy in the Near East, created the first sustainable link between the peoples of Europe and East Asia, and followed a religion that many consider to be the oldest form of monotheism in the world; but despite these accomplishments the Parthians are often overlooked in favor of the Achaemenid and Sassanid Persians who came before and after them respectively, not to mention the Romans themselves. Although the Parthians may not get top billing in most popular histories of the period, they left an indelible mark on the world that cannot be overstated.

Perhaps part of the reason why the Parthians have been overshadowed by other peoples is due to the nature of the primary sources used to reconstruct their history. Although the Parthians were literate, they wrote no histories of their dynasty and most of the extant ancient historical sources are somewhat biased since they were written by Roman and Greek historians. The Greek and Roman historians provide excellent accounts of some of the battles between the Romans and Parthians, but they are for the most part limited to warfare and view the situations almost totally from the Roman perspective. The Parthians built a number of monuments, temples, and tombs so modern archaeological excavations help scholars reconstruct some aspects of their city and court life, but again the evidence is limited and only of limited use alone. Thus, to construct an accurate chronology of the Parthian dynasty, modern scholars are forced to combine the Roman and Greek historians with the available numismatic evidence from the Parthian period since the Parthians made different coins for the reigns of most of their kings (Brosius 2010, 80). All that said, when historians combine all of the available primary sources concerning the Parthians, not only can an accurate chronology of their dynasty be compiled, but various aspects of their culture, such as economics and religion, are also made clear.

During the first half of the 1st millennium CE, an empire arose in Persia that extended its power and influence to Mesopotamia in the east, Arabia in the south, the Caucasus Mountains in the north, and as far east as India. This empire, known alternatively as the Sasanian Empire or Sassanid Empire, was the last of three great dynasties in Persia—the Achaemenid and the Parthian being the first two dynasties—before the rise of Islam. In fact, many scholars consider the Sasanian Empire to be the last great empire of the ancient Near East because once it had been obliterated, Islam became the standard religion of the region, ushering in the Middle Ages.

The Sasanian Empire was important for a number of reasons. Besides being the last of three great Persian dynasties, they carried on many Persian cultural traditions relating to religion and kingship. The Sasanians fostered and promoted the native religion of Zoroastrianism to the point of persecuting other religions from time to time. It was during the Sasanian period that the numerous Zoroastrian hymns, prayers, and rituals were collected under one book, known as the *Avesta*.

Thanks to the Sasanians' efforts with regard to religion, modern scholars know much more about Zoroastrianism than they would have if the religion continued to disseminate orally. Their efforts also protected Zoroastrian knowledge in later years after the dynasty was long gone and Islam became ascendant in Persia.

The Sasanians, like the Achaemenids and Parthians, also carried forth the Persian conflicts with the Hellenic world. Although the Achaemenids fought the Macedonian Greeks and the

Parthians challenged the imperial Romans for control of Mesopotamia, the Sasanians faced Rome in its later stages of collapse and subsequently fought the revitalized Byzantine Empire. An examination of Sasanian chronology and culture reveals that it was a much more important dynasty and empire than most may think.

The split between the two forms of Islam was already in the process of forming upon the death of the Prophet Muhammad. Muhammad had constructed around himself not only a potent new religious movement but also a powerful young state called the Ummah (the "Community" for lack of a better translation). Belonging to the Islamic faith also meant belonging to the Ummah, which was governed by its own laws and had many of its own institutions. In his own lifetime, Muhammad had ruled the Ummah through what sociologists call "charismatic authority," a term coined by Max Weber that is defined as "resting on devotion to the exceptional sanctity, heroism or exemplary character of an individual person, and of the normative patterns or order revealed or ordained by him." Hence, Muslims believe Muhammad ruled because he was uniquely chosen and endowed by God as the exemplar of all humanity, giving him a unique (though not perfect or infallible) ability to govern humanity. This was a holistic form of governance because the Prophet did not simply deliver God's words (what became the Holy Qur'an), nor did he simply pronounce upon court cases and create laws. He did all those things, but he also presented in his own person the embodiment of the best that humanity could aspire to. He was fully human, but the finest, most pious example that humans would ever produce[1].

One of the problems with charismatic authority, as Max Weber recognized and pointed out, is that charismatic authority is fragile because it cannot last beyond the lifespan of the charismatic individual without major changes. As a result, it is often difficult to create continuity after the death of a charismatic leader. Plenty of societies or movements have experienced collapse or massive upheaval after the death of a charismatic leader, such as France after Napoleon and the ancient world after Alexander the Great.

The process of converting a charismatic authority into a more stable, long-term form of government is called "routinizing charisma." In this process, the society attempts to keep some of the legitimizing elements of the deceased leader in place while also creating ways to choose new leaders. This can be agonizing, especially since new leaders rarely live up to or replace the one who has come before. That said, history has provided several successful examples, such as the Roman Empire after Julius Caesar, the Christian Church after Jesus, and the Islamic Republic of Iran after Ayatollah Khomeini.

Amid the upheaval in the Islamic world following Muhammad's death, the Umayyad Caliphate lasted for less than a century, but in that time it managed to become one of the most influential of the major caliphates established following him. Its official existence was from 661-750, and the

---

1   "Max Weber's Conceptualization of Charismatic Authority: Its Influence on Organizational Research" by Jay
     A. Conger in *Leadership Quarterly* V 4, I 3-4, pp 277-288

rulers were the male members of the Umayyad dynasty, roughly translated from Arabic as the "Sons of Umayyah." Its primary base of power was in Syria following the creation of a dynastic, hereditary rule headed by one of Syria's long-lasting governors, Muawiya ibn Abi Sufyan.

Like the other caliphates around that time, the Umayyads existed in a constant state of internal struggle and external conflict. Battles over succession, especially over which lineages possessed the more legitimate claim to power, plagued the early years of the caliphate in Syria. The most significant were the First Muslim Civil War in 661 and the Second Civil War in 680. The official right to become caliph passed between branches of the Umayyad clan, but Syria and Damascus continued to be the main seats of power even as the kingdom expanded to include the Iberian Peninsula, the Transoxiana, the Maghreb, and Sindh.

The Umayyad Caliphate became renowned for being a center of authoritarian power, education, and cultural development. The population was multiethnic and consisted of local peoples conquered throughout Africa, Europe, and Asia, including regional Christians and Jews. At its greatest extent, the empire extended over an area of 4,300,000 sq. miles, with over 33,000,000 residents. It was one of the largest known empires in history, even considering modern developments, and a precursor to the Golden Age of Islam.

Scholars throughout history have remained divided on the best way to interpret the legacy left by the Umayyads. On the one hand, they were able to unite a massive array of people and exert control over millions of square miles. On the other hand, they became infamous for their treatment of religious and ethnic minorities, were seen as turning away from God in favor of material excess, and managed to be overthrown by the millions they isolated through their policies. Through it all, they offered lessons for future Muslim kingdoms about the dangers of trying to combine religious beliefs with secular administration in a diverse world, and ultimately, the Umayyads would be replaced by the far more intelligent and crafty Abbasids, who managed to wield powerful tools like propaganda to undermine their opponents.

In terms of geopolitics, perhaps the most seminal event of the Middle Ages was the successful Ottoman siege of Constantinople in 1453. The city had been an imperial capital as far back as the 4th century, when Constantine the Great shifted the power center of the Roman Empire there, effectively establishing two almost equally powerful halves of antiquity's greatest empire. Constantinople would continue to serve as the capital of the Byzantine Empire even after the Western half of the Roman Empire collapsed in the late 5th century. Naturally, the Ottoman Empire would also use Constantinople as the capital of its empire after their conquest effectively ended the Byzantine Empire, and thanks to its strategic location, it has been a trading center for years and remains one today under the Turkish name of Istanbul.

The end of the Byzantine Empire had a profound effect not only on the Middle East but Europe as well. Constantinople had played a crucial part in the Crusades, and the fall of the Byzantines meant that the Ottomans now shared a border with Europe. The Islamic empire was viewed as a threat by the predominantly Christian continent to their west, and it took little time for different European nations to start clashing with the powerful Turks. In fact, the Ottomans would clash with Russians, Austrians, Venetians, Polish, and more before collapsing as a result of World War I, when they were part of the Central powers.

The Ottoman conquest of Constantinople also played a decisive role in fostering the Renaissance in Western Europe. The Byzantine Empire's influence had helped ensure that it was the custodian of various ancient texts, most notably from the ancient Greeks, and when Constantinople fell, Byzantine refugees flocked west to seek refuge in Europe. Those refugees brought books that helped spark an interest in antiquity that fueled the Italian Renaissance and essentially put an end to the Middle Ages altogether.

In the wake of taking Constantinople, the Ottoman Empire would spend the next few centuries expanding its size, power, and influence, bumping up against Eastern Europe and becoming one of the world's most important geopolitical players. It was a rise that would not truly start to wane until the 19th century.

The long agony of the "sick man of Europe,"[2] an expression used by the Tsar of Russia to depict the falling Ottoman Empire, could almost blind people to its incredible power and history. Preserving its mixed heritage, coming from both its geographic position rising above the ashes of the Byzantine Empire and the tradition inherited from the Muslim Conquests, the Ottoman Empire lasted more than six centuries. Its soldiers fought, died, and conquered lands on three different continents, making it one of the few stable multi-ethnic empires in history, and likely one of the last. Thus, it's somewhat inevitable that the history of its decline is at the heart of complex geopolitical disputes, as well as sectarian tensions that are still key to understanding the Middle East, North Africa and the Balkans.

When studying the fall of the Ottoman Empire, historians have argued over the breaking point that saw a leading global power slowly become a decadent empire. The failed Battle of Vienna in 1683 is certainly an important turning point for the expanding empire, as the defeat of Grand Vizier Kara Mustafa Pasha at the hands of a coalition led by the Austrian Habsburg dynasty, Holy Roman Empire and Polish-Lithuanian commonwealth marked the end of Ottoman expansionism. It was also the beginning of a slow decline during which the Ottoman Empire suffered multiple military defeats, found itself mired by corruption, and had to deal with the increasingly mutinous Janissaries (the Empire's initial foot soldiers).

Despite it all, the Ottoman Empire would survive for over 200 more years, and in the last century of its life it strove to reform its military, administration and economy until it was finally dissolved. Years before the final collapse of the Empire, the Tanzimat ("Reorganization"), a period of swiping reforms, led to significant changes in the country's military apparatus, among others, which certainly explains the initial success the Ottoman Empire was able to achieve against its rivals. Similarly, the drafting of a new Constitution (*Kanûn-u Esâsî*, basic law*)* in 1876, despite it being shot down by Sultan Abdul Hamid II just two years later, as well as its revival by the "Young Turks" movement in 1908, highlights the understanding among Ottoman elites that change was needed, and their belief that such change was possible.

Looking at the events of the empire's last two centuries, and interpreting the fall of the Ottoman Empire as a slow but long decline is what could be called the "accepted narrative." At the start of World War I, the Ottoman Empire was often described as a dwindling power, mired by administrative corruption, using inferior technology, and plagued by poor leadership. The general idea is that the Ottoman Empire was "lagging behind," likely coming from the clear stagnation of the Empire between 1683 and 1826. Yet it can be argued that this portrayal is often misleading and fails to give a fuller picture of the state of the Ottoman Empire. The fact that the other existing multicultural Empire, namely the Austro-Hungarian Empire, also did not survive World War I should put into question this "accepted narrative." Looking at the reforms, technological advances and modernization efforts made by the Ottoman elite between 1826 and the beginning of World War I, one could really wonder why such a thirst for change failed to save the Ottomans when similar measures taken by other nations, such as Japan during the Meiji era, did in fact result in the rise of a global power in the 20th century.

During the period that preceded its collapse, the Ottoman Empire was at the heart of a growing rivalry between two of the competing global powers of the time, England and France. The two powers asserted their influence over a declining empire, the history of which is anchored in Europe as much as in Asia. However, while the two powers were instrumental in the final defeat and collapse of the Ottoman Empire, their stance toward what came to be known as the "Eastern Question" – the fate of the Ottoman Empire – is not one of clear enmity. Both England and France found, at times, reasons to extend the life of the sick man of Europe until it finally sided with their shared enemies. Russia's stance toward the Ottoman Empire is much more clear-cut; the rising Asian and European powers saw the Ottomans as a rival, which they strove to contain, divide and finally destroy for more than 300 years in a series of wars against their old adversary.

Last but not least, the rise of nationalism among peoples under Ottoman domination was a key factor in the dissolution of the empire. At the end of the 19th century, shortly before its final collapse, the territory of the Ottoman Empire dwindled due to the growing call for independence coming from different ethnicities it ruled for hundreds of years. The Empire's inclusiveness, which marked it as a direct successor of the Byzantine Empire, was most certainly challenged by an aging leadership. The Ottoman Empire's inability to create a shared identity, a weak central state, and growing inner dissensions were some of the main factors explaining its long demise. Such a failure also explains the need for the creation of a new form of identity, which was ultimately provided by Mustafa Kemal, the founding father of modern Turkey.

Overall, the history of the dissolution can be defined as a race between the Empire's growing "illness" on one side (the Ottoman's inability to appease and federate the various people within its territory), and constant attempts to find a cure in the form of broad reforms. These questions are often presented together, but that tends to shift the focus outward, onto the various peoples and their aspirations, along with Europe's growing influence over the fate of the Ottoman Empire. To consider both the "illness" and the cure, it's necessary to separate them, before moving on to the direct cause of the empire's dissolution (World War I) and its heritage.

On February 1, 1979, amid great fanfare, exiled cleric Ayatollah Ruhollah Khomeini landed in Tehran. The return of the leader of the revolution to his home country was one of the final markers of the Iranian Revolution, a national phenomenon that had global implications.

The Iranian Revolution of 1979 has been described as an epochal event, called the peak of 20th century Islamic revivalism and revitalization, and analyzed as the one key incident that continues to impact politics across Iran, the Middle East, and the even the world as a whole. As a phenomenon that led to the creation of the first modern Islamic Republic in the world, the revolution marked the victory of Islam over secular politics, and Iran quickly became the aspiring model for Islamic fundamentalists and revivalists across the globe, regardless of nationality, culture, or religious sect. When Ayatollah Khomeini was declared ruler in December 1979 and the judicial system originally modeled on that of the West was swiftly replaced by one purely based on Islamic law, much of the world was in shock that such a religiously driven revolution could succeed so quickly, especially when it had such sweeping consequences beyond the realm of religion.

Revolutions are nothing new, but most revolutions, especially those in the West, have tended to remain secular. Even when religious ideology and themes were present, as in the English Civil War of the 1640s, these were not dominant driving forces behind the revolution, nor were they a significant factor in its immediate results.[3] Even outside the West, this has mostly proven to be true; the nationalist revolution and war for independence in Turkey, led by Mustafa Kemal Ataturk, was a battle for separation of church and state that called for democratic principles of equality, and the result was the formation of a modern and secular Turkey.

However, the revolution that swept across Iran proved to be starkly different from past revolutions of the world. Its most influential leaders came from the orthodox clergy, and its most pronounced important goals were the ouster of the monarch, who was deemed anti-Islam and blasphemous, and the complete return of Iranian government and society to fundamental Islamic principles. As one of the leading scholars on Iran, Nikki R. Keddie, wrote, this revolution was "aberrant," refusing to fit into the theoretical and academic ideas of what modern revolutions should be like.[4] Yet, there is no doubt that the Iranian Revolution ultimately led to a complete

---

[3] Nikki R. Keddie, "Iranian Revolutions in Comparative Perspective," *The American Historical Review* 88, no. 3 (Jun 1983): 579.

overhaul and restructuring of the age-old political, economic, social, religious, and ideological orders in Iran. Former Iranian Finance Minister Jahangir Amuzegar put it aptly, "The historical oddity, if not uniqueness, of the Iranian revolution can be seen in its four salient features: its unforeseen rapid rise; its wide base of urban support; its vague ideological character; and, above all, its ultimate singular objective, to oust the Shah."[5]

Furthermore, while the focus of the revolution was primarily about Islam, the revolution was also colored by disdain for the West, distaste for autocracy, and a yearning for religious and cultural identity. Though these are features of many other revolutions, the Iranian one was particularly unprecedented in the suddenness and rapidity of its occurrence, as well as the sheer amount of mass popular support it gained. Much of the world, including the U.S. and its Western allies, were initially caught off guard by the sudden occurrence and unanticipated strength of the revolution.

Of course, the world is now observing exceedingly religious revolutions today, including the Arab Spring of 2011, the Islamist movement that swept Egypt in 2012, and the radical Islamic fundamentalist groups that are fighting for territories in Iraq and Syria. The nature of these revolutions makes understanding the Iranian Revolution's causes and effects all the more important.

---

[4] Ibid., 580.

[5] Yuram Abdullah Weiler, "A Singular Success: The Uniqueness of the Islamic Revolution in Iran," *Tehran Times,* February 13, 2014, http://www.tehrantimes.com/component/content/article/52-guests/114075-a-singular-success-the-uniqueness-of-the-islamic-revolution-in-iran.

The Empires of Persia: The History and Legacy of the Dynasties that Ruled Persia from Antiquity to Today

The Rise of the Islamic Republic

Online Resources

Further Reading

The Foundation of the Persian Empire

The Persians had humble beginnings among the Indo-European nomadic tribes that lived in the plains of central Eurasia. They originally coexisted alongside a number of prominent Indo-European tribes, including the Medes, Khwarezmians, Sogdians, Bactrians, and Heretians.[6] However, around 550 BCE, Cyrus, a tribal leader, set off on a campaign of conquests. With his charisma, and with what the Greeks called the "fear he inspired and the terror he struck in all men," Cyrus took control of more and more territory, eventually overthrowing their primary rival, the Medes.[7]

An engraving depicting Cyrus the Great

Cyrus the Great, as he became known, subsequently founded the Persian Empire and reigned

[6] Kia, M. (2016) *The Persian Empire: A Historical Encyclopedia*. Santa Barbara: ABC - CLIO
[7] Tatum, J. (2014) *Xenophon's Imperial Fiction: On The Education of Cyrus*. Princeton : Princeton University Press

as the first king of the Achaemenid Dynasty from approximately 550-530 BCE. In just 30 years he laid the foundations of an empire whose borders would stretch from India in the east, to Greece on the Mediterranean, down to Egypt and Ethiopia, and north to what is now Russia. More than 30 different peoples were brought together under the rule of the man that called himself the "King of the World."

A map depicting the enormous extent of the Achaemenid Empire

Cyrus established his palace at the ancient city of Pasargadae. This site represented the birth of the Achaemenid rule, demonstrated Persian culture at its most sophisticated and refined, and influenced both the artistic and architectural layout and lifestyle of other urban centers in Persia. The city was founded in 550 BCE and served as the empire's first capital, but it was later abandoned by the Persian kings in favor of Susa and Persepolis. Irrigation channels were dug into the earth, leading towards the city's most stunning feature: its royal gardens.[8] The entire area in front of Cyrus's residential palace was cultivated as a walled garden called the *pairidaēza* – a word that was later adopted by the Ancient Greek and Latin languages, and which gives English the modern word "paradise."

---

[8] Stronach, D. (1978) *Pasargadae: A Report on the Excavations Conducted by the British Institute of Persian Studies from 1961–63*. Oxford: Oxford University Press

Mohammad Reza Domiri Ganji's picture of the Tomb of Cyrus in Pasargadae

Cyrus was famous throughout the ancient world for his love of gardens, to the extent that the ancient Greek writer Xenophon noted that "in all the districts that he [Cyrus] resides in, he takes great care that there are paradises full of all the beautiful things that the soil will produce."[9] No archaeologist has ever found evidence of the legendary hanging gardens of Babylon, so those of Cyrus's palace represent the earliest evidence of a formal garden found anywhere in the world. Gardens similar to this one were widely found across the empire during successive dynasties.

---

[9] Briant, P. (2002) *From Cyrus to Alexander: A History of the Persian Empire*. Winona Lake: Eisenbrauns

These gardens were seen as representations of the perfection of life, where the flowing water would have been refreshing and cool in the hot climate.[10]

Herodotus, one of the earliest Greek historians, also wrote that "the Persians adopt foreign customs more readily than any other people."[11] This sentence, written perhaps with a touch of contempt, actually reveals one of the most positive and impressive aspects of the Persian Empire. In the time of Cyrus, the economy in Asia was expanding and the people wanted stability. There was a widespread desire for ecumenism, meaning people wanted to be part of a unified world. The first to appreciate the value of this concept and to put it into practice was Cyrus. Found in Pasargadae was a sculpture of a winged genie that appears in the form of a typical Assyrian figure, dressed as an Elamite and wearing a showy Egyptian headdress.[12] The evidence suggests that the concept of a unified world, or perhaps a desire to belong to one, had originated in Persia. It also suggests that the Persians found pleasure in trying out the different lifestyles of the empire's many peoples.[13]

The Persian Empire extended into Europe under the rule of Cyrus's successors, and many other great cities were founded in modern Iran under their rule. Cambyses II added Egypt to the empire, and he was succeeded by his cousin, Darius the Great, who ruled for 36 years between 550 and 486 BCE. Under his rule the empire reached its greatest extent, stretching from the Indus Valley and Central Asia on the east to Libya and the Danube River on the west.

---

[10] Stronach, D. (2012) "Parterres and stone watercourses at Pasargadae: notes on the Achaemenid contribution to garden design." *The Journal of Garden History*, 14:1. 3 - 12
[11] Herodotus, *On The Customs of the Persians*
[12] Stronach, 1978
[13] Kia, 2016

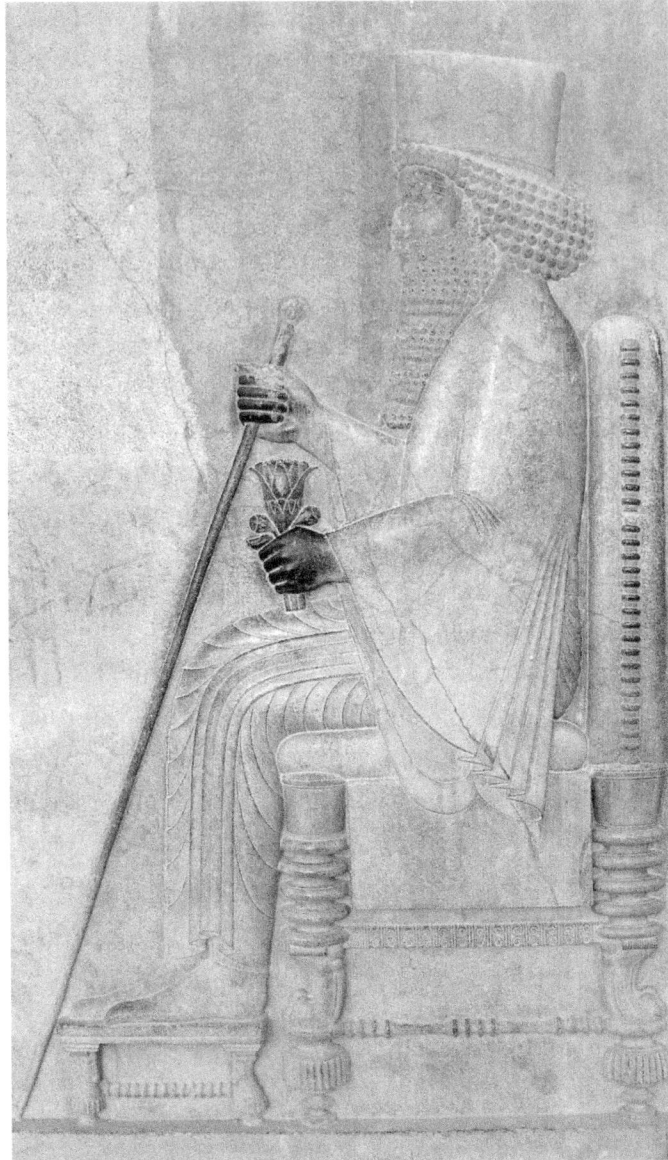

A relief in Persepolis that depicts Darius

Darius spent the earliest years of his rule stymieing revolts across the Persian territory, and he appointed satraps (local governors) to oversee the maintenance of order and collection of taxes in the diverse regions of the empire. Realizing that many of their subject peoples were just as advanced as the Persians, these satraps served as representatives of the empire but otherwise allowed local customs and laws to continue existing, as long as they swore obedience to the Persian king and paid their taxes. Darius also ordered the construction of an extensive network of roads that expedited communication and trade across his realm.

10 years after Pasargadae was founded by Cyrus, Darius I initiated a new era marked by the transfer of the Achaemenid capital to Persepolis. Historical records indicate that under Darius I the proto-Elamite city of Susa grew in splendor, becoming an imperial capital along with

Persepolis. At Susa, a great number of building foundations and the remains of massive columns attest to the presence of one of the largest palatial cities of Persia, equal in grandeur to Persepolis.[14]

It was also during this time that the importance of other parts of Mesopotamia gradually declined, with the Persian lands in modern Iran serving as the new center of cultural and political hegemony in central Asia. Nonetheless, even as the Persians were building great cities and gardens, they were still essentially a nomadic people. Like many groups in modern-day Iran, Persian communities would spend the winter months tending to their herds on the plains, and spend the hot summer months in the cool of the mountains.[15] For the Greeks, the Persians' nomadic lifestyle was a cause for mockery – escaping from the summer heat was taken as evidence of Persian unmanliness.[16] What the Greeks never understood, though, was that traveling was a key part of the Persian way of life. Their nomadic traditions always remained even after the construction of their cities – they were as at home in a tent as they were in the monumental structures of urban centers. Even around great settlements like Persepolis, there would have been a city of tents for those that came and went from the hinterland. Within these tents, one can imagine that ancient Persian life would not be too dissimilar to the kinds of images that can be seen today: cooking, the rearing of animals, the collecting of foodstuffs, and the weaving of clothing and carpets.

Hansueli Krapf's picture of the ruins of Darius's palace

---

[14] Potts, D. T. (1999) *The archaeology of Elam: formation and transformation of an ancient Iranian state.* Cambridge: Cambridge University Press

[15] Sporone, B. (1972) "The Status of Nomadism as a Cultural Phenomenon in the Middle East." *Journal of Asian and African Studies*, 7:1.

[16] Briant, 2002

Elnaz Sabar's picture of the ruins of Tachara, Darius's palace

Moreover, the Persian kings did not stay in a single place throughout the entire year. Persepolis was covered in snow for most of the winter, and thus impractical for many of the governmental functions. With such a vast empire to direct, the government could not simply shut down during this time of the year. Instead, they transferred operations to Susa – the bona fide second imperial capital in its own right.[17] They migrated seasonally, residing in Susa during the colder months and in Persepolis during the summer. These two cities were not only the political, economic, and administrative centers in the heartland of the empire but also regarded as sacred capitals. Pasargadae was used during coronation ceremonies, and Persepolis also had a key ceremonial role, having been founded as a site to hold the great annual feast of Nowruz, the Persian New Year's celebration.[18] People streamed into the city for the festival of Nowruz from neighboring areas and put up their tents in the suburbs of the capital as activities took place both outside and inside the palace grounds. The king initiated the Nowruz feast when his subjects bore him upon his throne from one capital to the other. Because of this, Persians called Persepolis Takht-i Jamshēd, which translated to "the Throne of Jamshid" (in reference to the popular mythological figure Jamshid).[19]

---

[17] Mitchell, L. and Melville, C. (2012) *Every Inch a King: Comparative Studies on Kings and Kingship in the Ancient and Medieval Worlds*. Leiden: Brill

[18] Sancisi-Weerdenburg, H. (1991) *Nowruz in Persepolis*. JW Drijvers.

Persepolis and Persian Culture

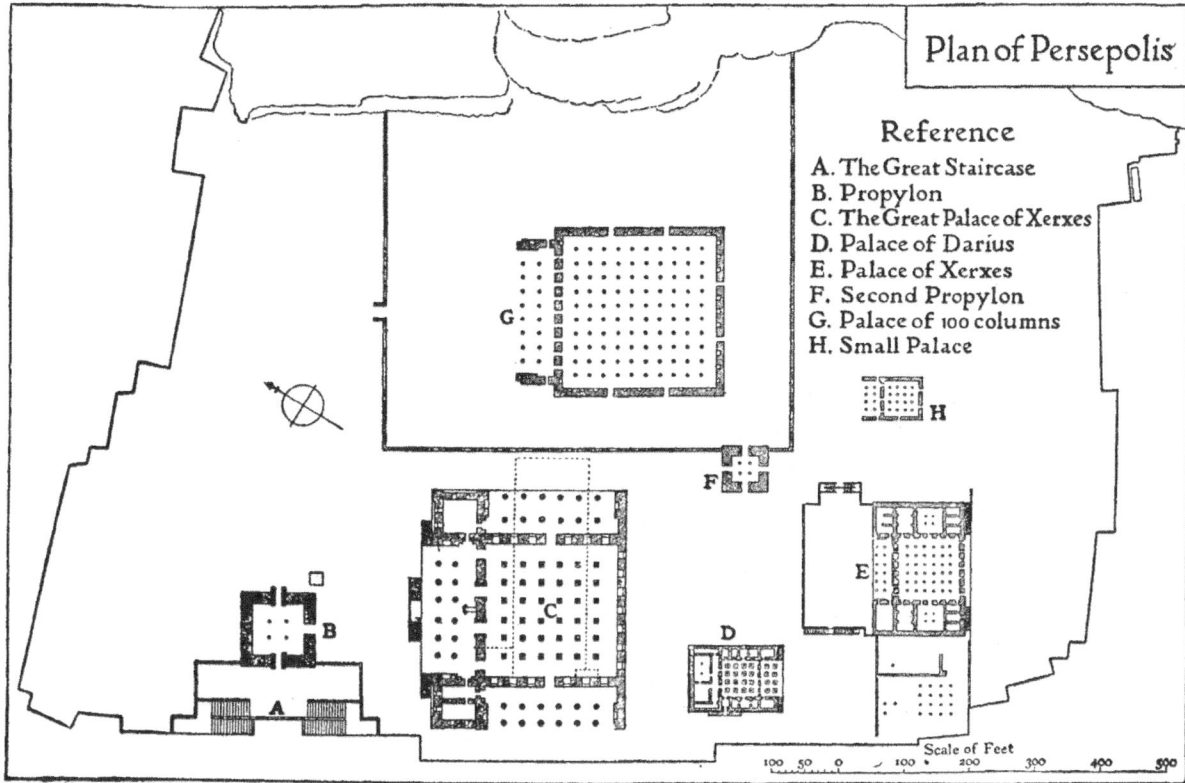

A blueprint layout of Persepolis

Positioned in the heart of the continent-sized Persian Empire was Persepolis, the greatest of all Persian cities and the key to understanding their empire's greatest achievements. "Persepolis" is the Greek designation for the acropolis of the city that was once originally called Pérsēs ("The Persians), but today it is generally applied to both the city and its acropolis. The name is attested in Achaemenid inscriptions, but after the fall of the Persian Empire and the destruction of the city, the population was no longer able to read the royal documents and inscriptions. The name of the city was gradually forgotten, and later the Sassanids called it *Sad Stun* ("The One Hundred Columned").

---

[19] Barnett, R. D. (1957) "Persepolis." *Iraq, 19:1*, 55 - 77.

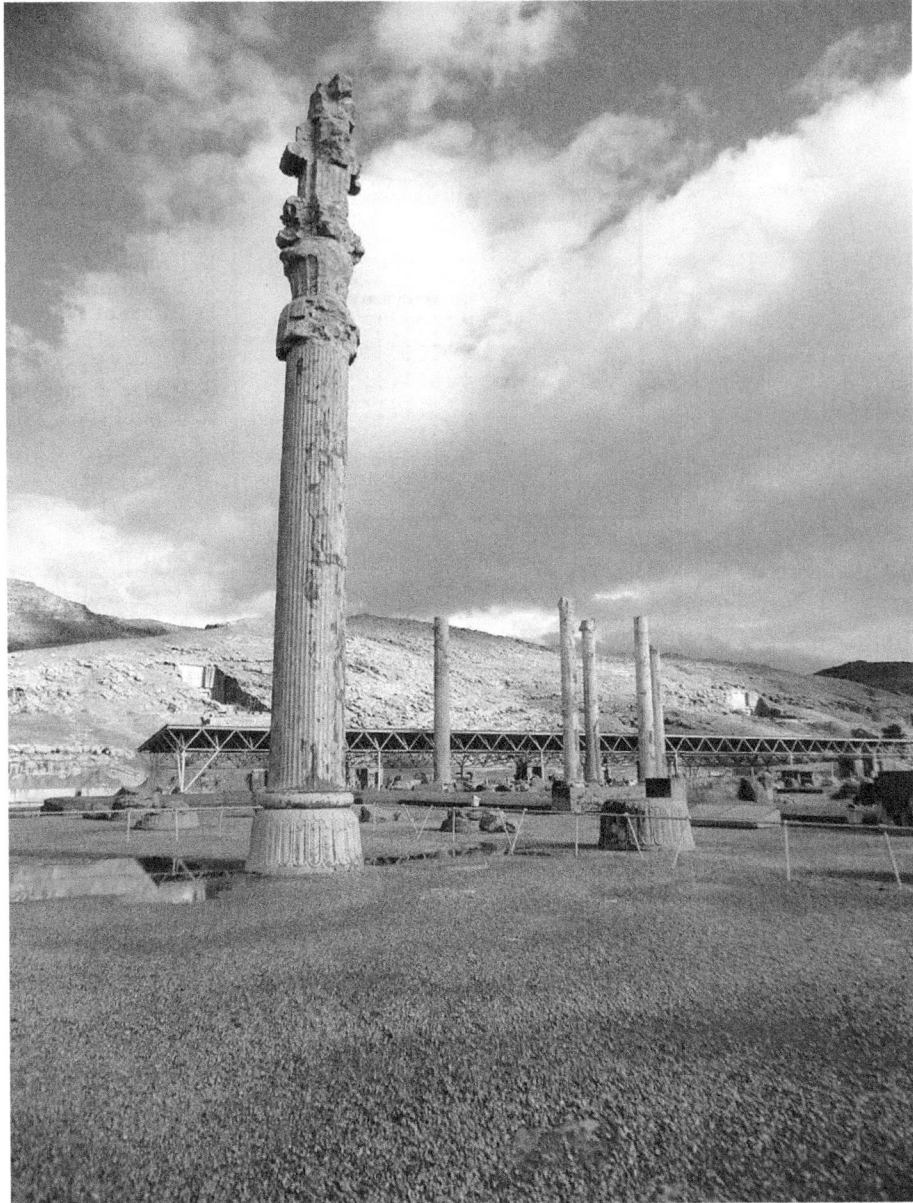

Columns at Persepolis

Persepolis is located in the Fars Province of modern-day Iran, approximately 70 miles northeast of modern-day Shiraz. Ancient Persia was composed of a broad range of ecozones, including plateaus, rainforests, deserts, plains, and mountain ranges – each containing a diversity of flora and fauna, and a climate ranging from arid to sub-tropical. The characteristics of the landscape in and around Persepolis were major factors in the site's growth and success. In particular, the city's success depended strictly upon its relationship with the ecology, climate, and resources of the Marvdasht Plain, a remote and barren land surrounded by sharp cliffs and fertile foothills of the Zagros Mountains, and part of the Kur River Basin.[20] This area was settled

---

[20] Hartnell, T. M. (2012) "Persepolis in context: A landscape study of political economy in ancient Persia."

around the first millennium BCE. The climate of the region affected Persepolis dramatically. During the rainy season of the Iranian winter the surrounding landscape became muddy and impassible. Therefore, most activity in the city took place during the warmer spring and summer seasons.

Archaeologists have been able to attribute most of the structures and phases of construction in Persepolis to the reign of one emperor. Persepolis was founded shortly before 500 BCE by Darius the Great, the fourth king of the Achaemenid Dynasty. The first period of construction took place between 518 and 490 BCE. During this time, the monumental terrace was constructed along with the Apadana audience hall and Treasury building, with the eastern stairs serving as the access point.[21] King after king added to Darius's creation. The second period of construction began from around 490 BCE as Darius initiated the construction of the Taçara, "winter palace" and the Gate of All Nations with its stairway, and expanded the Apadana. Many of these structures were completed during the third period of construction between 480 and 470 BCE, under the rule of his son, Xerxes I. Xerxes I, the greatest foe of the Greeks, succeeded Darius in 486 and ruled until 465 BCE.

Ruins of the Apadana in Persepolis

ProQuest.
[21] Wilber, D. N. (1989) *Persepolis: The Archaeology of Parsa, Seat of the Persian Kings*. Princeton: Darwin Press

Arya Mahasattva's picture of a relief on the Apadana that depicts an Armenian bearing tribute to the Persians

A relief depicting Xerxes

Jona Lendering's picture of a relief of Xerxes located at Persepolis

The largest part of Persepolis – a sort of second city – was built by the succeeding emperors of Xerxes down to Darius III. Under Xerxes's rule the Hadiš, Queen's Quarters, Tripylon, and Southern Buildings were constructed. After Xerxes, Persepolis continued to expand considerably, and friezes and bas-reliefs of this period depict it as a time of great celebration and expansion of the empire. This gives a sense of how strong and solid the empire was – quite the opposite of the barbarian images that the ancient Greeks handed down to Western civilization. Under the rule of Artaxerxes I, the Hall of One Hundred Columns was constructed, along with his palace and the garrison quarters.[22] The final phase of construction took place from the turn of the century to Alexander's invasion in 334 BCE.[23] During this time the royal tombs of Artaxerxes II and Artaxerxes III were excavated, the Palace of Artaxerxes III was constructed along with the Hall of Thirty Two Columns, and a new road and gate were started.

Masoud Khalife's picture of the ruins of Artaxerxes I's palace

In approximately 518 BCE, Darius selected a huge rock on the northwestern side of a hill called Kouh-e Rahmat ("Mountain of Mercy") for the construction of an immense terrace, upon which a fort, palaces, audience halls, and a treasury would later be built.[24] Large sections of the original rock were cut away, with the stone carved into immense stone blocks, and these blocks were used together with rough boulders, smaller stones, and mud to construct the terrace. It took almost a century for this giant platform to be completed, but when it did, it covered an area of more than 125,000 square meters.

Due to its massive size, the construction of the palatial complex took place in a series of stages. The finished terrace was between 45-55 feet high, with the southern part lower than the rest. This area was where the original access point was located.[25] Water channels were dug into the

---

[22] Wilber, 1989
[23] Wilber, 1989
[24] Kia, 2016

bedrock and the hillside, with an outlet dug in the form of a long and deep moat located behind the eastern wall. Originally, there was a fortification wall that went around its entire circumference, including the ridge and crest of the adjacent Kouh-e Rahmat.[26]

The terrace was later accessed by a series of monumental double-staircases on the northwestern side of the acropolis platform. The construction of the staircases was ordered by Xerxes. Each flight had 111 steps and each step was about 20 feet wide and 38 centimeters deep, but with a very shallow rise of just 10 centimeters. The steps were deliberately given broad width and short height so that the large number of military and civil officers, and representatives of the subject nations who came to the city, could climb with ease and in groups, as seen in the frieze of the Tripylon staircase.[27]

A. Davey's picture of the double staircase

Located east of these stairs was the Gate of All Nations, the monumental entrance portal that provided access to the ceremonial core of the city. Two massive guardian bulls supported the pillars of the west doorway. These were images of kingship and royal strength known as *lamassu* that had been adopted from the Babylonian civilization and became widely used throughout the Persian homeland.[28] They announced to visitors that they were entering the heart of royal Persian

[25] Wilber, 1989

[26] Aminzadeh, B., and Samani, F. (2006) "Identifying the boundaries of the historical site of Persepolis using remote sensing." *Remote Sensing of Environment, 102*:1. 52 - 62

[27] Aminzadeh and Samani, 2006

[28] Codella, K.C. (2007) *Achaemenid Monumental Gateways at Pasargadae, Susa and Persepolis.* Berkeley:

power. The gate was covered in a cedar wood roof, and its doors were adorned with gold fittings.[29] Walking through the enormous structure, visitors were asked to stand and wait in a four columned hall, sitting on benches of black marble that abutted the walls. These walls were covered in glazed tiles that were decorated with patterns of lotus flowers, palm trees, and stars. Here, the foreign delegates would be arranged in groups depending on the distance they had traveled to reach Persepolis before being allowed to access the imperial platform.[30] A master of ceremonies would stand on a platform abutting one of the walls, observing the hall and within view of the king's palace, where a representative would give him a signal to send forth the delegates.[31] They would then proceed through the southern doorway. Persian dignitaries, in contrast to those from vassal states outside of the Persian heartland, would pass through the eastern doorway, the pillars of which were supported by additional human-headed *lamassu* bulls.[32]

A relief with a lotus flower

University of California Press
[29] Codella, 2007
[30] Codella, 2007
[31] Codella, 2007
[32] Codella, 2007

A. Davey's picture of a relief depicting lotus flowers

Fulvio Spada's picture of a lamassu at the Gate of All Nations

At the heart of Persepolis was the Apadana, an audience hall where the Persian king received his subjects – and where the mysteries of the city truly begin. The Apadana took 30 years to complete and covered an area of 3,600 square meters – almost as large as a modern-day football field. It is believed that the enormous hall could have accommodated up to 10,000 people. Its walls were nearly six meters thick.[33] Today, only 14 of the original columns still stand, but in its original state, 72 columns, each over 80 feet high, held up another massive cedar wood ceiling. Each column was supported by a square base with a fluted shaft and a capital in the form of a

---

[33] Wilber, 1989

double-headed bull (unusually the capitals of the eastern portico had a double-headed lion instead).[34] The floor would likely have been covered in costly carpets and rugs, and the walls would have been adorned with glazed tiles, decorated with variegated floral motifs, rows of cedar and palm trees, files of soldiers, and even cuneiform inscriptions.[35]

---

[34] Wilber, 1989

[35] Root, M. C. (1985) "The Parthenon Frieze and the Apadana Reliefs at Persepolis: Reassessing a Programmatic Relationship." *American Journal of Archaeology, 89:1.* 103 - 120

An imagined reconstruction of the Apadana

Ruins of the Apadana

The construction of this extraordinary palace was a remarkable achievement, so Darius the Great ordered a trilingual inscription in the Old Persian, Akkadian, and Elamite languages to be prepared. It listed his name and the extent of his realm, and was copied onto four pairs of gold and silver tablets. Each pair of tablets were placed within a stone box and deposited inside the foundation wall at each of the four corners of the hall.[36] King Xerxes made some modifications to the Apadana, as attested by an inscription on glazed bricks discovered there that state, "The great king Xerxes says: By the grace of Ahuramazda, much that had been ordered by King Darius, my father, was well. It was also by the grace of Ahuramazda that I completed these works and made it excellent."[37] However, it is unknown precisely what these later works were.

The Apadana was where the Persian kings received tribute from all of the peoples of their empire, and where they could portray themselves as conquerors of the world. After climbing the staircases and through the deep portico, the foreign dignitaries would have been led through a massive set of doorways, each 60 feet high and covered with sheets of decorative gold patterns, lions, and bulls. Unfortunately, nothing remains today apart from the massive doorsills. Visitors

---

[36] Root, 1985

[37] Livius (no date) "Achaemenid Royal Inscriptions: XPg." (http://www.livius.org/aa-ac/achaemenians/XPg.html)

would have had to go through a specific series of ceremonial actions when they entered the great hall, as indicated by the bas-reliefs carved throughout the acropolis. They would have fallen to their knees in front of the king, and then immediately prostrated themselves on the ground, before giving the gifts or tribute and slowly backing out of the great throne room.[38]

The most beautiful and important surviving part of the Apadana is the eastern portico frieze, which is decorated with exquisite sculptured bas-reliefs. This frieze was likely created in the final years of the 6th century BCE and is believed to have been the work of *Yaunâ* sculptors from Greece.[39] The inner façade of the Apadana eastern portico frieze that faces the courtyard, is decorated with lines of soldiers, dignitaries, and courtiers adorning one wing, and twenty-three gift-bearing delegations on another. The northern part of the frieze depicts a troupe of dignitaries from within the Persian homeland marching alongside horsemen and charioteers. At the center are eight armed men and a winged sun.

On the southern area of the frieze is depicted a procession of dignitaries from all over the Persian Empire traveling to Persepolis to give gifts and pay tribute to the great Persian king. 23 nations have been identified in this stairway frieze, and among those represented are Thracians from Southeast Europe, Syrians and Cappadocians from the Levant and Anatolia, Aryans, Bactrians, and Sogdians from the East, Arabs from the South, Babylonians from ancient Mesopotamia, and Libyans from Africa.[40] The nations were identified by their styles of dress or facial features; the Medes were those with round caps, the Persians had straight caps, and the Elamites had their distinctive robes.[41] They are shown bringing objects and commodities from different parts of the empire, such as fine horses, shaggy mountain goats, camels, ivory tusks, carts gold, and jewelry.

---

[38] Root, 1985

[39] Root, M. C. (2007) Reading Persepolis in Greek: Gifts of the Yauna. *Persian Responses: Political and Cultural Interaction with (in) the Achaemenid Empire*, 177 - 224

[40] Root, 1985

[41] Root, 1985

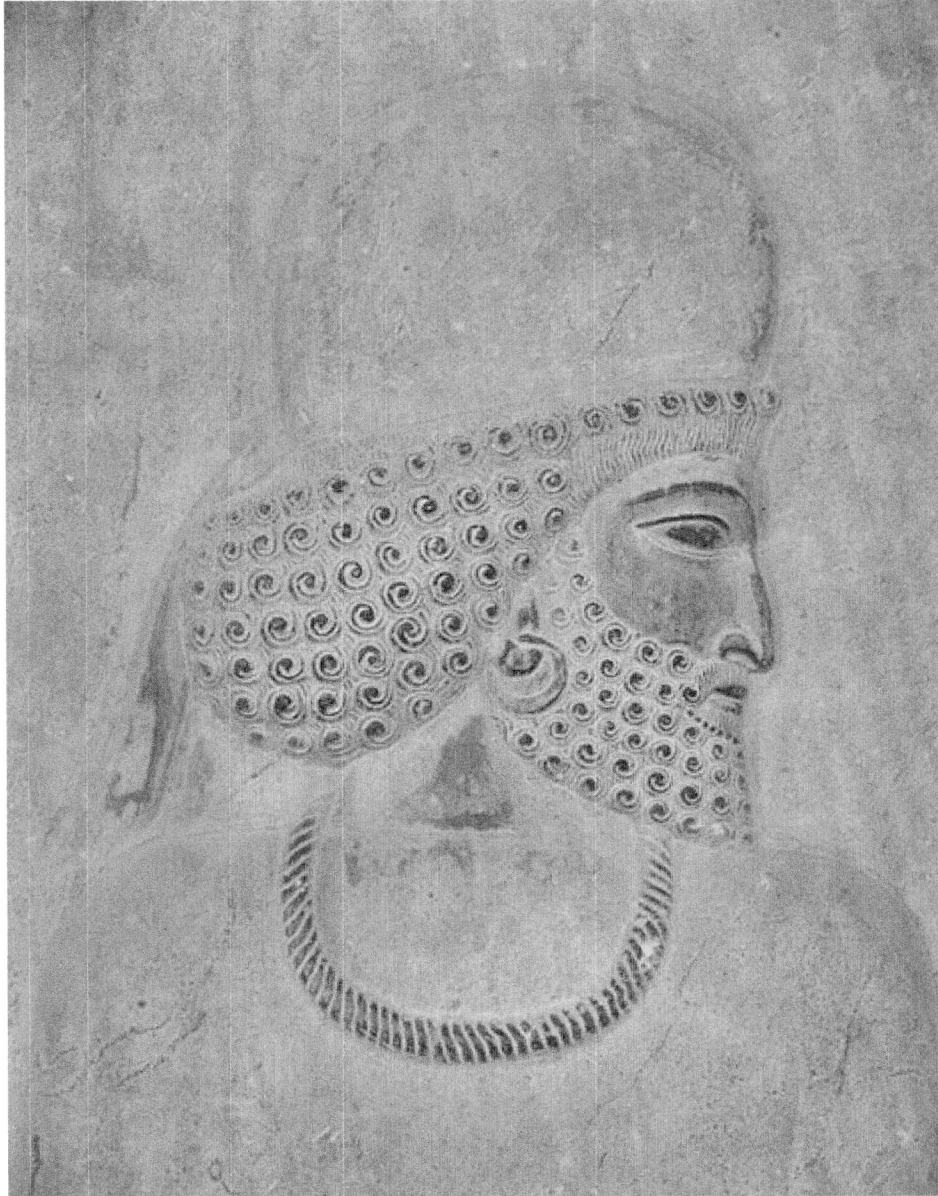

Albor Zagros' picture of a depiction of a Mede

Phillip Malwald's picture of Armenians bringing wine to the king

Bon Tenbal's picture of Medes and Persians

Some of the figures possess characteristics that mark them as figures of great importance. For example, one Elamite is wearing a diadem in his curly hair and brings with him lions to offer to the Persian leader, all of which are signs of royalty.[42] Some of the objects that are shown on the friezes have been discovered by archaeologists, such as a tall golden vessel with handles in the shape of griffins. Most of these dignitaries are shown carrying a lotus-like flower, and some hold round objects, both of which are still associated with the Nowruz festival.[43] This displayed both the wealth and power of the Persian Empire.

The frieze was also covered in symbolic imagery. Floral rosettes with 12 petals are shown, likely symbolizing the 12 months of the year, as well as cypress trees and an evergreen plant that was considered auspicious and paradoxical by the Persians.[44] These have been interpreted as symbols of perpetual happiness and prosperity. A lion attacking a bull is shown beneath the sculpted cypress trees, with the lion's head depicted frontally – a perspective that is very unusual compared to the side-on profiles of the figures shown elsewhere across the city. The most accepted interpretation of this scene is its astronomical association. The lion Leo was one of the signs of the Persian zodiac and was associated with the sun.[45] The bull Taurus was also one of the star signs that had been identified by this time. These stars were closely associated with the Vernal Equinox, which in the Persian calendar marked the start of the Nowruz festival.[46] It may also have signified "eternity," the symbolism of which would not have been lost among those attending ceremonies at the site that were designed to strengthen the ties between the diverse parts of the empire.

This frieze indicates that Persepolis was less a military capital, and instead first and foremost a symbolic and ceremonial place. From all over the empire, subject peoples came here to give their gifts to the king. The formal presentation of tribute confirmed the loyalty of the subject nations and the power of the king. A walk to the king followed a specific route through the complex, intended to maximize the impact of the architecture. Thousands of years later, it's still possible to imagine the cacophony of noise that would have been caused by the procession as they climbed the great staircases of the unfamiliar city before they finally reached the Gate of All Nations. Coming from the far-flung corners of the empire, few of these people would have ever seen a structure like this, ensuring that every visitor in ancient times who was allowed to climb to the royal terrace would have been in total awe.

The Royal Treasury was one of the first buildings to be constructed on the platform. Its

---

[42] Root, 1985
[43] Sancisi-Weerdenburg, 1991
[44] Root, 1985
[45] Hartner, W. (1965) "The Earliest History of the Constellations in the near East and the Motif of the Lion-Bull Combat." *Journal of Near Eastern Studies, 24:* ½. 1 - 16
[46] Hartner, 1965

function was interpreted from the artifacts discovered there, among which was a cache of 750 clay tablets inscribed with texts in the Elamite language.[47] These tablets preserved the record of payments to those employed in Persepolis. Needless to say, this archive is crucial because it sheds light on the administration of the work and conditions of the laborers at Persepolis, providing information on the division of work, the ethnic background of many employees, and their classification according to skills and gender.[48] Both men and women were hired as laborers at Persepolis and were paid in kind or cash according to their skills and nature of their work.[49] The tablets also record the staff of the Treasury itself. They indicate that more than 1,300 people worked there.[50]

Also found in the Treasury was a statue of Penelope, wife of the legendary Greek figure Odysseus. The statue may have been stolen from Greece during the campaigns there led by Darius I in 480 BCE, or it might have been gifted to the king by a foreign dignitary.[51]

The second-largest palace of Persepolis was a splendid building with a central hall containing 100 hundred columns, which gave the structure its name: the Hall of 100 Columns. Its construction was started by Xerxes and completed by his son, Artaxerxes I. The columns of the building were laid out in 10 rows of 10 columns each, built of a local dark-grey stone. Each had a bell-shaped base, fluted shaft, and was adorned on the top with floral designs and a gilded double-headed bull, upon whose backs rested the cedar rafters that supported the ceiling. The hall was over 200 feet long and 200 feet wide, and access was provided by four main doorways, two to the south and two to the north.[52] The doorways to the south were decorated with the figures of the king in audience, with subjects carrying his throne. Those to the north depict five rows of 10 figures, each shown from one perspective of their profile on either side of the doorway. These one hundred individuals represented the most senior officials of the empire – an analogy to the symbolism of the hundred columns within the hall.[53]

---

[47] Cameron, G. G. (1958) "Persepolis Treasury Tablets old and new." *Journal of Near Eastern Studies, 17*:3. 161 - 176
[48] Cameron, 1958
[49] Cameron, 1958
[50] Cameron, 1958
[51] Olmstead, C. M. (1950) "A Greek lady from Persepolis." *American Journal of Archaeology, 54*: 1. 10 - 18
[52] Wilber, 1989
[53] Wilber, 1989

Luis Argerich's picture of a column with heads of bulls

It's believed that this structure was an additional audience hall, though at an unknown point in time it was converted into storage rooms. Not everyone was allowed to approach the king. Sometimes visitors would have to be content with a glimpse of the emperor. According to bas-reliefs, when the king sat on his throne, he was enclosed in curtains and shrouded in shadow. The sparkling of his golden scepter was the signal that granted the right to speak. Only a select few would have been allowed to approach the king and pay homage to him with a deferential kiss known as *proskynesis*.[54]

Some of the most beautiful works of Persian art have been found in the Hall of 100 Columns. Their art was depicted in a very stylized manner, from the way they rendered the curls of hair to the extraordinarily detailed animals with evocative facial expressions.[55] There is also evidence that the friezes were painted in bright colors. The costumes for all of the foreign delegates are rendered in such detail that it is clear the Persian artists were fascinated by the variety of peoples they witnessed visiting the city. Also found in the building was the miniature bust of a young prince made of lapis lazuli and eyes of precious stones, now lost. Another work of art there was a small tile ornamented with an eagle with outstretched wings – the royal ensign of the Persian Empire.[56]

After presiding over the grand procession in the Apadana, the king would withdraw to the central palace known as the Tripylon (the "Triple Gate"), a private room for the king and his councilors located in between the Apadana and Hall of 100 Columns.[57] The building is composed of a main hall supported by four massive columns, each decorated with capitals sculpted in the shape of *lamassu* bulls. The eastern doorway depicts the mirror images of a ceremonial scene showing the Persian king seated on a royal chair, with his crown prince standing behind him.[58] They are both upon a massive platform that is being carried into the hall by 28 people – an image that may allude to what happened inside the structure. The north and south doors of the Tripylon led to the king's private apartments; these were also heavily decorated, this time showing the king leaving the building.

It was here that the king would meet with his trusted aides to improve the organization of his empire. In this chamber, the council resolved to build new roads, chart new sea routes, establish a unified system of weights and measures (evidence of which has been discovered in the Treasury), and adopt a common currency using bi-metal coins of gold and silver. That said, some scholars argue that this structure was nothing more than a monumental corridor connecting the Apadana and Hall of 100 Columns.

One of the first palaces built on the Persepolis platform was the Taçara ("winter palace"), located to the southwest of the Apadana and facing south. This was intended to serve as the private residence of Darius, but he died before construction was completed, so it was finished by his son, Xerxes.[59] The façade of the building was almost exactly modeled after Achaemenid royal tombs from Darius onwards, and its lintels carved in an Egyptian style also showed a striking resemblance to the palace of the Sasanian king Ardašir I in the city of Firuzabad.[60] Bas-

[54] Balcer, J. M. (1978) "Alexander's Burning of Persepolis." *Iranica Antiqua, 13.*

[55] Pope, A. U., Ackerman, P., and Besterman, T. (1964) *A survey of Persian art from prehistoric times to the present.* Oxford : Oxford University Press.

[56] Cahill, N. (1985) "The Treasury at Persepolis: gift-giving at the city of the Persians." *American Journal of Archaeology,* 373 - 389.

[57] Wilber, 1989

[58] Wilber, 1989

[59] Llewellyn-Jones, L. (2013) *King and court in ancient Persia 559 to 331 BCE.* Edinburgh: Edinburgh University Press

reliefs were carved into the door frames and façade depicting the king entering the building carried by a retinue of servants. Other motifs show the king's warriors slaying lions, winged bulls, and other beasts.[61] The columns and ceiling of this palace were probably wooden, though no trace of them has survived. There were many royal inscriptions carved into the walls, doorways, window frames, and even on doorknobs of the palace. The floor was paved with red tiles and likely covered in beautiful carpets. One particularly splendid room within this complex was a room dimly lit by light streaming through the window spaces which then reflected off of the highly polished stonework within. The architectural work was created with such a refined polish and beauty that people called it "the Mirror Hall."[62]

Sometime after 375 BCE, Artaxerxes III added a gate and staircase on the western side of the palace.[63] Upon the doorframe, he had inscribed messages that proclaimed his royal lineage and the buildings constructed during his reign. It is believed that a garden was also cultivated during this period, as small water channels were installed close to the gate,[64] and the clay tablets found in Persepolis list the different trees and plants that were planted here.[65] They showed that the composition of the garden was deeply symbolic. There were seedlings for thousands of different types of plants – including mulberries, olives, and dates – that had been collected by the king. These were trees that he had imported from all over his empire to reflect the size and extent of his power in this garden space. This garden was another form of political statement, because by making plants grow in an otherwise barren landscape, and by creating something ordered in an otherwise chaotic environment, the Persian kings showed all who came that they were the masters of the world.[66]

Close to the Mirror Hall was the palace of Xerxes, built on the south side of the terrace. Known as the Hadiš, it measured over 7,500 square feet, making it twice as large as the palace of Darius.[67] The main hall in the palace featured 36 columns, and surrounding it were three rooms on its eastern side, and three on its western side. On the northern side was a wide portico facing the Apadana. The decorative scheme of this building was similar to that of Darius's palace, with bas-reliefs that depicted the king being carried by servants as he entered and exited his residence. Located in between the palace of Darius and that of Xerxes is a very well preserved interconnecting stairway frieze depicting Ahura Mazda flanked on each side by sphinxes and members of the king's bodyguard. According to Classical writers, this elite core of the Persian army consisted of 10,000 foot soldiers carefully selected to protect the emperor. The number

---

[60] Llewellyn-Jones, 2013

[61] Wilber, 1989

[62] Golabchi, M., and Khorramirouz, M. (2009) "Assessment of structural components of Iranian heritage building: Persepolis." *Struct Stud Repairs Maint Herit Archit, 11.* 161 - 172

[63] Wilber, 1989

[64] Stronach, D. (1990) "The garden as a political statement: Some case studies from the Near East in the first millennium BC." *Bulletin of the Asia Institute, 4.* 171 - 180.

[65] Stronach, 1990

[66] Stronach, 1990

[67] Wilber, 1989

always remained at 10,000, because as soon as one died or was injured another immediately replaced him. For this reason, the corps was known as "The Immortals," or the "apple bearers."[68] Based on the depictions of these troops at the Palace of Xerxes and on glazed bricks at Susa, their uniforms were very colorful and shone with brilliant golden and floral designs.[69] The king they defended represented the unified state, and the sole ruler capable of imposing order onto the world. In some parts of the empire, he was even viewed as a divinity.

The aforementioned halls represent the most well-known structures on the acropolis, but many other buildings were constructed there. There were various residential areas and small private palaces scattered throughout the acropolis. On the lower southern side of the platform was a complex known as the Southern Buildings, which may have been used as store rooms or residential quarters for slaves and servants.[70] These were built by Xerxes between approximately 480 and 470 BCE. It is believed that they stand on top of the earliest point of access to the acropolis.

Located west of the palaces of Darius and Xerxes was a series of structures known today as the Garrison Quarters, though it is unknown precisely what their function once was. These were constructed during the reign of Artaxerxes I and feature a very well-preserved kitchen area, complete with a mud-brick oven.[71]

East of Xerxes's palace and west of the Treasury is the so-called Queen's Quarters, an L-shaped complex also constructed during the period of Xerxes' rule. Although it has been called a "harem," these institutions did not exist in Persia during the Achaemenid period of rule; the title was given by later European explorers drawing upon fanciful stories of the Persian king's 360 wives as described by the Greeks.[72]

Although less well-preserved in comparison to those of Darius and Xerxes, King Artaxerxes III had his own splendid palace constructed on the acropolis during his reign. His palace was located in between the palace of Xerxes and the Apadana. The floor plan was roughly identical with that of Darius's palace. The western section of the palace was decorated with a series of horned stone crenellations.[73] Artaxerxes III also constructed a structure known as the Hall of 32 Columns on the acropolis, though its function is not known.

To the north of the Hall of 100 Columns is an unfinished gate started under the rule of Artaxerxes III, which was originally intended to be a counterpart to the Gate of All Nations. It is believed that from the mid-4th century on this served as the main access point to the terrace, with

---

[68] Charles, M. B. (2011) "Immortals and Apple Bearers: towards a better understanding of Achaemenid infantry units." *The Classical Quarterly, 61*:1, 114 - 133.
[69] Charles, 2011
[70] Wilber, 1989
[71] Wilber, 1989
[72] In reality, the Persian king may have had up to four wives, as indicated by inscribed tablets found in Persepolis.
[73] Wilber, 1989

a thoroughfare known today as the "Army Road" or "Procession Road" leading from this entrance to the Gate of All Nations.[74] Located along the road were unfinished capitals carved in the shape of unusual eagle-headed griffins, believed to represent the *Huma* bird of Persian mythology.[75]

The incomplete status of the gate has provided scholars with a glimpse at the process by which many of the structures in Persepolis were built. For example, unfinished slabs were laid over one another before being carved into shape because the artists did not want to damage the lower parts with falling chips as they were working on the upper sections.

There were also a series of fortifications separating the acropolis from the lower city of Pérsēs, which surrounded the ceremonial core of Persepolis to the south, west, and northwest.[76] This area was likely occupied before Darius started construction of the terrace, though little is known about its earliest history. The lower city was an entire city of servant's houses, artisan's workshops, and everything else that served life in the king's court. Much of this is still waiting to be revealed by archaeologists, and for their secrets to be discovered.

The limited archaeological studies have revealed the foundations of a few large buildings, most of which were built in the traditional Persian style of square-shaped mud bricks much like those of the acropolis. Many of the door jambs were made of stone, which was very abundant in Persepolis perched, as it was, on a terrace of rock. One is particularly well-preserved, showing a floor plan that consisted of a residential core including a central hall surrounded by smaller rooms, with a square courtyard accessed by a short flight of stairs.[77]

The lower city seems to have been looted and razed during the period of Alexander's conquest and remained uninhabited after his armies had moved on.

---

[74] Wilber, 1989
[75] Codella, 2007
[76] Wilber, 1989
[77] Wilber, 1989

Masoud Khalife's picture of the ruins on the eastern side of Persepolis

In Persia, if someone wanted to offer tribute to a deity, they would have been hard pressed to do so because there were no temples. All over Persia, altars have been found standing alone on open hilltops, and the traces left by fires during sacrifices can still be found. Along with other evidence, these have contributed to historians' understanding of the Persian religion.

For the Persians, all of creation was divine – the sky, the earth, and all of its elements. The Persians considered natural phenomena, such as water, wind, earth, and fire, as sacred attributes.[78]

---

[78] Henkelman, W. (2008) *The other gods who are: studies in Elamite-Iranian acculturation based on the Persepolis Fortification texts*. Nederlands instituut voor het Nabije Oosten.

Hence, sacrifices were not held in an enclosed temple, but outside under the open sky. They offered their sacrifices to the sun, the sky, the moon, the earth, and fire. The earliest believers may have worshiped these as deities, thanks to their association with some of the most fundamental aspects of daily life.

However, around the 8th century BCE, fundamental changes occurred in religious beliefs across the region, as demonstrated in the *Shahnameh* (the "Book of Kings") – an epic history of the Iranian people written sometime in the late first millennium CE by the Persian poet Ferdowsi. In this, it is made perfectly clear that these people had begun to believe in a sort of monotheism, which had been reformed and made more ethical by Zoroaster (Zarathustra) sometime during this time.[79] Although little is known of Zoroaster's life, other than that he was Persian, his teachings were not actually compiled and documented until as late as the third century CE – many centuries after his death. Nonetheless, his teachings of a dualistic religion, and of the eternal conflict between good/truth and evil/deception, had a profound impact on Persian society. Their faith was directed towards the worship of a single deity known as Ahura Mazda, who incarnated the supreme good. Other deities were reinterpreted as being nothing more than demons and devils.

A depiction of Zoroastrian symbols

Zoroastrianism became the principle religion of the Achaemenid dynasty. On the southern retaining wall of the acropolis terrace, there are two inscriptions that describe the extent and nature of its connection to Persian royal power. Both are written in the Aryan alphabet, a script created under the orders of King Darius I to be used for Achaemenid royal inscriptions. These

---

[79] Ferdowsi, A. (2016) *Shahnameh: The Persian book of kings*. Penguin

attest to the importance of Ahura Mazda to the rulers of Persepolis.[80] Ahura Mazda was the principle Zoroastrian god, the lord of wisdom who was worshiped at fire temples. However, the Persians did not force the people of their empire to believe in Ahura Mazda. They allowed freedom of worship; sacrifices could be dedicated to any god they wished. The Jewish book of Ezra offers an independent account, in which the Persians are praised for liberating the Jews and allowing them to practice their religion freely.[81]

Two Achaemenid kings, Artaxerxes II and Artaxerxes III, had their tombs cut into the rock above Persepolis, on the sacred Kuh-e Mehr (Mountain of Mithra), which was known as the Kuh-e Ramat (Mount of Mercy) from the 13th century on.[82] This site was closely associated with the ancient Persian deity Mithra, god of oases and of the sun.[83] There were an additional four Achaemenid royal tombs excavated at Naqš-i Rustam, a necropolis located approximately twelve kilometers to the northwest of Persepolis. A few miles from Persepolis, archaeologists discovered a well-preserved small building with a square foundation, known today as the Cube of Zoroaster.[84] What it was is still a mystery, sparking vigorous debate among scholars, not just because of its unknown origin but also for its location close to the walls of Mount Naqsh-e Rustam. There are several hypotheses regarding this site; some say that it is a temple of fire, and others believe that it is a watchtower.[85] The most alluring idea is that it was once a library where sacred texts were kept.[86]

---

[80] Pope, A. U. (1957) "Persepolis as a ritual city." *Archaeology, 10*:2, 123 - 130

[81] Littman, R. J. (1975) "The Religious Policy of Xerxes and the" Book of Esther"." *The Jewish Quarterly Review, 65*:3, 145 - 155

[82] Schmidt, E. F. (2009) *Persepolis III: the royal tombs and other monuments*. Chicago: Chicago University Press.

[83] Kia, 2016

[84] Schmitt, R. (Ed.). (2000) *The Old Persian Inscriptions of Naqsh-i Rustam and Persepolis* (Vol. 1). London: School of Oriental and African Studies.

[85] Schmitt, 2000

[86] Schmitt, 2000

O. Mustafin's picture of the Tomb of Artaxerxes III

Upon closer inspection, a number of figures were found carved into the rock face. They appear to be in mourning for the death of their emperor, as evidenced by the cross-shaped incisions carved high in the rock face, each with an entrance elevated far from the ground. This is where kings Darius I, Xerxes, Artaxerxes I, and Darius II were buried, most in stone sarcophagi. Kings Artaxerxes IV and Darius III may also have been buried in the tomb of Artaxerxes II.

All six of these tombs share a similar form and decorative scheme, and are believed to have all been copied from that of Darius I.[87] They also share a resemblance with the carved façade of the

---

[87] Schmitt, 2000

Tachara; the king is shown on the tomb register as standing upon a platform that is carried by his servants. Depicted on these tombs are bas-reliefs that show the Persian king making sacrifices to a flame and to the god Ahura Mazda. In front of the tomb of Darius I is a well-preserved water basin, which is believed to have been used in funeral ceremonies.[88]

From Persepolis, the Persian kings managed their vast empire, and they were unique in how they envisaged how an empire should be run. Compared to the general consensus of the ancient world, in which cultures would seek to conquer, obliterate, and rebuild according to their own terms, this process was not the case with Persia, where political objectives were ensured through tolerance of cultural diversity. If subject nations paid their taxes and tribute to the Persian king, that was all that was required for them to continue living according to their own customs and cultural setting.

To avoid confusing babble, a common language was adopted during ceremonies and official acts: Old Persian. By using a language that they themselves had to study and learn, the Persians once again displayed their desire to create a common world that all would be able to belong to. Old Persian was the official language of the Persian bureaucracy – an important step between the creation of an empire encompassing many peoples to a state composed of a single people.[89]

The Persian representation of the empire as being multifaceted and tolerant of diversity was a dramatic departure from the imperial precedents of their forbearers. The subjects of earlier empires, such as of the Babylonian and Assyrian Empires, had also spoken and written many languages, but when it came to putting inscriptions into palaces and monuments of the rulers the inscriptions were that of the rulers. In this way, the identity of the empire was expressed in the terms of the rulers. The languages of the Achaemenid inscriptions, by contrast, were unprecedented symbols of the relationships between rulers and the ruled, as they were frequently provided in both the official Old Persian language and the languages of their vassal states, namely Elamite and Akkadian.[90]

By allowing subject nations to live their own lives, the Persians ensured that a multiethnic and multilingual empire flourished in relative peace for 250 years. That said, it obviously took more than tolerance to maintain control over a territory that stretched nearly 3,000 miles from west to east. Empires need an infrastructure in order to maintain control.

50 miles outside of Persepolis, carved into the side of a hill, is an ancient Persian road leading to the city, and the sides of the road are up to 30 feet high.[91] Such feats of engineering were repeated across the empire, where a network of roads and highways allowed the Persians to get

---

[88] Schmitt, 2000

[89] Kia, 2016

[90] Kia, 2016

[91] Mostafavi, M. T. (1967) "The Achaemenid royal road post stations between Susa and Persepolis." *A survey of Persian art, 16*, 3008-3010.

information, people, and materials from one corner of the empire to wherever the king was as quickly as possible. Even the Greeks could not fail to be impressed by the Persian road system, which stretched from Persepolis to Susa, and to Ecbatana via Pasargadae, and then 1,500 miles to the west to Ephesus on the Mediterranean.[92] Roads also went east to India. The Greeks were particularly amazed by the messengers that traveled along these roads, keeping the Persian kings at Persepolis informed of everything that occurred in the empire. The great Greek historian Herodotus wrote that "no mortal thing travels faster than these Persian couriers."[93]

Such speed was possible because of another Persian innovation: the staging post. Thanks to this system, a messenger would ride on one horse and be able to quickly change animals at these garrisons located approximately every 20 miles along the highways before continuing their journey straight away.[94] Manned by Persian soldiers, the staging posts also ensured that for the first time in antiquity, traders and travelers could move around a vast tract of land in relative safety.

Much is known about the nature and structure of imperial power through the art discovered in the city. Archaeological investigations discovered two particularly interesting sculptured scenes showing the royal audience, one of which is stored in the Iran National Museum and the other in the Persepolis Treasury. Both of these had originally ornamented the central façade of the Apadana stairways but were later removed to the treasury for unknown reasons.[95] The king appointed members of his family or his most trusted men to select positions. King Darius I is displayed enthroned beneath a canopy, and the heir to the throne, Xerxes, stands alongside several senior officials behind him. One of these officials is likely Pharnaces, the son of Arsames and the chief economic official, who was responsible for the payment of food gifts to the residents and visitors of the city.[96] The master of ceremonies stood before the throne and reported on the proceedings of the festivals. Ushers are depicted introducing the groups of gift-bearing delegations as they enter.

The exchange of gifts was, therefore, a key element in the Persian mechanisms of power and royal ideology, and the Apadana served as the principle location at which this took place.[97] It was, therefore, no surprise that Alexander the Great targeted this structure in particular to be destroyed.

One particularly interesting inscription discovered in the Queen's Quarters indicated that there might have been an element of competition when it came to a ruler's succession. Describing the ascension of Xerxes to the Persian throne after the death of Darius I, it reads, "My father Darius

[92] Mostafavi, 1967
[93] Kia, 2016
[94] Kia, 2016
[95] Root, 1985
[96] Root, 1985
[97] Llewellyn-Jones, 2013

had other sons, but – thus was Ahuramazda's desire – my father Darius made me the largest after himself. When my father Darius went away from the throne, by the grace of Ahuramazda I became king on my father's throne."[98]

Researchers from the Oriental Institute of the University of Chicago began to excavate the acropolis in 1931, and in 1933 they discovered fragments of tablets in two rooms of a gatehouse at the edge of the stone terrace. These became known as the Persepolis Fortification Tablets, as they had been discovered in the foundations of the ruined fortification wall that once surrounded the terrace. 30,000 fragments and whole tablets were found, which together provide one of the few sources of information about the workings of the empire that were written by the Persians themselves – information that we would otherwise never have access to. They were written in several languages, and composed of four main types of document: cuneiform texts in the Elamite language with impressions of seals; documents written in the Aramaic language and script also with seal impressions; pieces with seal impressions but no text; and various miscellaneous and unique pieces in Greek, Phrygian, Akkadian, and the only tablet written in Old Persian ever discovered. Like a treasure trove of coins, these were stored together in antiquity and found together in modern times.

What do these tablets tell people about Persepolis? They were not about the deeds and characters of kings, or armies on the march, or the eunuchs and harem intrigues, or other things that Hellenistic writers and artists were interested in. They are mostly the receipts and invoices of the empire during a narrow time of fewer than 20 years around 500 BCE.[99] More specifically, they are the record of one particular aspect of the Persian Empire: the provision of food by a centralized body. They describe transactions involving a range of grains, beer, wine, animals, fruits, and vegetables for people that were on the Persian government's payrolls, including workers, craftsmen, clerks, travelers, and members of the king's own family. One records "one and a half-shekels of silver for carpenters making sculptures," and another details "one jug of wine each to the seventy-four Syrian laborers working on the columned hall."[100]

With their road infrastructure, the Persians could establish an extensive trading network across their empire, through which they acquired the luxury goods to maintain the loyalty of their elite. The purpose of luxury at Persepolis was mainly linked to their perceptions of power and the propaganda of kingship. To have superfluous articles of expensive clothing, or to have one's palace strewn with textiles, an expression of power and wealth through the conspicuous consumption of material goods.[101]

In that vein, one custom that both fascinated and appalled the Greeks was the Persian feast. Most of what is known of the Persian feast comes from Greek sources, who described the

---

[98] Livius (no date) "Achaemenid Royal Inscriptions: XPf." (http://www.livius.org/aa-ac/achaemenians/XPf.html)
[99] Kia, 2016
[100] Hallock, R. T. (1969) *Persepolis fortification tablets*. Chicago: University of Chicago Press.
[101] Mitchell and Melville, 2012

opulence of the objects used, and the amount of drinking that was an essential part of the proceedings. The Persians lived according to a principle of telling the truth – something that the Greeks, begrudgingly, admired in them. Drinking during feasts had an important social role; they tended to get very drunk, because they believed that only in doing so they would tell the truth and be able to effectively settle arguments.[102] Feasting brought groups together as a community, with everyone partaking in the same food and engaging in the same experience.

Perhaps not surprisingly, the Persians were renowned for their luxury. Records and archaeological evidence indicate that they purchased spices, gold, purple dyes, and reams of the finest textiles. Although all that remains today are bare stone pillars and walls, the halls and palaces of Persepolis were once splendidly decorated in sumptuous textiles.[103] These fabrics were a way of expressing status and would have been found on walls, all over the floors, and the furniture.[104]

The cost of the site must have been immeasurable, judging from its immense scale, the opulence of its decoration, and luxury of the ceremonies and events that took place there. It seems the Persians were able to afford it through state investment, and making sure the fertile region of the Persian homeland flourished under the Achaemenid rule. Agriculture served as their main form of income, and the Persepolis Fortification Tablets indicate that grain and other produce served as the primary means of paying taxes.

In addition to the tributes and taxes paid by their vassals within the empire, the Persian royalty profited from the extensive trade that took place across their realm along the land-based routes known as the Silk Road and maritime trade routes via the Persian Gulf. Due to their position, the Persians frequently acted as middlemen in transactions between their neighbors. Their economy made use of a system of standardized coinage, and they even had a form of banking system by which the market could be made secure.[105]

Gift giving was how the Persian kings reinforced the loyalty of their subjects, but they also had other, less benign, ways of exercising power. A bas-relief at Behistun, in northwestern Iran, shows the Persian king at his most ruthless. King Darius the Great is shown enslaving those who threatened his throne, and the prominent position of the image served as a public warning to those who may have considered resisting him.[106] Many ancient Greek accounts also suggest that the Persians ruled with an iron fist, including descriptions of how the Persians cut off the limbs and even noses of their prisoners.

---

[102] Yarshater, E. (1960) "The theme of wine-drinking and the concept of the beloved in early Persian poetry." *Studia Islamica*, 13, 43 - 53.

[103] Hartnell, 2012

[104] Hartnell, 2012

[105] Kia, 2016

[106] Olmstead, A. T. (1938) "Darius and his Behistun inscription." *The American Journal of Semitic Languages and Literatures*, 55: 4, 392 - 416.

However, the bas-reliefs at Persepolis seem to present a very different perspective. There the figures do not display the expected rigidity of court rule or enslavement; instead, they appear relaxed, chatting and encouraging one another. They are depicted as holding one another's hands or shoulders, providing an image of peace and harmony. There are no battle scenes depicted in the city, and no violence in any form is demonstrated. Tolerant, peaceful, and wealthy, the Achaemenid kings believed that they were the masters of all that they surveyed.

The First Persian War

In 500 BCE, the major Greek city-states Sparta and Athens were not terribly interested in the affairs of the Achaemenid Persian Empire, and for the most part, the status of the Ionian Greeks, who were under Persian control, also mattered very little to them. Sparta stood at the head of an alliance/league of Peloponnesian city-states who were more concerned with their region, while Athens had recently abolished tyranny and was learning the intricacies of democratic government (Forrest 2001, 37).

While Athens was uninvolved, perhaps following the cue of their Athenian cousins, some of the Ionian, Aeolian, and Doric city-states in Anatolia revolted against their own tyrants, which was tantamount to rebellion against their Persian overlords (Forrest 2001, 37). Herodotus provided the best account of the Ionian Revolt, which was largely instigated by a former tyrant named Aristagoras, who believed that a successful revolt would place him in a powerful position. Herodotus wrote, "Certain substantial citizens of Naxos, forced by the commons to leave the island, took refuge in Miletus, which had been put under Aristagoras, son of Molpagoras, as deputy governor. He was nephew and son-in-law of Histiaeus, the son of Lysagoras, who was being detained by Darius at Susa . . . The first thing they did when they got there was to ask Aristagoras to lend them some troops, in the hope of recovering their position at home. This suggested to Aristagoras that if he helped the exiles to return he himself would be ruler of Naxos; so using their friendship with Histiaeus to cloak his purpose, he made them an offer." (Herodotus, *The Histories*, V, 30).

Aristagoras had a keen sense of political acumen and a feel for the times, as a large part of his strategy was to gain the favor of the Ionians Greeks by promising the reward of democracy. First, he had to abdicate his own tyranny, which he did in public fashion. According to Herodotus, "To induce the Milesians to support him, he began by professing to abdicate his tyranny in favor of a popular government, and then went on to do the same thing in the other Ionian states, where he got rid of the tyrants." (Herodotus, *The Histories*, V, 37).

At the same time, Aristagoras knew that enticing the Ionian states to rebel would not be enough to defeat the mighty Achaemenid Empire. For that, he would need the support of one, or both, of the Ionian's mainland Greek cousins. However, Aristagoras' efforts to obtain the aid of Sparta and Athens against the Persians would lead to his demise and set the Athenians on a crash course with the Persians that would reach its apex at Marathon.

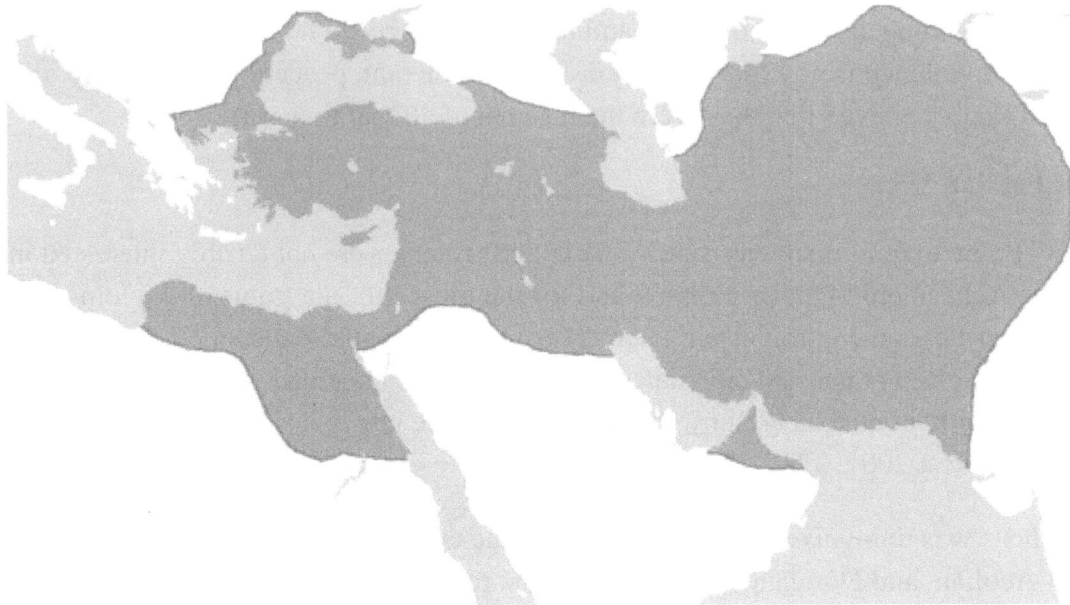

A map depicting the enormous extent of the Achaemenid Empire

Perhaps owing to the fierce reputation of the Spartan warriors, or simply due to the fact that Sparta was farthest from Ionia, Aristagoras visited Sparta first to plead for assistance against the Persians. At the time, Sparta's government was a type of republican-monarchy, in which adult males had voting rights at their councils but two kings presided over the city and largely decided on affairs of state such as diplomacy and war (Plutarch, *Lycurgus*, 7). When Aristagoras finally made it to Sparta, he met with the only reigning king of the time, Cleomenes, and at first tried to appeal to his patriotism, then his pride, and finally his greed. Herodotus' account of Aristagoras' plea to Cleomenes reads, "I hope Cleomenes, that you will not be too much surprised at my anxiety to visit you. The circumstances are these. That Ionians should have become slaves in place of free men is a bitter shame and grief not only to us, but to the rest of Greece, and especially to you, who are the leaders of the Greek world. We beg you, therefore, in the name of the gods of Greece, to save from slavery your Ionian kinsmen. It will be an easy task, for these foreigners have little taste for war, and you are the finest soldiers in the world. The Persian weapons are bows and short spears; they fight in trousers and turbans – that will   show you how easy they are to beat! Moreover, the inhabitants of that continent are richer than all the rest of the world put together – they have everything, gold, silver, bronze, elaborately embroidered clothes and beasts of burden and slaves. All this you may have if you wish." (Herodotus, *The Histories*, V, 49).

Cleomenes' interest was apparently piqued until Aristagoras showed him a map of the vast Achaemenid Empire, to which the Spartan replied, "Your proposal to take Lacedaemonians a three months' journey from the sea is a highly improper one." (Herodotus, *The Histories*, V, 50).

Unfazed by the Spartans' denial of his proposal, Aristagoras began to sail back to Ionia, but he stopped in Athens to present the citizens of that city-state with a similar offer. Aristagoras approached the Athenians at an opportune time, as they had recently expelled their tyrant Hippias, who was supported by the Persians, so they were already inclined to campaign against them (Herodotus, *The Histories*, V, 97). Aristagoras used many of the same arguments he tried with the Spartans, including the weakness of the Persian military and the riches of the Achaemenid Empire, but he also appealed to common ancestry that the Athenians and Ionians shared. Herodotus noted, "In addition to this he pointed out that Miletus had been founded by Athenian settlers, so it was only natural that the Athenians, powerful as they were, should help her in her need. Once persuaded to accede to Aristagoras' appeal, the Athenians passed a decree for the dispatch of twenty ships to Ionia, under the command of Melanthius, a distinguished Athenian." (Herodotus, *The Histories*, V, 97).

Athenian support for the Ionian cause was lukewarm at best, and the entire Ionian coalition soon crumbled under the weight of the mighty Achaemenid Empire. When the Persians were finally able to reestablish their rule over the rebellious Ionian city-states, Aristagoras fled and later died in exile, and the rebellious cities, especially Miletus, suffered under brutal punitive measures. (Herodotus, *The Histories*, V, 126). Herodotus graphically wrote about the punishment the Persians meted out to the Ionians: "Once the towns were in their hands, the best-looking boys were chosen for castration and made into eunuchs; the most beautiful girls were dragged from their homes and sent to Darius' court, and the towns themselves, temples and all, were burnt to the ground." (Herodotus, *The Histories*, VI, 32).

The ruthless suppression of the Ionian Revolt by the Achaemenid Persians proved to be the first act in the greater Greco-Persian Wars, and if the Athenians thought that their limited involvement in the affair would mitigate the ire of the Persian king Darius I (ca. 550-486 BCE), they were sorely mistaken. Through their involvement in the Ionian Revolt, despite the fact it was minimal for the most part, the Athenians set themselves at odds with the Persian emperor, putting them on a crash course that would culminate at the Battle of Marathon about nine years later.

An ancient depiction of Darius I

At the beginning of the 5th century BCE, the Greek city-states were as prone to fight each other as they were non-Greeks. The Persians on the other hand commanded the greatest empire the known world had ever witnessed – the Achaemenid Empire – which spanned from Bactria (present day Afghanistan) in the east to Egypt in the west (Briant 2002, 366). Besides possessing the already ancient and venerated kingdom of Egypt, the Achaemenid Persians also controlled the city of Babylon and the regions of Mesopotamia and the Levant, which were home to such illustrious previous cultures as Israel, the Phoenicians, and the Assyrians just to name a few. When viewed from this perspective, the Greek Ionian city-states were a small fraction of the total empire, and the more distant Athenians may have appeared to the Persians as little more than minor interlopers who were playing a dangerous game that was out of their league. That said, despite the fact that the Persians in general may have disregarded any military threat that the Athenians posed, Ionia was still viewed as an important part of the Achaemenid Empire.

The Athenians no doubt raised the ire of Darius I when they supported the Ionian Revolt, but their direct interference in the affairs of the Achaemenid Empire was not their first transgression against the Persians. Before the Athenians inserted themselves into the Ionian Revolt, they were involved in a war with Sparta, and when that did not go well for them, they looked to Persia for an alliance. The Athenians sent envoys to the city of Sardis in Ionia to meet with the Persian governor, Artapherenes, who requested that the Greeks give a symbolic gift of earth and water to him. Herodotus explained, "To strengthen their position they sent representatives to Sardis, in the hope of concluding an alliance with Persia. When they got there and delivered their message, Artapherenes the son of Hystaspes, the governor, asked in reply who these Athenians were that sought an alliance with Persia, and in what part of the world they lived. Then, having been told, he put the Persian case in a nutshell by remarking that, if the Athenians would signify their submission by the usual gift of earth and water, then Darius would make a pact with them; otherwise they had better go home. Eager that the pact should be concluded, the envoys acted on their own initiative and accepted Artapherenes' terms – for which they were severely censured on their return to Athens." (Herodotus, *The Histories*, V, 73).

As Herodotus wrote, the Athenian envoys were admonished for their act of obeisance towards the Persians, but the political damage had been done; the Athenians broke Persian protocol and tradition when they offered earth and water but did not give their obedience. Furthermore, around the time of the Athenian earth and water fiasco, Hippias, the tyrant who was expelled from Athens in 510 BCE, showed up in Sardis and urged Artapherenes and the Persians to restore him as tyrant of Athens (Olmstead 1948, 151-52). In fact, when the Persians finally set forward with their invasion plan of Greece, Hippias was with the Persian fleet, which indicates that the invasion was at least partially intended to restore Athens to tyranny (Doenges 1998, 2).

By breaking the standard Persian political protocol, the Athenians had placed themselves on the imperial radar of the Persians, but when they supported the Ionian Revolt, Darius I took the matter personally. The Persians were not the only one who committed atrocities during the Ionian Revolt, as a combined force of Ionian Greeks and Athenians captured and sacked the city of Sardis and reduced its temple to rubble. When Darius I learned of the Athenians role in the sack of Sardis, he exploded. According to Herodotus, "The story goes that when Darius learnt of the disaster, he did not give a thought to the Ionians, knowing perfectly well that the punishment for their revolt would come; but he asked who the Athenians were, and then, on being told, called for his bow. He took it, set an arrow on the string, shot it up into the air and cried: 'Grant, O God, that I may punish the Athenians.'" (Herodotus, *The Histories,* V, 105).

To Darius I, the matter was settled: the Athenians must be taught a lesson and brought under the yoke of the Achaemenid Empire. That said, in the ancient world, it took a lot of time and resources to plan a large-scale military campaign, and the Persian invasion of Greece was no exception. The heart of the Achaemenid Empire was thousands of miles from Greece, so any major invasion would involve many logistical concerns, especially transportation of troops and resources, but Darius I was up for the challenge. The Persian army was led by the general Mardonius, who mustered his forces on land and sea in Ionia in 491 BCE, and his expedition into

Greece would be the largest military expedition that world had ever seen. In fact, it was most likely intended to subjugate not only Athens but all of Greece.

From Ionia, Mardonius led the Persian army north along the Aegean coastline until they marched through Thrace and Macedonia. At this point, they encountered a storm that destroyed most of their ships (Herodotus, *The Histories*, VI, 44). The disastrous loss of the Persian fleet only proved to be a temporary setback though, as the rich Achaemenid Empire was able to muster a new army, which was led by a general named Datis. Datis was ordered by Darius I to "reduce Athens and Eretria to slavery and to bring the slaves before the king." (Herodotus, *The Histories*, VI, 94).

Datis had many advantages over the Greeks, as he commanded overwhelming naval superiority and had the military intelligence of Hippias, the former tyrant of Athens, at his disposal (Doenges 1998, 2). Instead of following Mardonius' route the previous year around the Aegean, Datis led the Persian army by ships directly across the Aegean, reducing the island of Naxos to slavery but sparing Delos (Herodotus, *The Histories*, VI, 95-98).

When Datis and the Persians arrived in Greece, they first set their sights on laying waste to Eretria. According to Herodotus, the Eretrians prepared themselves for a long siege but were betrayed by some of their own people: "The Eretrians had no intention of leaving their defenses to meet the coming attack in the open; their one concern (the proposal not to abandon the town having been carried) was to defend their walls – if they could . . . then on the seventh, two well-known Eretrians, Euphorbus the son of Alcimachus and Philagrus the son of Cyneas, betrayed the town to the enemy. The Persians entered, and stripped the temples bare and burnt them in revenge for the burnt temples of Sardis, and, in accordance with Darius' orders, carried off all the inhabitants as slaves." (Herodotus, *The* Histories, VI, 101)

With Eretria reduced to rubble, Datis then turned his attention south to the Attica peninsula and the city of Athens, but unlike the Eretrians, the Athenians would be better prepared and would leave their city to meet the Persians on the plain near Marathon.

Although Athens was a decent sized city-state for the Hellenic world, it was puny compared to the Achaemenid Empire, making it impossible to make up for the numerical disparity in a number of ways. Nonetheless, Athens was still formidable. All Athenian citizens between the ages of 18-42 were eligible for military service (Sage 1996, 38), and the army was sub-divided by tribes, which were then commanded by lieutenants known as *taxiarchs* (Sage 1996, 38). Although the requirements for and basic structure of the Athenian military are known, much less is known about the men's training. During the period of the Battle of Marathon, there is no evidence for any formal training of hoplites in Athens, and the only Greek city-state where any significant training is recorded comes from Sparta (Sage 1996, 35). In other words, the Athenian military at the time of the Battle of Marathon was a sort of "home guard," where each male citizen was responsible for his part militarily and thus always prepared for war.

Herodotus is the most complete primary source concerning the Battle of Marathon, but others do exist or at least once did, that can help complement Herodotus' account. The oldest sources that depicted the Battle of Marathon were actually a series of pictures that were painted in the Poecile Stoa by the artists Micon and Paenus around 460 BCE, about 30 years after the battle (Hammond 1968, 26). Unfortunately, the pictures are no longer extant, but the Greek geographer Pausanias gave a partial description in his geographic survey of Greece: "At the end of the painting are those who fought at Marathon; the Boeotians of Plataea and the Attic contingent are coming to blows with the foreigners. In this place neither side has the better, but the centre of the fighting shows the foreigners in flight and pushing one another into the morass, while at the end of the painting are the Phoenician ships, and the Greeks killing the foreigners who are scrambling into them." (Pausanias, *Description of Greece*, I, 5.3). Pausanias' description of the Poecile Stoa is useful because it corroborates Herodotus' accounts, namely that the Plataeans were the only other Greeks besides the Athenians who fought the Persians. It also indicates the chaos of the Persians' retreat.

The Battle of Marathon itself is believed to have taken place in September 490 BCE (Hammond 1968), and it is also thought to be the first amphibious battle in world history (Doenges 1998, 4). The Persians landed their invasion force near Marathon because it was believed to be good ground for them to maneuver their cavalry, which the Persian commander Datis believed would give him the edge over the Greek hoplites (Hammond 1968, 33). Although the plain around Marathon was good ground for cavalry and was no doubt a large part of the Persian decision to land there, its proximity to Eretria also played a role. Herodotus wrote, "The part of Attic territory nearest Eretria – and also the best ground for cavalry to maneuver in – was at Marathon. To Marathon, therefore, Hippias the son of Pisistratus directed the invading army, and the Athenians, as soon as the news arrived, hurried to meet it. The Athenian troops were commanded by ten generals, of whom the tenth was Miltiades." (Herodotus, *The Histories*, VI, 102-103).

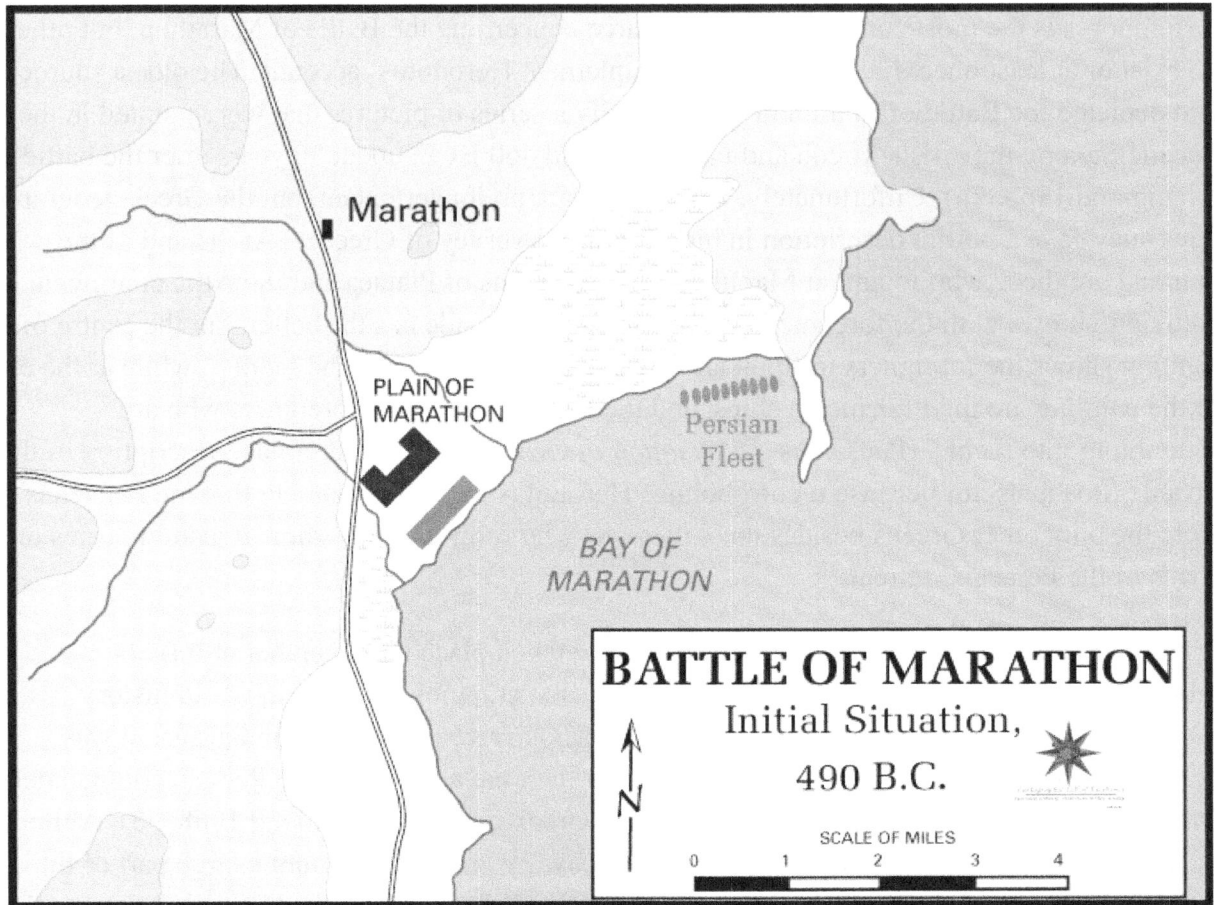

Disposition of the forces at Marathon

The appearance of the former Athenian tyrant, Hippias, is also important because he apparently provided useful intelligence to Datis and the Persians that revealed Marathon to be the best place for cavalry operations. It was also close to the recently conquered Eretria, and the close proximity to Eretria was logistically important to the Persians and their potential success not only at Marathon but also if they were to subject all of Attica and possibly Greece itself. Since the Persian army was so far removed from the nearest Achaemenid colonies (which were across the Aegean in Ionia), they were forced to use Eretria as a temporary base and source of their supply lines (Hammond 1968, 32). The short distance between Eretria and Marathon across the bay also provided a safe and quick route for the Persians to move goods and men.

As a result, the Persians assembled their army near Marathon, but the exact size of the army is still open to conjecture. Unfortunately, Herodotus never gave a number for the combatants in the Persian army – only ships – so modern historians are forced to make educated guesses based on the size of the field, the number that Herodotus listed as killed, and the number of Persian ships. A recent study estimates that the number of Persian fighting men may have been around 12,000-15,000 men, which would not be much more than the army the Greeks fielded at Marathon (Doenges 1998, 6), but earlier studies, such as Hammond's, places the total number of the

Persian army as high as 90,000. That said, Hammond noted that many of them would have been sailors and not infantry (Hammond 1968, 33).

Numbers aside, the two forces fought in a completely different way, which each side had perfected over decades, perhaps centuries, in their respective theaters of war. The Persian army was formed of contingents mustered from the furthest reaches of its vast empire, and though one might expect what was, in effect, a "multinational" force to adopt vastly different styles of fighting, ancient historians writing of the battle indicate there was a degree of standardization in their equipment. That said, it is possible the ancient historians who wrote of the battle, all of whom were Greek, decided to lump all Persian forces together by assuming one unit would have much the same equipment as the next, as was the case for the Greek soldiers. The Persian army that faced the Spartans and their Greek allies at Thermopylae was made up of infantry, cavalry and chariot units, each of them apparently equipped in a similar fashion. The infantry was what would be categorized by military historians as "light", thus not bearing heavy armor or weapons. Each individual Persian infantryman would be equipped with a light, short thrusting spear (which could also be thrown if necessary), a shortsword or saber, a light double-curved bow and a wicker shield. Shield sizes appear to have varied from unit to unit, but archaeological evidence from Persian sculpture seems to suggest that, generally speaking, the shields would cover the soldiers wielding them from knee to neck, while not being wide enough to create significant overlap with the ranks on either side.

Wicker might seem like a foolish material to construct a shield out of, but it was in fact remarkably effective in its own right. The wicker was, of course, extremely light, making it very easy to wield, but it was also effective in stopping slashes from light weapons and could also trap thrust weapons that penetrated it, making them extremely hard to withdraw. The cavalry and charioteers also shared similar equipment, being armed with longer curved sabers for slashing, double-curved bows and javelins. It appears as though some units, particularly those from the Persian heartland, were also armed with double-headed axes, fearsome weapons which would have in all likelihood made them the Persian shock troops.

Armor for the Persian soldiers appears to have also been fairly standardized as well. This is because for much of the Persian infantry it was virtually non-existent. Though it's hard to imagine today, especially considering the Persians were going up against heavily armored hoplites, Persian soldiers appear to have worn no greaves, vambraces or any other form of arm or leg armor, and most units seem to have forgone helmets in favor of knotted rags about their heads, or light caps of metal or leather. To protect their torsos, the soldiers either wore nothing at all, or light back-and-breasts of leather, chain mail, or (very rarely) bronze scales. The elite Persian infantry, recruited from the Persian heartlands, and the famous "Immortals", the Emperor's 10,000 strong personal guard, might have been more heavily armored, but generally speaking they were far from protected.

The reasons for this extremely light equipment are simple: aside from the monumental cost of equipping such a massive army like the one the Persians fielded with heavy armor and weapons, they were simply not suited to the climate in which the Persian army conducted much of its operations. The scorching desert plains of Asia Minor and Egypt, the near-impassable mountains of Afghanistan and the Hindu Kush, and the sweltering heat of the Punjab were not battlefields suited for heavy iron, steel or bronze armor, which weighed soldiers down and, in such extremes of temperature, might well carry them off altogether from heatstroke or fatigue. Thus, the standard Persian tactic was to shower similarly lightly-armed opponents with waves of arrows and javelins from a distance before closing with the weakened ranks of the enemy and cutting them to pieces with their short swords and sabers. The cavalry and charioteers would also most likely fight in a similar fashion, rather than in the knee-to-knee heavy cavalry charge of the middle ages or the Napoleonic battlefields more familiar to the West.

The Greeks, by contrast, fought in a vastly different manner. To begin with, while many of the Persian soldiers were conscripts (with the exception of some elite corps, like the Immortals, service in which was one of the greatest honors available in the Persian Empire), all of the Greek infantrymen were volunteers, and generally far better-trained ones. Each city-state required its volunteers to undertake city-wide annual or bi-annual military exercises, and the Spartans, the backbone of the Greek force, literally spent their entire life training and preparing for war, with manual labor entrusted to their serfs, the helots. It is not entirely clear why Sparta placed such a great emphasis on having a militaristic society, but it resulted in making military fitness a preoccupation for the Spartans from birth. Spartan babies with even the slightest hint of physical deformities were left to die, while the fortunate ones began their military training at the age of 7 years old. Every Spartan male had to join the army at 18.

Thus, the backbone of the Greek way of war was the citizen-soldier, and aside from some notable exceptions, like Boeotia, they fielded armies made up almost exclusively of infantry. While that might sound like a disadvantage against more diverse opposing forces that included archers or chariots, the Greeks weren't using just any infantry. Their main strength was the hoplite – a soldier about as different from his Persian counterpart as could possibly be.

Most historians believe that the hoplite became the dominant infantry soldier in nearly all the Greek city-states around the 8th century BCE Hoplites were responsible for acquiring their own equipment, so not every hoplite might have been equally armed, but considering the style of warfare, they needed as much uniformity as possible.

Like the Persian infantry, the hoplites also carried spears, but while the Persian weapons were short and light, the Greek spears were thick shafts anywhere between seven and nine feet long. These spears were topped by a 9-inch spearhead, with a "lizard-sticker" buttspike at the bottom which could be used as a secondary spearhead if the main weapon was snapped off, or to plant the spear upright when at rest. Each hoplite also carried a shortsword, designed specifically for thrusting in the close confines of a melee (the Spartan weapon, the *xiphos,* was so short as to be virtually a dagger, its blade barely over a foot long). Unlike the Persian infantry, the hoplites did not carry bows. Though the Greeks did employ light infantry, in the form of slingers, javelineers and archers, their role was extremely secondary to that of the heavy infantry.

This was largely due to the armor which each hoplite wore into battle, which consisted of bronze greaves covering the wearer from ankle to knee, a skirt of leather or quilted linen to protect the groin area, and a heavy breastplate made either of bronze or quilted linen under overlapping bronze scales. To protect their heads, the hoplites wore the famous helmet that is perhaps their most iconic feature, a full-face bronze helmet with high flaring cheek-pieces and a thick nasal that obscured and protected their faces completely, topped by a horsehair crest that added another foot to their height. Helmets were worn front-to-back for line infantry and sideways for officers, to make them more recognizable to their own troops in the heat of battle.

Armored from head to foot in iron and bronze, the hoplite was the tank of his age, but the most important feature of his equipment was undoubtedly his shield. Weighing in at over 30 pounds, the *hoplon* or *aspis* was a great wooden bowl over three feet in diameter, made of heavy oak fronted with bronze and covering each hoplite from knee to neck, as well as providing a significant overlap with the shields of his companions in the battle-line. Obviously, these armaments did not lend themselves to the style of fighting the Persians favored. There could be no standing off and engaging the enemy at a distance with the Greek hoplites carrying short swords and thrusting spears, and because of the weight of their equipment (which was up to 70-90 pounds all told),

Greek art depicting hoplites fighting

19ᵗʰ Century illustration of a Hoplite

For the Greeks, a hoplite was only as strong as the hoplite next to him; without hoplites on the sides, both flanks were exposed, and heavy infantry units are not mobile. Thus, the Greeks implemented the phalanx formation, one of history's most important military innovations. The phalanx was a line of infantry as wide across as the battlefield dictated, anything from five to 30 men deep, with each rank of men officered by a veteran. The formation also included an additional, expert file-closer at the back of each file, to keep the formation cohesive.

The phalanx advanced slowly to maintain its tight formation and unit cohesion, speeding up in unison just before reaching combat. The vast hoplite shields overlapped one another significantly, forming an uninterrupted wall of oak and bronze over which the first rank, while holding out their shields, would use their short swords to stab at the enemy in front of him, while the ranks immediately behind the first rank would slash at enemies with their spears over the top of the first line. Because each soldier's right flank was shielded by his companion's shield (all shields were strapped to the left arm, to preserve the integrity of the formation; left-handed fighters did not exist), the phalanx, especially in the case of less well-trained units, had a tendency to edge to the right, which the Greeks countered by placing their elite troops to the right as a bulwark. The rows in back of the first line would also use their shields to help hold up the hoplites in the front and help them maintain their balance. The formation and method of attack was designed to physically overpower the enemy and scare them, lowering their morale. The phalanx as a fighting unit fell out of favor by the height of the Roman Empire, but the principles behind it remained in use for subsequent infantry formations lasting past the American Civil War. As the Greeks relied on the hoplite to defend other hoplites and concentrate their attack, infantry units in the gunpowder age relied on concentrated gunfire to stun and scare the enemy. And as military commanders learned time and again throughout the ages, if soldiers were not packed shoulder to shoulder in a tight formation, they were far more likely to flee.

Ultimately, though this is a subject of some contention, much of the consensus argues that the main strength of the hoplite phalanx was its utter inexorability when it operated as a cohesive, immaculately drilled unit – an unstoppable juggernaut which relied less on the initial clash of shield-walls (hoplites never advanced at a run, to preserve their formation) than on the relentless pushing force of their advance to shatter the enemy formation.

The first major decision that the Athenians would face was to either prepare the city's defenses for a siege or wait for help from other Greeks, such as the Spartans, to arrive. The other choice was to meet the much larger Persian force on the battlefield near Marathon. There was merit to both arguments, and in true Greek fashion both sides were heard, but ultimately it was the general Miltiades who swayed the opinion of the other generals to meet the Persians on the battlefield: "Amongst the Athenian commanders opinion was divided: some were against risking a battle, on the ground that the Athenian force was too small to stand a chance of success; others

– and amongst them Miltiades – urged it . . . To Callimachus, therefore, Miltiades turned. 'It is now in your hands, Callimachus,' he said, 'either to enslave Athens, or to make her free and to leave behind you for all future generations a memory more glorious than even Harmodius and Aristogeiton left. Never in our history have we Athenians been in such peril as now. If we submit to the Persians, Hippias will be restored to power – and there is little doubt what misery must then ensue: but if we fight and win, then this city of ours may well grow to pre-eminence amongst all the cities of Greece' . . . Miltiades' words prevailed, and by the vote of Callimachus the War Archon the decision to fight was made." (Herodotus, *The Histories*, VI, 109-110).

The Athenians thus decided to meet the Persians on the battlefield, and it is generally believed that they took the northern route from Athens to Marathon, which is about 25 miles long (Doegnes 1998, 7). The only other road to Marathon was slightly longer at about 28 miles and would have left the Greeks more exposed to a cavalry attack (Doegnes 1998, 7). After the Greeks arrived, the two sides faced each other in an uneasy calm that lasted for a few days before the battle, which helped the Greeks fortify their forces and better prepare for battle.

Once the Greeks arrived on the plain, they camped at a site that was considered to be sacred to the hero Hercules, and they were then joined by the Plataean Greek contingent. According to Herodotus, "The Athenian troops were drawn up on a piece of ground sacred to Heracles, when they were joined by the Plataeans, who came to support them with every available man." (Herodotus, *The Histories*, VI, 108).

The total number of Greeks who were camped at the plain near Marathon is estimated to be around 10,000 total, with about 1,000 of the hoplites being Plataeans (Hammond 1968, 34). Although most of the Athenian hoplites traveled to Marathon to confront the Persians, a small skeleton crew stayed behind in Athens in order to defend the city in case the Persian forces split and part attacked the city (Hammond 1968, 34).

Datis and the Persians were eager to engage the Greeks in battle as they had the advantage with numbers and cavalry, but the Greeks were not yet done with their preparations that would help give them the ultimate advantage. In the days before the actual battle, the Greeks probably gradually advanced their position, felling trees along the way and then using those trees to obstruct the Persian cavalry (Hammond 1968, 39). Thus, by the time the Greeks had advanced to the actual battlefield, they tried to be protected in their rear and flanks by the rugged hillsides, which effectively made the Persian cavalry useless (Hammond 1968, 39). This strategy was a major factor in how the Greeks won the battle, because the vaunted and feared Persian cavalry played almost no role in the Battle of Marathon, and the Greek hoplites were much better armored and trained than the average Persian soldiers, who wore little armor.

In essence, Miltiades and the Greeks knew that in order to defeat the larger Persian army they had to plan accordingly and win the battle before the first blow was struck, while Datis became too reliant on his cavalry and was unwilling to improvise. Still, while the decisions made by

Miltiades and Datis before the actual battle may have ultimately decided the victor, the two sides still had to fight, and it turned out to be an epic battle that has rightfully earned its legendary reputation.

In pre-modern warfare, the standard order of battle usually involved the belligerent armies lining up in shield wall, or *phalanx*, across from each other and then fighting with the ultimate goal of breaking through the enemy's line. Herodotus' description of the Battle of Marathon appears to follow this method: "When it did come, the Athenian army moved into position for the coming struggle. The right wing was commanded by Callimachus – for it was the regular practice at that time in Athens that the War Archon should lead the right wing; then followed the tribes, in their regular order; and, finally, on the left wing, were the Plataeans." (Herodotus, *The Histories*, VI, 111).

The fact that the Athenian field marshal (War Archon), Callimachus, was on one of the wings instead of the center is another important aspect of the battle that will be discussed further below, but as the two armies met, the Greeks were forced to compensate for their numerical inferiority, so Callimachus, Miltiades and the other Greek generals were faced with a choice: concentrate their forces in the center (where the initial Persian thrust would probably be focused) or place the majority of their forces on the wings in order to prevent being flanked. According to Herodotus, the Greeks chose the second option: "One result of the disposition of Athenian troops before the battle was the weakening of their center by the effort to extend the line sufficiently to cover the whole Persian front; the two wings were strong, but the line in the centre was only a few ranks deep. The dispositions made, and the preliminary sacrifice promising success, the word was given to move, and the Athenians advanced at a run towards the enemy, not less than a mile away . . . They were the first Greeks, so far as we know, to charge at a run, and the first who dared to look without flinching at Persian dress and the men who wore it; for until that day came, no Greek could hear even the word Persian without terror." (Herodotus, *The Histories*, VI, 112).

Perhaps the most interesting and strategically important aspect of this passage is the fact that the Greeks ran to meet the Persians. At first, one may think that running to meet the enemy on the battlefield would be disadvantageous, especially a mile away, because it could tire the runners out, but there are some advantages to the strategy as well. Combatants in pre-modern battles had to be in good physical shape given the nature of the hand-to-hand fighting, so a brisk run to meet the enemy would raise soldiers' heart rates and help get them in the proper frame of mind as the battle began. In effect, the mile or so that the Greek hoplites ran across the plain of Marathon to meet the Persian army was a warm-up for the main event, which was the actual battle.

Modern scholars have also pointed out that when the Greeks sprinted to meet the Persians, they eliminated one of the advantages that the Persians had: cavalry. Once the two armies became engaged and the Greek flanks were protected by the hilly terrain, the Persian cavalry threat was eliminated (Hammond 1968, 40). The other Persian advantage – numerical superiority – was countered by the Greek formation of the battle line, which would prove to be the ultimate undoing of Datis and his army.

However, once the battle began, it was not long before the thin Greek center collapsed. A burial mound that was discovered and excavated in modern times marks where the Greek center stood, and also where the Greeks suffered most of their casualties (Hammond 1968, 18). Herodotus' account tells how the Persians pushed through the center: "The struggle at Marathon was long and drawn out. In the centre, held by the Persians themselves and the Sacae, the advantage was with the foreigners, who were so far successful as to break the Greek line and pursue the fugitives inland from the sea; but the Athenians on one wing and the Plataeans on the other were both victorious . . . Drawing their two wings together into a single unit, they turned their attention to the Persians who had broken through in the center." (Herodotus, *The Histories*, VI, 113).

The wings were instrumental to Greek victory, as they essentially ceded the center to the Persians but then collapsed on their enemy from the wings. Herodotus, who had no military experience and was not well versed in military affairs, does not mention if the Greeks planned the maneuver in such a way, but logic would seem to indicate that they did. Up until this point in the battle, everything that Miltiades and Callimachus did was precise and well-thought out, from the road they took to Marathon, to where they chose to camp, and even the decision to sprint to engage the Persians. As such, it would be hard to believe that the Greek generals did not plan to collapse the wings as well. Hammond noted, "Now it is obvious that the action of the Athenians and the Plataeans on the wings, which were separated from one another by a considerable distance, had been preconcerted; for Miltiades, having thinned his centre and packed his wings, must have anticipated the actual developments in the fighting and issued orders in advance to the effect that the men on the wings, if and when victorious, were to turn towards the centre, to form line and to go to the aid of the Greek troops of the centre." (Hammond 1968, 29).

Hannibal's victory against the Romans at Cannae has often been considered the seminal use of a pincers attack of this type, and it is still considered a masterpiece of generalship that was imitated about 2,000 years later by Napoleon at Austerlitz, but if Hammond is correct, Miltiades and Callimachus orchestrated a pincers attack at Marathon centuries before Hannibal did. Either way, it's clear that Miltiades and the other Greek generals aided their cause and evened the odds by planning for contingencies. On the other hand, despite numerous advantages, Datis and the Persians were unable to capitalize on their superior numbers at the center of the line, and their cavalry was useless (Doenges 1998, 12).

Once the Greek flanks collapsed on the Persian center, Datis knew that phase of the battle was lost, so he ordered the Persians to retreat to the ships. Herodotus wrote very little about the Persian retreat other than that the Greeks captured seven Persians ships and that two Greek generals, Callimachus and Stesilaus, were killed pursuing the Persians (Herodotus, *The Histories*, VI, 114-115), but Pausanias helps fill in the gaps. He wrote that the disastrous Persian retreat may have been partially due to them not knowing the terrain and running into a marsh: "There is at Marathon a lake which for the most part is marshy. Into this ignorance of the roads made the foreigners fall in their flight, and it is said that this accident was the cause of their great losses." (Pausanias, *Geography of Greece*, I, 32,7).

Datis and the Persians were losing, but they were not yet defeated, so he and his surviving army that made it to the ships set sail around the Attic peninsula for Athens (Morkot 1996, 75). The quickest way for the Persians to reach Athens from Marathon was by land, and preferably on horseback, but once the Greeks defeated them at Marathon, they had to sail the entire way to Athens (Hodge 2001, 247). At this point, the Greek victory on the battlefield of Marathon was assured, but all may have been lost if Datis and the Persians could reach Athens before them. Plutarch succinctly captured the Greek urgency as they raced back to Athens on foot: "When the Athenians had routed the Barbarians and driven them aboard their ships, and saw that they were sailing away, not toward the islands, but into the gulf toward Attica under compulsion of wind and wave, then they were afraid lest the enemy find Athens empty of defenders, and so they hastened homeward with nine tribes, and reached the city that very day. But Aristides was left behind at Marathon with his own tribe, to guard the captives and the booty." (Plutarch, *Aristides*, 4-5).

One of the most legendary aspects of the Battle of Marathon, at least in terms of how it resonates in modern society, is the story of the runner named Phillippides or Pheidippides. According to the later Greek historian Plutarch and the 2nd century CE Greek writer Lucian, Pheidippides ran a little over 26 miles from the battlefield of Marathon to Athens in order to tell the citizens of that city that the Greeks had won the battle. Lucian wrote, "Phillippides, the one who acted as courier, is sad to have used it first in our sense when he brought the news of victory from Marathon and addressed the magistrates in session when they were anxious how the battle had ended; "Joy to you, we've won." he said, and there and then he died, breathing his last breath with that, "Joy to you." (Lucian, *A Slip of the Tongue in Greeting*, 3).

After the Battle of Marathon, Darius I was not done with his punitive plans for Athens. According to Herodotus, the Persian loss at Marathon only incensed the Achaemenid king even more: "When the news of the battle of Marathon reached Darius, son of Hystaspes and king of Persia, his anger against Athens, already great enough on account of the assault on Sardis, was even greater, and he was more than ever determined to make war on Greece. Without loss of time he dispatched couriers to the various states under his dominion with orders to raise an army much larger than before; and also warships, transports, horses, and grain. So the royal command went round; and all Asia was in an uproar for three years, with the best men being enrolled in the army for the invasion of Greece, and with the preparations. In the year after that, a rebellion in Egypt, which had been conquered by Cambyses, served only to hard Darius' resolve to go to war, not only against Greece but against Egypt too." (Herodotus, *The Histories*, VII, 1).

Darius would never get his chance to exact revenge against the Athenians, as he died soon after in 487 BCE (Forrest 2001, 41), but the Greco-Persian Wars would continue with his son and successor, Xerxes, who would lead an even greater army into Greece.

Achaemenid Persian historical records say nothing of the Battle of Marathon and little concerning the Greco-Persian wars, which is not surprising since the Persian historical tradition was essentially inherited from other ancient Near Eastern traditions that depicted the sovereign as always victorious (Cameron 1983, 80-81). Even had the Persians followed more modern or Hellenic historiographical traditions, they still would have ignored their loss at Marathon due to its one-sidedness. According to Herodotus, the final casualty count of the battle was 5,400 Persians killed while the Greeks only lost 192 men (Herodotus, *The Histories*, VI, 117).

The Second Persian War

Although it is known that Xerxes I became Darius I's successor, the method of succession remains problematic for modern scholarship (Briant 2002, 518-25) and is an important factor when considering reasons why the Persian king initiated the second round of the Greco-Persian Wars. Herodotus (The Histories, VII, 2-4), gives a long account of Xerxes accession to the throne, which he attributed to a combination of the crown prince's mother, Atossa, and the fact that Xerxes was born while Darius I was king, unlike his older brothers who were born before he was king. Old Persian cuneiform inscriptions from the ancient Persian city of Persepolis attribute Xerxes' rise to power to the god Ahuramazda. A text known as "Xerxes Persepolis a" (XPa) states, "Saith Xerxes the King: Other sons of Darius there were, (but) – thus unto Ahuramazda was the desire – Darius my father made me the greatest after himself. When my father Darius went away from the throne, by the will of Ahuramazda I became king on my father's throne. When I became king, I built much excellent (construction). What had been built by my father, that I protected, and other building I added." (Kent 1953, 150).

The text is clearly aimed at proving the new king's legitimacy to rule the Achaemenid Empire, which suggests that there may have been questions within the royal family about Xerxes' right to rule. The text also relates that Xerxes dedicated at least a portion of his time and resources to building projects, which was a way that many kings from various ancient Near Eastern cultures legitimized their rule.

Given that he had rebellions to suppress and possibly questions about his legitimate right to rule, it's fair to wonder why Xerxes embarked on a Herculean effort to invade Greece shortly after his father had been defeated. In answering that question, Herodotus relates in detail that when Xerxes came to power in 486 BCE, his geopolitical interests were to the south of Greece, in Egypt. As Xerxes prepared his punitive expedition against the Egyptians, the Persian general Mardonius, who was famous for losing the Persian fleet in Greece during the reign of Darius I, convinced the Great King to also invade Greece. Herodotus wrote, "Xerxes at first not at all interested in invading Greece but began by building up an army for a campaign in Egypt. But Mardonius – the son of Gobryas and Darius' sister and thus cousin to the king – who was present in court and had more influence with Xerxes than anyone else in the country, used constantly to talk to him on the subject. 'Master,' he would say, 'the Athenians have done us great injury, and it is only right they should be punished for their crimes. By all means finish the talks you already have in hand; but when you have tamed the arrogance of Egypt, then lead an army against Athens. Do that, and your name will be held in honour all over the world, and people will think twice in future before they invade your country.' And to the argument for revenge he would add that Europe was a very beautiful place; it produced every kind of garden tree; the land there was everything that land should be – it was, in short, too good for any mortal except the Persian king." (Herodotus, The Histories, VII, 5).

Mardonius' influence was apparently effective, because Xerxes heeded the call to arms with the further incentives of upholding family honor and retribution for the Athenians' destruction of the city of Sardis during the Ionian revolt. Xerxes proclaimed, "I will bridge the Hellespont and march an army through Europe into Greece, and punish the Athenians for the outrage they committed upon my father and upon us. As you saw, Darius himself was making his preparations for war against these men; but death prevented him from carrying out his purpose. I therefore on his behalf, and for the benefit of all my subjects, will not rest until I have taken Athens and burnt it to the ground, in revenge for the injury which the Athenians without provocation once did to me and my father. These men, you remember, came to Sardis with Aristagoras the Milesian, a slave of ours, and burnt the temples and sacred groves." (Herodotus, The Histories, VII, 8).

These two passages reveal both Xerxes' initial reluctance to attack Greece and his passionate personality, both of which were important for how the fighting turned out, but either way, once the emperor was in favor of an invasion of Europe, the great Persian army would have to be mobilized and moved from Asia to Europe.

The Persian army's mobilization and mustering was no doubt the largest type in history until that time and was probably the largest until the First Crusade about 1,500 years later. The logistical feat of just assembling the army took years, and according to Herodotus, the amount of materials consumed by the army was immense. The historian wrote, "For the four years following the conquest of Egypt the mustering of troops and the provision of stores and equipment continued, and toward the close of the fifth Xerxes, at the head of his enormous army, began his march. . . All these armies together, with others like them, would not have equaled the army of Xerxes. Was there a nation in Asia that he did not take with him to Greece? Save for the great rivers, was there a stream his army drank from that was not drunk dry? Some nations provided ships, others formed infantry units; from some cavalry was requisitioned, from others horse-transports and crews; from others, again, triremes for floating bridges, or provisions and naval craft of various kinds." (Herodotus, The Histories, VII, 20-21).

The mustering of the army took place in Sardis from 484-481 BCE, after which they then set out in the spring of 480 for their long trek to Greece following the Aegean coastline. Before the army left Sardis, Xerxes sent representatives throughout Greece to demand the symbolic "earth and water" from the various kingdoms and city-states (Herodotus, The Histories, VII, 32). Earth and water, if given, was a symbol of a ruler's obeisance and fealty towards the Persian king; the Persian king in turn agreed to leave the subordinate ruler in power and to do no harm to any of his temples or people (Briant 2002, 145). At the same time, however, Xerxes sent no demand for earth and water to the two most important Greek city-states – Athens and Sparta – because the Persian messengers were killed when his father, Darius I, sent demands for earth and water during the first war (Herodotus, The Histories, VII, 133). It would also have been contrary to the partly punitive aspect of Xerxes' expedition against Athens to demand earth and water, since Xerxes did not want the obedience of the Athenians but to destroy and enslave them.

According to Herodotus, the entire army – soldiers, sailors, marines, and various support personnel – numbered 1,700,000 (Herodotus, The Histories, VII, 60) and it took them an entire week to bridge and cross the Hellespont, which is a channel in the Aegean that separates Asia from Europe (Herodotus, The Histories, VII, 56). While it's almost certain that number was inflated, the most important number concerning the size of the Persian army in relation to the Battle of Salamis was the 1207 triremes (war ships) that Herodotus said comprised the Persian fleet. Since Persia was a landlocked country, nearly the entire navy was gathered from other peoples, including 300 of the ships being manned by Phoenicians and 200 sailed by Egyptians (Herodotus, The Histories, VII, 89-96).

Of course, Xerxes and the Persians were not the only ones who prepared for the coming war. As the great Persian army began its long march into Europe, the Greeks, particularly the Athenians, also made preparations that would ultimately ensure their victory at the Battle of Salamis. Recognizing that war was in all likelihood an inevitability, the Athenians had begun the construction of a giant fleet, but because Athens could not hope to bear the expense of both treasure and manpower of funding both a standing army and a fleet, they had sought support elsewhere. The chief Greek states, ignoring the ambassadors that Xerxes sent to demand earth and water in 481 BCE, met at Corinth to decide on what was to be done. Their resolve was an indication of the measure of the crisis they faced, for the Greek city-states were notoriously fractious and only came together in times of the greatest emergency.

At the Hellespont, Xerxes planned to cross the straits via a gigantic bridge of boats, an incredibly ambitious endeavor and one that ends with one of antiquity's most colorful legends. Herodotus reported that the Persians' first attempt to bridge the Hellespont failed after a storm destroyed the flax and papyrus cables of the bridges. Enraged, Xerxes ordered his men to whip the Hellespont with 300 lashes and throw fetters into the water.

Illustration of Xerxes ordering his men to whip the Hellespont, 1909

After the meeting at Corinth, a force of 10,000 allied troops, under the command of the Spartans, was sent to blockade the pass of Tempe, in Thessaly, only to discover that Xerxes had stolen a march on them. Despite the first failure, the Persians had actually accomplished the unthinkable and physically bridged the Hellespont in 480 BCE, crossing into northern Greece to the south of the hoplites waiting at Tempe. There was now only one way to stop Xerxes; to cross into Greece proper, the Persians would be forced to travel through the narrow defile of the mountain pass at Thermopylae, a site which had already seen its fair share of battle due to its strategic nature. If the Greeks could hold Xerxes off at Thermopylae, and concurrently if the allied fleet could stop the Persian navy at Artemisium to prevent a bypass, then the invasion of Greece could be defeated.

The Spartans, as expected, were put in command of all allied land forces. Their prowess in battle, born of the fact that all Spartan citizens trained from boyhood in the ruthless warrior academy of the *agoge* to be perfect in the pursuit of feats of athletics and arms (and something they were able to do free of constraints as they delegated all manual labor to the helots) was legendary, and their fame rightly acquired. The Spartan hoplites were very rarely defeated, and the sight of their red-cloaked hoplites, with the Lambdas (Greek letter "L", shaped line an inverted "V", for Laekedaemon, the Spartan heartland) stark on their shields, was often enough to prompt enemies to flee the field altogether.

The Greeks set about making their preparations while Xerxes' army advanced south through Thessaly and Macedonia, a horde to end all hordes. There has been intense speculation and debate among historians as to just how large the Persian army was, with ancient accounts reporting that it drank rivers dry and stripped entire regions of their crops. Though Herodotus and the other Greek sources talk of a force numbering anything between a million and two and a half million fighting men, with equivalent numbers of support personnel, these figures are in all likelihood exaggerated, the product of either Greek propaganda or Persian misinformation. Modern scholars believe Xerxes' army was a more manageable but still extremely formidable 300,000-500,000 men, and the lowest modern estimates put the number at 100,000. Even the celebrated Spartans would have their work cut out for them.

Indeed, the campaign might well be over before it had properly begun, for the timing of Xerxes' advance could not have been more unfortunate for the Greeks. As the Persians approached Thermopylae, the Spartans were engaged in celebrating the festival of Carneia, the traditional period of peacetime in Laekedaemon during which time no armies could march, on pain of offending the Gods in the gravest way possible. One of the two Spartan kings, Leonidas (the Spartans always had two monarchs, so that if one should fall in battle Sparta would still have a ruler), beseeched the Ephors, the Spartan high priests, for a special permission to dispatch a unit to Thermopylae. Given the extraordinary circumstances, the Ephors granted him the right to take the King's Bodyguard, a unit of three hundred men, to war.

Leonidas was sure he was marching to his death, since the renowned oracle at Delphi had predicted that Sparta must mourn a king in order to achieve victory. According to ancient accounts, the oracle foretold:

"For you, inhabitants of wide-wayed Sparta,
Either your great and glorious city must be wasted by Persian men,
Or if not that, then the bound of Lacedaemon must mourn a dead king, from Heracles' line.
The might of bulls or lions will not restrain him with opposing strength; for he has the might of Zeus.
I declare that he will not be restrained until he utterly tears apart one of these."

Seeking to fulfill the prophecy, Leonidas personally picked 300, all of which had living sons so their bloodlines would not be extinguished. According to Plutarch, when Leonidas was asked upon his departure by his wife Gorgo, Queen of Sparta, what she should do in his absence, he replied, "Marry a good man and bear good children."

Statue of Leonidas

The Spartans were willingly creating a suicide unit, but to the men who joined Leonidas it was undoubtedly a high honor to be selected. The ancient Roman historian Plutarch captured the essence of the Spartans' thinking and culture in recounting a story about one of the men who was not chosen, "When Paedaretus was not chosen to be one of the Three Hundred, an honor which ranked highest in the State, he departed cheerful and smiling, with the remark that he was glad if the State possessed three hundred citizens who were better than himself."

Thus, in the summer of 480 BCE, Leonidas and his men marched towards Thermopylae. Alongside the vaunted 300 Spartans were a further 600 of the *perioikoi,* the Spartan "peers", which enjoyed similar rights to full-blooded Spartan citizens, and an equal number of helot servants and light infantrymen, for a total of 1,500. The Spartans were quickly joined along the march by another 3,000 hoplites from Corinth, Arcadia, Mantinea, Tegea and Mycenae, and more troops joined them as they progressed out of the Peloponnese and into Northern Greece. The Thespians sent 700 hoplites, the Thebans 400, and when the allied army reached Thermopylae the Phokians and Locrians, who inhabited the lands directly to the south of the pass, sent all 2,000 men they had, according to Herodotus. Thus, to bolster Leonidas' ranks, the Greeks either had around 6,000 men according to Herodotus or 7,500 according to ancient historian Diodorus Sicilus. Whatever the actual number, the Greeks were facing what even modern historians have estimated as being upwards of half a million men. Based on modern estimates, at best the Greeks were facing odds of 20-1, but it's more likely there were 50-80 Persians for every Greek.

Obviously the Greeks heading toward Thermopylae knew they were going to be outnumbered by an astounding amount ahead of time, so they were obviously determined to stand and fight there no matter how many men Xerxes had. As Plutarch so aptly put it, "The Spartans used to ask about the enemy, it was not important how many there are, but where the enemy was." But the Greeks weren't heading to Thermopylae simply to die a glorious death; they chose it because it was the best defensive ground.

To bolster their defense, the Greeks planned to occupy the narrowest point of the pass at Thermopylae, what was known as the "Middle Gate". At that spot, there still stood the ruins of an ancient wall built by the Phokians, which would help the defense of the pass. Some of the Peloponnesian allies, once they had surveyed the site, offered the opinion that they should abandon Phokis and Locris to their fate and fall back to the isthmus of Corinth, where it would be easier to summon reinforcement, but Leonidas was adamant that they must make their stand at Thermopylae, or not at all, not least because he had 2,000 Phokian and Locrian soldiers at his orders now. But Leonidas' considerations were tactical as well as political. Simply put, Thermopylae, "The Hot Gates" in Greek (named from the hot springs that made it a sought-after spa location for travellers from all across Greece), was the best possible place for a numerically inferior enemy to contest Xerxes' passage. Though the geography of the pass has changed considerably over the millennia, in ancient times it consisted of a track running at the bottom of a defile about 100 yards across, snaking its way along the coast. To one side of the path, the land fell away sheer to the rocky coast below, while to the other the pass was hemmed in by impassable cliffs. There was a single mountain path which could allow a small force to bypass Thermopylae, a fact which the Greeks knew but the Persians did not. Accordingly, Leonidas dispatched a thousand of his men to guard the path, while he arrayed the rest of his troops defensively across the narrow aperture known as the Middle Gate (there were three such tightenings of the pass all told) with the hastily reinforced Phokian wall as a fallback defensive position. In the narrow pass, Xerxes' massive advantage in numbers would be nullified. Now all Leonidas and his men could do was wait.

Some time after Leonidas, his Spartans and their allies had set up their defensive position at Thermopylae, and with the allied fleet standing to off Artemisium, Xerxes' army finally arrived. In August of 480 BCE, the Spartan scouts (possibly the *Skiritai,* the celebrated Spartan light infantry, who always fought on the extreme left of the Spartan battle-line, directly opposite the enemy elite troops) spotted a great horde of armed men moving on the far side of the Malian Gulf. Tens, then hundreds of thousands of armed men, followed by an equal or even greater number of slaves and camp followers, and more bullocks, horses, camels and assorted cattle than the assembled Greeks had ever seen in their lives.

Xerxes' horde was big enough to blacken the ground from horizon to horizon, and all that stood between it and Greece were six, perhaps seven thousand hoplites. Yet, remarkably, or perhaps as a testament for the respect he had for Greek heavy infantry, Xerxes did not attack at once. Instead, he chose to talk. He dispatched an envoy to the Leonidas and the Greeks, asking them to stand down and grant him passage, and promising that the Spartans themselves would receive untold honors if they would but submit. The Greeks, Xerxes' envoy argued, would still be free; inclusion in the Persian Empire would mean riches and privilege for all. Leonidas, however, did not see things quite that way. Capitulation, he and the Greek allied generals argued, was tantamount to slavery. At Leonidas' stubborn refusal to see sense, Xerxes' envoy grew irate and insisted the Spartans and their allies lay down their weapons. According to Plutarch, Leonidas replied with the famous phrase "molōn labé", "Come and take them."

The words molṑn labé inscribed on the marble of the Leonidas Monument at Thermopylae. Today this is the motto of the Greek 1st Army Corps.

Five days passed while the Greeks waited and Xerxes determined what was to be done. His navy could not hope to force the passage at the straits of Artemisium without suffering extremely heavy casualties, and might well be turned back altogether. Likewise, outflanking the small Greek force at Thermopylae appeared impossible. The Persians would have no choice, then, except to make a fight of it. On the morning of the fifth day after the Persian army's arrival, Xerxes gave his orders. 5,000 archers moved forward into position towards the Greek encampment at the Phokian wall. The battle of Thermopylae had begun.

With the Spartans in the vanguard, Leonidas ordered the Greeks to take up the phalanx formation across the pass and arrayed them before the wall as the Persian archers advanced to within a hundred yards of the Greeks. From there, the Persians unleashed a colossal volley of arrows against them. Like all good archers, it is likely that at that range the Persians could shoot three volleys while their first arrow was still in the air, and the Greeks soon found themselves under a veritable hail of darts. However, to the Persians' great consternation, the Greeks literally shrugged them off. The light Persian bows were a far cry from the longbows or compound bows of the English and Mongols, which could punch through armor at three hundred yards, and the Greeks' thick bronze shields, helmets and armor completely protected them from the storm of arrows, which the ancient historians claimed caused only a few light flesh-wounds. Shaken, Xerxes ordered his archers to fall back and sent in his hammer-blow: ten thousand of his best infantry, natives of the Persian heartland of Media and Cissia, which included among their officers a number of Xerxes' own relatives, scions of the royal family. It was time for the Spartans to prove why they were the best heavy infantry in the world.

Like a wave, the Medes and Cissians swept forward towards the Greek positions, where the Spartans, *Periokoi*, and other Peloponnesians had taken up their place in the van with Leonidas, who was in his 60th year and thus considerably older than he has historically been portrayed. Nevertheless, like a wave hitting a cliff, as the Persians smashed against the Greek phalanx they broke. The Persians had just encountered the famous "Wall of Bronze", and these initial attackers were powerless against it. Their courage and valor could not be disputed, but their training and equipment were completely inadequate to the task. The Persians had shorter spears, making it hard for them to even reach the Greek phalanx before getting speared themselves. And even if they did make contact, the lighter shields and shorter spears and swords of the Persians prevented them from effectively engaging the Greek hoplites. Their light spears shivered against the great bronze-fronted shields and thick armor of the hoplites, their sabers and short swords cut ineffectually at the crested helmets and bronze-wrapped shins, and their own light armor and wicker shields could do nothing to prevent the heavy Greek spears from punching through them like paper, splitting the men wielding them.

Despite their advantage in numbers and the great number of men they poured into the pass, try as they might the Persians could make no headway against the Greek forces. Indeed, they soon found themselves on the receiving end of what the hoplites had spent countless soul-numbing hours practicing: *Othismos*. This was the "mass shove" of the hoplite phalanx, which began pushing the Persians in their front backwards and chewing up their line like a meat-grinder. Thousands of the Medes and Cissians were cut down, while still more were crushed to death by the press of men or were literally hurled off the cliffs to drown or smash into the rocks below. According to Herodotus, this was achieved at the cost of only a few Spartan dead. The carnage was so catastrophic for the Persians that Xerxes, who was watching the battle from the heights above, leapt up from his chair three times in mortal anguish for his men, who were being cut to pieces in the defile below. The Greek historian Ctesias wrote that the Persians' first wave was "cut to ribbons", yet only only two or three Spartans were dead.

Fighting in the phalanx, even for trained warriors, was incredibly taxing physically. The need to be constantly reactive, often at a split second's notice, in order to block a thrust or slash or strike back in turn, coupled with wearing over 60 pounds of armor and constantly shoving against a solid-packed mass of men was so exhausting that it could only be endured for a handful of minutes at a time, even by the Spartans. Because of this, the Greek troops rotated their units (generally divided by city of origin) in and out of the battle-line to ensure a constant supply of fresh hoplites to the meat-grinder of the phalanx. According to Herodotus, this was also an indication that the Greeks had sufficient numbers to block the entire pass. The Greek soldiers were so exhausted from fighting that, as soon as they were relieved, they dropped to the ground as though dead, while the helots rushed to assist them. The ground, which had been hard-packed and parched in summer, was churned with blood.

In the early afternoon, a lull fell on the battlefield as the Persian forces pulled back, which allowed the Greeks a chance to catch their breath and tend to the small wounds which, despite their armor, were a natural consequence of fighting in the Phalanx. Given that fighting in the phalanx formation consisted largely of a confused shoving brawl where weapons burst into fragments of wood and iron and people lunged with knives, swords, spears and axes, it's quite likely that a significant number of wounds would be the result of "friendly fire" by overly enthusiastic fellow hoplites. And though they reportedly suffered few casualties in the first wave of fighting, the Greeks were impressed by the bravery of the Persians, who despite being decidedly outmatched had continued to hurl themselves at the phalanx, even tearing with their own bare hands at the weapons and shields of the enemy in an attempt to disarm them so that their comrades might get a spear-thrust in.

The Medes and Cissians had acquitted themselves nobly if futilely, and they had been bloodily repulsed, but Xerxes was far from done. The Spartans and their allies had barely dented his great horde, and now he dispatched the hammer-blow that he assumed would fell them in earnest. Against troops already bone-weary from the morning's battle, he sent in his famed 10,000 man crack unit, the Immortals. Unlike the Medes and Cissians, the Immortals advanced into battle in tomb-like, utter silence (as the Spartans did themselves), in a deliberate attempt to avoid battle-frenzy and instill fear into the waiting enemy. The Greek hoplites rose to their feet, shouldered their shields, and took up their positions in the phalanx. The Persians were coming again.

Depiction of the Immortals in the Palace of Darius I

The Persians' elite corps remains the subject of much intrigue, including over the origins of their name. It was Herodotus who referred to the force as the "Immortals", claiming that the name referred to the fact that the force was always 10,000 strong, and that there was thus always a new member to replace a wounded or dead one. Though there is evidence from Persia that the unit did exist, no name was attached to them, and modern historians believe that Herodotus and/or his source mistook the name Anûšiya ("companions") with Anauša ('Immortals')."

Herodotus wrote in his *Histories* of all the extra perks the Immortals received, including concubines and food designated only for them, but they were about to receive the same treatment from the Greeks that their counterparts had received earlier. Xerxes may very well have hoped or even assumed that his vaunted Immortals would make short shrift of the tired Greeks, especially because it was not even the Spartans but one of the allied contingents who first rose to take their place in the battle-line against them. However, once again the superior training and armament of the hoplites proved decisive. Though slightly more heavily armored than their Mede and Cissian counterparts, the Immortals were no match for the phalanx, who suckered the Immortals deeper into the pass by feigning a retreat and tempting the Persians to chase after them. Once again, Xerxes was forced to watch in horror as his vaunted infantry was cut to ribbons in the pass.

At last, as darkness fell, the decimated Immortals fell back, yielding the field of battle to the Greeks, who were so tired that many of them needed their comrades to physically force food and water into their mouths because they were incapable of taking sustenance themselves.

Though the night passed without incident, the dawn of the second day of the battle brought no respite for the Greeks. Though his elite shock troops had failed, Xerxes still had tens of thousands or even hundreds of thousands of completely fresh troops to throw at the Hot Gates. Counting on the fact that the Spartans and their allies would be exhausted and/or injured by wounds, and incapable of putting up a spirited resistance, Xerxes launched an all-out assault against the Phokian wall.

Yet again, Xerxes could not have been more wrong. Driven to extremes of valor and endurance by a desire to match up to the notorious Spartans, the allied Greeks performed like prodigies on the second day, and once again the phalanx proved to be a bulwark that could take any amount of enemy damage, shrugging off the Persian attacks without faltering. Now, however, fatigue began to tell in earnest, and as the Greeks became more sluggish, the number of casualties began to rise. Dozens were killed, and many more wounded, including a significant number of Spartans. Despite their casualties and exhaustion, however, the Greeks managed to push back the advancing Persians once more and, towards midday, Xerxes' men fell back to their encampment, now by all accounts terrified by the apparent utter invincibility of their foes.

It was at this crucial moment, when Xerxes was pondering if even attrition could destroy the Spartans and their allies, that he received what amounted to a gift from the gods. A native of Thracis named Ephialtes deserted to his side and revealed to his generals that there existed a remote mountain path, through which the Persians could march to the rear of Thermopylae. This would allow the Persians to envelop the defending Greek forces and destroy them. Ephialtes' name would later become so reviled as a traitor that his name virtually disappears from Greek histories altogether, indicating the shame associated with it. Even in modern Greece, the name Ephialtes is synonymous with traitor, and his name has become the word for "nightmare" in modern Greek.

According to Herodotus, two other men were accused of betraying the hidden trail to the Persians: Onetas, a native of Carystus and son of Phanagoras; and Corydallus, a native of Anticyra. However, Herodotus was certain that it was actually Ephialtes because, as he wrote, "the deputies of the Greeks, the Pylagorae, who must have had the best means for ascertaining the truth, did not offer the reward on the heads of Onetas and Corydallus, but for that of Ephialtes of Trachis."

Whatever the case, Xerxes no longer needed to force his way past the hoplites guarding the Hot Gates. Now he could simply outflank them and appear in both their front and rear. At dawn of the third day of the battle, General Mardonius, at the head of 10,000 Immortals (whose numbers were immediately filled by selecting eligible recruits from other units) and a further 10,000 Persian troops, moved up the path that Ephialtes had revealed, surprising the 1,000 Phokian hoplites who were guarding it. Faced with overwhelming odds and without a similarly effective defensive position to protect, the Phokians fell back to a hilltop nearby, where they planned to make a final stand, but the Persians contented themselves with keeping them at a distance with volleys of arrows while the main force proceeded at the double down the path.

A Phokian runner raced ahead of them, bearing the grave news to Leonidas; in a few hours at most, his troops would be encircled. Staring calamity in the face, Leonidas convened a council of war with his surviving generals. Despite their previous successes, all the Greeks knew that staying to fight meant death. Accordingly, many of the generals leading the Greek contingents chose retreat as the only viable option, but not Leonidas. With the weight of prophecy, Spartan military tradition, and simple common tactical sense on his shoulders, he bade the other Greek contingents disperse, but he and his Spartans were determined to stand and die. According to Plutarch, Leonidas exhorted his men, "Eat well, for tonight we dine in Hades."

The reason for Leonidas' decision is simple, and it has less to do with bombast and the will of the gods than it does with a desire not to see his entire command annihilated. By fighting a rearguard action, he could ensure that the slow-moving hoplites would be able to escape before Xerxes' cavalry, unleashed on the vast plains behind Thermopylae, could run them down and cut them to pieces. Thus, those who would stay behind to fight were doing so in an effort to save those who fled.

Whether it was because so many other Greeks were just as brave as the Spartans or because they realized the tactical situation, what was left of the 700 Thespians refused to leave even when ordered to do so, as did 400 Thebans. The helots who had accompanied the Spartans into battle also refused to retreat. Thus, while the majority of the Greek forces departed the battlefield, a mixed unit of around 1,700 men stayed back to defend the pass against Xerxes and the Persians.

As daylight washed across the battlefield, Xerxes made his customary morning sacrifices and, having established that the Immortals were now advancing towards the rear of what remained of the Greek forces, ordered a fresh wave of ten thousand infantry to advance against the Phokian wall.

This time, however, the Greeks did not remain on the defensive. Rather, in a last, desperate, glorious attempt to take as many of the enemy with them as they could, they advanced into the wider part of the path, meeting the Persians where every Greek spear and sword could be brought to bear. The struggle was brutal and vicious, and despite the odds it lasted for hours as the Greeks inflicted carnage upon the Persian forces but began to be slowly whittled down. According to Herodotus, when all their spears were shattered, and even their buttspikes had been smashed to kindling, the Greeks fought on with swords, daggers and captured Persian weapons, continuing a desperate melee where all form of fighting order broke down completely.

At the height of this fighting, Leonidas himself was killed, feathered with shafts by Persian archers, and a massive running fight broke out between the Greeks, desperate to keep his body in their possession, and the Persians who sought to despoil it. It was at this point, when the fighting was at its most bitter, that two of Xerxes' own brothers were killed, but both sides could not sustain a massacre of such ferocity for long. Greeks and Persians alike fell back to draw breath and, with the Immortals now approaching from their rear, the remnants of the Greek force dragged their dead and wounded back to a hill not far behind the Phokian wall to make one final stand.

It was at this point that Herodotus claims the Thebans had a change of heart. Historians have largely assumed the Thebans were brought as hostages to Thermopylae, as Herodotus himself suggested, which makes it unclear why the departing Greeks didn't take the hostages back with them. Some historians speculate the Thebans that remained were loyal to the Greek cause, but here Herodotus seems to dispel that notion in writing that they "moved away from their companions, and with hands upraised, advanced toward the barbarians..." Shouting that they surrendered, they advanced towards the Persians, casting their weapons aside. Many were cut down either out of vengeance or because the Persians suspected a trick, but eventually the rest were seized and borne away in chains.

The final act of the drama was about to unfold. The Persians swept in against the beleaguered Greeks who stood, back to back, atop the knoll they had chosen to die on. Their armor was in pieces, their shields stove in or long gone, and their weapons were little more than sticks and blunted, twisted pieces of metal. Herodotus described the final scene, "Here they defended themselves to the last, those who still had swords using them, and the others resisting with their hands and teeth." Finally, furious at the losses he had suffered, Xerxes ordered his men to fall back and, with his archers standing in at a distance, had the remaining Greeks slaughtered with a hail of arrows.

With the desperate fighting finally over, the Greeks had lost between two and three thousand men, but they had succeeded in holding the pass for three days and inflicted several times their number of casualties. It was a defeat, obviously, but one that had the flavor of victory. In fact, Thermopylae so enraged Xerxes that he ignored Persian customs honoring valiant enemy warriors and had Leonidas' corpse beheaded and crucified. Though the Greeks who had stayed behind to contest the passage of Xerxes' troops had perished to the last man, their sacrifice would echo throughout Greece, an inspiration for the men preparing for the battles yet to come, when the fate of all the Hellenic world would be decided.

Thermopylae had been the gates of Greece, and after the battle Xerxes advanced with both his army and navy into the heart of his enemies' territory. Greece's allied fleet retreated from its blockading position at Artemisium towards Salamis, where they helped ferry the Athenians away from their city and onto the island not far from the shore. Meanwhile, the Persian army advanced into the interior, putting Boeotia (including Thespiae) to the torch before marching on Athens itself. Finding the city deserted by almost all of its citizens, Xerxes vented his spite upon the

Greeks and took revenge for his father's defeat at Marathon by putting the entire city to the torch, forcing the Athenian citizens to watch as their city was turned to rubble.

In the aftermath of the campaign, a stone lion was erected on the site of the last stand of Leonidas' men at Thermopylae, and most of the bodies were interred there, Spartan, Helot and Allied (although Leonidas' bones were eventually returned to Sparta). Over them was laid a plaque bearing the epitaph written by the celebrated poet Simonides, one that has since spawned countless variations like, "Go tell the Spartans, stranger passing by, that here, according to their laws, we lie".

Ancient Athens is remembered militarily for its prowess on the sea, but if not for some fortuitous circumstances, the Athenians would never have become a maritime power and the Persians may have won the Battle of Salamis. In 483 BE, while the Persian army was mustering in Sardis, a large deposit of silver was discovered about 25 miles south east of Athens in a place that would later be named Laurium (Hale 2009, 7). This serendipitous discovery by the Athenians proved to be a boon to their economy, but the city leaders came to an impasse over how to spend the money; most of the city leaders wanted to put the 600,000 drachmas of silver towards a dole fund, but Themistocles, the great hero of the Battle of Salamis, had other ideas (Hale 2009, 11). Themistocles argued that the silver surplus should be used to build a navy, which the Athenians in turn would use to fight the Greek city-state of Aegina. Herodotus explained, "Themistocles, however, persuaded them to give up this idea and, instead of distributing the money, to spend it on the construction of two hundred warships for use in the war with Aegina. The outbreak of this war at that moment saved Greece by forcing Athens to become a maritime power." (Herodotus, The Histories, VII, 144).

Depiction of Themistocles

Herodotus' account is corroborated by the later historian and biographer Plutarch, who also gives more details concerning Themistocles' intelligence and personality. Plutarch wrote, "And so, in the first place, whereas the Athenians were wont to divide up among themselves the revenue coming from the silver mines at Laureium, he, and he alone, dared to come before the people with a motion that this division be given up, and that with these moneys triremes be constructed for the war against Aegina. This was the fiercest war then troubling Hellas, and the islanders controlled the sea, owing to the number of their ships. Wherefore all the more easily did Themistocles carry his point, not by trying to terrify the citizens with dreadful pictures of Darius or the Persians – these were too far away and inspired no very serious fear of their coming, but by making opportune use of the bitter jealousy which they cherished toward Aegina in order to secure armament he desired. The result was that with these moneys they built a hundred triremes, with which they actually fought at Salamis against Xerxes." (Plutarch, Themistocles, IV, 1-2).

Themistocles' oratory skills, intelligence, and guile convinced the other Athenian leaders to go with his plan, which ultimately saved their city from the Persians, but he was also successful in convincing them of the type of navy they should build. Themistocles specified that the navy would be comprised of fast, light triremes, which were designed for ramming, not carrying large numbers of marines (Hale 2009, 20). In Themistocles' judgment, it was the Persian navy that was its Achilles heel, so a well-trained and equipped Athenian navy would be the only way to defeat Xerxes and his army. Despite defeating the Persian army on the plane of Marathon, the force that Xerxes was bringing with him south on land was so much larger that the Greeks had thought to find another way to defeat the Persians this time around. The Persian navy was also vast, but unlike its army, which had a solid core of Persian fighters, it was primarily made up of subject peoples who were forced to fight (Hale 2009, 34).

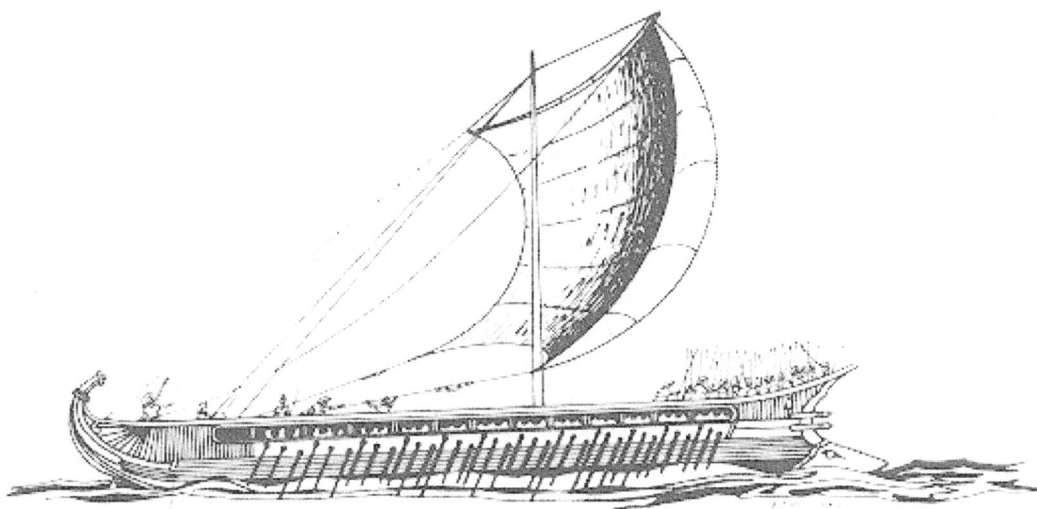

An illustration of a Greek trireme

Themistocles was able to build the Athenian navy through his silver tongue with the silver discovered in Attica, and he then used even more duplicitous methods to become the general of the Athenian fleet. According to Plutarch, there were not many men who desired to lead the Athenians against the Persians, due in large measure to fears of Persian reprisals should Xerxes defeat the Greeks. However, fear did not stop all candidates, and Themistocles and an apparently corrupt man named Epicydes were finalists for the position until the former used his guile to displace the latter. Plutarch explained, "At last, when the Mede was descending upon Hellas and the Athenians were deliberating who should be their general, all the rest, they say, voluntarily renounced their claims to the generalship, so panic-stricken were they at the danger; but Epicydes, the son of Euphemides, a popular leader who was powerful in speech but effeminate in spirit and open to bribes, set out to get the office, and was likely to prevail in the election; so Themistocles, fearing lest matters should got to utter ruin in case the leadership fell to such a man, bribed and bought off the ambition of Epicydes." (Plutarch, Themistocles, VI, 1).

With Themistocles firmly in the position as general, the Athenians had a capable leader who could defeat the Persian fleet. The Athenians also temporarily rescinded all ostracisms in 480 BCE, which allowed notable and wealthy citizens to return to defend their possessions. Athens later benefited from this policy at the Battle of Salamis since the formerly banished Aristides, the second most important Athenian at the battle, fought valiantly alongside his countrymen (Plutarch, Aristides, VIII, 1).

The Greeks then had two final acts of preparation to make before Xerxes and the Persian army arrived in Attica: they had to evacuate most of the Attic peninsula and consult their oracles. The ancient Greeks were a very religious people who saw the influence and actions of their gods in most events, great and small. Poseidon protected Greek mariners, Athena did the same to her eponymously named city, and Zeus sat on Mount Olympus presiding over all mortals and immortals alike. When the Greeks had important questions that pertained to worldly events and situations, they consulted oracles for answers, and the most important oracle in the Greek world was Apollo's oracle in the city of Delphi (Parker 2001, 320). Thus, the Athenians approached the oracle and asked directly what course of action they should take against the approaching Persian army, and Herodotus recorded that the oracle replied:

> "Why sit you, doomed ones? Fly to the world's end, leaving
>
> Home and the heights your city circles like a wheel.
>
> The head shall not remain in its place, nor the body,
>
> Nor the feet beneath, nor the hands, nor the parts between;
>
> But all is ruined, for fire and the headlong god of war
>
> Spending in a Syrian chariot shall bring you low.
>
> May a tower shall he destroy, not your alone,
>
> And give to pitiless fire many shrines of gods,
>
> Which even now stand sweating, with fear quivering,
>
> While over the roof-tops black blood runs streaming
>
> In prophecy of woe that needs must come. But rise.
>
> Haste from the sanctuary and bow your hearts to grief." (Herodotus, The Histories, VII. 140).

The oracle's answer both upset and confused the Athenians, who then decided to approach the oracle a second time with olive branches in their hands as signs of their supplication (Herodotus, The Histories, VII, 141). The second prophecy was still enigmatic, but it proved be the final statement on the matter. Herodotus wrote that this time, the oracle said:

> "Not wholly can Pallas win the heart of Olympian Zeus,
>
> Though she prays him with many prayers and all her subtlety;
>
> Yet will I speak to you this other word, as firm as adamant:
>
> Though all else shall be taken within the bound of Cercrops
>
> And the fastness of the holy mountain of Cithaeron,
>
> Yet Zeus the all-seeing grants to Athene's prayer
>
> That the wooden wall only shall not fall, but help you and
>
> your Children.
>
> But await not the host of horse and foot coming from Asia,
>
> Or be still, but turn your back and withdraw from the foe.
>
> Truly a day will come when you will meet him face to face.
>
> Divine Salamis, you will bring death to women's sons
>
> When the corn is scattered, or the harvest gathered in." (Herodotus, The
Histories, VII, 141).

The second prophecy was a bit clearer, but a new question arose: what was the wooden wall?
Determining what the oracle meant by the wooden wall immediately became a new source of
debate amongst the Athenians, and while one party believed that it referred to the wooden
palisade around the Acropolis in Athens, another faction believed it was in reference to the new
Athenian fleet (Herodotus, The Histories, VII, 142).

The Athenians, with their democratic nature, appeared to be at an impasse once more, and it
would be bridged not by a priest or oracle but by Athens' supreme commander and orator,
Themistocles. The Athenian commander had invested too much into the Athenian fleet to let it
slip away through a misinterpreted prophecy, so he did what any far-sighted military commander
would have done by interpreting the prophecy himself. Herodotus noted, " There was however, a
man in Athens who had recently come into prominence – Themistocles called Neocles' son; he
now came forward and declared that there was an important point in which the professional
interpreters were mistaken. If, he maintained, the disaster referred to was to strike the Athenians,
it would not have been expressed in such mild language. 'Hateful Salamis' would surely have
been a more likely phrase than 'divine Salamis', if the inhabitants of the country were doomed to
destruction there. On the contrary, the true interpretation was that the oracle referred not the

Athenians but to their enemies. The 'wooden wall' did, indeed, mean ships; so he advised his countrymen to prepare at once to meet the invader at sea." (Herodotus, The Histories, VII, 143).

Themistocles' charm, charisma, and oratorical skills prevailed once more as the Athenians decided to evacuate Athens and Attica and to make their stand on the sea in the narrow channel between the Attic peninsula and the island of Salamis, but before the Greeks would make their retreat further south to the island of Salamis and even further to the Peloponnesian peninsula, they had to form a formal alliance. Thus, as Xerxes and the Persian army was rampaging its way south through the kingdoms of Thrace and Macedon, a number of Greek city-states held a conference and formed the Hellenic League, with Sparta playing the role of military leader (Herodotus, The Histories, VII, 145). Once the Athenians had chosen a leader, built a navy, and recruited allies, it was time for them to put their plan into motion.

With the Persians marching south, the Greeks decided that they would meet Xerxes and his forces in order to give their people more time to evacuate Attica. After the meeting at Corinth, a force of 10,000 allied Greek troops, under the command of the Spartans, was sent to blockade the pass of Tempe in Thessaly, only to discover that Xerxes had stolen a march on them. Despite the first failure, the Persians had actually accomplished the unthinkable and physically bridged the Hellespont in 480 BCE, thereby crossing into northern Greece to the south of the hoplites waiting at Tempe. There was now only one way to stop Xerxes; to cross into Greece proper, the Persians would be forced to travel through the narrow defile of the mountain pass at Thermopylae, a site which had already seen its fair share of battle due to its strategic nature. If the Greeks could hold Xerxes off at Thermopylae, and concurrently if the allied fleet could stop the Persian navy at Artemisium to prevent a bypass, then the invasion of Greece could be defeated.

Thermopylae was clearly an important battle in the Greco-Persian Wars, but a naval engagement between the Persian and Athenian fleets that took place at the same time near the city of Artemisium had an even greater impact on the Battle of Salamis. Herodotus' account states that the Greeks were vastly outnumbered by the Persian fleet, but that the battle was a draw (Herodotus, The Histories, VIII, 8-200). Plutarch's account reveals more details, particularly how the Greeks used their experiences at Artemisium at the subsequent Battle of Salamis. He wrote, "The battles which were fought at that time with the ships of the Barbarians in the narrows were not decisive of the main issue, it is true, but they were of the greatest service to the Hellenes in giving them experience, since they were thus taught by actual achievements in the face of danger that neither multitudes of ships." (Plutarch, Themistocles, VIII, 1).

Plutarch's passage reveals two important aspects of naval warfare that the Athenians learned at Artemisium and would later use at Salamis. First, the Athenians, due to their inferior numbers, fought in the narrows against the Persian fleet, where the Persians' numerical superiority mattered less since only a limited number of ships could fight at one time in the bottleneck created by the narrows. Furthermore, the Greeks learned that they could stand in the face of a numerically superior enemy, and the confidence the Athenians gained from the Battle of Artemisium went a long way towards their victory at Salamis.

Despite the good showing of the Greek fleet at Artemisium, it only slowed the Persian advance temporarily and, if anything, provoked the wrath of Xerxes even more. When the Greek defense of Thermopylae failed, they fell back on their second defensive line, which spread across the Isthmus of Corinth on land, where the Peloponnesians (mainly Spartans) constructed a wall. The other end was at the Salamis strait (Hale 2009, 57). The Greeks yielded all land north of the line – essentially all of Attica – to Xerxes and the Persians.

Any Greeks who were unlucky enough to be caught north of the defensive line suffered greatly under the Persian army. Herodotus explained, "Along the valley of the Cephisus nothing was spared; Drymus, Charadra, Erochus, Tethronium, Amphicaea, Neon, Pedies, Trites, Elateia, Huampolis, Parapotamii – all these places were burnt to the ground, including Abae, where there was a temple of Apollo richly furnished with treasure and offerings of all kinds. There was an oracle there, as indeed there is today; the shrine belonging to it was plundered and burnt. A few Phocians were chased and caught near the mountains, and some women were raped successively by so many Persians that they died." (Herodotus, The Histories, VIII, 33).

Once the Persian army reached Panopes, it divided into two divisions; Xerxes led one division to Athens, while the other sacked the holy city of Delphi and its temple (Herodotus, The Histories, VIII, 34-5). When the Persians finally arrived in Athens, they found the city largely deserted except for a small force left to defend the Acropolis. After a successful siege, Xerxes leveled the final insult towards the Athenians by ordering the destruction of the Acropolis and its temples. Herodotus wrote, "But in the end the Persians solved their problem: a way of access to the Acropolis was found – for it was prophesied that all Athenian territory upon the continent of Greece must be overrun by the Persians. There is a place in front of the Acropolis, behind the way up to the gates, where the ascent is so steep that no guard was set, because it was not thought possible that any man would be able to climb it; here, by the shrine of Cercrops' daughter Aglaurus, some soldiers managed to scramble up the precipitous face of the cliff. . . Having left not one of them alive, they stripped the temple of its treasures and burnt everything on the Acropolis. Xerxes, now absolute master of Athens, dispatched a rider to Susa with news for Artabanus of his success." (Herodotus, The Histories, VIII, 53-54).

As it turned out, the most crucial battle would take place not on land but on water. The Battle of Salamis was fought in a narrow channel (much like the Battle of Artemisium) that separates the Attic peninsula from the island of Salamis. Despite the name Salamis being attributed to the island in modern times, there is some ambiguity in the ancient sources as to whether the reference was to the island or a town (Hammond 1956, 37).

The most detailed ancient source concerning the physical description and history of Salamis was written by the 1st century CE Greek geographer Pausanias, who wrote, "Salamis lies over against Eleusis, and stretches as far as the territory of Megara. It is said that the first to give this name to the island was Cychreus, who called it after his mother Salamis the daughter of Asopus, and afterwards it was colonised by the Aeginetans with Telamon. Philaeus, the son of Eurysaces, the son of Ajax, is said to have handed the island over to the Athenians, having been made an Athenian by them. Many years afterwards the Athenians drove out all the Salaminians, having discovered that they had been guilty of treachery in the war with Cassander." (Pausanias, Description of Greece, I, 35.1-2).

Obviously, since the battle was at sea, the exact positioning of the ships can only be implied from the historical sources, but two other notable landmarks from the Battle of Salamis can be located on land. Xerxes watched the entire battle from a throne on land (which will be discussed more thoroughly below) below Mount Aegaleos, so modern scholars place his exact position opposite the island of Salamis and above the temple known as the Heracleum, which was the narrowest part of the channel (Hammond 1956, 38). The island of Pysttalia, which was the site of the limited land fighting during the Battle of Salamis, lies at the mouth of the channel (Morkot 1996, 76) in front of the town of Salamis (Hammond 1956, 38).

Perhaps one of the most fascinating aspects of the physical layout of the channel of Salamis is how so many triremes were able to fit into such a tightly confined area. The size of both fleets can be deduced by the accounts of Herodotus and Plutarch, along with Aeschylus' drama *The Persians*. In fact, Plutarch cites Aeschylus as his source for the size of the Persian fleet (Plutarch, Themistocles, XIV, 1), but he only gives the number of Attic (Athenian) ships in his account, which he placed at 180 (Plutarch, Themistocles, XIV, 1). Herodotus' account concurs, as he wrote that the Athenians numbered 180 triremes and accounted for half of the Greek fleet (Herodotus, The Histories, VIII, 44). The passage where Aeschylus noted the numbers of both fleets was a scene where a Persian messenger related the disaster of the battle to Xerxes' mother, Atossa. The scene states, "If number of ships might gain the fight, believe me, queen, the victory had been ours. The Greeks could tell but ten time thirty ships, with other ten, of most select equipment. Xerxes numbered a thousand ships, two hundred sail and seven of rapid wing beside." (Aeschylus The Persians, 312). Based on all three of the ancient accounts, the modern historian N.G.L. Hammond placed the total number of Persian vessels at 1,407 and the Greeks at 380, which included some Greek defectors from the Persian fleet who came over to join their countrymen after the Battle of Artemisium (Hammond 1956, 40).

Despite the discrepancy in numbers, many major battles have been won before the battle even started through supreme planning and strategy, and the Battle of Salamis was no different in this respect. One of the most vital aspects of any military strategy is determining where and when the battle will be fought; if a commander is able to pick the place and time to engage his enemy, then he already has two advantages in his favor. As the Persian fleet advanced towards Salamis and the Persian army neared the Greek wall across the Isthmus of Corinth, not all of the Greeks (especially the Spartans and other Peloponnesians) were convinced that Salamis was an ideal location to engage the Persians, but Themistocles, the wise commander of the Athenians, knew that Greek victory depended on holding the channel near Salamis. Once again, he relied on his excellent oratory skills to convince his countrymen to make a stand. According to Herodotus, Themistocles said, "Now for my plan: it will bring, if you adopt it, the following advantages: first, we shall be fighting in narrow waters, and there, with our inferior numbers, we shall win, provided things go as we may reasonably expect. Fighting in a confined space favours us but the open sea favours the enemy. Secondly, Salamis, where we have put our women and children, will be preserved; and thirdly – for you the most important point of all – you will be fighting in defence of the Peloponnese by remaining here just as much as by withdrawing to the Isthmus – nor, if you have the sense to follow my advice, will you draw the Persian army to the Peloponnese. If we beat them at sea, as I expect we shall, they will not advance to attack you on the Isthmus, or come any further than Attica; they will retreat in disorder, and we shall gain by the preservation of Megara, Aegina, and Salamis – where an oracle has already foretold our victory." (Herodotus, The Histories, VIII, 60).

Not only is Themistocles' intelligence and knowledge of military strategy related in this passage but also a deep understanding of the Greek psyche. After the Battle of Artemisium, Themistocles knew what his fleet was capable of and what it needed to do to win at Salamis; fighting in a narrow channel benefited the numerically inferior Greek fleet as it prevented the Persian fleet from maneuvering a diekplous and surrounding them. The Athenian general also appealed to the Greeks' emotional states by pointing out that the Persians would not stop until they were beaten, and that the oracle at Delphi predicted their wooden wall (of ships) would be the victors.

The Spartans and other Peloponnesians appear to have been placated by Themistocles' speech, but the wily Athenian commander had one last machination planned that would go a long way toward Greek victory at Salamis. Themistocles realized that if the Greek army had no way to retreat, they would fight more fiercely. As the two fleets assembled and faced each other in the Salamis channel, Themistocles believed that many of the men, especially the Peloponnesians, might desert in order to go back and defend their homes, so to prevent this, Themistocles devised a plan that utilized a combination of deception and guile. Herodotus explained, "At this point Themistocles, feeling that he would be outvoted by the Peloponnesians, slipped quietly away from the meeting and sent a man over in a boat to the Persian fleet, with instructions upon what to say when he got there. The man – Sicinnus – was one of Themistocles' slaves and used to attend upon his sons . . . Following his instructions, then, Sicinnus made his way to the Persian commanders and said: 'I am the bearer of a secret communication from the Athenian commander, who is a well-wisher to your king and hopes for a Persian victory. He has told me to report to you that the Greeks are afraid and are planning to slip away. Only prevent them from slipping through your fingers, and you have at this moment an opportunity of unparalleled success. They are at daggers drawn with each other, and will offer no opposition – on the contrary, you will see the pro-Persians amongst them fighting the rest.'" (Herodotus, The Histories, VIII, 75).

In the cover of darkness Themistocles had no way of knowing if his plan worked until his fellow Athenian (and occasional political rival) Aristides sailed quietly through the Persian fleet from the allied Greek state of Aegina. Despite the well documented conflicts between the two esteemed Athenians, Aristides offered to put aside all differences and defer to Themistocles. Plutarch wrote, "'O Themistocles,' he said, 'if we are wise, we shall at last lay aside our vain and puerile contention, and begin a salutary and honourable rivalry with one another in emulous struggles to save Hellas, thou as commanding general, I as assistant counsellor, since at the very outset I learn that thou art the only one who has adopted the best policy, urging as thous dost to fight a decisive sea-fight here in the narrows as soon as may be.'" (Plutarch, Aristides, VIII, 3).

A statue depicting Aristides

This was actually a crucial point for the Greeks before the battle even began because Aristides, who would prove to be indispensable in the land battle, joined the Greek fleet and saw the virtue in Themistocles' trick, which was successful. Herodotus recounted that not only was Themistocles' plan successful (since the Persian fleet encircled the Greeks), he was also so supremely confident that he didn't care how the Greeks would react if they found out he was behind it: "'It was I who was responsible for this move of the enemy; for as our men would not fight here of their own free will, it was necessary to make them, whether they wanted to do so or not. But take them the good news yourself; if I tell them, they will think I have invented it and will not believe me. Please, then, go in and make the report yourself. If they believe you, well and good; if they do not, it's all the same; for if we are surrounded, as you say we are, escape is no longer possible.'" (Herodotus, The Histories, VIII, 80).

Themistocles' ploy proved to be effective since it ensured the Greeks were forced to fight to the last ship, but he also demonstrated his qualities as a commander by choosing when the battle commenced, and the ancient sources agree that when the Battle of Salamis took place was almost as important as where it was fought. According to Plutarch, Themistocles chose a time that benefited the sleek, low to the water Greek triremes: "Themistocles is thought to have divined the best time for fighting with no less success than the best place, inasmuch as he took care not to send his triremes bow on against the Barbarian vessels until the hour of the day had come which always brought the breeze fresh from the sea and a swell rolling through the strait. This breeze wrought no harm to the Hellenic ships, since they lay low in the water and were rather small; but for the Barbarian ships, with their towering sterns and lofty decks and sluggish movements in getting under way, it was fatal, since it smote them and slewed them round broadside to the Hellenes." (Plutarch, Themistocles, XIV, 1-2).

At dawn, before combat began, the leaders of both armies took their places. As mentioned above, Xerxes took a position of relative safety on the shore where he could observe the battle. According to Plutarch, "At break of day, Xerxes was seated on a high place and overlooking the disposition of his armament. This place was, according to Phanodemus, above the Heracleium, where only a narrow passage separates the island from Attica." (Plutarch, Themistocles, XIII, 1).

Xerxes stayed on his perch for the entire battle, never in danger, which stood in stark contrast to Themistocles, who took his place on a trireme amongst his men and roused them with his oratorical skills. Unfortunately, only a "compact version" (Zali 2013, 467) of the speech survives in Herodotus' account, and it is for the most part paraphrased. In the speech Themistocles used standard Greek rhetorical techniques (Zali 2013, 462) to exhort his men to demonstrate their better nature against their enemies, and despite the fact little of Themistocles's speech remains, it's easy to see how it fits into the overall picture of Greek victory at the Battle of Salamis. Themistocles – an expert at strategy and rhetoric – used all of his available skills to exhort the Greeks to fight fearlessly against overwhelming odds, and though the speech may not have been a decisive factor in the Greek victory at the Battle of Salamis, it was another plank in the "wooden wall" that the oracle prophesized.

One of the most interesting aspects of the Battle of Salamis, at least in terms of military maneuvers, is that no ancient source mentions a diekplous or an attempt at a diekplous by either navy (Wallinga 1990, 148). Some modern historians believe that the Phoenician ships that were at the rear ranks of the Persian fleet were expected to prevent a Greek diekplous (Hale 2009, 64), but one cannot say for sure based on the silence of the ancient sources.

The Greek fleet was drawn up in a single line against the Salamis shore, and while a careful look at the sources reveals that although the word diekplous was never used to describe maneuvers at Salamis, it was clearly on Themistocles' mind. It's apparent that the Athenian commander chose the narrow channel near Salamis, which was similar in topography to Artemisium, to prevent a Persian diekplous. It's possible that since the Greeks were successful at preventing one, the ancient sources simply never describe one when recounting the battle, but either way, the narrows clearly prevented the Persian fleet from performing the maneuver. For their part, the Greeks did not have the numbers to perform one.

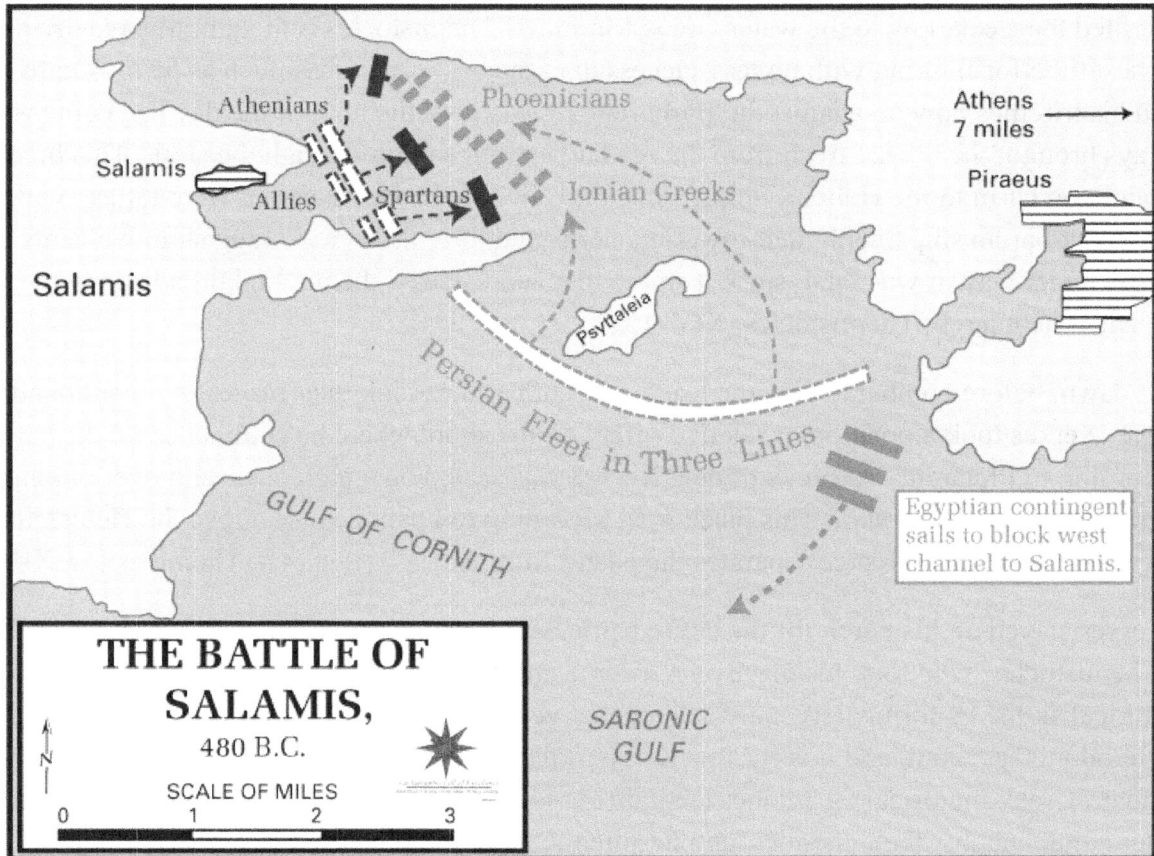

Map of the two navies' positions

The thin Greek line of triremes that faced the Persian fleet consisted of ships from Aegina on the right wing, Spartan ships in the middle, and the Athenian fleet on the left wing against the Phoenicians (Hale 2009, 65). As the Persian fleet moved forward to attack the Greeks, trumpets and war cries erupted from the Greek line. Aeschylus wrote, "Then the fierce trumpet's voice blazed o'er the main; and on the salt sea flood forthwith the oars, with measured plash, descended, and all their lines, with dexterous speed displayed, stood with opposing front. The right wing first, then the whole fleet bore down, and straight uprose a might shout. 'SONS OF THE GREEKS, ADVANCE! YOUR COUNTRY FREE, YOUR CHILDREN FREE, YOUR WIVES! THE ALTARS OF YOUR NATIVE GODS DELIVER, AND YOUR ANCESTRAL

TOMBS – ALL'S NOW AT STAKE!'" (Aeschylus, The Persians, 313).

The Persians, who were perhaps overanxious and overaggressive due to their numerical superiority, moved toward the Greek line, but the line held and even back rowed in a feigned retreat in order to face the Persian ships with their rams (Hale 2009, 67). The Persian fleet was then at a serious disadvantage despite their numbers, as their broadsides were exposed to the deadly Greek rams (Hale 2009, 47). This early engagement was written about by both Herodotus and Plutarch, but the details in their accounts differ slightly. Herodotus wrote, "The whole fleet now got under way, and in a moment the Persians were on them. The Greeks checked their way and began to back astern; and they were on the point of running aground when Ameinias of Pallene, in command of an Athenian ship, drove ahead and rammed an enemy vessel. Seeing the two ships foul of one another and locked together, the rest of the Greek fleet hurried to Ameinias' assistance, and the general action began." (Herodotus, The Histories, VIII, 84).

Plutarch's account of the early fighting at the Battle of Salamis does not mention Ameinias, but it appears to be more revealing in terms of general strategy and maneuvers. Plutarch noted, "Now the first man to capture an enemy's ship was Lycomedes, an Athenian captain, who cut off its figure-head and dedicated it to Apollo the Laurel-bearer at Phlya. Then the rest, put on an equality in numbers with their foes, because the Barbarians had to attack them by detachments in the narrow strait and so ran afoul of one another, routed them, though they resisted till the evening drew on." (Plutarch, Themistocles, XV, 2).

Although Plutarch's account is much more concise – in fact, his total account of the actual fighting is just this short passage – it is also more revealing in terms of the successful strategies employed by the Greeks. Again, the narrow strait/channel between Attica and Salamis played a crucial role in this battle as it proved to mitigate the Persians' numerical superiority. By creating a bottleneck in the channel, the Greeks only had to fight the Persians as they came at them a few at a time, which also prevented the Persians from performing a diekplous maneuver.

It was not long after the initial fighting broke out that the battle moved into its second, crucial, phase. Due to frustration at not being able to encircle the Greek fleet, poor commanders, or a combination of both, the Persian fleet quickly demonstrated its lack of discipline and broke its line (Hale 2009, 69). Once the Persian line broke, the Battle of Salamis was decided as the only individual ships in the Persian fleet that were a match for the Greeks, one on one, were helmed by the Phoenicians. As the Persian line broke and each ship was left to its own devices, the Greeks held strong and picked their individual battles wisely. Herodotus explained, "The Persian fleet suffered severely in the battle, the Athenians and Aeginetans accounting for a great many of their ships. Since the Greek fleet worked together as a whole, while the Persians had lost formation and were no longer fighting on any plan, that was what was bound to happen." (Herodotus, The Histories, VIII, 86).

In ship to ship combat, the Persians were no match for the Greeks, who continued to use their rams to sink their enemy's ships. In the few instances where the method of boarding and then fighting on the desk of ships was used, the Persians fared well because they carried many archers and javelin men and their ships were higher off the sea (Hammond 1956, 48), but such instances were the exception at Salamis.

Ship dashed against ship, till the Persian dead strewed the deep 'like flowers'

Early 20th century depiction of the Greek ships ramming Persian ships

Throughout the day, the Greeks continued to decimate the Persians one at a time using the ramming technique, but one commander in the Persian fleet stood out for her use of guile and intelligence. Since the Persians were so severely defeated at Salamis, none of their commanders are remembered very well except one: Artemisia of Halicarnassus. Artemisia was the queen of the city-state of Halicarnassus (ironically also the hometown of Herodotus), which was a part of the Caria satrapy in the Achaemenid Empire. By all accounts, Artemisia was a loyal subject of the Persians and even volunteered to lead a contingent from her city to follow Xerxes in his campaign against Greece in 480 BCE. Artemisia also fought against Themistocles and the Greeks at Artemisium, which is where she got her first taste of what the Persians were up against, but it was at Salamis where the queen became immortalized.

As fate would have it, Artemisia became famous for participating in a battle that she had advised the Persians against fighting. According to Herodotus, she said:

> "Tell the King to spare his ships and not do a naval battle because our enemies are much stronger than us in the sea, as men are to women. And why does he need to risk a naval battle? Athens for which he did undertake this expedition is his and the rest of Greece too. No man can stand against him and they who once resisted, were destroyed.

> If Xerxes chose not to rush into a naval encounter, but instead kept his ships close to the shore and either stayed there or moved them towards the Peloponnese, victory would be his. The Greeks can't hold out against him for very long. They will leave for their cities, because they don't have food in store on this island, as I have learned, and when our army will march against the Peloponnese they who have come from there will become worried and they will not stay here to fight to defend Athens.

> But if he hurries to engage I am afraid that the navy will be defeated and the land-forces will be weakened as well. In addition, he should also consider that he has certain untrustworthy allies, like the Egyptians, the Cyprians, the Kilikians and the Pamphylians, who are completely useless."

Interestingly, she gained her fame at the Battle of Salamis not through any excellent maneuvers or strategies but because of her cunning. After the Greeks broke the Persian line and it was everybody for themselves, Artemisia sprang into action. Herodotus explained, "I must however, mention Artemisia, on account of an exploit which still further increased her reputation with Xerxes . . . In this awkward situation she hit on a plan which turned out greatly to her advantage: with the Athenian close on her tail she drove ahead with all possible speed and rammed one of her friends . . . For the captain of the Athenian trireme, on seeing her ram an enemy, naturally supposed that her ship was a Greek one, or else a deserter which was fighting on the Greek side; so he abandoned the chase and turned to attack elsewhere." (Herodotus, The Histories, VIII, 87).

As the Battle of Salamis progressed and it became apparent to Xerxes that his navy had lost, the Great King tried one last ditch effort to win the day. Although he did not participate directly in the Battle of Salamis he watched the entire event from his perch, and the few Persian commanders that fought well were duly noted by Xerxes. Herodotus wrote, "Xerxes watched the course of the battle from the base of Mt Aegaleos, across the strait from Salamis; whenever he saw one of his officers behaving with distinction, he would find out his name, and his secretaries wrote it down, together with his city and parentage." (Herodotus, The Histories, VIII, 90). Indeed, it was from his mountain throne that he watched and was so impressed by Artemisia that he told one of his advisors "my men have turned into women, my women into men" (Herodotus, The Histories, VIII, 88).

While watching with anger as the Greeks annihilated his navy, Xerxes realized that he still had one card left to play: his immense land army. If Xerxes could somehow land his army on the island of Salamis, where all of the Athenian evacuees were located, then he could force the Athenians to terms, but he had few ships left to transport his army after the Greek fleet routed them, so he planned to bridge the channel. The narrow channel, which was an advantage for the Greeks, nearly turned into a disadvantage when Xerxes sent men to build a causeway across it. Plutarch explained, "After the sea-fight, Xerxes, sill furious at his failure, undertook to carry moles out into the sea on which he could lead his infantry across to Salamis against the Hellenes, damming up the intervening strait. (Plutarch, Themistocles, XVI, 1)

As clever as Xerxes' plan to bridge the strait of Salamis was, it never materialized as the few ships he had left quickly fell victim to Greek mop-up efforts. When it became obvious that they were defeated, the remaining Persian ships tried to sail for their original base at Phalerum on the Attic peninsula, near the mouth of the Salamis channel. The ancient sources reveal that few prisoners were taken, which suggests that among all the other strategies Themistocles planned, he told the Greeks to take no one alive. Thus, according to Herodotus, this phase of the battle was little more than a massacre: "When the Persian route began and they were trying to get back to Phalerum, the Aeginetan squadron, which was waiting to catch them in the narrows, did memorable service. The enemy was in hopeless confusion; such ships as offered resistance or tried to escape were cut to pieces by the Athenians, while the Aeginetans caught those which attempted to get clear, so that any ship which escaped the one enemy promptly fell amongst the other." (Herodotus, The Histories, VIII, 91).

Herodotus' account of the massacre of the Persian sailors by the Greeks can be corroborated by Aeschylus. The war veteran and dramatist wrote about the carnage from the perspective of a Persian: "Meanwhile the Greeks stroke after stroke dealt dexterous all around, till our ships showed their keels, and the blue sea was seen no more, with multitude of shops and corpses covered. All the shores were strewn, and the rough rocks, with dead; till, in the end, each ship in the barbaric host, that yet had oars, in most disordered flight rowed off. As men that fish for tunnies, so the Greeks, with broken booms, and fragments of the wreck, struck our snared men, and hacked them." (Aeschylus, The Persians, 313).

This phase of the Battle of Salamis may be the most difficult for people today to comprehend since the killing of prisoners of war is now deemed a war crime, and there is no doubt Themistocles was aware of and probably ordered the killing of all captured and fleeing Persians. In fact, this move may have been well thought out by the Athenian commander; after all, although most of the women and children of Attica were safely evacuated to Salamis, the Athenians who fought in the Battle of Salamis still faced uncertainties when they returned home. Would their homes and field still be intact? Would their sacred temples and shrines still be there when they wanted to give offerings? These were unknown to the Greeks when the battle commenced, but they could probably assume that the Persians devastated Attica.

The massacre also dealt with a logistical problem for the Greeks, who had nowhere and no way of caring for hundreds if not thousands of prisoners. Thus, just like they did at the Battle of Marathon, they simply killed any survivors.

While the Greeks were destroying the last of the Persian fleet, the last phase of the Battle of Salamis took place. As the day turned to night and Xerxes was trying to bridge the channel between Salamis and Attica, Persian transports ferried 400 of their elite soldiers to the island of Pysttaleia, and although somewhat peripheral to the eventual outcome of the Battle of Salamis, the island of Pysttaleia was important to both the Persians and Greeks and may have played a bigger role in the overall battle if the Persians would have been able to hold it. Pysttaleia is at the mouth of the channel of Salamis, which meant that if the Persians could have held the island, they may have been able to cross to Salamis and perhaps draw the Greeks onto land, where they would not have been so outclassed. At the same time, the island was important to the Greeks for spiritual reasons, as the Athenians believed it to be the sacred abode of the god Pan (Hale 2009, 63). The religious significance of the island should not be underestimated either, especially in the wake of the Persian destruction of so many Greek temples previously. After all, the Greeks had extra incentive to prevent them from defiling any more sacred spaces.

According to Plutarch, Aristides was the first Greek to notice Persians on Pysttaleia: "While the captains of the Hellenes were acting on this plan, Aristides noticed that Pysttaleia, a small island lying in the straits in front of Salamis, was full of the enemy. He therefore embarked in small boats the most ardent and the most warlike of the citizens, made a landing on Pysttaleia, joined battle with the Barbarians, and slew them all, save the few conspicuous men who were taken alive. Among these were three sons of the King's sister Sandaucé, whom he straightway sent to Themistocles, and it is said that, in obedience to some oracle or other, and at the bidding of Euphrantides the seer, they were sacrificed to Dionysus Carnivorous. Then Aristides lined the islet all round with his hoplites, and lay in wait for any who should be cast up there, that no friend might perish, and no foe escape." (Plutarch, Aristides, IX, 1-2).

With the fighting done, Herodotus wrote that there were not many Greek casualties, but he provided no numbers. He also wrote that the few Persians who survived the massacre drowned because they did not know how to swim (Herodotus, The Histories, VIII, 89). Among the multitude of Persians killed at the Battle of Salamis was Ariabinges, the son of Darius I and brother of Xerxes (Herodotus, The Histories, VIII, 89).

William Rainey's illustration depicting the death of Ariabinges

Meanwhile, having been massacred on both sea and land at Salamis, Xerxes and the Persian fleet quickly sailed back to Asia, but even still, the emperor had not abandoned his hopes for a conquest of Greece because the best of his army, under Mardonius, still remained in the field. However, the following year, in the summer of 479 BCE, the Persians faced a force of between 40,000 and 100,000 Greek infantry near the Boeotian city of Plataea. At the battle, the Greeks completely annihilated Mardonius' force of between 100,000-300,000 men, and Mardonius himself was killed. Around the same time, what remained of the Persian fleet was destroyed off Mycale. The Persian invasion was over, and no Persian army would ever set foot on Greek soil again.

The victory at Salamis was obviously a proud moment for the Greeks, especially the

Athenians, but the real rewards for Athens came in the succeeding years as the city became the pre-eminent force in the Greek world. Before the Persian Wars, Athens had no great traditions of philosophy, art, science, or historical writing, but after the Battle of Salamis, their culture began to flourish into what most moderns regard as the Golden Age of Athens (Hale 2009, xxv). The above opinion is not just confined to modern scholars; Plutarch also believed that it was Themistocles and his navy that brought Athens to greatness. He claimed, "But Themistocles did not, as Aristophanes, the comic poet says, 'knead the Pireus on to the city,' nay, he fastened the city of the Peraeus, and the land to the sea, And so it was that he increased the privileges of the common people as against the nobles, and filled them with boldness, since the controlling power came now into the hands of skippers and boastswins and pilots." (Plutarch, Themistocles, XIX, 3-4).

So it was that Themistocles and the Battle of Salamis transformed Athens. Previously a sleepy city-state that had just awoken from the nightmare of tyranny and was transitioning into early democracy, Athens subsequently became the world center of learning and culture. On the other hand, after the Battle of Salamis, Persia would begin its long decline.

A memorial commemorating the battle

Picture of a column dedicated to the Greek alliance to commemorate their victory in the war

Alexander the Great

The royal inscriptions found at Persepolis reinforce this image of a benevolent rule; they declare that the king loved peace, not war, and that subject peoples were allowed to practice their beliefs and customs. But was this merely Persian propaganda? After all, these were bas-reliefs commissioned by the king, and tablets written by his loyal – or fearful – servants.

In fact, there were plenty of people in the ancient world that despised everything the Persians stood for. The Persians themselves left little written history behind, so most of what is known about the empire and Persepolis has been gleaned from Greek accounts, but as the sworn enemies of the Persians, the Greeks liked to paint themselves as the creators of all things civilized and to portray the Persians as having been cruel, despotic, and backward. Inevitably, Western historians have identified better with the works of the Greco-Latin tradition, and thereby the importance of Persia in its historical setting has generally been downplayed.

Nevertheless, the Persians cannot be dismissed so easily. For 250 years they had ruled the largest empire the world had ever seen, even as the Greeks considered them an uncultured and warlike people. They liked to criticize the Persians for their perceived "softness,"[107] and one particularly pervasive trope was the portrayal of the Persians as barbarians. They viewed the Persians as a corrupting and effeminizing influence on all of the values that the Greeks stood for.[108] Alexander the Great warned his soldiers that "gluttony and opulence lead to much unmanliness. Those that eat such enormous meals are far too quickly beaten in battles."[109]

---

[107] Briant, 2002
[108] Briant, 2002
[109] Wiesehofer, J. (2001) *Ancient Persia*. London: IB Tauris.

Andrew Dunn's picture of a bust of Alexander the Great

Ultimately, it was Alexander the Great who was determined to end the corrupting influence of the Persians once and for all. In 334 BCE, he began a campaign that aimed to defeat the empire that had controlled most of the known world for the last few centuries.

At the first pitched battle between his army and that of the Persians, which took place at Issus in Turkey in 332 BCE, Alexander's Macedonian army scored a resounding victory over the forces of King Darius III of Persia, despite being greatly outnumbered.[110] Much had to do with the superior military tactics that the Macedonians employed against the Persians, since the latter were used to facing their foes in an open plain where their chariots could be best employed.[111]

---

[110] Heckel, W. (2007) *The Conquests of Alexander the Great*. Cambridge: Cambridge University Press
[111] Heckel, 2007

This victory opened the road for Alexander's campaigns in Syria and Phoenicia, where he received the surrender of all major cities except the island city of Tyre, which only fell after a prolonged siege.[112] Over the next two years, Alexander's superior military tactics allowed him to take over lands that were once under Persian control, and in 331 BCE he reached the Persian heartland itself.

Alexander fully understood the importance of Persepolis as the symbolic heart of the Persian Empire.[113] By the time Alexander had reached Persepolis, the Persian armies had been completely routed, and the 12th and last Persian king, Darius III, was dead. Alexander entered the monumental city unopposed – sources state that there was no military guard there to defend the population.[114] The ceremonial center that had for almost two centuries embodied Persia's dominance of the world was finally in Greek hands.

The luxury and opulence surrounding them were anathema to Alexander, who told his soldiers that they were now in the "most hateful of cities."[115] In triumph, Alexander held a banquet for some of his troops on the terrace. According to the Greek accounts, it was here that the city's fate was sealed; Alexander decided to destroy anything that might risk becoming a source of opposition to him as he continued his campaigns, and Persepolis was obviously one such risk.[116] His soldiers thus burned and looted the city, and the conflagration spread across the ceremonial terrace into the surrounding suburbs.

Once the city was burned down by Alexander's army, its remnants rapidly deteriorated and vanished. The Persian army was no longer strong enough to defend the empire, and the population had grown unhappy with the increasing levels of taxation they had suffered under the Persian kings. Alexander continued his campaigns to the east, bringing with him a Hellenistic culture that would dominate Central Asia for centuries.

Meanwhile, for the next several centuries, Persian cities lay neglected. With the original moat in Persepolis filled up, the rainwater flowing from the adjacent mountain gradually destroyed most of the eastern fortifications, and the debris piled up in the palace area, partially burying it in sediment. As in Mesopotamia, the principle building material of the terrace's substructures was dried mud-brick, so it quickly degraded due to the forces of weathering. Some of the mud-brick structures managed to survive to the present day in part, but only to a low height.

Conversely, the ashlar used for supporting elements, such as jambs and lintels of doorways, window-breastings, the bases of capitals, and sculptures, have easily survived the vicissitudes of time. Ironically, by burning down the city, Alexander helped preserve it, because many of the

[112] Heckel, 2007
[113] Borza, E. N. (1972) "Fire from heaven: Alexander at Persepolis." *Classical Philology*, 67:4, 233 - 245.
[114] Borza, 1972
[115] Borza, 1972
[116] Borza, 1972

structures remained perfectly preserved beneath the ashes produced by the fire, protecting them from the elements.[117]

Early European visitors saw the ruined city of Persepolis pretty much as the troops of Alexander the Great had left it. The first reliable drawings of the ancient city were made by a Dutch scholar and artist, Cornelius de Bruijn, who visited Persepolis between 1704 and 1705.[118] He inscribed his name upon the door frame of the Gate of All Nations, setting a precedent that many later travelers followed from the 18th century onwards.[119] De Bruijn was followed by Eugène Flandin and Pascal Coste of France, who made extensive literary and artistic descriptions of what they saw there.[120] There were also innumerable amateur explorers and treasure hunters who left no academic records but plundered much from the site.[121]

[117] Wilber, 1989

[118] Simpson, S. J. (2007) "Pottering around Persepolis: observations on early European visitors to the site." *Persian responses: political and cultural interaction with (in) the Achaemenid Empire*, 343-356.

[119] Simpson, 2007

[120] Simpson, 2007

[121] Simpson, 2007

18ᵗʰ century sketches of the ruins of Persepolis

One of the things they saw among the exposed monuments of the ruined city were inscriptions in a then unknown script, using characters composed of small wedge-shaped elements. This is known today as cuneiform, and a short text transcribed from the buildings there was the basis for the first steps in the partial decipherment of the Old Persian language. This decipherment was done by Georg Friedrich Grotefend, a teacher at the University of Göttingen in the earliest years of the 19ᵗʰ century.[122] By doing so, he confirmed what many other scholars had guessed during the last century: the monuments at Persepolis belonged to the kings of the Achaemenid Dynasty, whose names they knew only from being handed down by Greek and Roman authors.

---

[122] Daniels, P. T. (1995) "The decipherment of ancient Near Eastern scripts." *Civilizations of the ancient Near East*, *1*, 81 - 93.

Grotefend

For decades, inscriptions on the tomb of Darius the Great were an intriguing puzzle for archaeologists. High up on the mountain of Behistun, perched atop a tall ladder, English army officer Sir Henry Rawlinson valiantly transcribed the text. That was the easy part; it then took him 10 long years to decipher it.[123]

---

[123] Adkins, L. (2004) *Empires of the plain: Henry Rawlinson and the lost languages of Babylon*. Macmillan Press.

Rawlinson

Thanks to the work of this great archaeologist, the puzzle was solved in 1835, and with that a whole new world opened up to scholars: the history of the Persians, told this time through their own words. The text was written in three different languages and in two different scripts: cuneiform and Aryan. Aryan was an alphabet created under the orders of King Darius I that consists of 36 characters representing syllables, and an additional 8 ideograms used for certain concepts (namely king, country, good, god, earth, Ahura Mazda). One language was that of the empire's rulers, now called Old Persian. The other two were languages that originated with the empire's subjects: Elamite, which had been written and spoken in southwestern Iran long before Achaemenid rule, and Akkadian, the ancient language of the Babylonians and Assyrians.[124]

It was only in the 1930s that many of the wonders of Persepolis were finally uncovered through archaeological investigations. Persepolis was first extensively excavated by Ernst Herzfeld and Erich Schmidt of the Oriental Institute of the University of Chicago, and at the time, no one could dream of the regal splendors that their excavations would reveal to the world. Archaeologists found deep layers of burnt cedar, ebony, and teak wood while excavating the Apadana.[125] Whole staircases adorned with perfectly preserved bas-reliefs were seen for the very first time. In addition to the bas-reliefs, archaeologists found some artifacts that seemed less spectacular on first inspection but that would later prove vital in uncovering the secrets of the ancient Persians, such as the fragmented tablets.

The western wing of Xerxes' harem was reconstructed in the 1930s, designed by the German architect Professor Friedrich Krefter, and today serves as the headquarters of the Persepolis research foundation and museum. The structure is an almost perfect replication of what would have existed in the Achaemenid period, though it contains few of the objects that would have existed in the city during its Golden Age.[126] Persepolis had been plundered on many occasions throughout history, first by Alexander and then by many others. In addition, many valuable objects discovered there were carried away by foreign archaeologists. Even most of the better-preserved bas-reliefs and objects had been removed from their original contexts and taken to national or international museums.

Until recently, Iran was mostly closed to Western visitors. In 1973 a spike in oil prices caused Iran's economy to flood with foreign currencies, resulting in inflation and widespread corruption. By 1975 an economic recession had set in, which led to increasing unemployment and resentment of the ruling regime. From 1978 to 1979 the Iranian Revolution eventually resulted in the overthrow of Mohammad Reza Shah Pahlavi of the ruling Pahlavi dynasty.[127] The political turmoil of the 1980s made it almost impossible to travel there for research or fieldwork, but in the last few years, this has begun to change, allowing the study of ancient Persia to be done with renewed vigor.

Persepolis was added to UNESCO's World Heritage List in 1979, for being the example par excellence of the Achaemenid dynastic city, as well as a unique reflection of the art and culture of other nations that existed during their period of rule. Indeed, perhaps no other ancient site in the world reflects such a mixture of global art and culture as Persepolis. Since 1979, much attention has been directed to determining the borders of the city's hinterland, and for managing the increasing numbers of tourists that visit the fragile site. By 2000, more than 400,000 people were visiting Persepolis each year, bringing with them a range of conservation issues.[128] Further

---

[124] Adkins, 2004

[125] Schmidt, E. F. (1939) *The Treasury of Persepolis and other Discoveries in the Homeland of the Achaemenians.* Chicago: University of Chicago.

[126] Gershevitch, I. (1985) *The Cambridge History of Iran*, 2. Cambridge: Cambridge University Press.

[127] Sreberny, A., and Mohammadi, A. (1994) *Small media, big revolution: Communication, culture, and the Iranian revolution.* Minneapolis: University of Minnesota Press.

problems are caused by the urban spread of the nearby town of Marvdasht and other smaller villages surrounding the terrace, as well as the construction of various industries in the vicinity that risk polluting the site.[129] The long-term impact of these developments remain to be seen, but steps are being made to monitor and mitigate the risk of losing a site that, despite all odds, has lasted for so long.

As remarkable as Persepolis may be, history still has never given the Persian capital its due. It was one of the greatest architectural achievements of the ancient world. The complex was an architectural symphony, with each structure built to harmonize with one another. To prove their power, the Persian kings set out to create nothing less than paradise on Earth.

Beyond housing the royal entourage, these extraordinary buildings were used for a variety of purposes, and clues to the function of Persepolis lie carved into the walls and staircases of the city. In the scenes depicted in these stunning stone reliefs, the lives of those who lived in the city can be given a personality and identity.

As it turns out, the Greeks, whose civilization became the root of Western civilization as a whole and called the Persians barbarians, committed a gross act of vandalism and barbarity by destroying one of the most magnificent cities on the planet. Alexander's campaign may have destroyed Persepolis as a living city, but its story survived, always associated with those who built it and the individual who destroyed it. Moreover, the Persian approach to architecture, gardens, textiles, and luxury was copied by other civilizations – including the Greeks – and has survived to this day.

In the end, the Persians' greatest achievement of all was the empire itself. The characteristics of the Persian Empire were respect for their subjects, religious tolerance, and the promotion of trade, art, and culture. The first truly global empire in history was built and sustained on a model of tolerance and respect for other cultures that few great powers have ever matched.

---

[128] Aref, F. (2011) "Tourism industry for poverty reduction in Iran." *African Journal of Business Management*, 5: 11.

[129] Moradi-Jalal, M., Arianfar, S., Karney, B., and Colombo, A. (2010) *Water resource management for Iran's Persepolis complex*. Leiden: Springer Netherlands.

The Geographic and Ethnic Origins of the Parthians

Sculpture of a young boy in a Parthian outfit

Modern scholars generally classify the Parthians as a Persian dynasty, but they hailed from different origins than their Achaemenid Persian predecessors. Specifically, the Parthians were originally part of a tribe known as the Parni or Aparni, who originated on the eastern edge of the Caspian Sea (Colledge 1967, 25). After the death of Alexander the Great in 323 BCE, a vacuum was left from the number of kingdoms that he and his army toppled in their eastern campaign. A new political order emerged when various, formerly nomadic peoples migrated into to central Asia and established new kingdoms. The Parni were one of these formerly nomadic groups who migrated into the regions of Parthian and Bactria and became known as the Parthians (College

1967, 25).

The Parthians spoke a northern dialect of the Middle Persian language, which became known as "Asacid Phalavi" (College 1967, 68), but once they assumed power over the region and the plethora of different tribes and peoples, they made no attempts to impose their language on their subjects; in fact, it appears that the Parthians adjusted their linguistic background to a certain extent in order to make the dynastic transition more smoothly. Moreover, although the Parthians' native language was a form of Persian, they adopted Greek as the administrative language of their empire since it was the language of their predecessors, the Seleucids (Colledge 1967, 68). The Parthians never imposed the Persian language on their subjects though as they also allowed their subjects to keep their own native languages, but the Aramaic script, along with Greek, attained widespread use, especially in many official documents (Boyce 2001, 95). The linguistic and cultural diversity of the Parthian Empire was something that was passed down from the Achaemenids and Seleucids, and for the most part the Parthians followed in their predecessors' footsteps by treating those different peoples with a relatively light hand.

A map of the region at the end of the 3rd century BCE

Besides inheriting a number of different subject peoples, the Parthians also took hold of a number of different cities that were built by previous dynasties. The heart of the Parthian homeland was located in central Asia, roughly contiguous with modern day northeast Iran and western Afghanistan, and the Parthians inherited a number of notable cities that were built by the Seleucids, Achaemenids, and Elamites before them, such as Susa and Seleucia, but they also founded a number of their own impressive cities. The first Parthian king, Arsaces I (247-217 BCE), founded the city of Dara (Brosius 2010, 103), but it was the city of Nisa/Mithradatkert that was built by Mithridates I (171-138 BC) that became the first true capital of the Parthian

Empire (Brosius 2010, 103). Located in the mountains of northern Parthia, Mithradatkert not only served as an important political and administrative center in the Parthian Empire, but was perhaps one of the more important spiritual centers. It was at Mithradatkert where the tombs of the Parthian kings were located, which gave the city an extra level of importance throughout the lifespan of the Parthian dynasty (Brosius 2010, 111). The tombs provided a physical, focal point for the Parthians to demonstrate the legitimacy of their dynasty as well as an important part of their religion, which will be discussed below.

A coin depicting Arsaces I

A relief depicting Mithridates on horseback

Picture of the ruins of Nisa

Mithridates I proved to be a very energetic building king, as he also founded the city of Ctesiphon during his reign. Ctesiphon was the westernmost city built by the Parthians as it sat on the banks of the Tigris River in Mesopotamia across from the Seleucid city of Seleucis. The Parthians followed a practice similar to the Achaemenid Persians of having a capital circuit; the king and his court would travel from city to city depending on the season and circumstances, and wherever the king and his court were located was considered the capital. Due to its western location and proximity to the west, the Romans regarded Ctesiphon as the primary Parthian capital (Brosius 2010, 103), but the Romans were often largely ignorant of geographic locations within the Parthian heartland. Ctesiphon was essentially turned into a winter palace by king Orodes II's (58-38 BC) son, Pacorus (Colledge 1967, 67), but it remained an important city throughout the entire Parthian period.

Across the river from Ctesiphon was the former Seleucid capital of Seleucis, which was diminished in importance after the foundation of Ctesiphon but continued to serve as an administrative center and royal mint for the Parthians (Brosius 2010, 110). Eventually, Ctesiphon grew to a point where it engulfed Seleucis and the two became part of a larger ancient metropolitan area (Brosius 2010, 103).

The Parthian Government and Imperial Administration

The importance of the cities that the Parthians inherited from the Achaemenids and Seleucids should not be underestimated, but the greatest gift they received from their predecessors was their system of government.

At the head of the Parthian government was the king, whose rule was considered absolute and mandated by gods, but since the Parthian kings ruled such a vast and diverse empire (both culturally and geographically), it was imperative that they implement an efficient system to keep order. Fortunately for the Parthians, they had to do little in this respect since the Seleucids, who the Parthians conquered, already had a fairly sophisticated imperial administration in place that they in turn inherited from the Achaemenid Persians.

The Achaemenid Persians divided their empire into provinces, which are usually referred to by modern scholars with the ancient Greek word *satrapies*. The number of satrapies fluctuated, but there were usually somewhere between 20-25 of them. When Alexander the Great defeated the Achaemenid Persians, he destroyed their empire but not their imperial administration, because after his death his top generals divided the spoils and started new dynasties – Seleucis founded the Seleucid dynasty in Mesopotamia and for the most part based his new dynasty's administrative districts on the Achaemenid satrapal divisions (Colledge 1967, 57).

The Seleucids went further and subdivided the satrapies into *eparchies*, *hyparchies*, and fortified villages known as *stathmos* (Colledge 1967, 57). The Parthians adopted these Achaemenid and Seleucid divisions, but they also viewed their kingdom unofficially as being comprised of an Upper and Lower kingdom. The Upper kingdom of Parthia included Parthia proper and Armenia as two of the most important regions, while the Lower kingdom included Babylonia, Persis, and Elymais (Susa region) as the three most vital among many areas (Brosius 2010, 113).

One aspect where the Parthians differed from their predecessors was that they allowed some regions to retain more autonomy than others. For instance, Persis and Elymais were ruled by local kings, while the other provinces were overseen by a governor, or satrap, who was appointed by the Parthian king (Brosius 2010, 115). When the Parthian Empire was strong and the economic situation was good, this situation worked well, but during periods of instability the regional, semi-autonomous kings were able to assert more authority and even court outside forces, namely the Romans, for support.

The Parthians not only inherited the administrative divisions from their Achaemenid Persian and Seleucid predecessors, but also some aspects of royal ideology, as well as administrative techniques. For example, the Parthian kings continued the tradition of minting royal coins that was first initiated by the Achaemenids and continued with the Seleucids, and the coins not only served as currency during all three dynasties but also served to advertise the power of the Parthian kings throughout their realm (Brosius 2010, 101). The royal coins were often inscribed in the Seleucids' language of Greek, but that was not the only language the Parthians used in their administrative documents. A number of extant economic texts have been discovered in the Parthian city of the Nisa that were written in a variety of different languages, including Middle Persian, Greek, and Aramaic (Brosius 2010, 118).

The Parthian Economy and Trade

The high number of documents pertaining to trade is one indication of the Parthians' ancient entrepreneurial abilities, and their economy was one of the most noteworthy aspects of their empire. At the height of their power, the Parthians were as wealthy as the Romans to the west and the Chinese to the east, which was not primarily the result of their conquests but instead came through their control of important trade routes that linked the west and east. Since most of the Parthian Empire was landlocked, it relied on overland caravan routes to move commodities to and from the empire. A single trade caravan could include up to 1,000 Bactrian (two humped) camels that could carry 400-500 pounds of goods each (Brosius 2010, 123).

The extensive economic activity was conducted throughout the Parthian Empire and has been recorded on numerous documents, but modern archaeological excavations have also revealed that one of the more important economic regions was around the ancient city of Susa. The city of Susa was host to many different peoples and dynasties before the Parthians took control of it, from Elamites to the Achaemenid Persians and then the Seleucids, and they all understood the economic importance of the city. The agricultural region near the city was especially fertile, and the age of the city meant that the inhabitants were used to trade and had existing facilities to carry it out. By the time the Parthians took control of the Susa region most of its inhabitants were either Hellenized locals or Greeks (Wenke 1981, 306), so the idea of civilization and a sophisticated economy was nothing new to Susians. Archaeological evidence, in the form of coins and the remains of other commodities, demonstrate that Susa continued to be an important economic center during the Parthian period, especially for its agricultural output (Wenke 1981, 304).

Susa provided a vital economic link within the confines of the Parthian Empire, but the Parthians themselves provided the first true economic link between the western and eastern worlds. Before the Parthians came to power, the peoples of the Far East and those of Europe and the Near East knew very little about each other and contact was for the most part nonexistent. However, the Parthians bridged the gap between Asia and Europe when they established commercial and diplomatic relations with the Chinese Han dynasty (206 BC-AD 220) (Brosius 2010, 82). The Chinese emperors viewed the Parthians as both trading partners and allies against the numerous hordes that attempted to invade China, and the Chinese paid premiums for Parthian horses while the Parthians received silk, which was much coveted in the west (Brosius 2010, 83).

Indeed, it was during the Parthian Empire that the famed "Silk Route" came into maturity through the careful manipulation of the Parthians. The Silk Route is the term used for the many overland caravan routes that connected China with the Near East and the West, and as the name implies, the most prized commodity to flow through the Route was silk from China, which the Romans were willing to pay premiums for to convert into clothing and bedsheets. Nearly all of the overland caravan routes had to travel through Parthian territory, which the Parthians were able to exploit as middlemen in the trade process. As long as the Romans and other peoples of the west had a demand for Chinese silk, the Parthians grew wealthy.

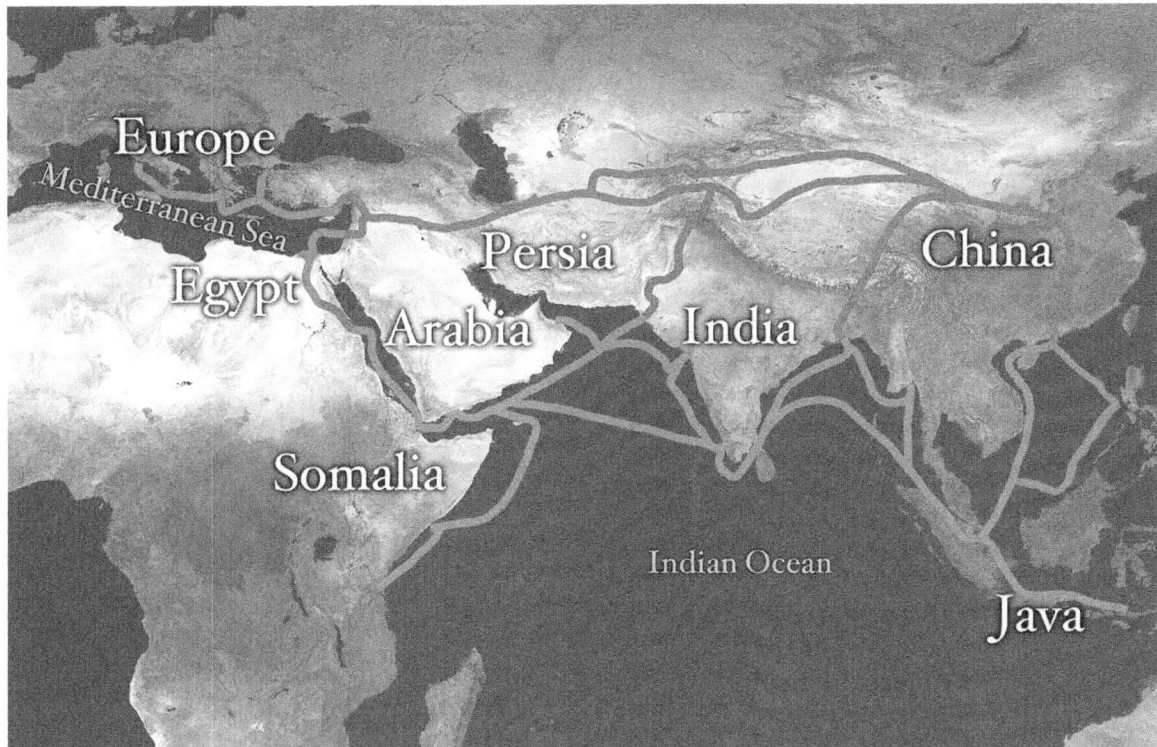

A map of the most famous routes on the Silk Road

When Augustus became emperor of Rome in 27 BC he ushered in an era known as the *Pax Romana*, or "Roman Peace." Augustus promoted free trade both within Roman territory and with Rome's neighbors. The many roads throughout the Empire became arteries that brought trade to and from Rome and maritime trade also increased exponentially during Augustus' rule (Temin 2006, 136). Particularly, silk became much more common throughout the Roman Empire during the reign of Augustus and in fact continued to be available throughout Roman territory until its fall (Thorley 1971, 71). But the Romans were only the westernmost terminus of the Silk Route; long before the silk reached Rome it had to pass through a number of different kingdoms among which the Parthians were the most important.

An ancient statue of Augustus

    After the Silk Road was firmly established around 90 CE, silk from northern China only had to pass through four kingdoms/empires: China, Kushan, Parthia, and Rome, so the logistics of the route were simple for the most part. The key role that the Parthians played in the facilitation of the Silk Road revolved around their control of the actual Chinese merchants and their product – once the Chinese merchants safely travelled through the Kushan kingdom, they were forced to stop and trade in the Parthian city of Merv (Thorley 1971, 75). The Chinese merchants would then take Parthian horses, lions, and/or a plethora of Roman commodities back to China while Parthian merchants would continue westward in order to trade with Roman merchants (Thorley 1971, 75-76). Although the Chinese knew of the Romans, who they referred to as T-tsin, they never had direct contact with them and were forced to deal with the Parthian intermediaries.

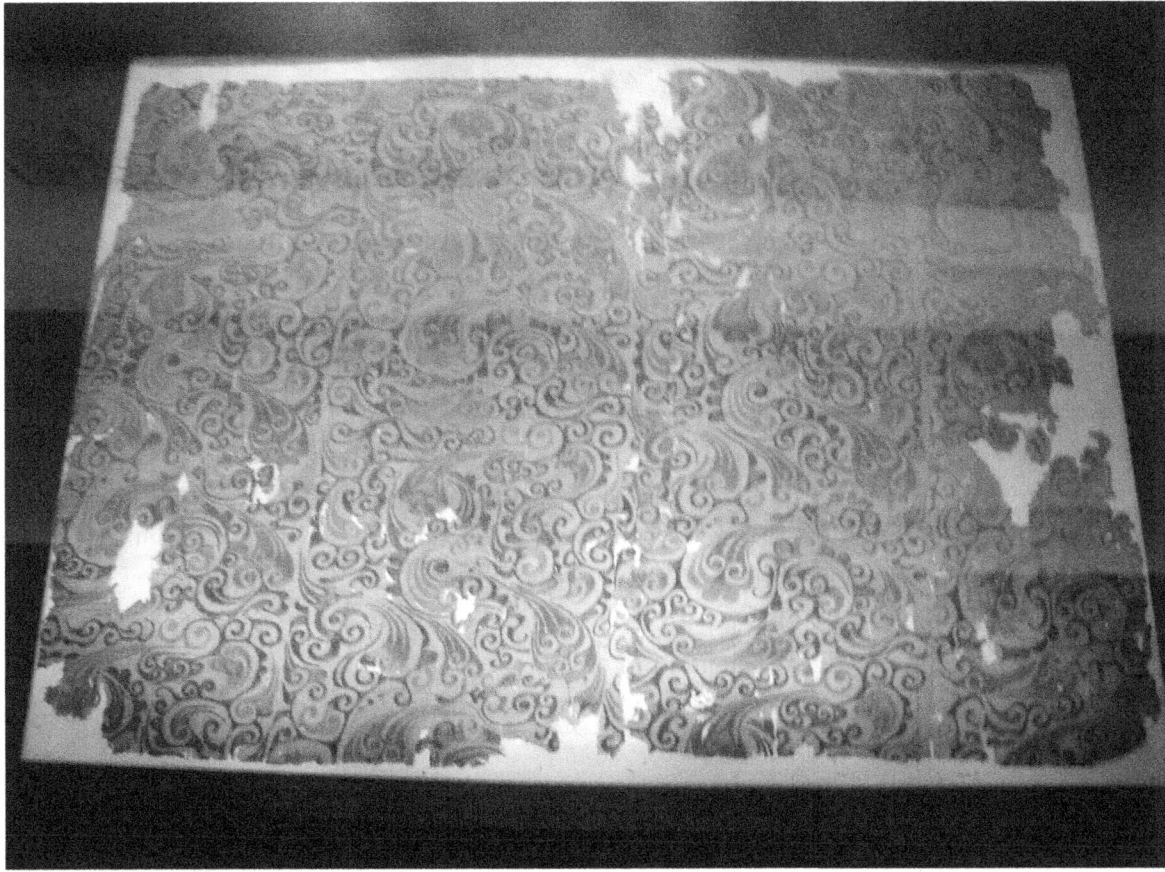

A picture of ancient Chinese silk from the 2ⁿᵈ century BCE

The Chinese coveted Roman gold and silver the most (Thorley 1971, 76), but ironically they also desired a manufactured version of the very silk that they sold to the Parthians and Romans. Today, most people know little about the process of silk manufacturing other than that it originates with the silk worm in some form, but the process of creating ancient silk garments in the ancient world was complex. The Chinese exported silk in a closely-woven, heavy form that was quite different from what the Romans, or modern people, consider silk (Thorley 1971, 77). Traders in Syria then unraveled and rewove the Chinese silk on looms to create a transparent gauze with other materials woven into it, which was essentially what is considered silk (Thorley 1971, 77). The Parthians were then able take the manufactured silk and sell it back to the Chinese at a nice profit (Thorley 1971, 77).

Although there are numerous written sources that document Parthian trade with the Chinese and various peoples of the west, there are no indications in those texts why the Parthians prohibited Chinese merchants to pass through their empire. Perhaps the Parthians were aware of the silk manufacturing process and wanted to keep it a secret in order to protect their lucrative position as middlemen on the Silk Route, or possibly they felt that allowing significant amount of foreigners on their roads posed a security risk. Whatever the reasons for the Parthians to control access to the Silk Route, it helped propel them to a wealthy status amongst their peers, but it also helped to contribute to their military power, which ultimately threatened the world's greatest empire: Rome.

War with Rome

As the Parthians grew richer due to their control of the Silk Road, they were able to use that wealth to build a state-of-the-art army and expand their borders. The period of Parthian expansion and international prestige can be traced to the reign of Mithridates I (171-139/8 BC), who took advantage of political instability in the west, which was primarily the result of the weakened status of the Seleucid dynasty (Brosius 2010, 86). In 141 BC Mithridates I was recognized as the king by the Babylonian elites, which marked the beginning of first Parthian influence and then outright control of Mesopotamia (Brosius 2010, 89). Mithridates I's successors, Pharates I (139/8-128 BC) and Artabanus I (128/7-124 BC), continued to expand Parthian control, although the Seleucid dynasty still challenged them in the west and nomadic invasions remained a problem in the northeast (Brosius 2010, 89). It was during the reign of Mithridates II (124-87 BC) that the Parthians were finally able to gain uncontested control of Mesopotamia and with it sent the Seleucid dynasty to the dust bin of history (Brosius 2010, 90). Once the Seleucid dynasty was destroyed the Parthians had to contend with the Romans for control of the Near East.

A coin depicting Mithridates I

Rome and Parthia engaged in a series of wars in the 1st century BCE, known as the Mithridatic Wars by the Romans, for control of the eastern Mediterranean region. Early on, the site of most of the battles and campaigns took place near the Euphrates River in Mesopotamia, but control of Armenia was usually the root cause of conflict (Brosius 2010, 82). The Romans often tried to install puppet pro-Roman kings on the Armenian throne, and they also frequently tried to foment discord within the Parthian court by supporting pretenders to the Parthian throne (Brosius 2010,

92). Needless to say the Parthians were not happy with the Romans' duplicitous dealings, which led to the numerous wars and conflicts between the two peoples.

One of the first major conflicts between the Romans and Parthians that was recorded by Greco-Roman writers took place during the late Republican Period. The famous biographer Plutarch wrote about how the Roman general Sulla embarked on a military campaign on the edge of Parthian territory and then met with some Parthian officials on the banks of the Euphrates River:

> "After his praetorship, he was sent out to Cappadocia, ostensibly to reinstate Ariobarzanes, but really to check the restless activities of Mithridates, who was adding to his dominion and power fully as much as he had inherited. Accordingly, he took out with him no large force of his own, but made use of the allies, whom he found eager to serve him, and after slaying many of the Cappadocians themselves, and yet more of the Armenians who came to their aid, he drove out Gordiusm and made Ariobarzanes king again.

> "As he lingered on the banks of the Euphrates, he received a visit from Orobazus, a Parthian, who came as an ambassador from king Arsaces, although up to this time the two nations had held no intercourse with one another. This also is thought to have been part of Sulla's great good fortune, that he should be the first Roman with whom the Parthians held conference when they wanted alliance and friendship. On this occasion, too, it is said that he ordered three chairs to be set, one for Ariobarznes, one for Orobazus, and one for himself, and that he sat between them both and gave them audience. For this the king of Parthia afterwards put Orobazus to death; and while some people commended Sulla for the airs which he assumed with the Barbarians, others accused him of vulgarity and ill-timed arrogance." (Plutarch, *Sulla*, V, 3-6).

An ancient bust of Sulla

Although this account is not as exciting as later ones that detail battles between the Romans and Parthians, it demonstrates a bit of the Roman arrogance and cultural misunderstanding that they became known for in other points of history. Sulla's slight toward the Parthian king would at least partially be responsible for number of wars between the two peoples that lasted until the end of the Parthian Empire, most of which took place during Rome's imperial phase.

One particular campaign during the late Republic cemented poor relations between the Romans and Parthians for over 200 years. Several years after Sulla's first foray into Parthian territory the Roman general and consul Crassus tried his hand at influencing the politics of Armenia and Mesopotamia. Crassus is best known for forming the First Triumvirate along with Pompey and Julius Caesar and playing an important role in the Civil Wars, but his role in the early conflicts between the Romans and Parthians was just as important. Under the consulship of Pompey, Rome supported a pretender to the Parthian throne, which naturally angered the legitimate Parthian king Orodes II (58/7-38 BCE) and led to war in 53 BCE that ended in disaster for the Romans (Brosius 2010, 94).

An ancient bust of Crassus

The failed Roman military campaign was detailed by both the 3rd century historian Cassius Dio and Plutarch. The Roman invasion began in Mesopotamia and the accounts reveal that hubris on the part of the Romans certainly played a role in their ultimate defeat. Dio wrote, "When Crassus had invaded Mesopotamia, as has been stated, Orodes sent envoys to him in

Syria to censure him for the invasion and to ask the causes of the war; at the same time he sent Surenas with an army to the captured and revolted districts. For the had it in mind to lead an expedition in person against that part of Armenia which had once belonged to Tigranes, in order that Artabazes, the son of Tigranes, the king of the land at that time, should send no assistance to the Romans through fear for his own land. Now Crassus said that he would tell him in Seleucia the causes of the war; this is a city in Mesopotamia which even at the present day has a very large Greek population." (Cassius Dio, *Roman History*, XL, 16, 1-2).

Once Crassus and the Romans were established in Mesopotamia, they arrogantly overlooked the Parthian army and were led into a trap. Dio's account explained, "It came about in this way. The Parthians confronted the Romans with most of their army hidden; for the ground was uneven in spots and wooded. Upon seeing them Crassus – not the commander, but the younger Crassus, who had come to his father from Gaul – felt scornful of them, since he supposed them to be alone, and so led out his cavalry against them, and when they turned purposely to fight, pursued them, thinking the victory was his; thus he was drawn far ways from the main army, and was then surrounded and cut down. When this had taken place, the Roman infantry did not turn back, but valiantly joined battle with the Parthians to avenge his death. Yet they accomplished nothing worthy of themselves because of the enemy's numbers and tactics, and particularly because Abgarus was plotting against them." (Cassius Dio, *Roman History*, XL, 21, 2-3; 22, 1-2).

Despite their dogged defense, Crassus and the Romans were forced to flee for their lives, but the Parthians were not done. According to Dio, the Parthian general Surenas feared that if Crassus was allowed to escape back into Roman territory that he would return with an even larger force and defeat the Parthians. In order to prevent this, Surenas resorted to devious methods to defeat the Roman general by requesting a parlay with Crassus and sending a horse to retrieve him. Dio noted what happened next: "So Crassus descended to the level ground and Surenas sent him a present of a horse, to make sure of his coming to him more quickly; and while Crassus even then delayed and considered what he should do, the barbarians took him forcibly and threw him on the horse. Meanwhile the Romans also laid hold of him, came to blows with the others, and for a time held their own; then aid came to the barbarians, and they prevailed; for their forces, which were in the plain and had been made ready beforehand brought help to their men before the Romans on the high ground could to theirs. And not only the others fell, but Crassus also was slain, either by one of this own men to prevent his capture alive, or by the enemy because he was badly wounded. This was his end. And the Parthians, as some say, poured molten gold into his mouth in mockery." (Cassius Dio, *Roman History*, XL, 27, 1-3). If the Parthians did in fact pour molten gold down Crassus' mouth, it was likely based on their knowledge that Crassus, one of the richest men in history, always thirsted for more wealth.

After Crassus' death, the Parthians were able to inflict one of the most devastating losses on the Roman army. In addition to losing a competent general and former consul, the Romans lost their prized eagle standards, and only 10,000 of their 42,000 men returned from the campaign

(Brosius 2010, 96).

The Parthians inflicted a heavy blow on the morale and military capabilities of the Romans in the east, but the unstable political situation in Rome contributed more to a period of peace between the two peoples than anything else. For most of the 1st century BCE, Rome was embroiled in a series of Civil Wars that left it vulnerable to the outside world, which is how Caesar was able to finish the Republic in the 40s BCE and Augustus was able to establish the Empire in 27 BCE.

After Crassus' failed campaign against Parthia in 53 BCE, the only other Roman action against Parthia was a failed expedition by Mark Antony which was never a real threat to the Parthian homeland, and when Augustus became emperor, he ushered in a new era of material prosperity known as the "Augustan Peace" (Temin 2006). Despite being a dictator with immense powers, such as the ability to veto the Senate, Augustus made every attempt to appear benevolent while securing his power base and establishing the Julio-Claudian Dynasty. Most of Augustus' time was spent in the realm of domestic policy and concerns; foreign affairs were a distant concern to the young emperor, and war became anathema to his political program.

An ancient bust of Antony

As a result of this, Augustus made peace with Parthia during the reign of king Pharaates IV (32-2 BC) in 20 BCE. The Roman-Parthian peace was exploited by Augustus as a victory, and later Romans wrote about how the Parthians groveled for peace and returned the standards they stole from Crassus. The early 2nd century Roman biographer Suetonius wrote, "The Parthians also were ready to grant Augustus' claims on Armenia and, when he demanded the surrender of the Eagles captured from Marcus Crassus and Mark Antony, not only returned them but offered hostages into the bargain; and once, because several rival princes were claiming the Parthian throne, they announced that they would elect whichever candidate he chose." (Suetonius, *Divus Augustus*, 22).

Like many narratives by ancient historians, this account is a mix of facts and hyperbole. The Parthians returned the standards, but there is no evidence to corroborate the claim that Augustus chose the next Parthian king. That said, both the accounts of Suetonius and the 2nd century Roman historian Tacitus relate that Augustus' successor, Tiberius (reigned 14-37), tried to influence the direction of the Parthian royal court. According to Suetonius, Tiberius' early foreign policy centered more on the attempted pacification of Germania, but Parthia was never far from his mind: "Tiberius was given another five years of tribunician power, with the task of pacifying Germany, and the Parthian envoys who visited Augustus at Rome with messages from their king were instructed to present themselves before Tiberius too, in Germany." (Suetonius, *Tiberius*, 16).

It was not long before Tiberius was faced with a formidable foe in the Parthian king Artabanus II (reigned 10-38), who forcefully overthrew his predecessor Vonones. Tiberius attempted to bribe Parthian officials and place spies in the Parthian court in order to place a friendlier king on the throne because Artabanus II apparently coveted the old boundaries of the Achaemenid Empire. Tacitus wrote, "In the consulate of Gaius Cestius and Marcus Sevillius, a number of Parthian nobles made their way to the capital without the knowledge of King Artabanus. That prince, loyal to Rome and temperate towards his subjects while he had Germanicus to fear, soon adopted an attitude of arrogance to ourselves and of cruelty to his countrymen. For he was emboldened by the campaigns he had successfully prosecuted against the surrounding nations; he disdained the old age of Tiberius as no longer fit for arms; and he coveted Armenia, on the throne of which (after the death of Artaxias) he installed his eldest son Arsaces, adding insult to injury by sending envoys to reclaim the treasure left by Vonones in Syria and Cilicia. At the same time, he referred in boastful and menacing terms to the old boundaries of the Persian and Macedonian empires, and to his intention of seizing the territories held first by Cyrus and afterwards by Alexander." (Tacitus, *The Annals*, VI, 31).

A coin depicting Artabanus II

Carole Raddato's picture of an ancient bust of Tiberius

Tiberius never led a major campaign against the Parthians, instead attempting, albeit unsuccessfully, to control his enemies through intrigue and espionage. The treasure of Vonones that Tacitus wrote about was apparently recovered later by Tiberius, according to Suetonius: "As for Vonones, the king of Parthia, whom his subjects had dethroned but who, under the impression that he was confiding himself to Roman protection, escaped to Antioch with a huge treasure, Tiberius treacherously robbed and killed him." (Suetonius, Tiberius, 49)

Artabanus II was apparently too strong of a leader for Tiberius and the Romans to seriously challenge, but the strength and stability that he brought to the Parthian Empire was short lived. At the height of his power, Artabanus II was assassinated by his own son, Gotarzes, whose actions thrust Parthia into a period of civil war. Once again, the Parthian sources are quiet concerning both the assassination and civil war, but Tacitus wrote an account on the confusing period in Parthian history. "That prince, king of Iberia and also brother of Mithridates, kept announcing that the Parthians were divided among themselves – the crown was in question, minor matters unregarded. For Gotarzes, among his numerous cruelties, had procured the murder of his brother Artabanus and his wife and son, with the result that the rest took alarm and called in Vardanes. He, with his usual alacrity for great adventures, covered three thousand stadia in two days; drove the unsuspecting and terrified Gotarzes into flight, and without hesitation seized the nearest satrapies – Seleucia alone refusing to acknowledge his supremacy." (Tacitus, *The Annals*, XI, 8-10).

Despite the instability in Parthia, the Romans were unable to take advantage of the situation, but the rivalry between the two great peoples continued. The lull in the hostilities between the Parthians and Romans ended when Trajan (reigned 98-117) became emperor of Rome and embarked on three campaigns against Parthia in 114, 115, and 116, which caused as much damage to the Parthians as any previous Roman campaigns. During Trajan's second campaign, he captured the Parthian city of Ctesiphon and was able to assert Roman control, albeit briefly, over Mesopotamia once more in 116 (Wenke 1981, 310). According to Dio, Trajan relied on engineering technology more than military might to conquer Ctesiphon: "Trajan had planned to conduct the Euphrates through a canal into the Tigris, in order that he might take his boats down by this route and use them to make a bridge. But learning that this river has a much higher elevation than the Tigris, he did not do so, fearing that the water might rush down in a flood and render the Euphrates unnavigable. So he used hauling-engines to drag the boats across the very narrow space that separates the two rivers (the whole stream of the Euphrates empties into a marsh and from there somehow joins the Tigris); then he crossed the Tigris and entered Ctesiphon. When he had taken possession of this place he was saluted imperator and established his right to the title of Parthicus. In addition to other honours voted to him by the senate, he was granted the privilege of celebrating as many triumphs as he should desire." (Cassius Dio, *Roman History*, LXVIII, 28, 1-3).

An ancient bust of Trajan

Although Trajan was given triumphs and columns were erected that proclaimed his victories in the Near East over the Parthians, the Romans were unable to hold onto Ctesiphon. In fact, the Parthian city would continue to be the focal point of conflict between the Romans and Parthians; the Roman general Avidius Cassius led a major campaign against Seleucia and Ctesiphon during the reign of Marcus Aurelius (reigned 161-180), but his army was forced to retreat when the Antonine Plague devastated his troops (Brosius 2010, 100).

Despite Rome's growing economic problems in the 3rd century, the emperors Septimus Severus, Caracalla, and Macrinus all led campaigns against Parthia. The Romans are often heralded by modern scholars for their efficiency, but their policy in regards to Parthia, especially in the 3rd century, can best be described as obstinate. Numerous Roman defeats at the hands of the Parthians under several different emperors never deterred a new emperor or general from embarking on the chimerical idea of defeating the Parthians once and for all. The Parthian king Vologases V (reigned 191/2-207/8) defended his kingdom from a vigorous campaign led by the Roman emperor Septimius Severus (reigned 193-211) around 198. While the Romans were fighting among themselves, the Parthians managed to retake Mesopotamia, which then became the focal point of Septimius Severus' campaign. Dio recounted, "After this Severus made a campaign against the Parthians. For while he had been occupied with the civil wars they had taken advantage of their immunity and had captured Mesopotamia, whither they had made an expedition in full force. . . As the Parthians did not await his arrival but retired homeward (their leader was Vologaesus, whose brother was accompanying Severus), he constructed boat on the Euphrates and proceeded forward partly by marching along the river. The boats thus built were exceedingly swift and speedy and well constructed, for the forest along the Euphrates and that region in general afforded him an abundant supply of timber. Thus he soon had seized Seleucia and Babylon, both of which had been abandoned. Later, upon capturing Ctesiphon, he permitted the soldiers to plunder the entire city, and he slew a vast number of people, besides taking as many as a hundred thousand captives. He did not, however, pursue Vologaesus, nor even occupy Ctesiphon, but, just as if the sole purpose of his campaign had been to plunder this place." (Cassius Dio, *Roman History*, LXXVI, 9, 1-4).

A bust of Severus

A coin depicting Vologases V

Dio's account may make it seem as though Vologases V and the Parthians retreated in fear from the Romans, but a closer examination reveals that they may have merely conducted a strategic retreat. As discussed above, the Parthian Empire was so vast that the Romans did not even comprehend its size properly, meaning it was possible Vologases V decided to retreat into the interior until Septimius Severus and his legions were sated by plunder. The Parthian king also probably knew of the social and economic problems that were plaguing Rome at the time, so he knew that the Romans would be unable to occupy any Parthian territory in Mesopotamia for very long.

Vologases V witnessed the growing weakness of Parthia's greatest enemy, but it was his successor, Vologases VI (208-228), who endured the last two major campaigns by the Romans against his people. Throughout this period, the growing weakness of Rome did not stop its emperors from embarking on new military campaigns. In fact, in the latter stages of the empire, Roman emperors became dependent on the legions for their support, which could sometimes be capricious as they often played the role of kingmaker. The result was that incompetent and often extremely violent emperors ruled Rome and constantly led the Empire into unwinnable campaigns.

Vologases VI had to contend with two Roman military campaigns, and the first was led by the emperor Caracalla (188-217) in 216. According to Dio, Caracalla (who Dio called Antonius) led a campaign deep into the Parthian homeland but accomplished little more than desecrate some Parthian tombs."So Antonius now ravaged a large section of the country around Media by making a sudden incursion, sacked many fortresses, won over Arbela, dug open the royal tombs of the Parthians, and scattered the bones about. . . When the Parthians and Medes, greatly angered by the treatment they had received, proceeded to raise a large army, he fell into the greatest terror. For, though he was most bold with his threats and most reckless in his undertakings, yet he was the greatest coward in the face of danger and the greatest weakling in the presence of hardships." (Cassius Dio, *Roman History*, LXXIX, 1, 2-4).

An ancient bust of Caracalla

The success of Caracalla's campaign into Parthia, like the other Roman ones before him, was for the most part pyrrhic, as the Romans were not able to keep any territory they gained. Caracalla was killed not long after in an assassination that may have been orchestrated by the head of the Praetorian Guards and eventual successor to the office of emperor, Macrinus (217-18). Perhaps not surprisingly, Macrinus continued Caracalla's inane policy towards Parthia by leading a campaign against Parthia in 218. Marcinus hoped to retake Mesopotamia, which the Parthians occupied after the death of Caracalla, but the Roman emperor's campaign ended in a stalemate. Of course, he still tried to use propaganda to turn it into a victory, as relayed by Dio:

"And the Parthian was not loath to come to terms, both for his reason and because his troops were exceedingly restive, due to their having been kept away from home an unusually long time as well as to the scarcity of food; for they had no food supplies available, either from stores previously made ready, since they do not make any such preparations, or from the country itself, inasmuch as the food either had been destroyed or else was in the forts. Macrinus, however did not forward a full account of all their arrangements to the senate, and consequently sacrifices of victory were voted in his honour and the name of Parthicus was bestowed upon him. But this he declined, being ashamed, apparently, to take a title from an enemy by home had been defeated." (Cassius Dio, *Roman History*, LXXIX, 27, 2-3).

Perhaps it was not Macrinus' conscience at all that prevented him from accepting the title because he was executed not long after his Parthian debacle. Either way, Marcrinus' campaign was the last time that the Romans and Parthians are known to have met on the battlefield according to records; the Parthian dynasty was almost finished, and Rome was well into its decay and its borders were contracting.

The numerous battles between the Romans and Parthians appear for the most part to be futile, but the 1st century BC Greco-Roman geographer Strabo wrote about one positive unintended side effect of the wars. Strabo is one of the best known of the ancient geographers, and his multivolume work has been preserved and translated over a number of generations into several different languages. The geographer's accounts not only give modern scholars a glimpse into how the Greeks and Romans viewed their neighbors and the land around them but also how they obtained that information. According to Strabo, the Parthians were responsible for giving people in the west new geographic information about previously unknown lands in the east. "Indeed, the spread of the empires of the Romans and of the Parthians has presented to geographers of to-day a considerable addition to our empirical knowledge of geography, just as did the campaign of Alexander to geographers of earlier times, as Eratosthenes points out. For Alexander opened up for us geographers a great part of Asia and all the northern part of Europe as far as the Ister River; the Romans have made known all the western part of Europe as far as the River Albis (which divides Germany into two parts), and the regions beyond the Ister as far as the Tyras River; and Mithridates, surnamed Eupator, and his generals have made known the regions beyond the Tyraas as far as Lake Maeotis and the line of coast that ends at Colchis; and, again the Parthians have increased our knowledge in regard to Hyrcania and Bactriana, and in regard to the Scythians who live north of Hyrcania and Bactriana, all of which countries were but imperfectly known to the earlier geographers. (Strabo, *Geography*, I, 2.1)

Although the Romans may not have liked the Parthians, they respected the knowledge that they had of the world and no doubt they also respected them as warriors. After all, those Parthian warriors were ultimately the ones who kept the Roman Empire from expanding further east.

Parthian Warfare and Military

A depiction of a Parthian infantryman

Since Parthia's battles with Rome comprise such a large and important part of Parthian history, historians have long been interested in Parthian military tactics, techniques, and weapons. Similar to other aspects of Parthian history, the Parthians left few written records that detailed how they conducted their military affairs, and because of this, modern scholars are forced to combine what few Parthian records do exist with Roman accounts and archaeological and art historical remains from Parthia to create an image of the Parthian army.

One Roman writer discussed Parthian warfare in detail: "The government of the nation, after their revolt from the Macedonian power, was in the hands of kings. Next to the royal authority is the order of the people, from which they take generals in war and magistrates in peace. Their language is something between those of the Scythians and Medes, being a compound of both. Their dress was formerly of a fashion peculiar to themselves; afterwards, when their power had increased, it was like that of the Medes, light and full flowing. The fashion of their arms is that of their own country and of Scythia. They have an army, not like other nations, of free men, but chiefly consisting of slaves, the members of whom daily increase, the power of manumission being allowed to none, and all their offspring, in consequence, being born slaves. These bondmen they bring up as carefully as their own children, and teach them, with great pains, the arts of riding and shooting with the bow. As any one is eminent in wealth, so he furnishes the king with a proportionate number of horsemen for war. Indeed when fifty thousand cavalry encountered Antony, as he was making war upon Parthia, only four hundred of them were free men. Of engaging with the enemy in close fight, and of taking cities by siege, they know nothing. They fight on horseback, either galloping forward or turning their backs. Often, too, they counterfeit flight, that they may throw their pursuers off their guard against being wounded by their arrows. The signal for battle among them is given, not by trumpet but by drum. Nor are they able to fight long; but they would be irresistible, if their vigour and perseverance were equal to the fury of their onset. In general they retire before the enemy in the very heat of the engagement, and, soon after their retreat, return to the battle afresh; so that, when you feel most certain that you have conquered them, you have still to meet the greatest danger from them. Their armour, and that of their horses, is formed of plates, lapping over one another like the feathers of a bird, and covers both man and horse entirely. Of gold and silver, except for adorning their arms, they make no use."

In the Parthian army equestrian and archery skills were paramount to any other since they needed to rely on mobility to traverse the vast distances of their empire. At the top of the Parthian military pyramid were the armed cavalrymen known as cataphracts. Cataphracts were almost always members of the nobility since they were the only ones who could afford the best horses and armor needed to make up this class (Brosius 2010, 116).

Perhaps the best primary source account of the Parthian military is a short but highly detailed one from Dio. "The Parthians make no use of a shield, but their forces consist of mounted archers and pikemen, mostly in full armour. Their infantry is small, made up of the weaker men; but even these are all archers. They practise from boyhood, and the climate and the land combine to aid both horsemanship and archery. The land, being for the most part level, is excellent for raising horses and very suitable for riding about on horse-back; at any rate, even in war they lead about whole droves of horses, so that they can use different ones at different times, can ride up suddenly from a distance and also retire to a distance speedily." (Dio, *Roman History*, XL,15, 3-4).

Dio's emphasis on the importance of equestrian abilities brings to mind an often referenced but little understood term: "the Parthian shot." The Parthian shot was a maneuver whereby the Parthian horseman would fire arrows from his bow as he retreated. The tactic so impressed the Romans that the term "Parthian shot" or "Parthian retreat" became common and eventually made its way into the modern lexicon, when it now usually refers to a verbal slight that someone gives towards the end of an argument or conversation.

Unfortunately, even though the Parthian Shot has been referenced numerous times throughout history, few physical depictions of it exist; the limited depictions of the Parthian Shot come primarily from non-Parthian sources, particularly Greek vases from the Hellenistic/Seleucid period. The esteemed Russian-American classical historian Michael Rostovtzeff examined pottery evidence from the Hellenistic period that depict Parthian horsemen. In one piece a man wearing traditional Parthian garb is riding a long, thin horse typical of the central Asian and south Russian steppes. The Parthian horseman is shown with his body and head turned shooting an arrow at his Greek adversary, who is at his behind (Rostovtzeff 1943, 177). Rostovtzeff correctly concluded that the figure depicted was a Parthian warrior engaged in the famed Parthian Shot or Parthian Retreat, but he carried his analysis further in order to determine the possible origin of the Parthian Shot. The historian added that the earliest known depictions of riders shooting in retreat were dated to the 8th and 7th centuries BCE and were products of Assyrian and Phoenician art, although these were often in the context of hunts (Rostovtzeff 1943, 180). He then pointed out that Chinese art from the Han Dynasty sometimes depicted mounted archers doing the Parthian Shot (Rostovtzeff 1943, 185).

An ancient sculpture depicting the Parthian Shot

Rostovtzeff's analysis of the origins and influence of the Parthian Shot are interesting, but it should be approached with a bit of skepticism. In terms of the origins of the Parthian Shot, if the Assyrians or Phoenicians invented the maneuver, then it's only fair to wonder why the Parthians' immediate successors, the Achaemenids and Seleucids, were never known to use it. Both the Achaemenids and Seleucids employed cavalry and the descendants of the Assyrians in their armies, so it would stand to reason that they would have used the Parthian Shot against their Greek and Roman enemies if they knew about it. Moreover, as Rostovtzeff pointed out, the Assyrian artistic depictions were of hunts, not warfare – an animal, perhaps confined, would prove to be a much easier target to do the Parthian Shot against then an enemy who is shooting back. Along those same lines, it is just as believable that the Parthians taught the maneuver to their Chinese trading partners. It is well known that the Silk Route was responsible for the movement of ideas, such as Buddhism and early Christianity, just as much as commodities, so it should not be surprising that the Parthians exported their unique military technique to Han

China.

Parthian Religion

A Parthian votive relief

In the ancient world, the Parthians were among the best merchants and warriors, but what set them apart from others was their religion. The Parthians' religion was similar to many of the religions of their Near Eastern neighbors in that ritual played a key role, but it differed greatly in terms of theology. The Parthian view towards the various religions within their empire was essentially a continuation of that of their Achaemenid successors: religious toleration and non-interference.

The religion that the Parthians practiced themselves was an early form of Zoroastrianism, which many argue is the oldest form of monotheism in the world. At the head of the Parthian religious order was a class of priests who carried out most of the religious rituals and formulated theological ideas. By all accounts, the priesthood was non-centralized and priests from each region exercised autonomy, so there was no Parthian-Zoroastrian religious hierarchy during the empire (Boyce 2001, 81).

The Parthian priesthood was probably inherited from the Achaemenid period, as were some other important aspects of the religion, but the Parthians also diverged from their successors in some important ways. For example, coinage was a general tradition that the Parthians took from the Achaemenids, but their use of religious iconography on the coins differed somewhat. The Achaemenids usually depicted their god, Ahura-Mazda, as a sun-disk, often with wings, on their coins and in other art in a way that was clearly influenced by earlier Egyptian and Mesopotamian artistic styles. Conversely, the Parthians typically depicted the divine in anthropomorphic style, which was more similar to the Hellenistic world (Boyce 2001, 82). This minor difference is probably indicative more of the Seleucids being the most immediate predecessors of the Parthians than any major theological shift, as other coins indicate that religious continuity from the Achaemenid through the Parthian dynasties was the rule.

Sacred fire altars were also common depictions on both Achaemenid and Parthian coins (Brosius 2010, 103). The depiction of sacred fire altars on coins appears to have become common about halfway through the Parthian Dynasty, during the reign of Vologases I (AD 51-80) (Colledge 1967, 51), and it was also during the reign of Vologases I that many of the books from the Zoroastrian holy scriptures known as the *Avesta* were first compiled (College 1967, 51).

The *Avesta* provides the modern reader with a glimpse into the theological motives that drove the Parthians, but the true essence of their religion was in the many arcane rituals that are still often misunderstood. The Parthians erected shrines, called *yazatas*, as sacred precincts where they believed Ahura-Mazada and some of the other lesser gods dwelled (Boyce 2001, 85). For the most part, they were similar to later Catholic shrines, but they were places of reverence more than ritual or worship, which was for the most part confined to the Parthian fire temples.

The oldest descriptions of Zoroastrian fire temples and the oldest identified fire temples themselves come from the Parthian period (Boyce 2001, 86). The Parthian fire temples were located at a place known as the "Hill of the Master" in what is now southeastern Iran, which appears to have been the focal point for Parthian religious activity (Boyce 2001, 86). Sacred fires were where Zoroastrian rituals took place as they served as the earthly avatar of their god.

The importance of fire in Zoroastrian religion is demonstrated in both the theological texts and role it played in liturgical rituals (Clark 2001, 82). Fire gave both light and heat to Zarathustra/Zoroaster, the prophet of Zoroastrianism, as he spread his message across ancient Iran. To the Parthians, as well as modern Zoroastrians, fire embodied both divine and regal aspects and was therefore to be treated with reverence and respect. Devout Zoroastrians would never turn their back on a fire and would never place anything in a fire that might pollute its purity, especially waste matter and corpses (Clark 2001, 94).

There have been a number of sacred fires during the lifespan of Zoroastrianism but the three greatest ones – named Adur Buzen-Mihr, Adur Farnbag, and Adur Gushnasp – were installed either late in the Achaemenid Dynasty or early in the Parthian Dynasty (Boyce 2001, 87). To the Parthians, Adur Burzen-Mihr was the favored fire as it was established in Parthia proper (Boyce 2001, 88). The fire was placed in a temple, and, according to Parthian tradition, one of Zarathustra/Zoroaster's followers, Vishtaspa, personally installed the fire in order to spread the new faith (Boyce 2001, 88).

Unfortunately, the Parthians wrote very little about their sacred fires, but Greek and Roman outsiders were impressed enough to write their own observations. An enigmatic Greek named Isidore of Charax wrote a journal of his travels along the Silk Route titled *The Parthian Stations*, and while most of the book concerns trade along the route, Isidore mentioned that a sacred fire was maintained where Arsaces, the founder of the Parthian Dynasty, first became king (Boyce 2001, 87). The earlier and better known 5th century BCE Greek historian Herodotus also wrote about sacred fires and the overall perception of Zoroastrianism to an outsider during the Achaemenid period. "The following are certain Persian customs which I can describe from personal knowledge. The erection of statues, temples, and altars is not an accepted practice amongst them, and anyone who does such a thing is considered a fool, because, presumably, the Persian religion is not anthropomorphic like the Greek. Zeus, in their system, is the whole circle of the heavens, and they sacrifice to him from the tops of mountains. They also worship the sun, moon, and earth, fire, water, and winds, which are their only original deities." (Herodotus, *The Histories*, I, 131). Herodotus followed the typical Greco-Roman convention of assigning the names of Greek and Roman deities to those he believed to be the foreign equivalent, so in this case Zeus, the head of the Greek pantheon, was associated with the Zoroastrian Ahura-Mazda.

Rituals concerning fire were perhaps the most important in the religion of the Parthians, but the funerary rituals they practiced were probably the most foreign to outsiders. Purity was an important concept in Zoroastrian religion, and Zoroastrian priests conscientiously observed protocols concerning purity when tending to fires, which included separating corpses from fires. To Zoroastrians, corpses are the embodiment of impurity and should never be touched, which is an idea that was followed well before the Parthians. The Parthians, much like their Achaemenid ancestors, entombed their dead nobles, but the majority of practicing Zoroastrians during the Parthian period probably practiced corpse exposure (Boyce 2001, 90). The practice of corpse exposure simply involves placing the deceased's corpse in an open area where vultures and dogs could devour the flesh and organs, after which the bones are then collected and placed in an ossuary (Boyce 2001, 90). This funerary ritual is still practiced today by the small Zoroastrian community in Mumbai, India (Clark 2001, 116), but it was mentioned briefly by the Roman historian Pempeius Trogus (Boyce 2001, 91).

A statue depicting a Parthian noble

Herodotus offered a more detailed description of the ritual from the Achaemenid period in his history. "There is another practice, however, concerning the burial of the dead, which is not spoken of openly and is something of a mystery: it is that a male Persian is never buried until the body has been torn by a bird or a dog. I know for certain that the Magi have this custom, for they are quite open about it. The Persians in general, however, cover a body with wax and then bury it. The Magi are a peculiar caste, quite different from the Egyptian priests and indeed from any other sort of person. The Egyptian priests make it an article of religion to kill no living creature except for sacrifice, but the Magi not only anything, except dogs and men, with their own hands but make a special point of doing so; ants, snakes, crawling animals, birds – no matter what, they kill them indiscriminately. Well, it is an ancient custom, do let them keep it." (Herodotus, *The Histories*, I, 140).

As noted by Herodotus, the magi were a specific caste of Zoroastrians during the Achaemenid period that carried out most of the religious rituals, and according to this passage, they were the ones who started the practice of ritual corpse exposure, which by the Parthian period appears to have become the standard funerary ritual for most Zoroastrians.

Although rituals were an important aspect of Parthian religion, they were contingent upon the theology that was articulated in the *Avesta*. The *Avesta* is not just one single book, but is a collection of scriptures that were compiled over the period of several centuries, similar to the processes that established the Old Testament and the New Testament for the Bible. The Parthian contribution to the *Avesta* is a book known as the Vendidad, or "Law against the Demons," which was compiled during the reign of Vologases I, who was also known as Valakhsh (Boyce 2001, 93). The Vendidad is concerned primarily with rules about ritual purity and what one should do if defiled by an impurity. Theologically speaking, the Vendidad is quite clear on these matters, especially as it pertains to corpses. "No corpse which has been carried away by dogs, birds, wolves, winds, or flies, defiles a man. Were these corpses which have been carried away by dogs, birds, wolves, winds, or flies, to defile men, then would almost all my corporeal world be little allied to purity, but become Khraojdat-urva and Pesho-tanus; on account of the multitude of corpses which have perished on this earth. Creator! A man pours water over a corn-field; the water flows over this field for the second, for the third time; after the fourth time a dog, or a panther, or a wolf, brings a corpse into the field; what is the punishment for this? Then answered Ahura-Mazda: no corpse which the dogs, birds, wolves, winds, or flies, have brought defiles a man." (Vendidad, Fargad V).

Interestingly, the Parthians, as well as all believers in Zoroastrianism, revered dogs despite their task of eating the polluted corpses. The Parthians believed that dogs fulfilled a sacred duty, but they also believed burial grounds were impure for a period of time. The Vendidad reads, "How long must the earth be left uncultivated on which dogs and men die? Then answered Ahura-Mazda: a year long, O pure Zarathustra! Shall the land remain uncultivated on which dogs and men die. The Mazdayacnians shall not till this land; they shall not pour water on it within a year when dogs and men die upon it." (Vendidad, Fargad VI)

Thus, the Parthians were mandated to practice rituals pertaining to purity in their lives and deaths in a way that made them thrive spiritually within the temporal world. Zoroastrian theological ideas of purity went beyond rituals though and extended to all living creatures.

Zoroastrianism is sometimes referred to as a *dualistic* religion in that its adherents worship the pure god Ahura-Mazda but still recognize an evil and impure god named Angra-Mainyu. The Parthians extended the theological idea of opposites, or poles, to the natural world around them, as some plants and animals were good and pure while others were evil and impure. Dogs were good animals, but there were also a number of evil animals that Zoroastrians were required to avoid. The historian Plutarch, who lived during the existence of the Parthian Empire, wrote about this dualism in his book on eastern mythology, *Isis and Osiris*. "They believe that among plants too, some belong to the good god and others to the evil daemon, and that among animals some, such as dogs, birds and land hedgehogs, belong to the good god, whereas water-rats belong to the bad deity, and for this reason they regard as happy whoever kills a great number of them. But they (the Persians) also relate many mythical details about the gods." (Boyce 1990, 108-9)

The idea of theological poles was also manifested in two important Persian words: *asha* and *drug*, which mean "truth" and "lie" respectively (Clark 2001, 5; 9). In Parthian-Zoroastrian theology, *asha* was associated with everything that was good and pure, while *drug* consisted of everything that was impure and evil.

The Parthians' strong religious beliefs also extended into their ideas of kingship to create an ideal that was most unique, even in the ancient Near East. Most of the peoples of the ancient Near East viewed their kings as either divine (such as Egypt) or as inspired and appointed by the divine, as in Mesopotamia. The Parthian view of kingship was closer to that practiced in Mesopotamia, but it was also different in many significant ways.

The concept of Parthian kingship, like Parthian religion in general, was essentially an extension of Achaemenid Persian kingship. As such, the king was believed to be the mortal vessel of Ahura Mazda, and it was his job to carry out the proper rituals and maintain purity throughout the temporal kingdom. In that vein, the Parthians seem to have followed the Achaemenids in crafting legends that validated and legitimized their dynasty; for example, the Parthians priests created a legend that stated that Arsaces, the first Parthian king, had six nobles who helped him take the throne. The legend shows another string of cultural continuity from the Achaemenid to the Parthian dynasty because the Achaemenids recognized six great Persian families in their empire. The number six is also theologically significant in Zoroastrianism because Ahura Mazda was attended to by six demigods in heaven (Boyce 2001, 87).

One of the more unique aspects of Achaemenid kingship that the Parthians followed was the practice of *khavaetvadatha*, or incestuous royal marriage (Boyce 2001, 97). The marriages included brother-sister, mother-son, and father-daughter pairings, and although there was no express endorsement of it in Zoroastrian theology, its practice no doubt comes from the concepts of purity inherent in Zoroastrianism. In a Greek document, Arsaces I was said to be married to his sister (Boyce 2001, 97), but the practice was only given a detailed account by Herodotus of the Achaemenid king Cambyses. According to Herodotus, the tradition began with the Achaemenids. "This woman was his sister by both parents, and also his wife, though it had never been a Persian custom for brothers and sisters to marry. . . He summoned the royal judges and asked them if there was any law in the country which allowed a man to marry his sister if he wished to do so. . . They could discover no law which allowed brother to marry sister, there was undoubtedly a law which permitted the king of Persia to do what he pleased. . . Cambyses accordingly married the sister he was in love with, and not long afterwards married another one as well – and this, the younger of the two, was the one who went with him to Egypt." (Herodotus, *The Histories*, III, 31).

Although most elements of Parthian religion and kingship appear to have been inherited from the Achaemenids, there were some aspects that were either native Parthian or came from elsewhere. The Parthians were culturally Persian and followed many of the traditions of their Achaemenid ancestors, but they originated from different tribes than the Achaemenids and were also influenced by other non-Persian peoples. Unlike the Achaemenids, the Parthians had extensive knowledge of and contact with different peoples in East Asia and they also were more influenced by the Greeks than the Achaemenids were. It has already been mentioned that Parthian coins followed the Hellenistic Seleucid style more than the Achaemenid, which is another source that depicts the Parthian concept of kingship. Some Parthian coins refer to the king as the "Brother of the Sun and Moon", which may be a reference to Ahura Mazda as the sun, but it could also be a reference to a pre-Zoroastrian nomadic deity (Colledge 1967, 103). The Parthians more than likely carried some elements of their pre-Zoroastrian religion with them into Persia, but for the most part they practiced a religion that was almost the same as the Achaemenids before and the Sassanids after them.

Religion clearly played an important role in Parthian culture, but their religion also influenced others. One of the more interesting aspects of Roman and Parthian history that continues to puzzle scholars is the nature of the Mithras cult and its potential origin in Persia. The Mithras cult was one of the many "mystery religions" that the Romans adopted, several of which came from cultures outside of Rome. Isis, an Egyptian goddess, and Cybele, an Anatolian goddess, were both popular with Roman women, while Mithras, which was a variation of the name of the Zoroastrian demigod Mithra, was popular with Roman soldiers and the political elite for over 400 years (Clark 2001, 157).

Since the Mithras cult, like all of the Roman mystery cult, were esoteric in nature, the exact nature of the influence the Parthians had on the cult remains unknown, but some archaeological evidence has led modern scholars to make educated deductions. Some believe that the conscription of Persian soldiers into the Roman army and continued contact between the Parthian and Romans led to some members of the ever eclectic Roman society adopting the cult directly from Parthian/Zoroastrian religion (Clark 2001, 157). This seems like the most plausible explanation, but others have argued that the Mithras cult was actually a Roman religion that was given a Parthian façade to make it appear more exotic in order to attract Romans who were enthralled with eastern spirituality (Clark 2001, 157).

The best evidence to determine the origins of the Mithras cult can be found in the many temples throughout Europe that the Romans erected to the god. Mithras temples, known as *mithraea*, were subterranean chambers where the secret rituals of the cult took place (Clark 2001, 158). The best evidence from extant mithraea are the reliefs on the altars, which depict a graphic mythological story. The altar reliefs usually depict the god/hero Mithra slaughtering a bull and often accompanied by a leaping dog (Clark 2001, 158). The references to Zoroastrian theology are unmistakable; the bull slaughter is similar to an account from a Zoroastrian text (the

Bundahishen), while dogs were viewed as *asha* animals in Zoroastrian theology and an important part of the funerary ritual (Clark 2001, 158). The detailed iconography on the Mithras altars suggests that the inventors of the Mithras cult had more than just a superficial knowledge of Zoroastrianism, which in turn indicates a provenance of the religion somewhere in Persian or Parthia.

Of course, if the Mithras cult began as a Roman interpretation of some elements of Zoroastrian theology then new questions are raised. Perhaps the most obvious question regards why the Romans would adopt one of their biggest enemies' gods. The answer to this question may never be revealed, but the fact that the Romans worshiped Mithra demonstrates the strength and vitality of Parthian culture. The numerous Roman-Parthian wars for the most part ended in stalemate with the borders, aside from Armenia, rarely changed, and both sides were weakened by internal problems; but there was clearly enough contact between the two to have their cultural concepts cross into the two empires.

A Mithraic relief from Ancient Rome

The Decline of the Parthian Empire

The exportation of Mithra to the west was one of Parthia's last great triumphs, because even as numerous Romans worshiped the Zoroastrian deity in underground chambers, the Parthian Empire was falling apart. As Rome entered into its precipitous decline in the 3rd century CE, so did its erstwhile enemy; but the end of the Parthian Empire was much more abrupt.

Although the Parthian dynasty ended quickly and is usually attributed to the last king of the dynasty, Vologases VI (207-228), numerous factors contributed to make the decline a foregone conclusion. The Antonine Plague of 165-180 CE proved to be an especially devastating illness to the Roman army in the east, but it was equally devastating to the civilian population of Europe once the soldiers returned home. All of the sources that describe the plagues' effects and extent are Roman, so it is unknown what effect the plague had on Parthia, but one can assume that it affected the Parthians equally. The plague ravaged Europe during the reign of the Parthian king Vologases IV (148-192), who is not known to have conducted any major campaigns, an indication that the Parthians also suffered from the plague. It stands to reason that given the centuries of animosity built up between the Romans and Parthians, if an opportunity made possible by the plague presented itself to the Parthians, they would have taken advantage of it by campaigning against the Romans.

The Parthians were almost certainly adversely affected by the Antonine Plague, but that alone would not have undone the empire. Perhaps the greatest external problems that the Parthians encountered were primarily those of their own creation: constant wars and conflicts with other peoples. The numerous Roman-Parthian wars are known to have been a drain on the Roman economy, and one can only imagine that a similar situation took hold in Parthia. As the Parthians fought the Romans for control of Mesopotamia and Armenia, they neglected their trade routes and other peoples, such as Kushan, grew stronger. For the most part, the Romans were never an existential threat to the Parthians, but when the Parthians focused most of their resources on western campaigns, they invited rebellion and instability into their empire.

Much of the instability would come within the Parthian nobility and the royal line. From the beginning of the Parthian dynasty, there were always pretenders to the throne, many of whom were supported by the Romans, but it was not until later in the dynasty that it became a problem. Questions and claims concerning royal succession in the later Parthian dynasty led to some apparent and tangible problems, such as assassinations and multiple claims to the throne. Osroes and Vologases III both claimed the Parthian throne simultaneously, as did Vologases VI and Artabanus IV (Brosius 2010, 202). Naturally, as the Parthian Empire grew weaker, the problems of succession and pretenders to the throne became amplified, to the point that they were no longer minor problems that could be ignored but existential issues that the Parthian kings could no longer effectively handle.

The chaotic political situation in the late Parthian Empire was just a reflection on the nature of the Parthian Empire itself, as it was one without a true national or central character. Though the Parthians followed a governmental system similar to that of the Seleucids and Achaemenids before them, the power of the Parthian central government was considerably weaker, and while the Parthians continued the satrapal system of their predecessors, they also allowed certain regions to retain their own kings as long as they supplied taxes and/or men for the Parthian military. Such a system could work well in times of peace and internal stability, but once the Parthian dynasty began to turn on itself, it also quickly lost control of its semi-autonomous kingdoms.

The Parthians also never demonstrated the kind of propaganda abilities of the Achaemenids when it came to advertising their power within the empire. The Achaemenid Persians were masters of ancient propaganda, and they depicted themselves as legitimate rulers on the temples and monuments of the peoples they conquered. The Achaemenids left their political mark on the temples of Egypt, Mesopotamia, and Anatolia in order to advertise their power to their new subjects. Although it is nearly impossible to determine how effective such measures were, it no doubt implanted an indelible mark in the minds of their subjects and served as a constant reminder of who wielded the power and central authority within the empire. The Parthians on the other hand left little evidence of their control in the lands of their subject peoples, so it's safe to assume that whenever the royal succession problems intensified, subjects furthest from Parthia thought little of who was in control.

As the situation grew more difficult within the Parthian dynasty, a new Persian dynasty rose in its place. In 224, Ardashir of Persis was proclaimed king of the Sassanid dynasty, which began a new era in the history of Persia (Colledge 1967, 173). Vologases VI may have survived nominally as king until 227, but Ardashir's accession is considered by most scholars to be the terminal point of the Parthian dynasty and empire. Since the Parthians were a Persian dynasty and not necessarily an ethnic group themselves, they continued to live in the Parthian heartland, but without the power they wielded for centuries. The Parthian dynasty may have collapsed, but vital elements of their culture continued on for centuries under the Sassanids. Most importantly the Sassanids continued the Zoroastrian religious tradition and continued tending to the sacred fires until the advent of Islam.

Early Sasanian History

The Sasanian Dynasty began in the hills of what is now southern Iran in the region known as Persis. From their city of Istakhr, the Sasanians had easy access to all of the Achaemenid monuments (Brosius 2010, 139), and although they could not read the cuneiform inscriptions on the monuments, the predecessors seemed to have given the early Sasanian kings and nobles not just a link to Persia's glorious past, but also something around which they could rally.

As the Sasanian nobles watched the Parthian Dynasty collapse before their eyes in the 3rd century CE, they decided to make their move. The first true Sasanian king and progenitor of the Sasanian Dynasty was Ardashir I (224-239/40), but interestingly, the dynasty took its name from a man named Sasan, who was the guardian of the sacred fire in the Anahita sanctuary at Istakhr (Brosius 2010, 139). It may seem surprising that the Sasanians were not named for their first, warlike king, but a closer look at the situation reveals it was actually quite logical. First, Sasanian kings were generally very pious Zoroastrians, so any individual associated with one of their sacred fires would be afforded an exceptionally high place in their culture. Second, the process placing Ardashir I in the position to defeat the Parthians was actually a very long one, and if anything, his rise represented the final step. The Sasanians slowly defeated their neighbors in an east to west direction while staying under the radar of their Parthian overlords (Brosius 2010, 140).

Classical Numismatic Group, Inc.'s picture of a coin depicting Ardashir I

When Ardashir I proclaimed the Sasanian dynasty as the legitimate rulers of Persia, Parthian King Artabanus V would not hand the crown over willingly. According to the early 3rd century Roman historian Cassius Dio, Ardashir I and Artabanus V fought at least three battles for the throne of Persia. The defining battle came at Hormuzjan in the region of Media on April 28, 224, where Artabanus V (213-224) died on the battlefield and Ardashir I proclaimed himself "King of Kings," following standard Near Eastern royal nomenclature (Brosius 2010, 14).

Dio wrote that after defeating Artabanus V, Ardashir I, whom he referred to as "Artaxerxes," attempted to wrest all of Mesopotamia and Armenia away from the Romans. "But the situation in Mesopotamia became still more alarming and inspired a more genuine fear in all, not merely the people in Rome, but the rest of mankind as well. For Artaxerxes, a Persian, after conquering the Parthians in three battles and killing their king, Artabanus, made a campaign against Hatra, in the endeavor to capture it as a base for attacking the Romans. He actually did make a breach in the wall, but when he lost a good many soldiers through an ambuscade, he moved against Media. Of this country, as also of Parthia, he acquired no small portion, partly by force and partly by intimidation, and then marched against Armenia. Here he suffered a reverse at the hands of the natives, some Medes, and the sons of Artabanus, and either fled, as some say, or, as others assert, retired to prepare a larger expedition. He accordingly became a source of fear to us; for he was encamped with a large army so as to threaten not only Mesopotamia but also Syria, and he boasted that he would win back everything that the ancient Persians had once held, as far as the Grecian Sea, claiming that all this was his rightful inheritance from his forefathers." (Cassius Dio, *Roman History*, LXXX, 3-4).

Almost as soon as he had been proclaimed king, Ardashir I initiated a policy of martial continuity with the Achaemenid Persians by engaging in open hostility with the Romans, who had inherited Hellenic culture from the Greeks. In order to be effective in their campaigns against the Romans, Ardashir I knew he had to rebuild the army, and for this, he followed Parthian precedent by placing the cavalry at the apex of his army, with both light and heavy units (Brosius 2010, 186). Cavalry had long been a tradition in Persia, dating back to the Achaemenids, but it was the Parthians who had truly raised cavalry tactics to the next level with their famed "Parthian shot." This tactic essentially saw horseback archers firing as they retreated, and the Sasanians learned to follow these military traditions quite effectively.

Ardashir I knew that if his dynasty was to last as long as the Achaemenid, he would have to also take the Parthian Dynasty into consideration and try to establish further strings of continuity. Besides organizing the Sasanian military along the Parthian model, Ardashir I also made the Parthian-Mesopotamian city of Ctesiphon a Sasanian capital. After taking control of Ctesiphon, Ardashir I had himself proclaimed king in a formal ceremony in the city, thereby establishing a clear line of continuity from the Parthian Dynasty to the Sasanian Dynasty (Brosius 2010, 142).

Sahand Ace's picture of a Sassanid relief depicting Ardashir I receiving the ring of kingship

Once the king had been safely ensconced in his seat of power, he was free to dedicate his time to cultural pursuits that made the Sasanians unique and powerful at the same time. Although Ardashir I followed many of the cultural precedents set by his Achaemenid and Parthian predecessors, he also established some norms that were different and thus represented Sasanian culture.

By all accounts, the Sasanians maintained a very religious dynasty, more so than their predecessors, as nearly everything they did—including their wars with the Romans and Byzantines—revolved around religion. One of the most unusual religious practices introduced by Ardashir I that was followed by many of his successors was *kvedodah*—the practice of royal incestuous marriage. The Sasanians were not the first people in the world to practice royal incestuous marriage—the Ptolemaic rulers of Egypt had done so more than 200 years prior—but the Sasanians had given the practice religious legitimacy. Ardashir I was the first king of the dynasty to practice *kevedodah* when he married his paternal half-sister, Denk (Boyce 2001, 111).

Although the practice was associated with Zoroastrianism, there are no direct references to the practice in any Zoroastrian text, which has left many modern scholars at pains to find its theological origins. There are also few historical texts that mention the practice. One of the earliest non-Sasanians to mention the practice was 7th century Coptic Bishop John of Nikiu, who references it in an anachronistic historical account of Persia. "And after the death of Belus, Ninus his father's brother reigned over Assyria. He married Semiramis his mother and made her his wife, and established this impure custom and transmitted it to his successors: and they are designated by this evil name till the present day. This conduct does not create a scandal amongst the Persians; for they take to wife their mothers and sisters and daughters." (Charles 2007, 18).

Among the Sasanian sources, only a few such marriages are attested (Brosius 2010, 173), but an inscription left by Zoroastrian High-Priest Kirider, who had served under several Sasanian kings after Ardashir I, mentions the practice in a religious context. The text states, "And with the support of the yazads and the King of kings, and by my act, many Vahram Fires were founded in the land of Iran, and many next-of-kin marriages were made." (Boyce 1990, 113).

Establishing the practice of *khvedodah* was certainly one of Ardahsir I's more interesting religious policies, but the aggressive king enacted other ideas promoting Zoroastrianism and connecting the Sasanians with their illustrious Achaemenid ancestors.

Ardashir I's promotion of Zoroastrian ideals throughout his kingdom was primarily carried out by the high-priest of the religion, known as the *herbad,* whose responsibility it was to see that the sacred fires were burning and Zoroastrian laws were being followed. Tansar was the herbad under Ardashir I and into Shapur I's reign (239/40-270/2). A letter written by Tansar details some religious policies carried out by Ardashir I: "Long afterwards Ardahsir son of Papak, son of Sasan, took the field...Apart from Ardavan, the man of most might and dignity at the time was Gushnasp, king of Parishwar and Tabaristan...When it became clear to Gushnasp that he could not avoid submitting and paying fealty, he wrote a letter to Tansar, chief herbad of Ardashir son of Papak. Tansar read the letter...and wrote the answer which follows: The chief herbad, Tansar, has received the letter of Gushnasp, prince and king of Tabaristan and Parishwar...He has studied each point, good and bad, and is pleased with it...In the beginning of time men enjoyed perfect understanding of the knowledge of religion...Yet it is not to be doubted that even then, through new happenings in their midst, they had need of a ruler of understanding; for till religion is interpreted by understanding by understanding it has no firm foundation...Punishments, you must know, are for three kinds of transgressions; first that of the creature against his God...when he turns from the faith and introduces a heresy into religion...For (this) the King of kings has established a law far better than that of the ancients. For in former days any man who turned from the faith was swiftly... put to death...The King of kings has ordered that such a man should be imprisoned, and that for the space of a year learned men should summon him at frequent intervals and advise him and lay arguments before him and destroy his doubts. If he become penitent and contrite and seek pardon of God, he is set free. If obstinacy and pride hold him back, then he is put to death...The truth is that after Darius (III) each of the 'kings of the peoples' [i.e. the Parthians' vassal kings] built his own [dynastic] fire temple. This was pure innovation, introduced by them without the authority of king of old. The King of kings has razed the temples, and confiscated the endowments, and had the fires carried back to their places of origin…In the space of fourteen years…he thus brought it about that he made water flow in every desert and established towns and crated groups of villages…Good order in the affairs of the people affects him more than the welfare of his own body and soul. Whoever considers his achievements…will agree that since the power of the world's Creator arched this azure sphere the world has not known so true a king." (Boyce 1990, 109-10)

The letter also relates Sasanian knowledge of earlier Persian dynasties by making mention of Darius (the Achaemenid emperor who led the First Persian War against the Greeks), demonstrating the importance Sasanians placed on both the past and religion. Ardashir I and the other early Sasanian kings also physically linked their dynasty to the Achaemenids by leaving inscriptions near Achaemenid monuments at Naqsh-I Rustam (Brosius 2010, 162).

Although there is no evidence the Sasanians were genealogically connected to the Achaemenids, they apparently felt the need to connect to the older dynasty in order to legitimize their rule in Persia. The policy was successful for the most part, as rebellions were extremely rare during the empire's first few centuries in power.

When Ardashir I died, the Sasanian crown passed peacefully and uneventfully to his son, Shapur I. The young king carried on the policies of his father during his long rule, promoting Zoroastrianism and fighting the Romans in Mesopotamia. Shapur I defeated the young Roman Emperor Gordian III (238-244) in Mesopotamia in 243 (Brosius 2010, 144). Not content with just one victory over the Romans, Shapur I pushed further east, taking cities in Syria from the Romans in 256 and 260. Shapur I proved so effective on the field of battle, at least against the Romans, that he was able to capture the Emperor Valerian (253-260), which set a new low for the Romans as it was the first time one of their emperors had been captured (Brosius 2010, 145).

Classical Numismatic Group, Inc.'s picture of a coin depicting Shapur I

When Shapur I was not fighting the Romans for control of Mesopotamia, he was following and adding to many of the religious policies his father had established. Shapur I continued the tradition of khvedodah by marrying his sister, Anahid (Boyce 2001, 111). He also continued to leave inscriptions near the Achaemenid monuments at Naqsh-I Rustam. In particular, an Achaemenid era tower became the favorite place for Shapur I and other Sasanian kings, who left several inscriptions there. Known to the locals as the Ka'ba of Zardusht, the inscriptions are usually in three languages: Parthian, Middle Persian, and Greek (Brosius 2010, 145). The multilingual facet of the inscriptions was another Achaemenid tradition continued by the Sasanians, although the Achaemenid inscriptions employed the cuneiform script in the languages of Old Persian, Akkadian, and Elamite.

One of Shapur I's inscriptions from the Ka'ba of Zardusht states that he is the king of all Iran, descended from the yazads, Zoroastrian angels, or demigods. The inscription states, "I, Lord Shabuhr, Mazda-worshipper, King of kings of Iran and non-Iran, whose race is of the yazads…And because with the help of the yazads we sought out and conquered these so many lands, there we have founded in each region many Vahram Fires, and have acted benevolently towards many priests, and have exalted the affairs of the yazads…Then even as we now are diligent in the affairs and service of the yazads, and are (ourselves) the domain of the yazads, and even as we with the help of the yazads sought out and conquered these lands, and achieved deeds of fame and courage, so let him also who shall be ruler after us be of good service and good intent towards the yazads, so that the yazads may be his friends as they have been ours." (Boyce 1990, 111)

Perhaps one of the most important domestic developments taking place during Shapur I's rule was the elevation of a man named Kirdir to the position of high-priest of the Zoroastrian religion. The first mention of Kirdir in any Sasanian text is dated to the reign of Shapur I (Sprengling 1940, 202), but it was during the reign of Bahram I (273-276) that the high-priest made his presence known throughout Persia. Historians believe that although Kirdir may have been important religiously during Shapur I's rule, he asserted himself politically after helping make Bahram I the Sasanian king (Brosius 2010, 147). A commoner by birth, Kirdir left many inscriptions in Middle Persian throughout Persia, which has helped scholars learn more about this ancient holy man (Boyce 2001, 109). It is known that he accompanied kings he served under on military expeditions against Rome (Boyce 2001, 110), and he is credited with following Tansar's theological justification of the practice of khvedodah (Boyce 2001, 111).

As Kirdir promoted Zoroastrianism virtues within the realm, he began to see more and more theological enemies who needed to be extricated from the land. When compared to other religions, Zoroastrianism usually defies most definitions, often ending up in a category by itself, and it is important to consider its place among other religions to understand why Kirdir led the persecution of non-Zoroastrians in Persia. Although Zoroastrianism is a revealed religion like Judaism, Christianity, and Buddhism, it was not a universal religion like the others because its adherents rarely proselytized the faith. The result was that nearly all Zoroastrians lived within the realm of the Sasanian Empire and most were ethnic Persians. It was also not a true "ethnic" religion like Judaism either; while nearly all of the followers of Zoroastrianism were Persians, nearly anyone could convert to the religion, meaning there were also followers from places far away from Persia. At first glance, it appears that Zoroastrianism is a monotheistic religion, but a further examination demonstrates it is not. And while the Persians never seemed concerned with proselytizing their faith to non-Persians, more than one Sasanian king and several high-priests, such as Kirdir, believed Zoroastrianism should be the only religion within the realm.

Kirdir was responsible for persecuting nearly every non-Zoroastrian religion within Persia, but he seemed to have a special distaste for the Manicheans, despite (or because of) the fact Manicheism was similar to Zoroastrianism in many ways. Manicheism was a revealed religion, started by a prophet named Mani, and its core theology held that the world was dualistic, thereby divided by good and evil. Although these basic ideals coincided with Zoroastrianism, Mani also preached that believers should lead an ascetic life, which was at odds with the worldly philosophy of Zoroastrianism (Boyce 2001, 111). The theological conflict resulted in Mani being imprisoned in the Sasanian capital, where he died in 276 (Brosius 2010, 147).

Kirdir believed that persecuting non-Zoroastrians was the right thing to do and proudly proclaimed so in an inscription on the Ka'ba Zardusht. It states, "And Jews and Buddhists and Brahmans and Aramaic and Greek-speaking Christians and Baptisers and Manichaeans were assailed in the land. And images were overthrown, and the dens of demons were [thus] destroyed, and the places and abodes of the yazads [i.e. fire temples] were established." (Boyce 1990, 112).

After Kirdir's death, the persecution of non-Zoroastrians in Persia subsided, as the next few Sasanian kings had to contend with a revitalized Rome led by two of its gre[...] Diocletian (284-305) and Constantine the Great (306-327). As Rome strug[...] economy in the early 3rd century, the Sasanian kings took the opportunity t[...] Roman lands in the east. Mesopotamia had always been a battlefield betwe[...] Persians, but the Sasanians thought the Roman client kingdom of Armenia [...]

Thus, Sasanian King Narseh (ruled 293-302) decided to try his luck agai[...] Diocletian, their emperor, around the year 295, initiating an offensive agai[...] Armenia and heading south to Mesopotamia. The campaign in Mesopotam[...] Narseh, as the Roman commander led his troops in a haphazard attack the [...] down. The Roman Emperor Julian (355-363) wrote of the events in a pane[...] Constantine the Great: "Did not the Caesar incur a disgraceful defeat whe[...] his own account? It was not till the ruler of the whole world turned his att[...] directing thither all the forces of the empire, occupying all the passes with[...] of hoplites, both veteran and new recruits, and employing every sort of m[...]

fear drove them to accept terms of peace." (Julian, *Panegyric in Honour of Constantius*, 18)

Classical Numismatic Group, Inc.'s picture of a coin depicting Emperor Julian

The Romans subsequently reinforced their forces and held the Syrian city of Nisbis, which Narseh promptly besieged. The siege of Nisbis proved to be a turning point in the war. Julian wrote, "But the Persians ever since the last campaign had been watching for just such an opportunity, and had planned to conquer Syria, by a single invasion. So they mustered all forces, every age, sex, and condition, and marched against us, men and mere boys, old men and crowds of women and slaves, who followed not merely to assist in the war, but in vast numbers beyond what was needed…But the magnitude of your preparations made it manifest that their expectations were but vanity. They began the siege and completely surrounded the city with dykes, and then the river Mygdonius flowed in and flooded the ground about the walls, as they say the Nile floods Egypt. The siege-engines were brought up against the ramparts on boats, and their plan was that one force should   sail to attack the walls while the other kept shooting on the city's defenders from the mounds…After spending four months, he retreated with an army that had lost many thousands, and he how had always seemed to be irresistible was glad to keep the peace, and to use as a bulwark for his own safety the fact that you had no time to spare and that our own affairs were in confusion." (Julian, *Panegyric in Honour of Constantius*, 26-28)

Narseh was forced to accept Diocletian's peace in the year 298, which conceded all Sasanian land west of the Tigris River to Rome (Brosius 2010, 148). The Sasanians were beaten in the west, but not quite defeated. Theirs was still a new and vigorous dynasty and empire in 298, while Rome was rotting from internal problems.

G. Dallorto's picture of a bust of Diocletian

When Narseh's grandson, Shapur II (309-379), came to the Sasanian throne, he was only an infant (Boyce 2001, 118). It was during Shapur II's rule when the nobles became much more powerful, to the point that they would eventually choose several of the later Sasanian kings. As the young king learned the arts of diplomacy and war early in his reign, Constantine the Great made overtures of peace toward Persia, and Rome and Persia experienced a period of extended peace until he died in 337, which essentially erased the agreements he had made with the Sasanians (Brosius 2010, 149).

Jean-Christophe Benoist's picture of an ancient bust of Constantine the Great

Perhaps sensing that Constantine's successors were nowhere near his capabilities, or possibly impelled by the nobles, Shapur II renewed hostilities with Rome over Armenia and Mesopotamia. Shapur II returned to Nisibis to finish what his grandfather had started, but he was stymied by the city's defenses on three separate occasions in 338, 346, and 350 (Brosius 2010, 149).

Though the reasons for Shapur II's failures in Mesopotamia are not clear, it was probably due to a combination of the king's lack of leadership abilities and the fact that the Sasanians were being assailed from multiple directions. Various nomadic hordes, some of which were related to the Huns who had attacked Rome, made several incursions into Sasanian territory from the southern, eastern, and northern borders during Shapur II's reign (Brosius 2010, 151).

In terms of Shapur II's lack of leadership skills, what the primary sources do not say is perhaps just as telling as what it recorded. Unlike most of his predecessors, Shapur II left no major monumental inscriptions. It is not known why he did not add his name to the Ka'ab Zardusht, but it may have to do with his preoccupation with Mesopotamia and Armenia. In his quest to win those lands, Shapur II simply neglected his domestic duties, but at the same time, his lack of monumental inscriptions seemingly set a sort of precedent because most of the latter Sasanian kings followed suit by not leaving inscriptions either (Boyce 2001, 118).

Although the king left no Persian-language inscriptions detailing his domestic policies, a number of non-Sasanian sources have survived that paint the picture of an anti-Christian zealot whose actions would have made Kirdir blush. Constantine the Great is remembered for many things, but perhaps none more than his decision to end the persecution of the Christians. Although the emperor was only baptized on his deathbed, his efforts to legalize Christianity across the Roman Empire effectively made Rome a Christian kingdom. Shapur II began the persecution of Christians in 322 (Boyce 2001, 119), but he accelerated the process after Constantine died and war resumed with Rome. To Shapur II and an increasing number of Sasanians, Christianity became synonymous with Rome. All Christian sects, even ones birthed far from Europe, were seen by the Sasanians as anathema to their civilization, with its followers viewed as a potential fifth column.

The anti-Christian persecution continued for the remainder of Shapur II's rule, only subsiding in the chaos that followed. After Shapur II, three kings ruled for a total of 20 years. The nobility exercised immense power during this period, deposing and even assassinating kings who did not do as they were told (Brosius 2010, 151).

Sassanian Religion

A clay head depicting a Zoroastrian priest

More important than the numerous wars fought by the Sasanians against Rome for control over Mesopotamia was the religion they followed and promoted. As noted above, the Sasanians were ardent followers of the Zoroastrian religion, which, like the Abrahamic religions, is a revealed faith with a prophet and holy books but not necessarily a universal religion. It is believed that a form of Zoroastrianism was practiced as far back as the Achaemenid Dynasty and refined, to a certain extent, under the Parthians, but it was under the Sasanians that the religion became fully articulated in writing. Nearly all of the Sasanian kings who left significant historical records behind professed to be pious followers of the faith.

The Sasanian kings did whatever they could to promote Zoroastrianism, to the point of making it a state religion, so it is necessary to understand the historical and theological background of Zoroastrianism. Zoroastrianism was established in Persia through the preaching of the prophet known as Zoroaster or Zarathustra. Unfortunately, there is no consensus among historians concerning when Zarathustra lived and disseminated his message, with some believing him to have lived as early as 2000 BCE, while others have argued he did not live until the Achaemenid period. The latter argument is disregarded by most scholars since the Achaemenids made numerous mentions of Ahura Mazda in their monumental texts, which means they were already practicing Zoroastrians, or at least, practicing proto-Zoroastrians, by the 6th century BCE. Based on the available evidence, it seems logical to believe that Zarathustra lived sometime between 1500 BCE and the early 6th century BCE (Malandra 1983, 16), which would have made him a contemporary of Aryan-Vedic India society and a potential contemporary of the early Achaemenid kings.

Whenever Zarathustra walked along the hills of Persia, it cannot be denied that his new religion had an immense impact on the people. The new religion was a combination of rituals not so different than those practiced by Aryans in northern India and a new set of morality codes that had been designed to uplift the Persian people. Zoroastrianism is often referred to as a monotheistic religion and possibly an influence on early Christianity, but such claims are a bit simplistic and often misleading. The message Zarathustra preached can best be described as dualism; he taught that for all of the evil in the world, there was a corresponding good, and the two were constantly at war. Zoroastrianism held there were, in fact, many gods and demigods, but Ahura Mazda—also referred to as Ohrmazd—was the supreme creator and solar god who was almost exclusively worshipped. At the opposite spectrum was Angramainyu, or Arhriman, who was similar to the Christian devil in many ways. Along with the two primary gods were countless other gods or demigods, divided into camps of good and evil. The yazads were similar to angels, and some, such as Mithra, were revered to the point of worship, while the devs were demons that worked in concert with Angramainyu (Malandra 1983, 19).

The Zoroastrian religious book, the *Avesta,* contains a passage where Ahura Mazda explains this dualism to Zarathustra:

> "Ahura-Mazda spake to the holy Zarathustra.
>
> I created, O holy Zarathustra, a place, a Creation of delight, [but] nowhere was created a possibility [of approach].
>
> For had I not, O holy Zarathustra, created a place, a creation of delight, where nowhere was created a possibility.

The whole corporeal world would have gone after Airyana-vashja [A place, a Creation of delight, not so delightful as the first (have I created); the second, an opposition of the same—one destroying men (Has Angra-mainyu created)]." (Bleeck 2005, I, 3)

A relief depicting Ahura Mazda giving the ring of kingship to Shapur II while Mithra stands behind the emperor

Although this theology had been in existence long before the Sasanians came to power, it was during their rule that the *Avesta* was first put into writing. Like the Bible, the *Avesta* is comprised of several different books that had been recited orally for generations before being put into writing at different times. Specifically, the *Avesta* is comprised of 21 "divisions" known as *nasks* (Malandra 1983, 26), which are further divided thematically. The sections known as the "Gathas" are Zoroastrian songs. The "Yashts" are also songs, but they are dedicated to specific Zoroastrian gods. The "Vendidad" is a collection of verses that concern laws, which is where many of the Zoroastrian ideas about fire and purity are articulated, as well as pseudo-history and myths, many of them cosmological in nature (Malandra 1983, 27).

The complete *Avesta* is written in a form of the Persian language generally referred to by modern scholars as "Avestan," but there were other Zoroastrian religious texts written in Middle Persian. The Middle Persian texts, known as the "Zand" or "Zend," were essentially translations of the *Avesta,* so they are often referred to as the "Zend-Avesta," but they are not considered as authoritative as the true *Avesta* (Boyce 2001, 113).

Since the *Avesta* originated as a series of oral traditions, it is difficult to pinpoint when it was first composed. Grammatical studies have suggested that the earliest portions of the *Avesta*, known as the "Old *Avesta*," were first uttered around 1200 BCE (which would seem to confirm that date for Zarathustra's life), while it is believed that "Younger *Avesta*" was first comprised around 800 BCE (Boyce 1990, xiii).

As mentioned above, it was during the Sasanian period when the disparate texts were finally compiled into writing to form the definitive *Avesta*. It is believed that the early Sasanian kings had chroniclers put all of the known oral texts into writing, combined with the few that had been written to complete the book (Malandra 1983, 30). A high-priest and Ardashir I's advisor, Tansar, is believed to have authorized which texts were admitted to the final version and which ones were omitted (Boyce 2001, 103).

The final version of the *Avesta* was unlike most other previous religious texts of the ancient Near East. Near Eastern religious texts prior to the Sasanians focused either on ritual or morality, but the *Avesta* wove the two elements together in a seamless way. Most of the religions of the ancient Near East before Christianity and Manicheism were highly ritualistic, often commenting very little on issues of morality in their texts. Although much of the *Avesta* is concerned with ritualistic aspects surrounding purity, there are numerous references in the Vendidad concerning how a follower should lead a moral life. One passage states:

> "Creator! With how much does the contract when broken affect which is committed by the joining hands?
>
> Then answered Ahura-Mazda: With six hundred similar punishments which it brings upon the nearest relations…
>
> Creator! If a man strikes a hard sore on a man,
>
> What is the punishment for it?
>
> Then answered Ahura-Mazda: Strike thirty strokes with the horse-goad, thirty with the Craosho-charna." (Bleeck 2005, I, 33-35).

The passage highlights that in Zoroastrianism, like most religions, violence against others was condemned, but the passage also highlights the importance of contracts, known as *mithras*. Contracts were very important in Zoroastrianism, so much that there was a god of contracts, Mithra, who even became popular among Roman soldiers.

The importance of contracts is a reflection of the Sasanian/Zoroastrian beliefs in dualism and the eternal struggle of the truth or *asha* against the lie or *drugh* (Malandra 1983, 47). Essentially, the morality of Zoroastrianism was primarily concerned with observing the purity laws and fighting the evil devs (Boyce 1990, 2), thereby keeping proper balance in the universe. One of the Yashts from the "younger" *Avesta* summarizes how the lie can affect purity in the world:

> "How does one separate one's self from the path of the pure, how from that of the wicked? Then answered Ahura-Mazda: if he utters my Manthra, keeps in mind reciting, draws a circle uttering, guards his own body.

> I will for thee: every Druga which runs about openly, every one which is concealed, every one which pollutes—for thee every Druga, for the Aryan land will I   smite away, for thee will I bind the Druga with cords [?] I will curse away the Drugas.

> I will say to the pure man, he shall draw three circles, right, round circles shall he draw, round will I say to the pure man, nine circle shall he draw, nine say I to the pure man." (Bleeck 2005, III, 31).

Thus, the one who knows the true path of Ahura Mazda will be protected by the god from the lie through numerous circles, but bringing these circles of power to reality involved more than just a belief - Sasanian Zoroastrianism posited that in order for a moral person to fight the devs, he must perform the proper rituals along in addition to having a pure heart.

Having a good heart and mind was only part of the Sasanians' war against evil. They also believed that to be a good Zoroastrian, one must follow the proper rituals, which could be as simple as a prayer, as Zarathustra was told by Ahura Mazda:

> "Zarathustra asked Ahura-Mazda: Ahura-Mazda, Heavenly, Holiest, Creator of the corporeal world, Pure One!

> How shall I purify the dwelling?

> How shall I purify the fire, how the water, how the earth, how the cattle, how the trees,   how the pure man, how the pure woman, how the stars, how the moon, how the sun, how   the lights without beginning, how all the good things which Ahura-Mazda has created,   which have a pure origin?

> Then answered Ahura-Mazda: Thou shalt pronounce the prayer of purification O Zarathustra.

> Then will these dwellings be pure." (Bleeck 2005, I, 95).

To the Sasanians, the most important religious ritual they performed was the creation and care of sacred fires they believed to be the earthly avatar of Ahura Mazda.

Although it is well-known that the Zoroastrian sacred fires are the earthly representation of Ahura Mazda, it is not known when the first ones were established. John of Nikiu mentioned the Zoroastrian fires in a passage of his history, but again, it is anachronistic and wrong on many points. He wrote, "And as Perseus was surprised at what had befallen, forthwith from that fire he kindled a fire and preserved it. And this fire he took and brought to Persia on his return and placed it in the kingdom of Assyria. And the Persians made it a god and honoured [sic] it and built it a temple and named it 'The immortal fire.' And they say that fire is a son of the Sun enveloped in crystal." (Charles 2007, 23).

John of Nikiu was correct in his statement that the Persians worshipped the sacred fires and associated their god with the sun. Another non-Persian chronicler, the 6th century Byzantine historian Procopius, also noted as much. In a passage where he described the surrender of a city by a Sasanian general named Perozes who served under Sasanian King Kavad I (488-496; 499-531), the general first consulted Zoroastrians priests, known as the magi, in order to comply with Persian theological beliefs. Procopius explained, "Perozes should consent to prostrate himself before him as having proved himself master, and, taking the oaths traditional among the Persians, should give pledges that they would never again take the field against the nation of the Ephthalitae. When Perozes heard this, he held a consultation with the Magi who were present and enquired of them whether he must comply with the terms dictated by the enemy. The Magi replied that, as to the oath, he should settle the matter according to his own pleasure; as for the rest, however, he should circumvent his enemy by craft. And they reminded him that it was the custom among the Persians to prostrate themselves before the rising sun each day; he should therefore, watch the time closely and meet the leader of the Ephthalitae at dawn, and…turning toward the rising sun, make his obeisance." (Procopius, *History of the Wars*, I, iii, 18-21).

Procopius also wrote about how Sasanian King Khosrow I (Chosroes) revered the regnal fire in Persia, and he made a connection between the Sasanians and ancient Romans. "Now it happened that Chosroes had come from Assyria to a place toward the north called Adarbiganon, from which he was planning to make an invasion into the Roman domain through Persarmenia. In that place is the great sanctuary of fire, which the Persians reverence above all other gods. There the fire is guarded unquenched by the Magi, and they perform carefully a great number of sacred rites, and in particular they consult an oracle on those matters which are of the greatest of importance. This is the fire which the Romans worshipped under the name of Hestia in ancient times." (Procopius, *History of the Wars*, II, XXIV, 1-3).

John of Nikiu and Procopius knew about the Sasanian sacred fires because they were so important to the dynasty. With that said, while Procopius understood the significance of the sacred fires more than John, neither historian understood their true theological significance. All

Persian dynasties built special temples for the sacred fires, but the Sasanians appear to have had more of a special reverence for them than their predecessors did. For instance, the fire temples built by the Achaemenids and Parthians often also held cult statues and icons of various gods. Early in the Sasanian Dynasty, the high-priests removed the icons and statues and replaced them with sacred fires (Boyce 2001, 107).

The Sasanians also systematically made the establishment of sacred fires more uniform. Private individuals, no matter how pious, were not allowed to establish fires. Moreover, only one regnal fire was allowed to burn at a time, but several smaller fires were established under official sanction (Boyce 2001, 108), and the role of establishing official fires was under the purview of the Zoroastrian high-priest or herbad. Although few sources remain that detail these responsibilities, one inscription of Kirdir's relates that the program was actually quite extensive and extended beyond the borders of Persia. During Shapur I's western campaigns, the Sasanians observed sacred fires in the Caucasus region, and there were claims that sacred fires burned as far away as Albania in Europe.

Modern scholars believe that many of the sacred fires outside of Persia were initially established by the Achaemenids (Boyce 2001, 110), but regardless, Kirdir made sure the far-flung sacred fires were cared for under his watch. The high-priest wrote, "And I caused many fires and priestly colleges to flourish in Iran, and also in non-Iranian lands. There were fires and priests in the non-Iranian lands which were reached by the army of the King of kings. The provincial capital Antioch and the province of Syria, and the districts dependent on Syria; the provincial capital Tarsus and the province of Cilicia, and the districts dependent on Cilicia; the provincial capital Caesarea Pontus, and the province of Armenia, and Georgia and Albania and Balasagan, up to the 'Gate of the Alans'—these were plundered and burnt and laid waste by Shabur, King of kings, with his armies. There too, at the command of the King of kings, I reduced to order the priests and fires which were in those lands. And I did not allow [harm] be done them, or captives made. And whoever had thus been made captive, him indeed I took and sent back to his own land." (Boyce 1990, 113).

Whether the fires were first established by the Achaemenids or the Sasanians (as Kirdir had claimed) is less important than the fact there were some so far from Persia. The sacred fires clearly were a powerful force to the believers of Zoroastrianism, especially the Sasanians, who tried their best to appear as pious followers of the faith.

As important as the sacred fires were to the Sasanians, their funerary practices played just as a significant role in their religion in many ways. Zoroastrian funerary practices were like none other at the time or since, for that matter. The belief in purity reinforced in so many verses in the *Avesta* greatly influenced how the Sasanians disposed of their dead. According to Zoroastrian religion, corpses were considered to be among the most unclean of all things, so special precautions had to be made when disposing of them (Boyce 2001, 44). Zoroastrianism held that once a person was deceased, the soul needed to leave immediately, and the only way to do that was to expose the corpse to dogs, vultures, and other animals.

The Sasanian era Vendidad is very specific as to how a corpse is polluted and how much time should pass before it should be disposed of:

> "Zarathustra asked Ahura-Mazda: Ahura-Mazda, the Heavenly, the Holy, Creator of the corporeal world. Pure One!
>
> When does the Drukhs Nacus rush to the dead men?
>
> Then answered Ahura-Mazda: immediately after death, O holy Zarathustra! Consciousness departs.
>
> The Drukhs Nacus rushes hither from the region of the North, in the form of a fly, pernicious when she comes bringing immense filth from her anus, as (do) the most hideous of the Khrafetras.
>
> Creator! When these [corspes] have been slain by dogs, wolves, sorcerers, by wounds, by falls, by men, by violence, by anguish, after how long a time does Drukhs Nacus arrive?
>
> Then answered Ahura-Mazda: After the next division of the day." (Bleeck 2005, I, 57).

After the ritual was complete, the deceased's bones were collected and placed in an ossuary. The prohibition on touching dead corpses is clearly stated in the Vendidad. One verse states:

> "No corpse which has been carried away by dogs, birds, wolves, winds, or flies, defiles a man.
>
> Were these corpses which have been carried away by dogs, birds, wolves, winds, or flies, to defile men,
>
> Then would almost all my corporeal world be little allied to purity." (Bleeck 2005, I, 40).

Unfortunately, Sasanian and Avestan texts only reference the ritual from a Zoroastrian perspective, so many details about the process are lacking. Again, to understand the process a bit better, one must turn to non-Sasanian sources, only a few of which mention the practice of exposure. For example, Procopius mentioned an instance, and the 5th century BCE Greek historian Herodotus wrote about the ritual during the Achaemenid period. Herodotus's passage was fairly detailed and informative: "There is another practice, however, concerning the burial of the dead, which is not spoken of openly and is something of a mystery; it is that a male Persian is never buried until the body has been torn by a bird or a dog. I know for certain that the Magi have this custom, for they are quite open about it. The Persians in general, however, cover a body with wax and then bury it. The Magi are a peculiar caste." (Herodotus, *The Histories*, I, 140).

The practice that Herodotus mentions of covering the body with wax was reserved for the Achaemenid kings, who were interred in tombs. In their quest to appear legitimate and connected to the Achaemenids, the Sasanians also embalmed their dead kings in tombs while the rest of their people practiced corpse exposure (Boyce 2001, 120-1).

The passage in which Procopius mentions the ritual of exposure concerned a Sasanian general under Kavad I named Seoses, who had been sentenced to death for straying from Zoroastrianism. "Now the whole Persian council gathered to sit in judgement moved more by envy than by respect for the law. For they were thoroughly hostile to his office, which was unfamiliar to them, and also were embittered by the natural temper of the man. For while Seoses was a man quite impossible to bribe, and a most exact respecter of justice, he was afflicted with a degree of arrogance not to be compared with that of any other. This quality, indeed, seems to be inbred in the Persian officials, but in Seoses even they thought that the malady had developed to an altogether extraordinary degree. So his accusers said all those things which have been indicated above, and added to this that the man was by no means willing to live in the established fashion or to uphold the institutions of the Persians. For he both reverenced strange divinities, and lately, when his wife had died, he had buried her, though it was forbidden by the laws of the Persians ever to hide in the earth the bodies of the dead. The judges therefore condemned the man to death." (Procopius, *History of the Wars*, I, xi, 32-36).

Other Aspects of Sasanian Culture

Zoroastrianism clearly played a major role in the culture of Sasanian Persia, if not the most important role, as it influenced everything from their laws to their daily life activities. With that said, Zoroastrianism was not the only aspect of Sasanian culture.

One thing nearly all pre-modern cultures have in common is the importance of the priest class in the collection and dissemination of knowledge. Priests served as the leaders of their peoples' faiths, but they were also often scientists, philosophers, and doctors, and the libraries serving as receptacles of religious texts doubled as storage units of historical and scientific knowledge. In this respect, the Zoroastrian priests of Sasanian Persia were no different than those of the other cultures who came before them.

Since Persia is located at the crossroads where East meets West, and it was along the Silk Road, Zoroastrian priests in the Sasanian era were able to collect ideas from as far west as Greece and Rome and as far east as India (Boyce 2001, 113). A late Sasanian text claims that the collection of non-religious academic texts began during the reign of Shapur I. "Shabur, King of kings, son of Ardashir, further collected the non-religious writings on medicine, astronomy, movement, time, space, substance, accident, becoming, decay, transformation, logic and other crafts and skills which were dispersed throughout India, Byzantium and other lands, and collated them with the Avesta, and commanded that a copy should be made of all those writings which were flawless, to be deposited in the Royal Treasury." (Boyce 1990, 114).

The above text and most others that relate to Sasanian academic pursuits come from the reign of Khosrow I (501-579), who took a special interest in learning. Khosrow I also took advantage of changes in the Roman Empire. When the last Roman emperor in the West was deposed in 476, Europe was thrust into a period of chaos generally referred to as the Dark Ages. Germanic warlords fought for control of the West, while power in the East was transferred to Constantinople and the Byzantine Empire, whose kings continued to refer to themselves as Roman emperors.

When Justinian the Great (527-565) came to the throne, he wielded power in a way that had not been seen in Rome for hundreds of years. As part of his efforts to make Constantinople the "second Rome," he closed down the philosophical school in Athens with the hope that the great thinkers would come to Constantinople. Some of those scholars did, in fact, move to Constantinople, but others were enticed by Khosrow I to come to Persia and add to the growing corpus of knowledge he had acquired (Brosius 2010, 172).

Petar Milosevic's picture of a contemporary mosaic depicting Justinian the Great

Just as the Sasanian kings brought in philosophers, scientists, and intellectuals from a number of different places throughout the ancient world, their subjects were just as diverse. The Sasanians themselves were Persians, but their kingdom extended far beyond Persia and included Arabs, Armenians, Turks, and a number of other Asiatic peoples. In this sense, the Sasanians carried on another tradition established by the Achaemenids by ruling over a vast territory with a diverse number of subject peoples. The Sasanians' recognition of the diversity of their empire is reflected in the multilingual inscriptions they left at the Ka'aba Zardusht and the tolerance they generally showed for other religions, with a few exceptions mentioned earlier. With that said, the Parthian language was gradually limited until during the middle of the 4th century, when its written use was probably outlawed (Boyce 2001, 116). It is unknown why the Sasanians outlawed the written use of their predecessors' language, but it might have been due to the fact that the *Avesta* had finally been compiled during the Sasanian Dynasty, which meant their language would be the cultural winner.

Although not as important as their religion, trade played an important role in Sasanian culture. The Sasanians inherited the Silk Road from the Parthians and were therefore able to continue to profit from it, outside of a few minor disturbances by nomadic bands from the north and east. But unlike the Parthians, the Sasanians conducted trade in other methods besides overland routes. Archaeological and textual evidence shows that the Sasanians developed long-range trade routes stretching from India to Sasanian possessions in the Arabian Peninsula, particularly in the country now known as Yemen (Brosius 2010, 182). Sasanian trade routes impressed the Byzantine Greeks, as noted by Procopius, who wrote, "For it was impossible to buy silk from the Indians, for the Persian merchants always locate themselves at the very harbours [sic] where the Indian ships first put in, [since they inhabit the adjoining country], and are accustomed to buy the whole cargoes; and it seemed to the Homeritae a difficult thing to cross a country which was a desert and which extended so far that a long time was required for the journey across it, and then to go against a people much more warlike than themselves. Later on Abramus too, when at length he had established his power most securely, promised the Emperor Justinian many times to invade the land of Persia, but only once began the journey and then straightaway turned back." (Procopius, *History of the Wars*, I, XX).

As the passage relates, the Sasanians faced Justinian in during the 6th century, and he proved to be the most formidable foe the Sasanians had confronted since Diocletian.

Later Sasanian History

The conflict between the Sasanians and Romans ebbed after the middle of the 4th century for a number of reasons. The Sasanians had more pressing problems with the emergence of Asiatic tribes to their north and east, while the Romans were in the midst of fighting off primarily Germanic tribes on their northern border. The Romans ultimately lost the fight, and the base of power gradually moved to Constantinople after Constantine's reign.

During the reign of Kavad I, in about 506, the Sasanians entered into another short-term peace treaty with the Byzantine Empire. Apparently, this treaty was not the result of the Sasanians being defeated by the Byzantines in any battle, but more of a move to protect their flank. Nomadic Asiatic tribes, which Procopius referred to generally as "Huns," continued to create problems for the Sasanians, so Kavad I called for the treaty after giving back the city of Amida to the Byzantines. Procopius explained, "Because they had shewn themselves wanting in obedience to them, when it was possible to capture as prisoners of war such a multitude of Persians and the son of Glones and the city itself, while they had in consequence attached to themselves signal disgrace by carrying Roman money to the enemy, and had taken Amida from the Persians by purchasing it with silver. After this the Persians, since their war with the Huns kept dragging on, entered into a treaty with the Romans, which was arranged by them for seven years, and was made by the Roman Celer and the Persian Aspebedes; both armies then retired homeward and remained at peace." (Procopius, *History of the Wars*, I, ix, 23-24).

Once the Sasanians had vanquished their nomadic enemies and Constantinople had established itself as the new power in the Mediterranean, their peace treaty would not last. Eventually, the two powers would engage in a series of wars that would prove more destructive than the prior ones, even as they did not prove any more decisive.

Justinian the Great's Sasanian counterpart was Khosrow I Anoshirvan (531-579), who proved to be just as ambitious as the Byzantine emperor. After reorganizing the military and establishing internal peace in Persia, Khosrow I turned his attention to reacquiring lost possessions in Mesopotamia and Armenia.

Classical Numismatic Group, Inc.'s picture of a coin depicting Khosrow I

The renewed conflict between Persia and the Byzantines began the same year Khosrow I came to power and continued into the first few years of the reign of his successor, Hormizd IV (579-590) (Frendo 2008, 223). The first major battle took place in 531 along the banks of the Euphrates River, where the Sasanians advanced with their full army into the region but were repulsed by the Byzantine forces. Procopius described the fight: "Finally the Persians made their bivouac on the bank of the Euphrates just opposite the city of Callinicus, From there they were about to march through a country absolutely uninhabited by man, and thus to quit the land of the Romans; for they purposed no longer to proceed as before, keeping to the bank of the river. The Romans had passed the night in the city of Sura, and, removing from there, they came upon the enemy just in the act of preparing for the departure. Now the fest of Easter was near and would take place on the following day…He then formed the phalanx with a single front, disposing his men as follows: on the left wing by the river he stationed all the infantry, while on the right where the ground rose sharply he placed Arethas and all his Saracens; he himself with the cavalry took his position in the centre. Thus the Romans arrayed themselves…Then by mutual agreement all the best of the Persian army advanced to attack the Roman right wing, where Arethas and the Saracens had been stationed. But they broke their formation and moved apart, so that they got the reputation of having betrayed the Romans to the Persians. For without awaiting the oncoming enemy they all straightway beat a hasty retreat. So the Persians in this way broke through the enemy's line and immediately got in the rear of the Roman cavalry…Many a time after giving up, the Persians would advance against them determined to break up and destroy their line, but they always retired again from the assault unsuccessful. For their horses, annoyed by the clashing of the shields, reared up and made confusion for themselves and their riders. Thus both sides continued the struggle until it had become late in the day. And when night had already come on, the Persian withdrew to their camp, and Belisarius accompanied by some few men found a freight-boat and crossed over to the island in the river, while the other Romans reached the same place by swimming. On the following day many freight-boats were brought to the Romans from the city of Callinicus and they were conveyed thither in them, and the Persians, after despoiling the dead, all departed homeward. However they did not find their own dead less numerous than the enemy's." (Procopius, *History of the Wars*, I, xviiii, 13-50).

Khosrow I's defeat in Mesopotamia was only temporary, though, as the Sasanian king proved to be extremely resilient. 9 years after his major defeat in Mesopotamia, Khosrow I led his army back into the Fertile Crescent, but instead of attacking Byzantine positions in Mesopotamia, he went for the Levant. Khosrow I's target was the ancient city of Antioch, which held strategic and symbolic significance as a wealthy city and a center of trade. It was also an early Christian ecclesiastical center, which was not lost on Khosrow I, and it was known in the Byzantine annals as "Chosroes." Procopius wrote, "Not long after this the Persian army also came. There they all pitched their tents and made camp fronting on the River Orontes and not very far from the stream. Chosroes then sent Paulus up beside the fortifications and demanded money from the men of Antioch, saying that for ten centenaria of gold he would depart from there, and it was obvious that he would accept even less than this for his withdrawal…But on the morrow the populace of Antioch [for they are not seriously disposed, but are always engaged in jesting and disorderly performance] heaped insults upon Chosroes from the battlements and taunted him with unseemly laughter…On the following day, accordingly, he led up all the Persians against the wall and commanded a portion of the army to make assaults at different points along the river, and he himself with the most of the men and best troops directed an attack against the height…But the Persians, with no one opposing them, set ladders against the wall and mounted with no difficulty…For the Persians did not spare persons of any age and were slaying all whom they met, old and young alike…Thus the inhabitants of Antioch were visited with every form of misfortune." (Procopius, *History of the Wars*, II, viii).

Once he'd laid waste to Antioch, Khosrow I moved his army south, towards Jerusalem. According to Procopius, Khosrow I's real target was Jerusalem, but since it was so far into Byzantine territory, he had to take other strategic points first. During the 6th century, Jerusalem was safely within Byzantine territory, and Justinian made it his personal duty to protect the city from the infidels, which added another religious dimension to the already religiously charged conflict between the Sasanian Empire and the Byzantine Empire. Procopius noted, "And his purpose was to lead the army straight for Palestine, in order that he might plunder all their treasures and especially those in Jerusalem. For he had it from hearsay that this was an especially goodly land and peopled by wealthy inhabitants. And all the Romans, both officers and soldiers, were far from entertaining any thought of confronting the enemy or of standing in the way of their passage, but manning their strongholds as each one could, they thought it sufficient to preserve them and save themselves." (Procopius, *History of the Wars*, II, xx, 18-19).

Khosrow I was stopped by Justinian's forces before he was able to make it to Jerusalem, so the conflict moved to the kingdom of Lazika in the north, on the southern slope of the Caucasus Mountains, roughly congruent with the modern nation-state of Georgia. The Sasanian forces arrived in the region but were surprised by and routed by the Byzantine forces. According to Procopius, "Now the five thousand, upon coming nearer to the frontier of Lazica, encamped in a body beside the small bands and plundered the neighbouring [sic] country…And the Persians chose out a thousand men of repute among them and sent them forth, that no one might advance against the camp to harm it…The Romans, therefore, and the Lazi fell suddenly upon the thousand men, and not one of them succeeded in escaping, but the most of them were slain, while some also were captured…And the Romans and Lazi captured the camp and all the standards, and they also secured many weapons and a great deal of money as plunder, besides great numbers of horses and mules." (Procopius, *History of the Wars*, II, xxx).

Although Khosrow I was a very active military king, his campaigns were mostly ineffective, and the Sasanians did not gain or lose any significant territory during his reign. However, when Khorsow I was not fighting, he initiated a number of programs that helped make the kingdom stronger. Besides warfare, trade was a very important aspect of Khosrow I's rule. The king continued to profit from the Silk Road running through Sasanian territory, and he was the one who conquered Yemen and established a sea route from that land to India (Brosius 2010, 154-5). Khosrow I was also instrumental in remodeling the Sasanian army. The army was still largely dependent on its cavalry troops, but the king decided to decentralize the army by dividing it into quarters, with a commander for each cardinal direction of the empire (Brosius 2010, 155). The division of the Sasanian army into quarters was probably based on tradition as much as practicality; following in the footsteps of their Near Eastern predecessors, the Sasanian kings referred to themselves as the rulers of the four corners of the universe.

Khosrow I was truly a warrior king, but the primary sources also indicate he was as pious as any other Sasanian king. It was during Khorsow I's reign that the definitive canon of the *Avesta* had been compiled. It was also during his rule that the Avestan alphabet was created, and though it was only a liturgical language, it made it easier to modify and control from the top of the power hierarchy. During Khorsow I's reign, a standardized 46 letter Avestan alphabet was created for use by the priests (Boyce 2001, 134).

An Avestan text attributed to Khosrow I, which only survived as a later Arabic version, relates how the king personally viewed the Zoroastrian concepts of truth and purity. It states, "I give thanks unto God…for all the favours [sic] which he has shown me…Many benefits require in return a deep sense of obligation…And since I hold that gratitude should express itself in both word and deed, I have sought the course of action most pleasing to God, and have found that it consists in that whereby sky and earth continue to exist, the mountains remain immovable, the rivers flow, and the earth is kept pure: that is to say, in equity and justice." (Boyce 1990, 115).

Khosrow I's piousness was duplicated by the last few Sasanian kings, although none were as important as him. After his reign, the Sasanians once more fell into violence at the hands of the nobles. Kings were chosen by the nobles and murdered if they did not do as the nobles pleased. In fact, this process began before Khosrow I's reign ended, and it appears likely there was an attempt made on his life. Procopius wrote a detailed passage about the assassination attempt and the reasons behind it: "Straightway it came about that plots were formed against both rulers by their subjects; and I shall now explain how this happened. Chosroes, the son of Cabades, was a man of an unruly turn of mind and strangely fond of innovations. For this reason he himself was always full of excitement and alarms, and he was an unfailing cause of similar feelings in others. All, therefore, who were men of action among the Persians, in vexation at his administration, were purposing to establish over themselves another king form the house of Cabades. And since they longed earnestly for the rule of Zames, which was made impossible by the law by reason of the disfigurement of his eye, as has been stated, they found upon consideration that the best course for them was to establish in power his child Cabades, who bored the same name as his grandfather, while Zames, as guardian of the child, should administer the affairs of the Persians as he wished…But the plan was discovered and came to the knowledge of the king, and thus their proceedings were stopped. For Chosroes slew Zames himself and all his own brothers and those of Zames together with all their male offspring, and also all the Persian notable who had either begun or taken part in any way in the plot against him. Among these was Aspebedes, the brother of Chosroes' mother." (Procopius, *History of the Wars*, I, xxii, 1-6).

Khosrow I would have the last laugh, as he outlived all of his enemies and was able to pass the kingship on to his son, Hormizd IV (579-590). However, Hormizd IV did not rule as long as his father and left little impact on the history of the Sasanian Empire. Most of his activities were focused on continuing domestic reforms and further establishing the theology of Zoroastrianism. It was during Hormizd IV's rule that religious communal violence, especially toward Christians, appears to have reached a crescendo. The violence was apparently so bad that it threatened the stability of the dynasty itself, so much so that Hormizd IV felt compelled to do something about it. In a letter to the Zoroastrian priesthood, also known as "magi," Hormizd IV exhorted the religious leaders to put a lid on communal violence. Perhaps the king saw that centuries of war with Rome and the Byzantines did little for his kingdom. The king also indicated that by refraining from violence against Christians. they could possibly win more converts. His letter states, "Even as our royal throne cannot stand upon its two front legs without the back ones, so also our government cannot stand and be secure if we incense the Christians and the adherents of other religions, who are not of our faith. Cease, therefore, to harass the Christians, but exert yourselves diligently in doing good works, so that the Christians and the adherents of other religions, seeing that, may praise you for it, and feel themselves drawn to our religion." (Boyce 1990, 115).

It is interesting that Hormizd IV makes a reference to potential proselytization, even though Zoroastrianism was never a faith of missionaries. It seems that the king's request was more practical than anything; perhaps he knew that another round of war with the Byzantine Empire might deplete the royal coffers, or maybe he believed that Christianity would soon become the ascendant religion in the region.

Little did Hormizd IV know that it would not be the Christians who would threaten to annihilate his religion. Instead, a little-known sect that was forming hundreds of miles away in the deserts of Arabia.

The rise of Islam happened to coincide with the rule of the last great Sasanian king, Khosrow II (590-628). As a conqueror, Khosrow II did far more than Khosrow I and was more like Shapur I. Khosrow II sacked Jerusalem in 614 and conquered Egypt in 619, accomplishing what Khosrow I had been unable to do, but before Khosrow was able to carry out his successful conquests, he needed to deal with problems at home (Frendo 2008, 226). During the first year of Khosrow II's rule, another claimant, named Bahram VI Chubin, claimed the Sasanian throne. Although Bahram VI had the support of the king-making Sasanian nobles, Khosrow II proved to be more politically astute by currying favor with the Byzantine Emperor Maurice (582-602). Khosrow II defeated Bahram VI in battle (Brosius 2010, 157) and went on to enjoy nearly 10 years of peace with the Byzantine Empire.

It was not until Maurice had been assassinated that Khosrow II conducted his campaign against Byzantine possessions in the Near East. The end result of the Byzantine-Sasanian wars during Khosrow II's rule was much like what had taken place during the previous kings' reigns. But while this stalemate might not have changed the geopolitical situation in the past, an Islamic empire was on the move and looking for new land and converts.

The last Sasanian king was Yazdgird III (633-651), who was the unfortunate recipient of his predecessors' myopia in regards to Islam. As much as Khosrow II may be seen as the last great Sasanian king and conqueror, he did nothing to prepare his kingdom for the Arab onslaught. The Arab Muslim army took Babylon in 636, which set the stage for the epic battle between the Persians and Arabs at al-Qadisiya that same year. The battle was an overwhelming victory for the Arabs, who continued on to Persia and defeated the Sasanians once more at Nihavand in 642 (Brosius 2010, 159).

At that point, the Sasanians were leaderless, but they continued to resist the Arabs for a time. A 9th century Arabic manuscript detailed some of the problems the Arabs faced when they attempted to occupy Sasanian Persia: "Hudhaifah advanced as far as Ardabil, the capital of Adharbaijan, in which city was the marzban [i.e., Persian governor] thereof, and where the payment of its tax was made. The marzban had gathered there the militia…These resisted the Moslems [sic] fiercely for some days. Then the marzban made terms with Hudhaifah for all the people of Aharbaijan for 800,000 dirhams, the conditions being that he should not kill or enslave any of them, nor raze any fire temples…nor hinder the people of ash-Shiz in their peculiar custom of dancing on their festal days nor in observing their usual observances…When he arrived at Ardabil he found its people in possession of a treaty, but some of them had broken it, so he raided them, defeating and plundering them…The Ali ibn-abu-Talib appointed al-Ash'ath governor Adharbaijan…He established in Ardabil a number of Arabs who were   enrolled in the pension lists and the register, and made it a capital city, and built its mosque." (Boyce 1990, 115-6).

Once in total control of Persia, the Arabs were able to wipe the Sasanian Dynasty out and establish *sharia* law across the land. With that, Zoroastrianism suffered a quick demise in its homeland.

The Rashidun Caliphate

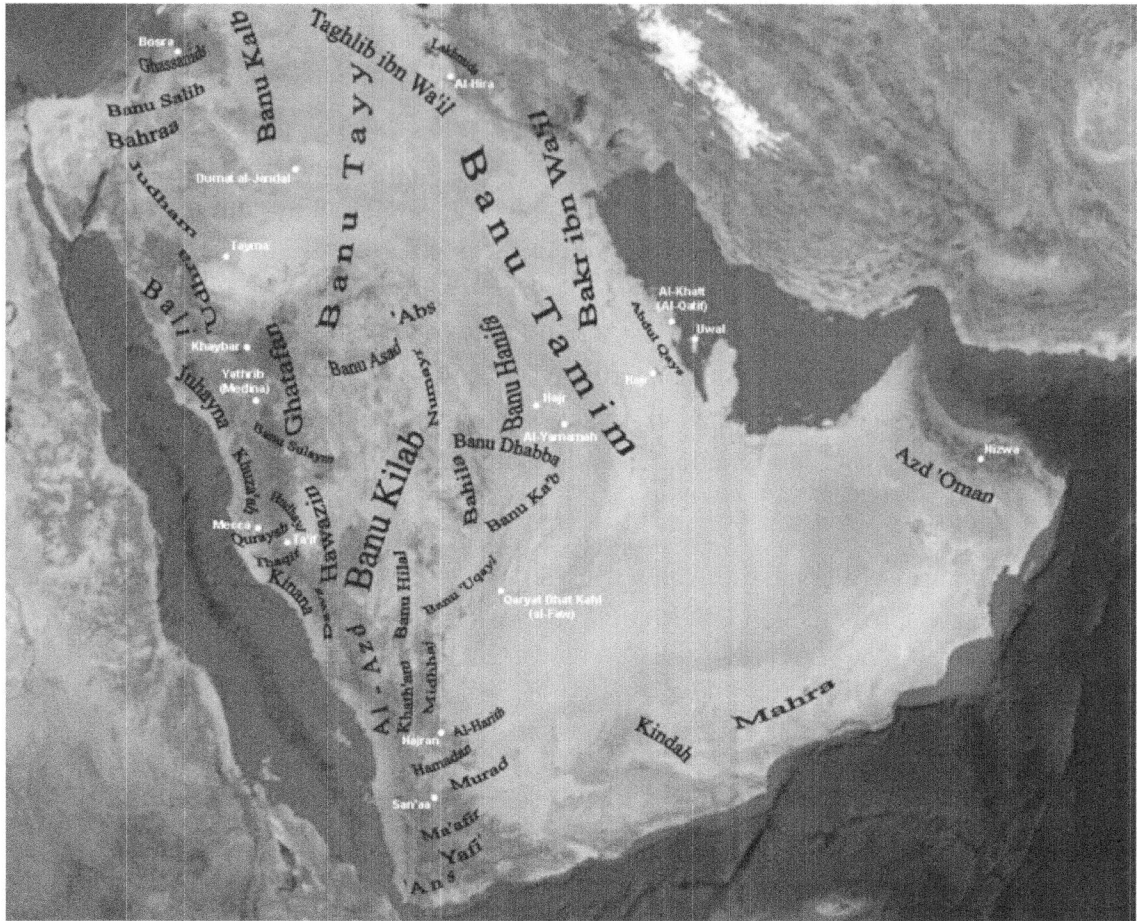

The Arabian Peninsula and the names of various tribes during Muhammad's life

When Muhammad died, the Ummah realized he could not be truly replaced and that there would never again be a man like him. That said, the Ummah hoped to find a leader that was still significantly superior to the ordinary man, and the most obvious candidates for superior people were the Prophet's family. Was there some way that the special qualities of Muhammad could be found amongst the members of his close family? Was there some special teaching or insight that Muhammad passed on to his family? Were Muhammad's teachings and the blessings of God only to be found within the Qur'an and the emulation of the life of the Prophet and therefore available equally to all Muslims? If there was something special about Muhammad, then special consideration should be given to the Prophet's family in the political life of the new Islamic state. However, if the leaders of the Ummah should be chosen based on their knowledge of the Qur'an, their piety, and their ability to administer and defend the community, then there was no need to turn just to Muhammad's family for leadership.

Ultimately, those who believed in a special place for the role of the Prophet's family became the Shias, while those who believed that all Muslims were equally capable in the eyes of God became the Sunnis. Even today, however, many rulers claim lineage to the Prophet as a form of legitimacy, including in Sunni states such as the modern Hashemite dynasty in Jordan.[130]

Within the Shia position - that there is something unique about the Prophet's line that gives them a special ability to rule - there is an important division that was not immediately apparent after the Prophet's death: is this uniqueness something that is born within them, or is it a special knowledge which comes from either a secret teaching or from insights gained from prolonged intimacy with Muhammad? This is important because if it is knowledge, then it can be codified and taught to those who are not his descendants, and it can also be lost by those who are.

While Muslims have continued to debate this issue, the Prophet and the Qur'an are ambivalent on it. On the one hand, there is a strong assertion of the equality of all Muslims, including the following passages:

> "O Mankind, We created you from a single (pair) of a male and a female and made you into nations and tribes, that you may know each other. Verily the most honored of you in the sight of God is he who is the most righteous of you (Quran 49:13)."

> "O people, Remember that your Lord is One. An Arab has no superiority over a non-Arab nor a non-Arab has any superiority over an Arab; also a black has no superiority over white, nor a white has any superiority over black, except by piety and good action (Taqwa). Indeed the best among you is the one with the best character (Taqwa). Listen to me. Did I convey this to you properly? People responded, Yes. O messenger of God, The Prophet then said, then each one of you who is there must convey this to everyone not present. (Excerpt from the Prophet's Last Sermon as in Baihiqi)"

> "The Prophet said: Let people stop boasting about their ancestors. One is only a pious believer or a miserable sinner. All men are sons of Adam, and Adam came from dust (Abu Dawud, Tirmidhi)."

On the other hand, these eminent sources also had something to say in support of the other side. There are a number of Hadith (sayings or teachings of the Prophet) that the Shia hold up to support their claims about Ali's special status as the heir-apparent of Muhammad. The first is the Hadith of the Pond of Kumm, when the Prophet gave a sermon in which he discussed how he would meet them in heaven: "I will ask you about the two weighty things that I have left for you when you come to me to see how you dealt with them. The greater weighty thing is Allah's book—the Holy Qur'an. One end is in Allah's hand and the other is in your hands. Keep it and you will not deviate. That other weighty thing is my family and my descendants."[131]

---

130   For the ancestry of the Jordanian Royal House, visit their official homepage: http://www.kinghussein.gov.jo/rfamily_hashemites.html

Another important argument is found in the Hadith of the Cloak, a story in which the Prophet wrapped Ali, Fatima and their two sons Husayn and Hasan in his cloak and declared that they were sinless and composed his family (and by extension were his inheritors). While there are a number of others, one that will come up later is the Hadith of the Twelve Successors, in which the Prophet taught that there would only be 12 legitimate Caliphs after him and a plethora of false caliphs, and that after the last of his successors the earth will end[132].

These religious interpretations remain an important part of the Sunni-Shia debate today, but in the early political context of the upheaval after the Prophet's death, these debates were not philosophical but were instead connected to different candidates for the mantle of Muhammad's successor. In fact, it is altogether possible that the candidates existed and were well-known before these justifications were developed to support them. Upon Muhammad's death, the debate was between two individuals: Abdullah ibn Abi Qhuhafah (commonly known as "Abu Bakr") and `Alī ibn Abī Ṭālib ("Ali").

---

131 The Sunnah of the Prophet can be found in English at: http://sunnah.com/
132 *Muhammad: A Prophet for Our Time* by Karen Armstrong (2007)

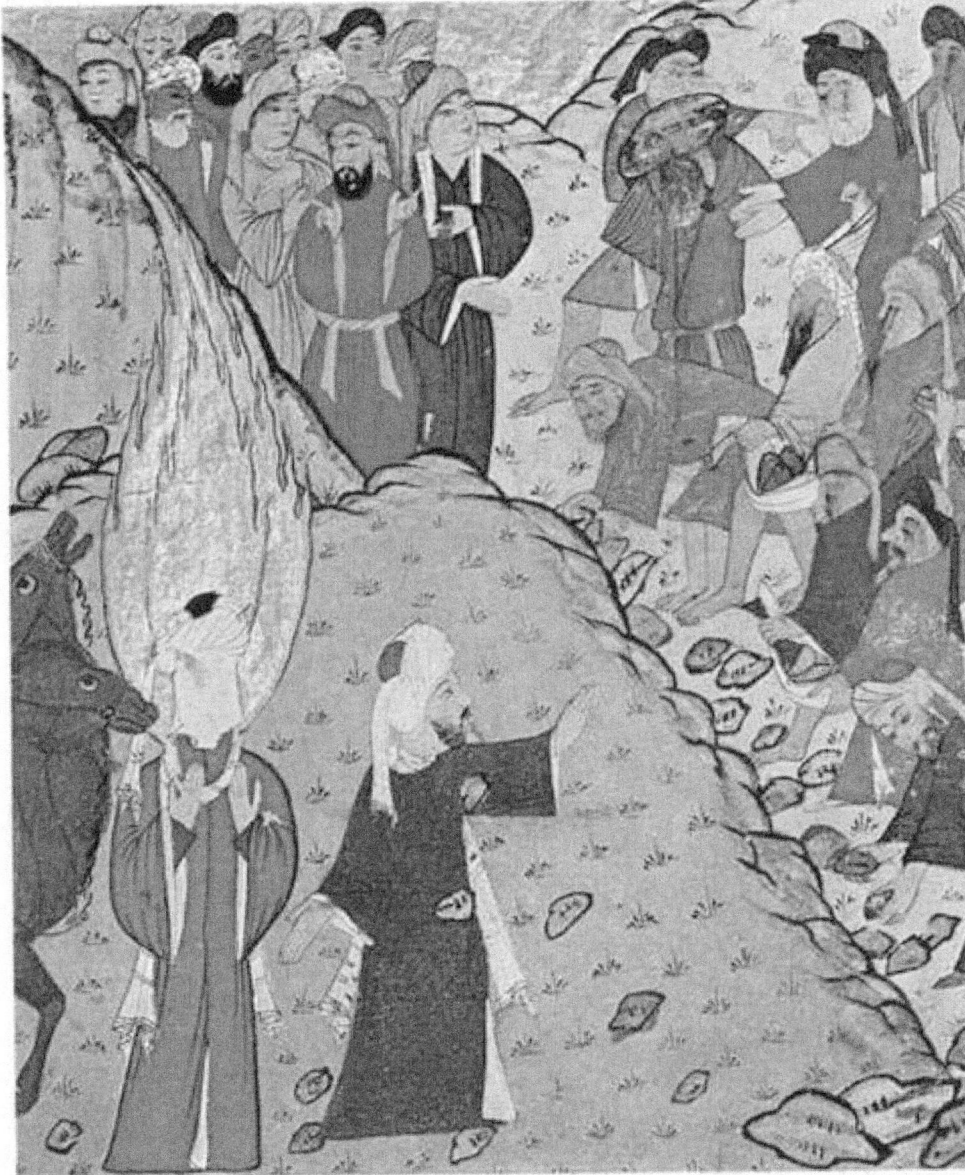

A 16th century depiction of Abu Bakr in Mecca

Both men were already eminent within the Ummah and featured prominently in the histories of the life of the Prophet. Abu Bakr was the father-in-law of the Prophet and - like Muhammad - was a merchant based in the city of Mecca before Muhammad declared his Prophethood. He was outside Mecca traveling with a caravan as Muhammad first announced his new faith, and when he returned to the city, Abu Bakr was the first convert to Islam from outside Muhammad's own family. This was a major step because Muhammad called upon Muslims to abandon narrow clan ties for connection to the larger Ummah, and Abu Bakr served as one of the Prophet's closest advisors. While his daughter Aisha was married to Muhammad, since the Arabs were (and remain) patrilineal, this meant that Aisha entered Muhammad's family (male line), but it also meant Muhammad did not enter Abu Bakr's family. As a result, Abu Bakr is not considered to be a kinsman of the Prophet.

Ali, on the other hand, was family. The cousin of the Prophet on the male line, he was also married to the Prophet's most beloved daughter, Fatima. According to Islamic histories, Ali was born in the Kaaba, the sacred shrine at the heart of the holy city of Mecca, and he was the first man to convert to Islam upon hearing Muhammad's message. Like Abu Bakr, Ali had served as the Prophet's lieutenant, especially in military matters. Ali had regularly led the Muslim troops into battle.

A 16ᵗʰ century depiction of Ali leading soldiers in battle

When the Prophet died in 632, choosing Muhammad's successor was a decision ultimately made by the Sahabah, a term used for the body of individuals who had known the Prophet during his life (in English, it is often called the "Companions of the Prophet"). It is difficult from such a distance to say exactly why the Sahabah preferred Abu Bakr over Ali, but there are several plausible arguments, and it's safe to assume that even Abu Bakr's supporters would have had different reasons for their allegiance to him. One is that Abu Bakr was considerably older than Ali, and in the strictly hierarchical society of Medieval Arabia, age and experience were vitally important. There is an old Arab saying that men are not wise until the age of 40,[133] and Ali was only 32 or 25 (depending on which source on his birth one reads).[134]

Another possible reason for excluding Ali from the center of power may have been based on the fact he was a member of the Prophet's family. Early Islam was a religion that placed a great emphasis on egalitarianism, especially since the Prophet and the Qur'an called upon Muslims to reject their old ties of clan, tribe, and ethnicity. It may have been that the Sahabah wanted precisely to avoid creating a hereditary dynasty within the Prophet's family as a supreme rejection of the old clannishness[135].

Whatever the reasons, Abu Bakr was chosen to become "caliph," a shortened form of the title "Khalifat Rasul Allah" ("Successors to the Messenger of God"). The Caliph inherited all of the Prophet's political authority and much of spiritual power as well.

Since the election of Abu Baker in 623, there have been hundreds of individuals from close to a dozen dynasties that have claimed the Caliphate, but only the first four are widely considered by Sunnis to have inherited the true spiritual mantle of the Prophet. These four men, all of whom were Sahabah (Companions of the Prophet in his life), are called the "Rashidun" (or "Rightly Guided" Caliphs), and their government is referred to as the Rashidun or Patriarchal Caliphate (632-661).

After the Prophet's death in 632, the Caliphate controlled the Arabian Peninsula, which today consists of Saudi Arabia, Yemen, Oman, the United Arab Emirates, and Qatar, but it expanded during the Rashidun period with the conquests of today's Iraq, Syria, Israel, the Palestinian territories, Jordan, Persia, Armenia, Egypt, Cyprus, Lebanon, Azerbaijan, Kuwait, and Bahrain, as well as portions of Afghanistan, Turkmenistan, Turkey, and Libya.

However, it was also during this period that the division between Sunnis and Shias was taking shape. Initially, it consisted of a political division, with the proto-Shia as something akin to a loyal opposition; they supported the overall system of the Caliphate, obeyed the Caliph's rulings and were pious Muslims, but they believed that Ali was the better candidate and may have had strong opinions about the special place of the family of the Prophet in public affairs.

---

133   This is a widespread belief in Arab lands, and was confirmed by the fact that Muhammad's Prophethood did not begin until his fortieth year.

134   "The Caliphate" in *Islam: Faith, Culture, History* (2002). By Paul Lunde. DK Publishing.

135   *No God But God: The Origins, Evolution and Future of Islam* by Resa Aslan (2011). Random House

One point of conflict during Abu Bakr's rule was over the oasis of Fadak. Located close to Mecca, it was one of the Muslim army's earliest conquests and had been under the direct control of Muhammad during his lifetime. At his death, his daughter Fatima (Ali's wife) claimed that it had been owned by Muhammad due to the right of conquest and that he had willed it to her. Abu Bakr, on the other hand, denied this claim and stated that a Prophet of God could not own property. Thus, Abu Bakr asserted that after the Prophet's death, the lands under his control reverted back to public ownership and were to be managed by the Caliph. While Fatima assented to Abu Bakr's ruling, she was furious over it, and it created a rift between her family and the Caliph. After this event, Ali and Fatima retreated from the public eye to become farmers, but before she died a few months later, Fatima gave a rousing speech in the Mosque of the Prophet before the Caliph and the assembled Sahabah in which she denounced their government as turning its back upon true Islam and praising her husband as an alternative. This event, known as the "Fadakyiah Sermon," can be considered the intellectual foundation of Shia Islam, and it continues to resonate with Shias today.[136]

---

136   For a Shia interpretation of these events, read: http://en.shafaqna.com/etrat/item/26306-fadak-an-outcry-beyond-a-bequest.html

A medieval depiction of Muhammad giving Fatima in marriage to Ali

Fadak continued to emerge as a point of contention throughout the Rashidun Caliphate and became a symbol of the shoddy treatment that Shias believe the family of Ali and Fatima - the true heirs of the Prophet - received at the hands of jealous, power-hungry proto-Sunni Caliphs. It still continues to be a rallying cry for those who seek to restore the birthright of Ali's line, such as the radical Shia Fadak satellite television station, which broadcasts anti-Sunni rhetoric from London.

Abu Bakr only ruled for two years, and after his death, he was replaced by his handpicked successor, the famously stern Umar (also written Omar). Umar addressed Muslims in the wake of Abu Bakr's death and said, "O ye faithful! Abu Bakr is no more amongst us. He has the satisfaction that he has successfully piloted the ship of the Muslim state to safety after negotiating the stormy sea. He successfully waged the apostasy wars, and thanks to him, Islam is now supreme in Arabia. After Abu Bakr, the mantle of the Caliphate has fallen on my shoulders. I swear it before God that I never coveted this office. I wished that it would have devolved on some other person more worthy than me. But now that in national interest, the responsibility for leading the Muslims has come to vest in me, I assure you that I will not run away from my post, and will make an earnest effort to discharge the onerous duties of the office to the best of my capacity in accordance with the injunctions of Islam. Allah has examined me from you and you from me, In the performance of my duties, I will seek guidance from the Holy Book, and will follow the examples set by the Holy Prophet and Abu Bakr. In this task I seek your assistance. If I follow the right path, follow me. If I deviate from the right path, correct me so that we are not led astray."

Succeeding to the caliphate in 634, Umar ruled until 644 and profoundly shaped the emerging Muslim state largely through his skill as a jurist and lawmaker. Under Umar, the Caliphate continued to expand, conquering the Levant, Egypt, coastal Libya and - crucially for the future history of Shias - the entire Persian Empire. Umar attempted some reconciliation with the extended family of Ali, but he still maintained Abu Bakr's position on Fatima's contested inheritance at the oasis of Fadak.

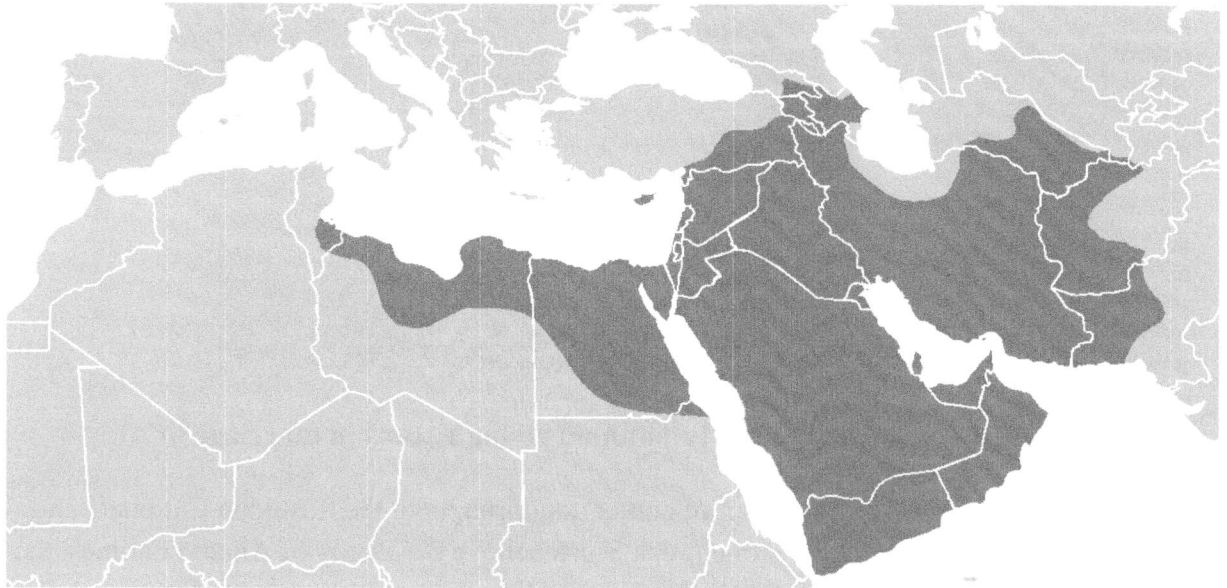

Mohammad Adil's map of the expansion of the Rashidun Caliphate

For the Sunnis, Umar has gone down in history as the greatest of the Faqih, an expert in "fiqh" (Islamic jurisprudence). During this period, the Ummah went through major changes as the number of Sahabah (Companions of the Prophet - those who heard Muhammad speak and had direct knowledge of his teachings) was decreasing both overall (as people like Abu Bakr died) and as a percentage of the overall population. This meant that the direct lessons of the Prophet and his example were becoming increasingly more difficult to teach, and as the Empire expanded, there was a greater need to apply Islamic law to an ever-growing number of cultural contexts. Umar and the scholars of his period began the process of collecting and codifying the Hadith (teachings of the Prophet) and creating a body of organized, universally-applicable laws for the new state[137].

While Sunnis and Shias differ on their interpretations of the Hadith, these collected sayings and acts of the Prophet are central to all forms of Islam and demonstrate how the word of God - the Qur'an - is applied in the life and words of a pious man as near perfect as a human could be. However, since the Prophet himself never wrote up a book of his teachings (Muslims consider the Qur'an a recitation from God given word-for-word to the Prophet), after his death there was a chaotic jumble of ideas. On top of that, the memories of the Sahabah began to falter as they grew older, and some Sahabah and non-Sahabah began to invent spurious "teachings."

What scholars have done for generations is collect and write down these Hadith and then sifted through the collections, examining the chain of oral transmission and the character of the transmitters to determine which Hadith they gave weight to. This also means that there are numerous similar (but often subtly or even dramatically) different versions of the same tale. The Sunni tend to be relatively liberal in accepting Hadith as their basic assumption; if a Sahabah reported a Hadith, they trust its veracity unless that individual can be shown to have abandoned Islam or the chain of transmission to the recorder was faulty. The Shia, on the other hand, interpret all of the Hadith through the prism of the treatment of the *Ahl al-Bayt* ("The People of the House"), a general term used for the descendents of Muhammad but used in Shia contexts only for Ali, Fatima and their descendents. Those among the minority that sided with Ali and Fatima against Abu Bakr and Umar in their disputes on inheritance and precedence are viewed by Shia faqih as the only legitimate sources of Hadith.

That said, during the era of Umar - before the open Sunni-Shia split - there were no such divisions made, so Muslim authorities were collecting Hadith not to compete with each other but to gather up the holy teachings before they faded from memory. In fact, at this point there were no theological differences between the proto-Sunni and the proto-Shia except for the relative importance they placed upon the political role of the Ahl al-Bayt, especially Ali.

In 644, Umar was murdered by a stab wound from a slave, and the fact that this slave was of Persian origin became a point of Sunni-Shia friction centuries later after Persia converted to Shi'ism under the Safavids. On his deathbed, Umar appointed a committee of six men to find his successor, and this committee included Ali and the eventual choice, Uthman ibn Affan. All six were part of the aging cohort of Sahabah and had been prominent political actors throughout the Prophet's reign and the succeeding caliphs.

137   *Islam: Faith, Culture, History* (2002). By Paul Lunde. DK Publishing. Pp 48-49

The committee had to come to consensus, and according to legends, Umar ordered his son to kill any single member of the committee who held out against consensus. One of the six, Zubayr, backed Ali, and another, Sa'd ib Abi Waqas, supported Uthman. The remaining candidate/committee member, Abdur Rahman, withdrew from the running and was appointed arbiter. The final committee member, Talhah, was not present because he had been in a distant part of the empire when Umar died.

Eventually, the committee gathered before the Ummah at the Friday night prayers in the Mosque of the Prophet in Mecca, and when Abdur Rahman gave his support to Uthman, it forced Ali's hand. The committee announced it had reached a consensus, but Shias continue to maintain that Ali never accepted Uthman because he knew that the Prophet had appointed him as the only legitimate successor.

Regardless, upon his ascension, Uthman continued the military campaigns of his predecessor and pushed Islamic armies into Khorasan (today's northwestern Afghanistan), Balochistan (southern Pakistan), Armenia, and northern Africa. His rule lasted for 12 years, but while the first half of his reign was peaceful, the second half witnessed growing discord that eventually led to open revolt. The Shia argue that even in the time of Uthman, the later tendencies of the Sunni caliphs towards rule not as the first among equals but as dynastic monarchs was evident. Uthman had appointed his family members to governorships, accepted rich gifts, and used monies from the public treasury for himself, all of which flew in the face of the rigid egalitarianism of the previous rulers.

All of the discord culminated in 656 with the assassination of Uthman and unrest across the empire. The assassination itself was a dramatic event known as the "Siege of Uthman," which consisted of angry citizens/rebels from outlying areas converging on Mecca with a set of demands for Uthman. Central to their complaints was Uthman's appointment of his extended family as governors. The exact events are still unclear, but it is possible that documents were faked by his cousin Marwan (who would later be Caliph) that ordered the rebel leaders executed. Ali was called upon by Uthman to intercede, but his attempts at negotiations failed, so the rebels continued to besiege Uthman within his home. The siege was a slow-motion affair of many days and largely without open bloodshed - Ali was even able to bring water to the Caliph – but in the end, rebels led by Muhammed ibn Abu Bakr broke in and killed the Caliph[138].

Not surprisingly, the nature of these revolts and the assassination is clouded by centuries of assertions by Sunni and Shia, especially since the development of radical Wahhabi Sunni theology in the 19th and 20th centuries. The Wahhabis (who are discussed in much greater detail in the final chapter) argue that the decline of Islam is due to the corruptions of the true faith, in particular by the Shia, who they view as heretical. These theologians and historians argue that

---

138   "'Uthman ibn 'Affan" in *The Encyclopedia Britannica* accessed online at:
        http://www.britannica.com/EBchecked/topic/620653/Uthman-ibn-Affan

the Caliph was brought down by a Jewish figure named Abd Allah ibn Saba' al-Ḥimyarī, and that he was funded by external enemies of the Islamic empire to sow divisions within the faith and undermine the Caliphate. They argue that the theological roots of Shi'ism comes from this individual, who led a revolt movement that assassinated Uthman in order to put the corrupted Ali on the throne and end the Empire's expansion. The Wahhabis point to connections between some of the rebels and Ali, including Muhammed ibn Abu Bakr, who was Ali's adopted son[139] and became a general for him when he was Caliph.

Shia historians, on the other hand, claim that Abd Allah ib Saba' al-Ḥimyarī is a fictional character created to disparage the Shia by claiming that their theology is Jewish in origin. This is considered an especially damning charge after the creation of the state of Israel in 1948. Moreover, the Shias insist that Abd Allah ib Saba' al-Ḥimyarī was concocted to place the blame for the end of the Rashidun Caliphate on their betrayal[140]. Instead, they argue that the Caliphate lost its path when it appointed a figure other than Ali as Caliph in the first place, and that the creeping growth of this corruption could be seen in Uthman's increasingly monarchic tendencies.

In 656, Uthman's death finally made Ali the leader of the Caliphate, and respect for Ali and for his caliphate is the last point of historical commonality between the Sunnis and the Shia before their trajectories took them in different directions. Changes had swept the Ummah (community of Muslims); the Prophet had died 34 years ago, and the community of his Companions - the Sahabah - were vanishing and losing their control over social and religious life. Thus, Ali took over an empire in the throes of revolt but managed to hold onto power for the next five years.

Immediately after the death of Uthman, the rebel factions declared Ali to be their Caliph, but Ali turned them down at first. As a result, the rebels demanded a Caliph be appointed, so the remaining members of the committee that appointed Uthman and were in Medina - Ali, Talhah, Zubayr[141] - met together in the Mosque of the Prophet with others of the Sahabah. This committee eventually appointed Ali the new Caliph, but there would be debate among those involved, as well as historians, as to whether this was done willingly or by force. Either way, the events at Medina were not unchallenged by those opposed to Ali, and conflicting rumors spread like wildfire across the Empire about the nature of Uthman's death and the appointment of Ali. The opposition gathered around Aisha, the Prophet's wife, and then around Muawiyah, the second cousin of Uthman and Marwan and the governor of Syria in Damascus[142]. Another lesser faction was based in Egypt around the governor of that province, Amr ibn al-As.

---

139   The first Caliph, Abu Bakr, was his biological father.
140   For a summary of the evidence in the debate, read: "Authentic References and Case Research of ibn al Saba's Existence" accessed online at: http://makashfa.wordpress.com/2012/12/16/authentic-references-and-case-research-of-ibn-al-sabas-existance/
141   Sa'd ib Abi Waqas, was governing Persia at the time.
142   He was not, however, one of Uthman's nepotistic appointments as he had been given his position by Umar.

In one form or another, the First Civil War (called a "Fitna") consumed Ali's reign and ultimately brought about his death. Around him gathered a group of loyal followers who became known as the *Shī'atu 'Alī*, a term that means Party of Ali, and over time, "Shiatu Ali" became shortened to "Shia," the term that continues to be used today. Hence, it can be said that while the roots of Shi'ism go back to even before the death of the Prophet, the Shia become an identifiable political group upon Ali's succession.

The first open battle in the conflict was the Battle of the Camel on November 7, 656. When Muawiyah sent his word that he would not recognize Ali, Aisha, Talhah and Zubayr (who were on pilgrimage together) traveled to Medina to ask Ali not to attack Muawiyah but to instead hunt the killers of Uthman. When they learned that Ali was not hunting the killers, they allied with Marwan and his kinfolk (the Umayyad clan). Ali learned of their movements and summoned groups from the Iraqi city of Kufa to aid him.

When the two armies met, it seemed that conflict would be avoided once all of the main parties agreed to a truce and settlement. However, during that night, unknown hotheads attacked the camps, sparking wider fighting. Both Zubayr and Talhah refused to participate, but Zubayr was killed by one of his soldiers and Talhah was killed by Marwan. The battle was fierce and included thousands on both sides, with the focus being on the capture of Aisha on her camel. Aisha eventually surrendered and was pardoned by Ali, and Marwan was captured.

A medieval depiction of the Battle of the Camel

    This solidified Ali's control over the heartland of the Caliphate but left the Umayyad clan and Muawiyah in rebellion in Syria. Thus, the civil war continued to rage as Ali attempted to conquer the rebellious provinces and hold the Caliphate together. Finally, the two armies met in 657 at the Battle of Siffin on the banks of the Euphrates River near present day Raqqa in Syria.[143] Once

---

143   There were roots of earlier conflicts here. The Byzantine and Persian Empires had long maintained proxy
       states in Syria and Iraq (respectively) and the two groups - both Arabic speaking - were old and bitter rivals even

again, they were slow to engage and preferred to attempt to settle their difficulties, but even though the two sides held off for months to negotiate, fighting eventually broke out. Thousands died on each side and both leaders retreated, so the conflict remained unresolved.

Eventually, Ali agreed to Muawiyah's call for arbitration according to the laws set down in the Qur'an, but when word spread that Ali agreed to negotiations as if Muawiyah was an equal, a faction of his most radical and fiercest supporters broke off and retreated to southern Iraq, becoming a sect called the Kharijites. In the end, Ali left the arbitration greatly weakened, making Muawiyah the symbolic victor. Ali retreated to his wartime capital in Iraqi Kufa, and Muawiyah headed to Damascus, where he was declared Caliph in 658. There were other campaigns in the aftermath of Siffin, but Muawiyah's influence gradually began to expand. Ali was further weakened by battles in 659 against the Kharijites, which eventually led to his assassination by the Kharijites in the Great Mosque of Kufa in 661.[144]

Even as the Sunnis and Shias continued to split, there were still some overlaps between the two, and there have always been periods of shared history that they agree upon. One example is the 4th Shia Imam Muhammad ibn Ali (677–732), who, despite being the head of the "Party of Ali," became a well-respected scholar in Sunni circles as well. However, the simmering conflict between the Umayyad Dynasty and their Shia challengers to the throne exploded during the reign of the Caliph Yazid I, the son of Muawiyah I who reigned from 661-680. When Yazid came to power, he represented a new element in the religious and political life of the Empire; he was a ruler born after the death of the Prophet (and thus was not one of the Companions), and he was the first to be appointed to his position by filling his father's seat. Ali's son Hasan had ruled as Caliph for a short period during the conflict after his father's death, but this had not been over the majority of the Caliphate and was barely long enough for him to surrender. Thus, Yazid I came to represent the political corruption that was seeping into the Caliphate.

Ali's elder son, Hasan, had died in 670, so he did not live to see Yazid come to power, but his younger brother, Hussein (also spelled Husayn), did. In 680, Hussein had been the prominent leader of the Shia for 10 years, and he refused to accept Yazid as Caliph, noting that the peace treaty that he had signed with Muawiyah to end the Fitna had expressly prohibited the Umayyads from appointing one of their own as successor. Hussein was 54 at the time, while Yazid was only 34, and he had been one of the Companions of the Prophet. Furthermore he was mentioned by name in the Hadith, and the Prophet was said to have given him special favor. His most important ally at the time was ibn Zubayr, the grandson of Abu Bakr (the first Rasidun Caliph).

Hussein gathered his allies at Mecca, far from the center of Umayyad power in Damascus but at the heart of the old traditional power bases. The people of Kufa, Ali's old capital, heard of

---

when absorbed into the Islamic Empire. Hence, when Muawiyah went into rebellion in Syria, many Iraqis from Kufa were more than willing to join the fight against him.

144   "'Ali" in the *Encyclopedia Britannica* accessed online at:
       http://www.britannica.com/EBchecked/topic/15223/Ali

Hussein's revolt and sent word to Mecca that they were ready to join the revolution. They further encouraged him to make Kufa his capital, and against the advice of ibn Zubayr, Hussein gathered his family and companions and headed towards Kufa.

Meanwhile, Yazid moved quickly to consolidate his power, including sending his lieutenants to Kufa to depose the local governor and attempt to control the city's crowds. He also sent armies to the roads between Mecca and Kufa, anticipating Hussein's movements. Once Yazid's forces encountered Hussein on the road, there was a tense period of negotiation and wary watchful encampments. According to Shia accounts, Hussein's party shared water with the Umayyad soldiers, but they refused to return mercy by forcing Hussein to encamp far from water sources and then killing Hussein's younger brother, Abbas. Both sides agree that the truce broke down, resulting in the Battle of Karbala, during which Hussein and 72 of his followers were killed and decapitated. The bodies of the dead were left in the desert, but the soldiers returned with the heads and the captured women and children to Damascus to deliver them to Yazid. In the process, Hussein's sister Zaynab rose to prominence by denouncing the Caliph and protecting the honor of the surviving female members of the family.

A depiction of important figures at the Battle of Karbala, with the central figure being Abbas

These shocking events were seared into the consciences of the people of Kufa and all of the Shia, not to mention many Sunnis who have come to view the Umayyad Dynasty as corrupt and tyrannical. The annual observance of Hussein's death is called Ashura, meaning "Tenth," referring to the fact that it is the 10th day of the Muslim month of Muharram. For the Shia, it is seen as a day commemorating triumph over, and opposition to, tyrannical government. According to legend, the first commemoration of Hussein's death was held in the prison in

Damascus and led by Zaynab, who has since become a symbol of strength, resistance to oppression, and piety.

The Battle of Karbala led to the rise of the Umayyad Caliphate, but eventually, a mosque – the Imam Husayn Shrine – was built in Karbala over the grave of Hussein, and it became the focal point of annual Ashura pilgrimages. Even outside of Karbala, Ashura has become a time when Shia march through the streets of their hometowns carrying banners, funeral biers, and performing an act called a Matam, which involves beating one's breast either with the open palm or holding an object like a knife or a chain, in lamentation for the dead. Ashura is the most obvious, public, and controversial marker of Shia identity, and the annual celebration of Ashura is always fraught with controversy and conflict. For one, it is a symbol of Shia-ness in nations where the Shia are often a minority (such as in India or Lebanon) or an oppressed majority (such as in Saddam Hussein's Iraq or contemporary Bahrain). On the other side, it is a symbol of opposition to oppression and has become a rallying point for dissent against tyrants (such as the Shah of Iran, Saddam Hussein or the government of Pakistan).

The Imam Husayn Shrine in Karbala, Iraq

The Umayyad Caliphate's Social Structure

Within the caliphate were four distinct social classes which controlled where a person could live, their position in society, and whether they were subjected to increased taxation and limited rights. These four classes were the Muslim Arabs, the Muslim non-Arabs, the *dhimmis*, and the slaves.

Not surprisingly, the Muslim Arabs dominated society and held the majority of significant positions within the caliphate, including administrators, governors, tax collectors, religious leaders, and prosperous traders. Despite Islamic teachings which stated all Muslims were equal, the Muslim Arabs did not mix or mingle with their non-Arab counterparts and kept themselves walled away in separate districts.

Underneath the Arabs were the Muslim non-Arabs, often individuals or native peoples who converted to Islam from another religion. These people were supposed to receive the same rights, protections, and opportunities as their Arab counterparts, but this was not the case. Almost no members of this social class managed to climb to significant positions in the military or government, and none were chosen as religious leaders.

The inequality between the Arab and non-Arab Muslims provided a constant form of strife and social unrest. The Umayyad Caliphate was successful in spreading Islam across North Africa, into Asia, and into the Iberian Peninsula of Europe, but as the years passed, more and more of the population was composed of non-Arab Muslims who demanded the rights they were promised for converting. Unfortunately, the governors did not want to acknowledge the converts, as they were making money by taxing them for following another religion. In other words, many administrators in the caliphate continued to treat the non-Arab Muslims as *dhimmis*.

Dhimmis were the third social class and constituted members of the population who refused to convert to Islam. They formed a large portion of the population and were often adherents of Christianity, Judaism, Zoroastrianism, and other local religions. Since they did not become Muslims, the *dhimmis* were forced to pay special religious taxes like the *jizya*. By paying, the *dhimmis* could live in relative peace as legally recognized second class citizens but were relegated to the poorer quarters. Despite their situation, many great Christian and Jewish theologians emerged from the Umayyad Caliphate and contributed greatly to the understanding of their religions.

The final class consisted of slaves. They were not considered citizens and possessed limited rights and protections, with their lives and safety often forfeit and in the control of their masters. The vast majority of slaves were captives taken during the long period of expansion and conquest of the Umayyads.

No empire would be complete or successful without an effective administration that established communication across the land, collected taxes, and carried out justice, but when the Umayyad Caliphate first developed, it struggled to form a cohesive system. The first four caliphs were tasked with developing a stable administration, and since it was one of the first Islamic states, the rulers did not have many regional empires on which to base their new caliphate. Instead, the caliphs chose to emulate the practices of the nearby Byzantine Empire, which possessed strong administrative institutions and powerful branches of government. These four branches were of political affairs, tax collection, religious administration, and military affairs.

To better administer to their territory, the Umayyads split the empire into multiple provinces, although the borders changed significantly over time. Each province had a governor appointed directly by the caliph. The governor then controlled the region and was responsible for all other civil or religious leaders in the domain, including religious officials and civil administrators. Even generals were supposed to adhere to the governor, but military leaders operated with more license than other officials. One of the most influential areas would be Khorasan, or the eastern territories. Although the Umayyad Caliphate did expand significantly to the west and managed to conquer the majority of the Iberian Peninsula, administrating such far areas would always be a major challenge.

The provinces economically operated with some independence from the central Umayyad administration. Local expenses were paid for with taxes gathered from the regional population and the remainder was sent to the central government in Damascus – although the location of the primary branch of government shifted several times throughout the years. Because the Umayyad Caliphate was plagued with civil wars and succession crises, many of the governors did not send their tax revenue to the central administration and were able to amass personal fortunes.[145]

When it came to the operation of the government, the original intent of the Umayyads was to limit positions of power to qualified Arab Muslims. However, as the empire rapidly expanded, the pool of qualified Arabs decreased significantly. Eventually, the caliphs were forced to let local government workers and administrators maintain their positions in conquered provinces to better manage the new territory. This meant Arab Muslims slowly lost some of their prestige in the empire, and also that administrative documents started to be written in languages other than Arabic, such as Persian, Coptic, and even Greek. It was not until the 8th century that all government work became consolidated and written in Arabic throughout the territories.[146]

Another issue the administration faced was attempting to decide upon a currency. Since the Umayyads spread and started to encompass and include other civilizations in their empire, they needed to find a way to unify the currency while balancing many different monetary systems. As a solution, the Umayyad Caliphate once again copied the nearby Byzantines and even used Byzantine copper and gold coins until monetary reforms were implemented around 700. The first Muslim coins in history were not minted until post-700, and these were created in Damascus. Gold coins were dinars and silver coins were dirhams. No individual copper coins were printed

---

[145] Hugh Kennedy, *The Prophet and the Age of the Caliphates: The Islamic Near East from the 6th to the 11th Century* (Second ed.). Harlow: Longman, 2004.
[146] Ibid.

at this point.

Finally, the central administration was divided into six Boards, also known as the Boards at the Center, which served the caliph and worked with him to govern the caliphate. These were the *Diwan al-Qudat* (Board of Justice), the *Diwan al-Jund* (Board of Military), the *Diwan al-Kharaj* (Board of Revenue), the *Diwan al-Khatam* (Board of Signet), *Diwan al-Barid* (Board of Posts), and the *Diwan al-Rasa'il* (Board of Correspondence).

The Sufyanids

Although Umayyad is the name of the entire caliphate and is often called a dynasty, many of the individual rulers themselves developed their own long-lasting personal dynasties based on hereditary bloodlines. Another important element to note about many of the Islamic caliphates is that each one believed to be of a dynasty or lineage shared with Muhammad. For the Umayyad family, who were also called the Banu Abd-Shams, tradition stated they shared a common ancestor with Muhammad named Abd Manaf ibn Qusai who came from Mecca. While Muhammad was descended from Abd Manaf's son Hashim, the Umayyads were of a different son, Abd-Shams. Both families were considered separate clans because of the traditional rules of patriarchal lineage, but of the same tribe, the Quraish.

Tradition dictated the Umayyads hated the Hashemites before the birth of Muhammad, and the deep animosity only worsened followed the Battle of Badr in 624. During the battle, three prominent leaders of the Umayyad clan were murdered in a three-on-three melee with leaders of the Hashemites. Legend states the leaders were Utbah ibn Rabi'ah, Walid ibn Utbah and Shaybah for the Umayyads and Ali, Hamza ibn Abdul-Muttalib and Ubaydah ibn al-Harith for the Hashemites.[147]

Despite the growing number of opponents, Abu Sufyan continued his mission to exterminate the growing number of Muslims in the region. He waged another battle in an attempt to curb the power of the Muslims of Medina and take revenge for the defeat at Badr. This second armed conflict became known as the Battle of Uhud and occurred throughout March 625. Abu Sufyan led his army of Qurayshi Meccans against the forces of Muhammad in Medina.

While the Meccans struggled to gain ground at Badr, Uhud was considered a success because the Muslims incurred greater losses than the Meccans despite having the home advantage. Islamic tradition often seeks to emphasize the supposed barbaric quality of the Meccans during the battle by including anecdotes about individual brutalities. One of the most well-known stories is that Abu Sufyan's wife, a woman named Hind, climbed on the battlefield and cut open the corpse of Hamza, a rival. She then removed his liver and tried to eat it. There is no historical

---

[147] Giorgio Levi Della Vida, "Umayya b. Abd Shams" ikn Bearman, P. J.; Bianquis, Th.; Bosworth, C. E.; van Donzel, E. & Heinrichs, W. P. (eds.). *The Encyclopaedia of Islam, New Edition, Volume X: T–U.* Leiden: E. J. Brill, 2000, p. 838.

reference for whether or not corpse desecration was common practice during these early struggles.

Unfortunately for the Meccans, their power would not last. In 629 , less than five years after the initial success in Mecca, Muhammad beat back Abu Sufyan and took control of the city. He announced general amnesty, at which point Abu Sufyan, Hind, and the rest of the family converted to Islam. Sources indicate their son would become the future caliph Muawiyah I. However, the Umayyads would not ascend to power until Uthman ibn Affan became the third caliph. Uthman ibn Affan was an early companion of Muhammad as well as being his son-in-law and second cousin.

As caliph, Uthman ruled from 644-656 but failed to establish a dynasty. Instead of passing down power to his sons, he chose to appoint members of his familial clan to notable positions of power in the region, including his first cousin Marwan ibn al-Hakam.[148] Marwan became the top advisor to the caliph, which drew the ire of the Hashemite companions of Muhammad. According to sources, Marwan and his father Al-Hakam ibn Abi al-As had both been exiled from Medina by Muhammad himself. The Hashemites were further angered at the promotion of Walid ibn Uqba, Marwan's half-brother, as governor of Kufa. Walid ibn Uqba was a notable drinker and was accused of leading prayer while under the influence. Finally, Abdullah ibn Saad became the governor of Egypt despite his lack of experience, replacing the more favored Amr ibn al-As.[149]

Besides these slights to the Hashemite clan, Caliph Uthman further chose to consolidate Muawiyah's governorship of Syria and granted him control over more territory. While Muawiyah proved to be a capable and successful leader, the Hashemites still resented Uthman's position. Muawiyah, meanwhile, would go on to develop one of the most disciplined armies on the continent, composed primarily of nearby Syrian Arabs. Over time, Uthman came to trust and rely upon Muawiyah more and more, eventually appointing him as the governor of Syria when the previous leader succumbed to a plague that killed 25,000 people.[150] By 649, Muawiyah chose to expand his power base and created a navy led by Christian sailors and Muslim troops. This navy proved capable and managed to defeat the Byzantine navy in 655, resulting in the opening of the Mediterranean Sea to trade and conquest. This opening would prove beneficial to later iterations of the Umayyads who sought to gain power in the region.[151]

While Uthman was caliph, he chose to relax many of the restrictions placed by his predecessor, Umar ibn Al-Khattab. Former caliph Umar ibn Al-Khattab (sometimes written as Omar with the title "Al-Farooq"), was one of the most pious and just rulers of the Umayyad Caliphate. He was an expert Muslim jurist and also one of the most powerful Muslim rulers in history. While he

---

[148] G. R. Hawting, *The First Dynasty of Islam: The Umayyad Caliphate AD 661–750 (2nd Edition)*, London and New York: Routledge, 2000.
[149] Ibid.
[150] Fred M. Donner, *The Early Islamic Conquests*, Princeton: Princeton University Press, 1981.
[151] Donner, *The Early Islamic Conquests,* 83-84.

held the throne, he enacted numerous policies designed to control the morals of his people, particularly administrators. He reformed the code of law, removed Christians and Jews from holy territory in Africa, and commanded his subordinates to control any vices they may have, including full abstinence of alcohol and full recognition of holy days.

Caliph Umar ibn Al-Khattab also implemented several other influential policies. If he believed any of his governors or commanders was becoming greedy, lustful, or power hungry, then the official was stripped of his position. Likewise, armies were forced to stay in encampments away from cities that were under attack. This way, Umar ibn Al-Khattab believed the soldiers and commanders would not be tempted to loot and pillage and would not turn away from the teachings of Allah. When Uthman came to power, he was more lenient with his governors.

Besides working with his administrators and allowing them to live more relaxed lives, Uthman also needed to deal with growing tensions between the different tribes of the Arab population. Although these differences had been discouraged while Muhammad was alive, they resurfaced over territorial disputes and claims to power. Iraq and Syria were most notable for issues, and the local Sassanid Empire continued to wage war against nearby Byzantium. Uthman's decisions ultimately led to his murder in 656 at the hands of an unknown assassin.

The next individual to rise to the position of caliph in the burgeoning Umayyad dynasty was a man known to history as Ali. Ali was the cousin and son-in-law of Muhammad – indicating he married his cousin's daughter. Once he took power, Ali switched the location of the capital from Medina to Kufa, which irritated a broad range of factions in the region. As noted earlier, Ali experienced initial success against the supporters of Aisha at the Battle of the Camel in 656, but he ran into trouble a year later (July 657) against Muawiyah.

For Muawiyah, his dynasty was the Sufyanids or "descendants of Abu Sufyan." They would reign from 661-684 and would only have three rulers: Muawiyah, his son, and his grandson. While Muawiyah ruled, the kingdom managed to maintain internal security while being able to expand externally. Only one major rebellion occurred when Huir ibn ʿAdi al-Kindi of Kufa, a former companion of Muhammad, supported the descendants of Ali. His movement was rapidly suppressed, however, by the governor of Iraq.

To maintain internal peace and stability, Muawiyah encouraged peaceful coexistence between Muslims and religious minorities like the Christians of Syria. Historians note the caliph's rule as being one of the only reigns characterized by "peace and prosperity for Christians and Arabs alike," and Muawiyah even employed Syrian Christians as advisors to the court.[152] At the same time, the Umayyad caliphate launched an aggressive and unceasing war against the nearby Byzantine Roman Empire for territory and resources.

---

[152] Kennedy, *The Prophet and the Age of the Caliphates*, p. 76.

Through superior numbers and tactics, the caliphate claimed Rhodes and Crete and assaulted the city of Constantinople itself. Ultimately, however, that assault was a failure and spawned a largescale Christian uprising by the Mardaites. The Mardaites were a group of early Christians who lived in the Nur Mountains. As the Umayyad caliphate and other Muslim groups sought to claim the region, the Mardaites adopted an aggressive fighting style and sided with the Byzantine Empire to push the invaders back. Their numbers swelled through the arrival of thousands of runaway slaves from Muslim territory, resulting in an ethnically diverse society and fighting force. The Mardaites were so deadly in combat that Muslim resources from the time refer to the fighters as being "sick" or "insane."[153] Through their presence, the Byzantine Empire managed to retain a hold on the Nur Mountains and even forced Muawiyah to pay tribute as part of a short-lived peace treaty.

The first Sufyanid caliph was not done with Asia. Over the next decade, Muawiyah would target Kabul, Bukhara, and Samarkand, leading to their conquest. All three would become a part of the growing Islamic empire of the 7th century. At the same time, when he wasn't trying to break further into Asia and Europe, Muawiyah focused on Africa. He was responsible for overseeing a large-scale military expansion throughout North Africa, which would be the foundation of Kairouan. Kairouan, sometimes spelled Qayrawan, was a significant center of early Sunni scholarship and education. It currently serves as the capital of Tunisia and played an important role in the Umayyad power structure in North Africa.

Eventually, Muawiyah fell ill and passed away. Yazid I, the eldest son of Muawiyah, rose to the throne and was crowned in 680, but his rule did not go unchallenged. Numerous prominent Muslims opposed the idea of hereditary succession, including Abd-Allah ibn al-Zubayr. Abd-Allah ibn al-Zubayr was the son of one of the original companions of Muhammad. Standing with him was Husayn ibn Ali, a younger son of the original Ali who opposed Muawiyah.

The challenge and ensuing conflict became known as the Second Fitna. During this civil war, Ibn al-Zubayr was forced to flee Medina for Mecca because of his political views. He remained there in opposition and exile until his death, unable to dislodge Yazid I from the throne. At the same time, Husayn was also forced to flee, unable to muster the forces necessary to combat the military of the Umayyad Caliphate. The people of Kufa invited him to lodge in the city, but Husayn and his family were intercepted, captured, and executed on their way during the Battle of Karbala. Yazid I sent his victorious soldiers to occupy Kufa and quash the rebellious spirit of the city.

However, Yazid I's victory was not complete. Once word of Husayn's death spread, opposition throughout the caliphate grew. Multiple movements and rebellions rose, especially when the Kharijites heard word of the unrest. Two central movements emerged with one centered in Medina and another in Basra. Yazid I was forced to invest his time and energy into suppressing

---

[153] Christos G. Makrypoulias, "Mardaites in Asia Minor," *Encyclopedia of the Hellenic World - Asia Minor*, 2005.

the growing unrest. In 683, he sent his army to confront the rebels of Medina at the Battle of al-Harra. Once they defeated their initial opponent, the army then went on to besiege Mecca. The soldiers pillaged the city and damaged several influential cultural centers, including the Grand Mosque of Medina and the Kaaba in nearby Mecca. Resentment among the people grew as they saw their heritage and religious centers attacked.

News traveled slowly through the Umayyad Caliphate, and before the army had broken into Medina and finished the siege of Mecca, Yazid I perished. Once word reached the generals, the Umayyad army was ordered to return to Damascus. Ibn al-Zubayr took control of Mecca while Yazid's son, Muawiyah II, took the throne, but few recognized his rule outside of Syria. Instead, two factions developed: the Confederation of Qays and the Quda'a. The Confederation supported Ibn al-Zubayr while the Quda'a recognized Marwan, a descendant of Umayya through the bloodline of Wa'il ibn Umayyah.[154] Both forces went to war, and the supporters of Marwan triumphed at the Battle of Marj Rahit, ensuring Marwan became caliph in 684.

The Marwanids

The line of succession begun by Marwan would become known as the Marwanids. The new caliph's first task upon ascending to the throne was to assert his authority and stymy the rival claims of Ibn al-Zubayr. Ibn al-Zubayr had a much greater base of support and was recognized as the caliph throughout the majority of the Islamic world. Marwan's solution was to retake the regions which supported Ibn al-Zubayr, beginning with Egypt. He succeeded in capturing the territory, but he died in 685, so his rule lasted a scant nine months.

Marwan's eldest son, Abd al-Malik, then became caliph. His early rule was marred by the revolt of Al-Mukhtar. Al-Mukhtar, full name Al-Mukhtar ibn Abi Ubayd Al-Thaqafi, a revolutionary in Kufa who supported the rule of the lineage of Ali. His goal was to promote Muhammad ibn al-Hanafiyyah, one of the sons of the deceased Ali, to the throne. Somewhat surprisingly, Ibn al-Hanafiyyah is believed to have had no connection to the revolt on his behalf and made no claims to the caliphate.

Al-Mukhtar commanded his troops to stop the armies of Abd al-Malik from reclaiming territory throughout Africa on behalf of the Umayyad Caliphate, and they engaged in multiple battles over the next year, but al-Mukhtar gained little ground. Although his armies defeated the Umayyads in battle near the Khazir River near Mosul in 686, al-Mukhtar and his revolutionaries were crushed the next year. With less opposition, the Umayyad troops managed to reconquer Iraq and marched upon the forces of Ibn al-Zubayr, who remained a threat until 692. In that year, Ibn al-Zubayr was defeated during an attack on Mecca.

---

[154] According to historic lineage, Marwan was the cousin of Muawiyah I. The battle for the caliphate was fought between a series of supporters and detractors of Muhammad and a select few families and clans who sought leadership amongst themselves.

Once he consolidated his power, Abd al-Malik turned to domestic policies and improvements. Chief among these was the construction of the Dome of the Rock in Jerusalem, which would be completed in 692. Because it was being built during the conflict with Ibn al-Zubayr, numerous historians believe the Dome of the Rock was intended to rival the Kaaba as a destination for dedicated pilgrims. At the same time, Abd al-Malik centralized the administration of the caliphate and established Arabic as the official language of government and business. He would then become the first creator of a distinct Muslim currency designed to replace the Byzantine and Sasanian coins used in the past.

A late 7th century Umayyad coin

An Umayyad coin weight

Later in his rule, Abd al-Malik adopted an aggressive foreign policy against Byzantium. He recommenced his predecessors' offensive warfare and marched upon Byzantine territory in 692, breaking the peace that had existed between the two powers since 680. The first major success for the Umayyads was the Battle of Sebastopolis, during which Byzantine leader Leontios led an army of 30,000 Slavs against the Muslim soldiers. Unfortunately for him, 20,000 Slavs defected during the conflict, resulting in a massive loss for Byzantium. Caliph Abd al-Malik thus reestablished control over Armenia and Caucasian Iberia and developed a more positive relationship with the native population of the region.[155]

Abd al-Malik remained an effective ruler until his death in 705. At this point, his son, Al-Walid I, became caliph. Although Al-Walid was an active builder and ruler, sponsoring the construction of both the Al-Masjid al-Nabawi and the Great Mosque of Damascus, he did not remain in power for long. That said, despite the fact he only ruled until 715, he gained several influential regions, particularly the Sindh and Punjab regions of the Indus River. Following the death of his best general, Muhammad bin Qasim, Al-Walid I retired from the project of conquering India and

---

[155] John F. Haldon, *Byzantium in the 7th century*, (Cambridge University Press, 1997), 72.

instead turned his remaining months in power to domestic pursuits. To protect his claims in the region of Iraq, he requested the Umayyad governor of the region to import additional Syrian troops.

When Al-Walid died in 715, he was replaced by his younger brother Sulayman. Sulayman was one of the least effective leaders of the Umayyad Caliphate, ruling for a scant two years. He is best known for his protracted siege of Constantinople, which resulted in a serious failure that ended serious expansionist ambitions against the Byzantine capital and the northern extents of the empire.

Another major defeat for Sulayman was against the Chinese Tang dynasty. The Umayyad Caliphate drew Chinese ire when they deposed the ikhshid of the Principality of Farghana and replaced him with a new ruler.[156] The deposed ikhshid fled to nearby Kucha and requested Chinese intervention to protect his sovereignty as well as that of the Tangs. Unwilling to allow Islamic influence to spread further into Asia, the Chinese sent General Zhang Xiaosong with 10,000 troops to Farghana.

Zhang Xiaosong routed the invading Umayyads and restored the ikhshid to power. However, the Umayyads were not done. In 717, they attacked Transoxiana in an attempt to thwart the Chinese military garrisons' hold in the region. The goal was to claim the Four Garrisons of Anxi district. The ensuing conflict was the Battle of Aksu, during which Umayyad commander Al-Yasukuni was forced to flee to Tashkent.[157] This was the final humiliating defeat for Sulayman.

Later that year, Sulayman's cousin Umar ibn Abd al-Aziz would become caliph. He became the only Umayyad caliph to be considered a genuine caliph or *khalifa* rather than just a worldly king, or *malik*. Umar became well-known and honored for his decision to tackle the fiscal problems associated with religious conversion to Islam. This was essential as the majority of the people living within the borders of the Umayyad Caliphate were not Muslim. Instead, they were Christian, Jewish, Zoroastrian, or members of smaller cults, religions, and ethnic groups.

As non-Muslims, the majority of the population was required to pay the *jizyah*, or a religious tax. This created a major problem for the administration as widespread popular conversion to Islam would be unprofitable and diminish state revenues. Regional and provincial governors thus actively discouraged individuals from converting. Umar's exact actions towards resolution are unknown. Historical sources indicate he proposed similar treatment for Arab and non-Arab Muslims at a time when Arab Muslims were treated as superior to converts from different ethnic backgrounds. He also eliminated several of the obstacles that prevented non-Arab conversion. Sources indicate this could mean removing troublesome provincial governors in favor of more devout or progressive administrators.

---

[156] The proper term Ikhshid was the title for the Iranian rulers of the region in the pre-Islamic and Early Islamic periods.
[157] Haldon, *Byzantium in the 7th century.*

Umar was one of the most influential leaders of the Umayyad Caliphate despite his short reign. He died in 720, a scant three years after his coronation. Without a direct heir, he would be succeeded by another son of Abd al-Malik, Yazid II. Yazid proved to be an unpopular caliph best known for his declaration of an iconoclastic edict that targeted Christian imagery. He ordered all Christian images destroyed throughout Umayyad territory, spawning civil unrest. Iraq revolted once again; this time led by rival Yazid ibn al-Muhallab. It was quickly quashed and Yazid II would only rule until his death in 724.

The last son of former ruler Abd al-Malik became caliph following Yazid II's demise. This son, Hisham, possessed the longest and most eventful rule out of all of his siblings. One of his first actions was to move the official court closer to the Byzantine border. The chosen location was Resafa in norther Syria. From Resafa, Hisham could resume hostilities with the Byzantine Empire. It was the first major action against the Byzantines since the failed siege of Constantinople. Instead of beginning with direct confrontation, Hashim ordered his troops to conduct short military campaigns and raids into Anatolia. Unfortunately, the Byzantine Empire responded by sending their own armies. At the Battle of Akroinon, the Umayyads suffered a major defeat and were unable to gain any new territory.

It was at this point in the caliphate's history that the Umayyads turned towards Europe. Using bases in North and Western Africa, the caliphs ordered their generals to collect willing converts from the Berbers and raid the coastal towns owned by the Visigoths. The Visigothic Christian kingdoms were spread out across the Iberian Peninsula – the location of modern Spain and Portugal. Permanent occupation by the Umayyads began as early as 711 and would continue northward into southeastern Gaul.

While expansion began under Al-Walid I, it would end with Hisham. In 732, the Arab army, bolstered by Berber soldiers, failed to defeat the Franks at the Battle of Tours. The Franks were a prominent combination of European ethnic groups populating the region of modern France, Belgium, and western Germany. They were often at odds with the neighboring Gauls, a Celtic people that had expanded into the region of Switzerland, Luxembourg, and part of France. Unfortunately for the Arabs, the Franks possessed a moderately centralized empire with a standing military that refused to back down in the face of enemy expansion.

The loss at the Battle of Tours would not be the most severe military defeat under the rule of Hisham. Seven years later, in 739, a major Berber revolt occurred in North Africa. Throughout the Umayyad Caliphate's expansion, the Berbers had formed the brunt of the military force, but even though the native western Africans had converted to Islam in large numbers, they were treated as second class citizens to Arabs. They did not receive recognition for their accomplishments, were not promoted like Arab soldiers, and often formed segregated regiments assigned to the worst tasks. The Berbers were no longer willing to accept Umayyad rule. Many of the soldiers stationed in Iberia rebelled and left their posts, shaking the power of the caliphate.

From the rebellion came some of the first Muslim states to exist outside of the caliphate, including Morocco.

Without the backing of the Berbers, Umayyad influence in Iberia dwindled. The Visigoth Christian kingdoms worked together to eliminate the Umayyad armies holding al-Andalus and pushed the caliphate back. By the middle of the 8th century, the Umayyads claimed only southern Iberia, while the Visigoths held strong in the north. At the same time, the Arab military began to crumble across the empire. In India, for example, the south Indian Chalukya dynasty defeated the encroaching Umayyad army while the north Indian Pratiharas dynasty did the same.[158]

These losses were the greatest of Hisham's career, but they were far from the only ones. In the 730s, the Umayyad Caliphate attempted to displace the Khazars and head into Eastern Europe, but they were soundly defeated at the Battle of Marj Ardabil. Even when the generals launched a massive invasion all the way to the Volga River, the Khazars remained undefeated, and the Umayyads were forced to limit their hopes for a northern expansion. Before this, Hisham had attempted to move east and subdue Tokharistan and Transoxiana, but the invasions failed miserably and increased the discontent of religious minorities who had been promised tax relief if they chose to convert to Islam. Revolts broke out throughout the empire.

The issue of taxation against religious minorities, as well as that of rights for non-Arab Muslims, continued to be the source of major problems in the Umayyad Caliphate. Further compounding these difficulties was the issue of succession, which had not been settled. Political rivals still vied for power, each with a claim of either religious superiority or a close tie to the Islamic prophet Muhammad. The poor rule of Hisham was the straw that broke the camel's back for various rebels and rivals throughout the empire, leading to the Third Fitna in 744.

The Third Fitna was yet another series of civil wars and political uprisings against not only the Marwanid line, but the Umayyad Caliphate as a whole. It began with the death of Hisham in 743. According to a decree by Yazid II, Hisham's successor was to be his brother al-Walid II. At first, the people seemed willing to accept their new caliph. Hisham had been unpopular and al-Walid II's first act upon coming to power was to increase military pay in attempt to appease the soldiers. However, he was also a man who desired earthly pleasures over spiritual enlightenment and religious devotion. He avoided his spiritual duties in favor of amassing more wealth and decorating his "desert palaces" like Qusayr Amra and Khirbat al- Mafjar.[159]

For many of his political rivals, al-Walid II's failure to uphold the fundamental tenets of Islam served only to breed resentment. Even within the Umayyad family itself, al-Walid II proved to be unpopular. Instead of appointing one of his numerous male cousins as his successor, the

---

[158] B. A. Litvinsky; A. H. Jalilov; A. I. Kolesnikov. "The Arab Conquest." In B.A. Litvinsky. (ed.). *History of civilizations of Central Asia, Volume III: The crossroads of civilizations: A.D. 250 to 750*, (Paris: UNESCO Publishing, 1996).

[159] Hawting, *The First Dynasty of Islam.*

caliph instead chose his two underage sons. When the family protested, al-Walid II ordered the flogging, imprisonment, and torture of his cousin, Sulayman ibn Hisham.[160] Further opposition on a large scale grew when al-Walid II persecuted the Qadariyya sect, a group of early Islamic theologians who assigned humans free will and absolved God of all evil in the world. He then became involved in the rivalries of the northern and southern Arab tribes, breeding resentment from all four factions involved in the disputes.

Tensions reached their peak in April 744, when Yazid III marched into Damascus. Yazid III was one of the sons of al-Walid I and possessed a claim to the Umayyad throne. His supporters, who had bolstered their ranks with Kalbis from the surrounding area, overthrew the guards and seized the town. Yazid III was declared the new caliph. Al-Walid II, who had been vacationing at one of his desert palaces, fled the region and arrived at al-Bakhra near Palmyra. He garnered little support from the local Kalbis and Qaysis, but managed to muster a small force. However, the majority fled when Yazid III's army arrived. Without protection, al-Walid II was captured, executed, and had his severed head sent as a trophy to Damascus. A local pro-Qaysi uprising then tried to march upon Damascus in an attempt to place the Sufyanid Abu Muhammad al-Sufyani on the throne, but it was easily defeated. Abu Muhammad found himself in prison alongside al-Walid II's sons.

Although he took the throne by force and only served for a brief period, Yazid III proved to be an exemplary caliph and one of the most efficient rulers the Umayyad Caliphate enjoyed. He modeled himself after the pious Umar II and earned the esteem and favor of the religious administrators who had denounced al-Walid II. He further supported the Qadariyya and worked to disassociate his reign from the autocratic tendencies of his predecessors by avoiding the excesses and abuses that drew ire in the past. This meant reducing taxes rather than increasing them, bringing soldiers home instead of sending them on long expansionist wars, not enriching the Umayyads and their family members and adherents, and not giving preference to the region of Syria. In other words, he wanted to create a fairer caliphate that focused less on the enrichment and glorification of the Umayyads and more on developing a focused, pious, and centralized empire.

Yazid III further distinguished himself by claiming the community chose him and therefore possessed the right to depose him if they were not pleased with his practices.[161] None of the previous Umayyad rulers could host such a claim or even incorporated the broad public – or at the least the influential men – in such a way. While this could have been a turning point for the autocratic rule of the Umayyad Caliphate, Yazid III was the first and last leader for several centuries to even attempt to incorporate broader public appeal into his tenets of rule.

Although he was successful, Yazid III did not live long. He died after only six months and left

---

[160] Ibid.
[161] Hawting, *The First Dynasty of Islam,* p. 95.

a power vacuum in his place. The figure who would emerge from the void was Marwan II. Marwan II supervised many of the campaigns against the Byzantine Empire and the native Khazars for many years. When he learned about the death of al-Walid II, he originally planned to claim the caliphate for himself. However, he was forced to put down a Kalbi rebellion instead. When Yazid III came to power, Marwan II was sent to Upper Mesopotamia and resided in Harran.

When Yazid III died, Marwan II saw his opportunity to become the new caliph. He gathered his forces and marched into Syria. To bolster his public support, Marwan II claimed to be fighting on the behalf of the imprisoned sons of al-Walid II. As their champion, he gathered numerous followers from the local Qaysis and Hims of the region and marched unopposed until he traveled between Baalbek and Damascus. There, he discovered another experienced general, Sulayman ibn Hisham, waiting for him. Sulayman headed the Dhakwaniyya private army and received support from the regional Kalbis. He attempted to prevent the advancement of Marwan II, but suffered a brutal loss and fled to Damascus to avoid being captured. Those he left behind were forced to pledge allegiance to the sons of al-Walid II before being executed by their compatriots for disloyalty to Sulayman.[162]

Without the imminent opposition of Sulayman, Marwan II entered the capital of Damascus in peace in December. Upon reaching the palace, he was declared caliph. To avoid reprisals and maintain peace throughout the region, Marwan II encouraged the administrative districts in Syria to choose their own governors and officials rather than picking them himself. This way, local rebels were able to exert some form of control over who possessed power. This decision reduced support for Marwan II's opponents, and Sulayman ibn Hisham eventually arrived in Damascus to submit.

Unfortunately, while Marwan II demonstrated some political savvy in the beginning of his reign, he quickly made the poor decision to move the capital of the caliphate from Damascus to Harran, effectively leaving Syria. According to historians, "[f]or the first time a caliph seemed to have abandoned Syria altogether."[163] It is important to note at this point that Damascus and Syria in general had been chosen as the capital for the Umayyads to control the underlying waves of rebellion and resentment existing in the region. By leaving, Marwan II fueled mistrust in his leadership and left a simmering population with the explosive potential of a powder keg. Almost immediately after his departure, Marwan II faced trouble in the form of a Kalbi revolt in Palestine in the summer of 745. He was forced to return to Syria and put down the revolt city by city, overthrowing and killing many of the local governors and leaders who strove to liberate the region from the larger control of the Umayyads.

At this point, Marwan II realized he needed to reaffirm his hold on the caliphate. With Syria in

[162] Hawting, *The First Dynasty of Islam,* p. 97.
[163] M.A. Shaban, *The Abbasid Revolution*, (Cambridge: Cambridge University Press, 1979).

his clutches, Marwan II ordered the other living members of the Umayyad dynasty to converge upon his palace and bear witness as he named his sons as his heirs in a hereditary line of succession. He then assembled a new army to send to Iraq to put down the revolts popping up throughout the territory. Yet again, he was unfortunate. As soon as the army reached Rusafa, it mutinied and instead accepted Sulayman ibn Hisham as the true leader of the caliphate. The army marched upon and took nearby Qinnasrin where it was joined by a mass of local rebels.

With the majority of his army defeated, Sulayman ibn Hisham was forced to once more escape, this time heading to Palmyra. Once there, he gathered some supplies and moved to Kufa. The surviving portion of his army did not join him. Instead, it withdrew to Hims, where Sulayman's brother took command. The brother, Sa'id, took too long to recuperate and collect his forces; Marwan arrived before Hims was prepared and besieged the city.

Throughout the winter of 745 and 746, Marwan attacked the city walls and wore down the remaining supporters of Sulayman. With supplies low, the army at Hims was forced to capitulate. With the opposing forces once more subdued, Marwan refused to show any more leniency to the Syrians. At this point, the Syrians had rebelled multiple times, forged an army, and destroyed many of the caliphate's resources in an attempt to change the line of succession. To reduce further rebellion, Marwan went between the Syrian towns, destroying the walls so they were unprotected. According to historical sources, some of the affected cities included Damascus and Jerusalem.

The Abbasid Revolution

Marwan's troubles were not limited to Syria. He faced significant opposition in Egypt and Iraq, where local governors attempted to restore the preeminence of their regions in the power of the Umayyad Caliphate. Although Marwan was able to suppress the rebellions and regain a semblance of control over the territories, his tribulations were not over. On the horizon loomed the Abbasid Revolution.

The Abbasid Revolution had its origins in 719, the year missionaries began to seek support in Khurasan for "a member of the House of the Prophet who shall be pleasing to everyone."[164] On the surface, the mission sounded like basic proselytism and the spreading of Islam. However, the missionaries were actually attempting to drum up support for the Abbasids. The Umayyad Caliphate was growing increasingly unpopular among the different Muslim sects, and the Abbasids began to receive support from Arabs and non-Arabs alike.[165] Non-Arabs were perhaps the most influential, as large numbers of Christians, Jews, and Zoroastrians were dissatisfied with their sociopolitical limitations in the current caliphate.

The Abbasids were descendants of Abbas ibn Abd al-Muttalib, one of the youngest uncles of

---

[164] Ira M. Lapidus, *A History of Islamic Societies*, (Cambridge: Cambridge University Press, 2002), p. 58.
[165] John Esposito (Ed.), *The Oxford History of Islam,* (Oxford: Oxford University Press, 1999).

Muhammad and a member of the same familial clan. They claimed to be the true successors of the prophet Muhammad and manipulated the tense political situation in the Umayyad Caliphate to bolster their position amongst the people. In addition to drumming up a powerful base among non-Arabs, the Abbasids and their supporters also drew power from discontented Shia Muslims and Sunni non-Arab Muslims who felt their religious views and social position were not respected by the current hereditary dynasty. These ranks were further bolstered by former members of the Shia rebellions that sprang up throughout Syria due to alliances and perceived wrongdoings during the Second and Third Fitnas.[166]

During the first half of the 8th century, Kufa rapidly became a center for opposition to the Umayyad dynasty. Of particular importance in the region were the supporters of Ali and the minority Shias. According to historians of the Islamic caliphates, the well-known Persian general Abu Muslim first met with Abbasid agents in the region around 741. At this point, he made initial overtures to join the opposition of the Umayyads and eventually worked his way to meeting Imam Ibrahim, the leader of the Abbasids, during a trip to Mecca.

Due to his military prowess and charismatic personality, Abu Muslim became the de facto leader of the Hashimiyya in Khurasan by 746. Instead of being an open rebellion against the Umayyads, the Hashimiyya developed an underground resistance movement alongside the Abbasids to slowly enlarge their popular support. Secret communicative networks were mapped out throughout the eastern half of the Umayyad Caliphate, and spies were used to not only drum up support for the Abbasids but also spread dissent and doubt about Umayyad leadership.

Buildup continued through the Zaydi Revolt in Iraq and the Berber Revolts in Iberia and Maghreb, during which the underclasses of the current Islamic caliphate began to rebel against partisan leadership and the Umayyad failure to treat converted Muslims the same as Arab Muslims. The Hashimiyya also remained active but secretive during the Ibadi rebellion in Hijaz and Yemen, the Third Fitna, and the revolt of al-Harith ibn Surayi in Khurasan.

Despite remaining secret, the Abbasids and their allies were highly effective at manipulating local politics and grudges to increase outward rebellion against the Umayyads. The Umayyad Caliphate, meanwhile, was besieged in all four corners of the empire and expended numerous resources attempting to regain control over territory that now stretched over three continents. Some modern historians, including G.R. Hawting, assert the Umayyads were stretched so thin they would have been unable to thwart the Abbasid machinations had they known of them in the first place.[167] Around the Revolt of Ibn Surayi in 746, the Abbasids were ready to make their move.

Ibn Surayj was the leader of a social and religious rebellion against the Umayyads. He began

---

[166] Ibid.
[167] Hala Mundhir Fattah, *A Brief History of Iraq,* (New York: Infobase Publishing, 2009), p. 77.

his initial revolt at Merv but failed to outmaneuver the caliphate's soldiers, resulting in the loss of many civilians and his own secretary and confidante. Eventually, ibn Surayj was able to discover some allies in the region, banding together with nearby rebel factions. Combined, the rebels were able to drive the Umayyad forces back from Merv to Nishapur. Unfortunately, Ibn Surayj was betrayed and lost his forces and by the summer of 747, the Umayyads sued for peace. The rebel victory was short lived though, as one of the sons of ibn Surayj assassinated the backstabbing rebels. Shi'ite revolts broke out throughout the region, and Abu Muslim took advantage of the chaos to launch his own rebellion in June 747.

On June 9, Abu Muslim raised the sign of the Black Standard and initiated an open rebellion against local Umayyad leaders in Merv.[168] At this point, Abu Muslim had over 10,000 soldiers under his control. By February 14, 748, he ousted the Umayyad governor Nasr ibn Sayyar and dispatched part of his army to the west where the soldiers marched upon Qumis. To bolster his ranks, Abu Muslim relied upon the Abbasid officers Qahtaba ibn Shabib al-Ta'i, Al-Hasan ibn Qahtaba, and Humayd ibn Qahtaba. These men, a father and his two sons, were tasked with pursuing ibn Sayyar and continuing to push him west, away from Abu Muslim's revolt.

Al-Ta'i became the most significant officer in the west while Abu Muslim remained in the east. With the aid of his sons, al-Ta'i defeated an Umayyad force of 10,000 at Gorgan in August and then captured the city of Rey where Ibn Sayyar had attempted to regroup with reinforcements. Unfortunately, the city fell and Ibn Sayyar died fleeing west to Hamedan. Al-Ta'i would appear on the scene shortly thereafter and defeat the 50,000 soldiers sent by the Umayyads to Isfahan, weakening the caliphate's power in the west.

The Umayyads' last stand would come at Khorasan. The remaining soldiers were survivors of Hamedan, along with the remnants of Ibn Sayyar's forces. At Nahavand, the military garrisoned and locked themselves in the city,[169] but relief contingents from Syria failed to arrive as Qahtaba cut them off. While his son laid siege to the Umayyad forces in Nahavand, Qahtaba cut a deal with the captured troops. The Syrian contingent pledged loyalty to the Abbasids and shared military secrets, resulting in the systematic execution of the Umayyad soldiers left in Khorasan. Umayyad power in the region crumbled, ending a ninety-year reign.

Around this time, Abu Muslim strengthened Abbasid control over the Muslim far east by facilitating more rebellions. The Abbasid rulers took advantage of their newfound power to appoint loyal governors in Bactria and Transoxiana. Anyone who could oppose their control was offered a peace deal, only to be double crossed and destroyed once they accepted and laid down their weapons.[170]

Once Khorasan was under their control, the Abbasids made a rapid transition into

---

[168] Richard N. Frye (Ed.), *The Cambridge History of Iran*, (Cambridge: Cambridge University Press, 1977).
[169] Matthew Gordon, *The Rise of Islam*, (Hackett Publishing Company, 2005).
[170] Ibid.

Mesopotamia. This region was one of the oldest and most coveted of the Umayyad holdings and was necessary to exert total power over the Muslim world. In August 749, Umayyad commander Yazid ibn Umar al-Fazari tried to intercept Abbasid al-Ta'i before he reached the city of Kufa. Before he could make it, a separate Abbasid military group raided al-Fazari's encampment. Al-Ta'i's forces took part, but the commander himself would perish in battle.

Losing men and supplies fast, al-Fazari was forced to flee to the nearby city of Wasit. His soldiers reinforced the garrisons and managed to resist the Siege of Wasit from August 749 until July of 750. The Abbasids viewed al-Fazari's position in the city as beneficial to their own aims. The usurpers were able to leave a small number of soldiers around the area to besiege Wasit, and the rest of the army was available to go on the offensive and attack the other Umayyad holdings.[171]

While Wasit was under siege, the Abbasids crossed the Euphrates River and marched on Kufa. Inside the city's walls, the son of a disgraced Umayyad official started a pro-Abbasid riot in the citadel. Sources agree the son acted to avenge his father's torture and execution at the hands of the Umayyads. When the Abbasid commander al-Hasan bin Qahtaba arrived in September of 749, he was able to walk through the gates and take Kufa with few casualties.

Once in Kufa, the Abbasids faced a minor challenge from one of their officers, Abu Salama. Abu Salama's connection to the Abbasids was tenuous, and he supported them mainly because of their financial backing. While in the city, he tried to drum up support for a rival Alid leader. One of his confidantes reported these actions to the Abbasids, and they responded rapidly. After a brief consensus, they anointed As-Saffah as the new caliph of Kufa and held an official ceremony at the mosque. As-Saffah was the great grandson of al-Abbas, the uncle of Muhammad. Abu Salama pledged his loyalty alongside twelve other military commanders to avoid embarrassment and the repercussions of his political leanings.[172]

While General Qahtaba was busy in Kufa, the Abbasids sent the combined forces of two more commanders, Abdallah ibn Ali and Abu Awn Abd al-Malik ibn Yazid, to broader Mesopotamia. Because the armies were approaching from different directions, they arranged to meet on the left bank of the Tigris River where they attacked Umayyad forces. This battle became known as the Battle of the Zab. Marwan II, the current caliph of the Umayyads, saw his army completely destroyed and after nine days on the field, he was forced to turn tale and flee, sealing the fate of the Umayyads. As Marwan II made his way through Syria and to Egypt, the Abbasid armies snapped up the Umayyad towns in quick succession.[173]

Eventually, Damascus fell in April 750. Marwan II and his family managed to flee the city but were tracked down in August and brought to Egypt by a small group of loyal soldiers. Historians debate what happened to all of the members of the family. Some claim every individual was

---

[171] Hawting, *The First Dynasty of Islam*, p. 116-117.
[172] Ibid.
[173] Ibid.

executed in Egypt, while some suggest a few of the younger women were allowed to live. Whatever the case may be, the Umayyad dynasty was over. Over the next few months, the final Umayyad military commanders were tracked. Although several were promised amnesty if they surrendered, all of them were executed instead.

The supporters of the Abbasids were from a variety of backgrounds and included almost every level of society, including full Arab Muslims, non-Arab Muslims, and dhimmis. There was also significant military backing, and many of the soldiers were Muslims of non-Arab descent who were tired of Umayyad authority and the caliphate's refusal to acknowledge them as equals to their Arab counterparts. Another common issue was the Umayyad decision to centralize authority and administration in regions where the ethnic peoples were accustomed to a nomadic lifestyle. Non-Muslim subjects revolted against religious discrimination. Although the Abbasids did not promise any changes to the Umayyad administration, many individuals thought someone new holding the reigns of the caliphate would bring necessary reform.[174]

To fully understand the causes of the Abbasid Revolution, it's important to examine the different demographics. Each one experienced varying levels of discontent, but also importantly had different amounts of power. Perhaps the most important were the Shia Muslims who felt the Umayyads did not respect their religious beliefs. Dissent continued to rise and reach a boiling point following the Battle of Karbala in 680. In the Battle of Karbala, the grandson of Muhammad – Husayn ibn Ali – was massacred alongside his family and friends. This event became the rallying cry of the Shias against the Umayyads, and the Abbasids manipulated the memory of Karbala to gain support among the Shia Muslims.[175]

However, although there was general discontent among the Shia Muslims, it would be the Hashimiyya movement that rallied Arab Muslims against the Umayyad dynasty. The original goal, as mentioned earlier, was to replace the Umayyads with a ruling family. The revolts of the Shias actually closely resembled the Shi'ite revolts and uprisings in the past, being centered in cities and led by more influential members of Arab society. However, the Hashimiyya was clear about their desire for an Alid ruler for the caliphate. As the revolts worsened and significant Shia commanders and leaders started to die in battle with the Umayyads, anti-Umayyad sentiment continued to grow. Even better for them, the Shi'ite oppositional leaders were captured and murdered by the Umayyads, leaving the Abbasids as the only realistic alternative to the Umayyads.[176]

Although the Abbasids did not want an Alid ruler, they kept quiet about their true loyalty. Instead, when meeting with other dissidents, they stated they wanted a ruler who was a descendant of Muhammad that the Muslim community would all approve of. Many of the Shi'ite

---

[174] Hawting, *The First Dynasty of Islam*, p. 106.
[175] Ibid.
[176] Gordon, *The Rise of Islam*, p. 46.

Muslims assumed this meant an Alid would ascend to the role of the caliph, and the Abbasids tacitly approved.[177] As time went on, more and more individual groups began to support the Abbasids, partially because they believed the Abbasids were the only group to have enough power to combat the Umayyads. Among their followers were the former supporters of revolutionary leader Mukhtar al-Thaqafi and many of the Kaysanite Shia.

Perhaps the second most influential group of supporters for the Abbasids were non-Arab Sunni Muslims. Many of these individuals converted during the period of the Umayyad conquest. They had been promised the same rights as their Arab counterparts upon conversion, but were treated as second class citizens under the Umayyad regime. In fact, the Umayyad state continues to be well remembered as an Arab-centric state that showed favored status to ethnic Arabs above all else.[178] As an example of how unfair the situation was, Arab Muslims dominated the bureaucracy and held almost all significant military positions. If Arab Muslims chose to live outside of Arabia proper, they were housed in special garrisoned fortresses that became cities within cities. Non-Arab Muslims, often called Mawali, could not live there. There were also strict rules about racially mixed marriages – Arab men could marry non-Arab women, but non-Arab men could not marry Arab women out of cultural concerns for purity.

Surprisingly, while non-Arab Muslims were a powerful group, they only made up 10% of the Umayyad population. The majority were non-Arab non-Muslims who had their territory conquered. However, it was not long before non-Arab Muslims began to outnumber the Arab Muslims, which terrified the Umayyad nobility. Of major concern was that converts would no longer pay the jizya tax stipulated by the Qur'an for non-Muslims. There was a legitimate fear the empire would go bankrupt and no longer be able to remain in control over such an expansive territory. Another issue was cultural. Islam was seen as property of the Arab aristocracy, and if they could not control it, then they would lose some of the sociopolitical power. Since the Umayyads denied equal rights to them, the non-Arab Muslims were happy to side with the Abbasids to gain more power.

Another major cause was the repression of Iranian culture. The Muslim conquest of Persia had disrupted an empire and toppled a powerful culture, and the Umayyad leaders saw an intense threat in that culture. They therefore adopted an anti-Iranian Arabization policy in an attempt to suppress the nobility, language, and religion. Even common people started to be banned from engaging in traditional cultural behaviors. Such actions led to widespread dissent and discontent.[179]

The Umayyads only worsened the situation by appointing controversial Arab governors who applied their own restrictions to their populations. Governor Al-Haijaj ibn Yusuf, in particular, used force to ban written and spoken Persian not only is his court, but also for the general

[177] Hawting, *The First Dynasty of Islam.*
[178] Halm Heinz, *Shi'ism,* (Edinburgh: Edinburgh University Press, 2004).
[179] Susanne Enderwitz, "Shu'ubiya" in *The Encyclopaedia of Islam*, vol. 9, pp. 513–514 (Leiden: Brill Publishers, 1997).

population. Historians even note that the actions of al-Haijaj caused the death of the unique Khwarezmian language, a dialect related to Persian. What did the governor do? When the Umayyad Empire expanded into the east Iranian Khwarezm, he ordered the execution of any person literate in the language, leaving behind only the illiterate.

Such actions made the Umayyad Caliphate supremely unpopular, particularly among other non-Muslims who experienced similar treatment. Support for the Abbasid Revolution became widespread throughout the early 8th century , and only worsened after 741. That year, the Umayyads decreed non-Muslims could not serve in any government posts, particularly ones that would have placed them in a position of power over Arab Muslims. To avoid making the same mistakes, the Abbasids tempered their policies so they possessed a Muslim character while still appealing to the non-Muslim majority.[180]

In order to gain popular support, the Abbasids needed to diversify their tactics and operate behind the scenes until they were able to drum up the manpower and resources required to take on an empire as large as the Umayyad Caliphate. When it came to the military, the Abbasids strove to create ethnic and racial equality by mixing individuals of different backgrounds in the same regiments. These orders were passed among the influential commanders. Historians have evidence that generals like Abu Muslim recruited officers of diverse backgrounds along the silk road and registered them based on location instead of ethno-national affiliations. Doing so diminished tribal and ethnic solidarity, and created a sense of communality among the Abbasid soldiers.

This commonality would be one of the Abbasids' greatest assets as it allowed them to appeal to a broad range of individuals throughout the Umayyad Caliphate. Every group that had complaints about the Umayyads found themselves supporting the Abbasids because they seemed to target some of the problems inherent in Umayyad society. In particular, the Abbasids painted themselves as champions of ethnic equality who would overturn the imbalanced society of the Umayyads.

Of course, the Abbasids would not have been able to sway so many ethnic groups without using one of the most powerful tools in all of history – propaganda. Historians believe the Abbasid Revolution is one of the most significant examples of early medieval propaganda and its effectiveness in toppling empires. The Abbasids were familiar with the powers of subliminal and liminal persuasion and were particularly effective at utilizing symbols. For example, the Black Standard, a traditional flag believed to have been flown by the prophet Muhammad, was unfurled openly at the start of the revolution. This carried with it heavy messianic overtones since Muhammad's family had started numerous failed rebellions.

---

[180] Aptin Khanbaghi, "The Fire, the Star and the Cross: Minority Religions in Medieval and Early Modern Iran," *International Library of Iranian Studies*, (London: I.B. Tauris, 2006), p. 19.

Tugging at religious heartstrings did not end there. The Abbasids were descendants of Muhammad's uncle Al-'Abbas ibn 'Abd al-Muttalib, and they held violent historical reenactments of the murder of Muhammad's grandson by the Umayyad ruler, Yazid I. After the displays, they promised retribution. It should be noted these techniques did not focus on just what the Abbasids intended to do once in power, but instead focused on the legacy of Muhammad's family. They played intensely on concepts of messianism and religious persecution, and even revised preexisting Muslim chronicles so there was more emphasis on the relationship between Muhammad and his uncle. They wanted power, and the Abbasids were willing to fight outside of the battlefield to get what they wanted. All told, historians estimate there were over seventy professional Abbasid propagandists spread throughout Khorasan alone. These seventy worked under twelve central leaders who reported directly to the Abbasids.[181]

Further, the Abbasid Revolution relied heavily on secrecy, a tactic that was absent in other unsuccessful rebellions against the Umayyad Caliphate. For example, while the Shi'ites and other rebellions used publicly known leaders and made clear demands, the Abbasids hid everything. Few people knew their plans, identities, or even existence. Even the man who would be the first Abbasid caliph, As-Saffah, refused to become public and receive his pledge of allegiance from the people until the Umayyad nobility were executed. The Abbasids took no chances.

The military leaders followed the same policy of secrecy. The most famous commander, Abu Muslim – full name Abu Muslim al-Khorasani – used a mysterious title that gave no meaningful information. When translated, the name literally meant "father of a Muslim from the large, flat area of the eastern Muslim empire."[182] Modern historians still have no clue about his actual identity, even if they all agree Abu Muslim was a single individual and not a series of generals operating under the same name.

Finally, the Abbasids relied upon ruthlessness and deception to eliminate the last of the Umayyads and claim total control over Khorasan and the rest of the former caliphate. They tracked down any remaining members of the Umayyad family and offered them pardons if they pledged loyalty to the Abbasids. Eighty Umayyads went to Jaffa expecting to be given amnesty and were instead massacred in a brutal public ceremony. The victors would go on to desecrate the tombs of the Umayyads in Syria to further undermine the former royal family.

Once the Umayyads were out of the way, the Abbasids turned on their former allies. Abu Muslim, the infamous general, was accused of treason and heresy by the second Abbasid caliph less than five years after the end of the revolution. The caliph, Al-Mansur, had Abu Muslim publicly executed at the palace in 755. This was a poor move, as Abu Muslim was admired and loved by many of the former rebels and the general public. Numerous rebellions broke out

---

[181] Bertold Spuler, *The Muslim World a Historical Survey*, p. 48.
[182] Ibid.

throughout Khorasan and Kurdistan, and Caliph al-Mansur became known for his coldness and brutality.

The Shi'ites were next. Although they had been crucial to the success of the revolution, the Abbasids commenced persecutions in earnest. This not only was done to eliminate a perceived rival, but also because the Abbasids attempted to portray themselves as being orthodox and just rulers in comparison to Umayyad excess. Religious minorities were thus deemed heretics and needed to be eliminated. Surprisingly, though non-Muslims were treated with more benevolence and were able to hold government positions, they could not live in the same neighborhoods as Muslims, leading to the diversity of Baghdad under the Abbasids. By 755, the Abbasids were thoroughly in control and there were no traces left of the Umayyads save for some family members who went into hiding.

The Umayyad Caliphate's Legacy

Ultimately, as the history details, the significance and legacy of the Umayyad Caliphate is up for interpretation by many historians of the Islamic caliphates and their expansion. The Umayyad Caliphate itself was characterized by incredible territorial expansion across multiple continents but was plagued by the administrative and cultural issues one can expect from trying to incorporate a diverse array of peoples and religions into a single empire. Although diverse, the Umayyad Caliphate favored Arab Muslims over all others and became known for material excess, lavish palaces, and strict societal norms.

Such an organization, however, was instrumental in the development of the first great Islamic empire. Arabic became the administrative language as well as the lingua franca across the entire region. State documents and currency lent Arabic more legitimacy and forced individuals who wanted to rise to learn Arabic if they wanted to gain any power in the region. Mass conversions further made Islam one of the most common religions in the region, which was quite a feat considering Muslims only formed less than 10% of the entire population.

To many, the Umayyad Caliphate has become synonymous with the start of the Arab Golden Age – a period of great cultural development. However, such an interpretation is decidedly modern. Shortly after the Umayyads were out of power, historians and archivists wrote great treatises on the corruption of the dynasty. While the Umayyads were seen as managing to turn a small religious institution into a dynastic empire, such a transition was seen as turning away from the rule of Muhammad. In particular, early Islamic historians believed the Umayyads had facilitated the worship of a king over the true deity, and had given in to indulgence and excess. Such beliefs were heavily influenced by the Abbasids who strove to eliminate any positives about their predecessors.

Still, there is much to learn from the Umayyad Caliphate. It was the first successful Islamic empire, and it paved the way for many more. It managed to unite territory across three expansive continents, and place Muslims at the forefront of technological and cultural development. Perhaps just as important, the Umayyads faced the kind of serious issues that arise when trying to develop a political regime out of a religious institution. The kings viewed themselves as given the divine right to rule through virtue of their blood and struggled to maintain austerity when given control over so many resources. This caliphate would obviously not be the last to do so, but it was definitely one of the first.

The Ottomans

The origins of the Ottoman Empire and the dynasty that founded it are surrounded by legends and mysteries. The mythology around Osman I and his closest family created an image of the dynasty, legitimizing their heritage and right to rule. While some of it surely is true, a lot of it may also be sheer exaggeration. Even the true origin of the Ottoman dynasty is heavily debated by modern historians. The general opinion is that the Ottomans descended from the Kayi tribe, a branch of the Oghuz Turks. This was never mentioned in any records actually written by the time of Osman I's life, but firstly 200 years later, which makes it a highly contested statement. Contemporaneous writers would claim Osman to be a descendant of the Kayi tribe to aggrandize him.

The Kayi Tribe was powerful, prosperous and played an important role in the Caucasus region, both at the time before Osman was born and for hundreds of years to come. To link the Ottoman dynasty with such a tribe would work as an incentive to keep up good relations with the actual Kayi tribe, and also inflate the story about how the Ottoman dynasty descended from power and political influence. It would also support the inherited right of the Ottoman dynasty to rule the area. Though this may never be clearly settled amongst historians today, we do know that Osman's family was one of many Oghuz Turkish people originating from what today is western Kazakhstan, just east of the Caspian Sea.

From there, the Seljuk tribe of Oghuz people moved southwest into Persia and founded their empire, slowly moving west towards the Byzantine Empire. When the Seljuk Empire disintegrated, many smaller states were formed all over Anatolia and Osman's father Ertugrul was a ruler of one of them. Legend has it that Ertugrul and his army of 400 horse-borne fighters accidentally came upon a battle between two foreign armies. Heroically he decided to intervene and support the side currently losing. With his help, they turned the battle and won. Ertugrul learned that he had been fighting on the side of the Sultan of Konya, from the capital of Rum, against the invading forces of the Mongolian armies.

As a reward for his actions, he was handed a piece of land in northwestern Anatolia, centered around the town of Sögut. The truth in this story is again under debate since it wasn't written down until much later. There is no clear evidence of how Ertugrul came in possession of the lands he ruled or what his relationship was with the Sultanate of Rum. All we can say for sure is that this became the embryo of the Ottoman Empire as Ertugrul settled down, got married and later also had a son, Osman. This happened sometime in the middle of the 13th century, but the exact date of Osman's birth was never recorded.

During the years of Osman's childhood, his father was the chief of his given lands but also subordinated the Sultanate of Rum. When Osman was 23, his father died and Osman inherited the title and power Ertugrul had earned. It was now nearing the end of the 13th century and the Sultanate of Rum, as well as the whole Seljuk Empire, was disintegrating. The rise and expansion of Osman's territory came more or less as a natural consequence, replacing one power with another. It was a gradual process going on for generations of the Ottoman dynasty and Osman's early conquerings were only a fraction of how large the empire would become. The necessity of expansion was in later years explained with the spreading of the Muslim faith. The truth behind this is a contaminated topic among modern historians and hard to verify. Islam is no longer considered to be a driving force for either Ertugrul or Osman. Ertugrul was not a Muslim, but many claim Osman's religious father-in-law converted him to the faith. The story of how Osman became a devout Muslim is of importance to the Ottoman legacy. It includes a prophecy where God himself appoints Osman and his descendants to glory and success. This was in later centuries used to legitimize the continued rule of his heirs. It was also Osman who named the whole empire and the following dynasty, still alive today. Osman is the Arabic version of the Turkish Uthman, or Athman, which scholars believe was Osman's real name. His name changed into Osman under influence from the Arabic and Persian Islamic culture, to signal his transcendence into a Muslim. Whether or not Osman was religious he decided to expand into Byzantine territory and kept peace with his Turkish neighbors. Until the actual dissolution of the Seljuk Empire, the Ottoman dynasty did not fight other Turkish tribes.

The Rise and Reign of Osman I

To try to pinpoint the descent and origins of the Ottoman dynasty and Osman himself is more or less impossible today. The sources are highly contaminated with propaganda like factoids about Osman's persona, his heroic actions and the constant success of his ambitions, written at the height of the Ottoman Empire hundreds of years after Osman's reign. There are hardly any actual records from his childhood and we know very little about his early years of conquest. Probably because at the time being, Osman's father and family were not considered particularly mighty or influential. Thus, the lack of contemporaneous writings implies the falsehood of the anachronistic records speaking of Osman's visions and also of his father's heroic intervention against the Mongol army. Anatolia consisted of many beyliks at the time, as well as different alliances between tribes from all over Eurasia, Eastern Europe, Middle East and as far away as Central Asia. The number of interconnections and movements between the different tribes are uncountable, which makes it harder to factually pin down the true origins of Osman's ancestors. Whoever the ascendants of Osman truly were one can safely say that his descendants, using his very name, would be well-known to historians and civilians for many centuries.

As stated above, Osman was born as the son of a chief in northwestern Anatolia, in the town of Söguk sometime around the middle of the 13th century. The exact year has not been confirmed by any reliable sources, but 1258 is usually mentioned as most likely. His mother is presumed to be Halime Hatun, but even this has not been securely confirmed, and hardly anything is recorded of who she was. We know safely that Osman grew up in his hometown with two brothers but until his marriage to Mal Hatun there's not much information of his whereabouts. As the firstborn son of a local chief, Osman was aware of the fact that he would someday inherit the position, and it is said he learned to ride and fight already as a child. The first story recorded by the 15th-century historians of the Ottoman Empire is the one about how Osman became a Muslim. It was during a visit at his good friend Sheik Edebali's house, who was a very religious man, that he found the Quran. Osman became interested and asked his friend what this book was. His friend, who was an influential religious man in the community told him it was the holy book of Islam.

Osman lay awake that night, reading and reading until he couldn't keep his eyes open anymore. He fell asleep at the auspicious hour of dawn and then dreamed of a tree, sprouting from his navel with branches reaching all over the world. People in the dream were happy and the landscape was beautiful. When he woke up in the morning he told Edebali about the strange dream who in turn explained that because Osman had read the book so intensely and honestly, God had chosen him and his descendants to be blessed with glory and honor for many generations to come. Sheikh Edebali then gladly gave Osman his daughter Mal Sultana to marry and of their love, many poems have been written. The union of the two families benefited Osman greatly according to later sources because Sheikh Edebali was associated with very devout and ascetic dervishes. Though the dervishes didn't have any riches or power, their relationship to Allah would help benefit the Ottoman dynasty. The story of how Osman was the first in the family to actually become a devout Muslim was important to legitimize him taking over the remnants of the Seljuk Empire.

Osman's dream wasn't written down until almost 200 years later, a time when such a story would be of importance to keep the Ottoman Empire united. The story was valuable to the unification of separate Muslim emirates and gave Osman the right to conquer them. Another tradition that bears Osman's name is the girding of the sword of Islam given to him by his father-in-law. Every sultan of the Ottoman Empire was girt with a ceremonial sword within two weeks of their accession to the throne, although not the same sword as Osman received from Edebali. Again, this practice was only introduced when Islam already had emerged as the prevalent ideology of the Ottoman Empire long after Osman's death, and again, the ceremony was mainly used to inflate the religious importance of the dynasty.

The year after his marriage to Mal Sultana, which probably took room in 1280, Osman's father passed away and left the 23-year-old son in charge of the beylik. The timing was perfect for Osman to become a world-famous conqueror and founder of an empire. In the west, the

Byzantine Empire was falling apart and many cities made easy targets for Osman's army. In the east, the Mongols were wreaking havoc, contributing to the decline of the Seljuk Empire, and forced many Turks to flee the territories under Mongol siege. A great many ghazi warriors and potential soldiers streamed into Osman's emirate and gladly joined him in his quest against the Byzantine Empire.

The tradition of Ghazi warriors has been compared with the idea of the crusades or jihad. The word means "to carry out a military expedition or raid" in Arabic, but some scholars also mean that it indicates that the ghazi warrior fought to spread Islam. This is another fact debated in modern research, and there are no contemporaneous sources confirming that Osman was fighting in the name of Islam or that he really was a devout Muslim. As stated, these implications were written down much later by religious history writers at a time when they wanted to portray the founder of the empire as God's chosen man. What is known about the ghazi warriors is that they most likely fought as mercenaries and hence changed sides to whoever could pay them at the moment. Whatever their reasons might have been, the ghazi warriors were important contributors to Osman's success. Osman also added the word ghazi to his name, as did eight of his successors. Whether all of them defined themselves as simply conquerors or as religious men, it is impossible to say. The adding of Ghazi to their name nonetheless indicated their expansionist intentions.

After Osman had gotten married and his father had passed away, he was a full-fledged leader of the beylik, with a strategically important territory and prosperous family ties through his marriage. The stream of warriors and refugees made Osman a ruler of more people than his father, and with more people, more lands were needed. To expand at the cost of the Byzantine Empire was a logical solution, and it is estimated that he started his expansionist campaign in the year 1288. His first target was two nearby fortresses, Karacahisar and Eskişehir. A decade later, in 1299, he conquered the two larger towns of Yarhisar and Bilecik from the crumbling Byzantine Empire. He made Yarhisar the new capital of the beylik and declared independence from the Seljuk Empire.

By then, the central rule of the empire was weak and the popular sultan had been forced to flee the lands a couple of decades earlier. In his wake, there was chaos and no strong ruling power. The newly born independent state under Osman was organized as a strong central government on the same principles as the previous Sultanate of Rum. Though many people in the peripheries were opposed to Osman's rule, he quickly lightened the tax burden of his new citizens which assuaged them and changed the negative opinion of him. He needed to establish trust and loyalty amongst the people who are furthest from the capital to stabilize the borders, and the low tax strategy worked well. He was also the first chief in the area to mint his own coins which points to Osman's ambition of creating a larger organized political entity.

After the declaration of independence, Osman continued to expand both southwest and north into Byzantine territory aiming to control the whole area between the Sea of Marmara and the Black Sea. He conquered towns along the coasts and the poorly organized Byzantine armies were coerced to draw back towards the Bosphorus. In 1308 he captured the last city on the Aegean coast, Ephesus, and thus achieved his goals of dominating the region. His mounted forces used multiple creative military strategies for defeating the enemies around the countryside of Bithynia and fought in ever-surprising formations. During his last years in life, he also had good help from his sons, especially the oldest, the heir to the throne Orhan. After a whole life on the battlefields with his father, Orhan had learned and fully mastered the ideas behind Osman's tactics.

The last successful campaign of Osman was the siege of Bursa, though his son was left in charge and Osman himself didn't participate physically. Orhan showed tenacity and chose to lay siege to the city instead of attacking and conquer it forcefully. The siege was successful and the city surrendered after two of years under the threat of starvation. This was the last and most important victory of Osman I's expansion in Anatolia, not fully complete until the same year Osman died, 1326. After Bursa fell under Ottoman rule, other cities in the vicinity soon followed suit. It became the new capital under Orhan and an important staging ground against further expansion to the west.

It is difficult to separate the legends surrounding Osman from facts, and little is known about his earliest endeavors. Osman gained some interest from contemporaneous writers with the capture of Ephesus and that's the first time he is mentioned in historical records from his own time. From 1308 there are reliable sources about how and what he managed to achieve, and the second half of his life is less mysterious than the first half. Osman's conquests gained importance because his son and grandson continued his expansionist ambitions and at the same time incorporated religious tolerance and political stability in their rule. No one could at the time was able to foresee what the Ottoman Empire would grow to be, though people already in an early stage took refuge under Osman and preferred him to many other rulers. When the Seljuk Empire finally disintegrated and collapsed in 1308 Osman's prosperous lands was a capacious, natural escape from raiding Mongols. After his death at the age of 68 his son, Orhan continued the expansion far beyond what his father had dreamed.

A picture of the tomb of Osman

Expansion and the Safavids

By the time of Osman's death and Orhan's ascension to the throne, there are more reliable sources, to be found. It's possible to retell certain historical dates and happenings correctly but still, Orhan's reign is also somewhat glorified and exaggerated by the history writers. Orhan was probably born in the year 1281, as the only son to Osman I and his first wife, Malhun Hatun. Before Orhan conquered Bursa in 1326 not much is known of him. He was over 40 years old when Osman died and left him in command of the territories he had conquered, all of which he, together with his brother Alaeddin took good care of. Alaeddin was the second son of Osman, but born of his second wife Rabia Bala Hatun, a woman of Arabic descent. There are still some divisive opinions about which of the two brothers actually were the oldest, but their different personalities are usually seen as a natural explanation for their partition of duties. Orhan became the chief as appointed by their father and later he made Alaeddin the vizier. Orhan was a military man, who had spent much of his adult life campaigning throughout Anatolia with Osman while Alaeddin was calm, benevolent, pious and more passive, and had received management training in administration and business.

The affinity between them stands out as something of an oddity in the Ottoman family. As the empire grew so did also the hunger for power, and the brothers of succeeding generations fought hard to claim the throne. In later years, the death of a sultan was cause for civil war to break out, and having your competing brothers murdered in cold blood. Alaeddin and Orhan, on the other hand, shared the duties and collaborated to rule the beylik even though Orhan was the one officially sitting on the throne. The story of how the brothers decided to share the burden is more or less fabricated to shine a glorifying light on them. The noble Orhan offered the throne to his brother, who, just as noble, turned it down stating their father had wanted Orhan as his heir. Orhan asked Alaeddin to become his vizier, a title he invented there and which simply means "bearer of a burden." This indicates that the brothers felt the inherited burden of responsibility from their father's accomplishments. Alaeddin accepted the title and only asked for a small patch of land close to Bursa while Orhan kept the rest of the lands under his rule. The records tell of how Orhan often sought Alaeddin's advice on administering and managing both the civil and the military institutions of the state. Together they shaped a strongly centralized government that became significant for the Ottoman Empire and modernized both politics, economy and military during its existence.

Before Alaeddin died in 1331 or 1332, he made important contributions to Orhan's rule. In 1329 he suggested to standardize a monetary system all over the beylik, to choose an official costume or outfit for the Ottomans and to reorganize the army. Coins with Orhan's name was stamped in the same year, white became the official color of the modest clothing worn by government and military officials, and the army was divided into smaller squadrons. This initiative implies that before there probably hadn't been any similar way to organize the soldiers, though it would later become the standard. With smaller units each led by an officer it was possible applying more advanced tactics and strategies in field battles. This system is usually attributed to Alaeddin in Ottoman records, though its origins still are under debate. He also suggested forming an army which only was summoned in wartime, and hence could contribute to society in other ways during times of peace. This is largely how modern armies use their soldiers today, but the idea was new for the time. The first experiment failed under Orhan's rule, because the armies lacked military training when needed. In later generations, these armies came in very useful.

Orhan had gotten married a first time in 1299, which resulted in two or three sons. Two of them reached fame and many sources can confirm their lives and whereabouts. Suleyman Pasha was the oldest and intended heir to the throne. He helped his father expanding his emirate mostly to the west and north taking big chunks of the Byzantine lands. After Bursa fell under Ottoman rule, the Byzantine commander chose to side with Orhan and their forces joined together. Orhan's armies kept deprecating the west and northern coastlines around the sea of Marmara and Bosporus. The Byzantine Emperor Andronicus III would not yield without a fight and was determined to stop Orhan in his advances and regain some of the lost lands.

The Battle of Pelekanon in 1329 was the first time the Byzantine armies met the Ottoman forces. The clash ended with a shattering defeat for the attacking Byzantines, although their numbers were larger and they possessed more experience from battle than the Ottomans.

Contemporaneous sources explain the crushing win with the Byzantine spirit already being broken by the empire's civil struggles while the confidence of the arising Turks made them fight with more vigor and conviction.

The Battle of Pelekanon marks a significant turning point in the history of the region. The Byzantine Empire never again tried to reclaim the lost territories on the Asian side of Bosphorus and more or less left Nicea and Nicomedia to be besieged and later incorporated into Orhan's beylik. By 1340 Orhan had also annexed the beylik of Karasi which was the first time he had chosen to march towards Turkish neighbors. He did so because the chief had passed away and the two sons of the chief were currently warring against each other to claim the title. Many soldiers and civilians had already died when Orhan decided to intervene for the sake of peace. One of the brothers was killed and the other captured and Orhan now ruled four provinces. Most of the cities within the beylik were peaceful and many former Christians quickly embraced Islam without coercion. The region needed to be stabilized in order to build the strong state apparatus as the foundation of an empire. Orhan had put all of Bithynia and the northwestern corner of Anatolia under his control without much resistance from the population.

After his brother's death in the early 1330s, Orhan had help of his two eldest sons Suleyman and Murad in expanding the emirate. In 1341, the Byzantine Emperor Andronicus III died and left an 8-year-old successor on the throne. The following civil war created a golden opportunity for the Ottomans to march further into the declining empire and inflict some irreparable damage. The fall of the empire would take another hundred years of power struggles, but there was no way to restore it to its former glory. A six-year-long civil war broke out on the Balkans, and since peace reigned in Orhan's lands, he chose to head further west attempting to create an Ottoman road to Europe.

The Byzantine Grand Domestic John VI Kantakouzenos, who was also the young emperor's custodian and acting as regent, recognized Orhan's potential and formed an alliance with the Ottoman chief. He gave his daughter Theodora in marriage and then used Orhan's help to usurp the throne and become Emperor of Byzantine in 1347. In exchange, Orhan gained the right to plunder Thrace and he started raiding the area regularly through the peninsula of Gallipoli. His oldest son Suleyman took charge of the plundering as Orhan himself was growing older and weaker. The raiding was fruitful and the Ottomans gained both land and riches, while the Byzantine emperor let them. This attracted thousands of uprooted Turkmen to head west and join in Suleyman's expeditions. The emperor of Byzantine had not intended for the Ottomans to actually take possession of Thrace, but that was, of course, inevitable. After Suleyman made Gallipoli into a permanent base for his raiding parties across present-day Bulgaria it didn't take long until John VI was more or less forced to sign over the lands to Orhan's family, a very prestigious win. Constantinople was now surrounded by Ottoman territory, albeit still under Byzantine rule.

It was by the end of Orhan's life that his oldest son died in an accident, which took a toll on Orhan's spirit. He withdrew from power and his last years were spent living quietly in Bursa. Before he died, his youngest son whom he had with Theodora, Sehzade Halil, was kidnapped by pirates along the Aegean coast. It is unclear if they knew who they were kidnapping but when realizing, they took refuge in a Byzantine fortress in Phocaea. After finding this out, Orhan appealed to the co-emperor Andronikos IV to rescue his son and promised in return to call off debts and withdraw his support for the Kantakouzenos family. Andronikus agreed and laid siege to Phocaea, which ended in Orhan paying 30,000 ducats as a ransom for his son. Halil was released in 1359 and it was decided he would marry another Byzantine princess to strengthen the ties between the two dynasties. The imperial family hoped to see Halil as the rightful heir to the beylik since the older brother Suleyman had died.

Their expectations would soon turn into disappointment when Murad was appointed successor to the throne and not the teenager born by Theodora. Murad took over the title and started ruling the emirate after Orhan's death. Orhan was the longest living and ruling chief of all the Ottoman leaders and died in 1362 at the age of 80. Shortly after Orhan's death Murad even had his half-brother executed accused of challenging Murad for the throne. The 16-year-old had already gotten married and produced two young boys who were now left fatherless. This was perhaps the start of brotherly distrust between the heirs of the Ottoman empire. The first sultans had neglected to formulate an order of succession and it was not until a hundred years later they constituted laws. Hence the throne was up for grabs by any of the sons when a sultan died, although usually some sort of pre-agreement had been made between the generations. Out of sight from the dead father the avaricious sons almost made it a habit to challenge each other for the throne. After Murad had executed his little brother, many more were to follow his example.

Murad was now the undisputed ruler of Osman's beylik, and the first major conquest attributed to him was that of Adrianople, the third most important city of the Byzantine Empire. As more sources have been found in later year,s it is now debated when the conquest really took place, and even who actually conquered Adrianople. It has been the general consensus that Murad laid siege to the city in either 1361 or 1362, but newer research holds 1367 or 1371 as more likely. There's also a possibility that it was not Ottoman Turks who conquered the city but some other group of the roaming ghazi warriors. It is also debated regarding when Murad moved his capital from Bursa to Adrianople, the general opinion being that Murad captured the city in 1362, renamed it Erdine and made it the new capital in 1363. Other sources say that the city still belonged to Byzantium by 1366 and was conquered in the 1370s by Murad's second lieutenant Lala Sahin Pasa, who also administered the city for some time after. The same source claims that Murad himself actually didn't enter Erdine until 1377, when the Byzantine Emperor Andronikos IV needed his help in a civil war. Erdine was the military center of the Ottomans in the Balkans, but Bursa was considered the capital until the conquest of Constantinople and the rebuilding of it into a new capital.

Murad I

Murad transformed the beylik into a sultanate in 1383 and declared himself sultan. His right hand, the second lieutenant Lala Sahin Pasa, became the governor of the western province Rumeli while Murad remained in control over Anatolia. At this point, he also instituted an army, referred to as Janissaries, and a recruiting system called Devshirme. This was possible thanks to the reorganization of the military, a seed which was planted by his uncle Alaeddin some 50 years earlier. The Janissaries were an elite infantry loyal only to the sultan. Their mission was to protect only him and in battles they were always the closest to him, forming a human shield. Originally they consisted of non-Muslim slaves, mainly Christian boys from Byzantium. Jewish boys were not taken as soldiers and Muslims could not, by law, be enslaved. Murad had instituted a tax of one fifth on all the slaves taken in war, and the idea of only taking boys fit for fighting was called Devshirme, or blood tax. The slaves went through a very strict training, first learning to speak Turkish and practicing Ottoman traditions by living with a family chosen by the sultan. The boys also were forcibly converted to Islam, forbidden from wearing a beard and lived under monastic circumstances in celibacy. They were overseen by eunuchs and trained in special schools, enhancing their personal abilities. The main difference between these and other slaves was that they were being paid for their services. This served as a motivator and kept the soldiers loyal.

The Janissaries were at first a hated institution by the subjugated Christian minorities. Rather than having their sons taken away, it happened that the parents disfigured their children so as to make them weak and unsuitable for Devshirme. But the status of the Janissaries grew. They became men of high learning and an ascetic nature, favored by the sultan. As they grew in numbers, they also became very influential in the capital and their skills as warriors made them feared far beyond the borders of the empire. The Janissary corps was the first of its kind and a groundbreaking contributor to the success of Ottoman warfare. At the time of Murad's reign, they were fewer and less respected than what they would become at a later stage, though they were quite significant for the conquering of the Balkans.

Not just the conquest of Erdine but also many other historical details in Murad's life is widely debated by historians today. Though it is difficult to prove the consecutive order of certain events in the fast-growing sultanate, it is certain that his reign was a bloody and expansive period, followed by more of the same by his successor. During the 1370s his second lieutenant and trusted friend Lala Sahin Pasa crushed the Serbian armies in the battle of Maritsa though they were heavily outnumbered. Using superior strategies and a surprise night-time attack, the Serbs were close to being annihilated and their king killed in the campaign. Little remained of the Serbian Empire and the lands were easily taken over by the Ottomans. They then aimed north and started raiding Bulgaria's southern borders. The Bulgarian king more or less acquiesced to vassalage, something that the Serbians, Macedonians and some of the Greek rulers already had done, though the Ottomans kept deprecating their borders. After capturing both Sofia and Nis by the year 1386, Murad was forced to return to Anatolia to settle rising troubles in the home province. In his wake, the bitter rulers of the Balkans formed an alliance and went to war against the Ottoman forces. Two of the Bulgarian princes, along with the Serbian Prince Lazar and more allies from Kosovo, Macedonia and Bosnia won their first battle against the Ottomans and took back Nis in 1388. Murad quickly responded by launching new campaigns in his recently conquered territories which resulted in the Battle of Kosovo in 1389.

The Battle of Kosovo was the apogee of Murad's fighting in the Balkans and turned into a bloodbath with significant losses on both sides. It was in the midst of summer, June 1389, that the two foes met slightly north of modern-day Pristina in the open fields of Kosovo. Records of the actual battle itself are scarce, but historians have managed to reconstruct a likely chain of events thanks to written down strategies, numbers, and information from other, similar battles.

The Serbian and Turkish sources often contradict each other, and what modern history books retell about the events are based on the general assumption and what most likely is true. Murad arrived backed up by a neighboring beylik from Anatolia, and together they had mustered an army of nearly 40,000 men. The Serbian Prince Lazar had, together with allies from Kosovo and Bosnia, an army the size of 30,000 men. As some sources claim, it is also likely that the Knight Hospitaller from Croatia fought on the Serbian side, and anachronistic records state that the Serbian army was larger than Murad's. Murad had both his sons with him, Bayezid and Yakub, commanding one wing each.

Initially, it looked like the Serbs would prevail and the Ottoman forces conceded heavy losses during the first hours. However, in a frenzy of bloodthirst and revenge, Bayezid led his wing in a counterattack towards the knights, whose heavy armor became a hindrance for their retreat. Bayezid slaughtered a great number of the Serbian soldiers, and Prince Lazar's allied Vuc Brankovic from Kosovo fled the field trying to rescue as many men as possible. At this point, Prince Lazar had probably been captured or killed in the heat of the battle. At the end, there was not much left of either army, the Serbian Prince Lazar had died, and Sultan Murad had been killed. There are three common stories about how and when he was killed - either in battle by Lazar, by one of the 12 Serbian lords who broke through Ottoman lines, or by an assassin in his own tent after the battle was won. No matter which story is true, it resulted in the oldest son Bayezid strangling his brother Yakud on the spot, so as to be the sole heir to the throne. Hence he pursued in his father's footsteps, as his father had also started his reign by killing his brother.

After the war, the Serbs didn't have enough troops left to defend their territory. Bayezid sent for more armies from the east and within a short period of time, most of the principalities became Ottoman vassals.

Murad I had died at the age of 62, and his organs were buried in the battlefield in Kosovo, while his body was transported and buried in Bursa. His legacy included a lot more than just new lands, and apart from his military reorganization, he also created the council of ministers called Divan, over which the grand vizier presided. This became the ruling political entity in the sultanate. He united the smaller emirates into two larger provinces, Rumeli and Anatolia, each ruled by a strong provincial vizier. The military court was also Murad's doing, and he introduced a legal system. At the same time, he expanded the sultanate in Anatolia but even more to the west of the Bosphorus, to include most of the Balkans and Bulgaria. When he died he left the sultanate ready to rule for his son Bayezid.

Bayezid I

It would seem as if much of the hard work already had been done by the time Bayezid came to power in the Ottoman Sultanate. The difficult first century of expanding and stabilizing the new state had passed, and many of the foundational institutions been formed by Murad and Orhan. The military and government had been efficiently organized and now Bayezid needed to emulate his predecessors. After the battle of Kosovo and the losses of thousands of soldiers, as well his father, Bayezid continued to raid the Balkans. He maintained the borders to the south and coerced the Albanian, Macedonian and Serbian princes into vassalage. By marrying the daughter of the deceased Prince Lazar, he established a new bond with her brother, the soon-to-be-despot Stefan Lazarevic. After endorsing Stefan he left him in charge of the Balkan territories and returned to Anatolia to settle unrest in his homelands.

In 1390 he managed to conquer six different beyliks to the north and east of his territory before the winter fell, the first time an Ottoman ruler had decided to annex Turkish lands. It was partially because of his skills as a warrior and because of his fiery temper he gained the nickname Yildirim, lightning bolt.

The annexation of the Anatolian lands didn't come without consequences. Both Turkmen loyal to the Ottoman dynasty and outside of their territories expressed dissatisfaction and Bayezid sought peace with the larger emirate Karaman in 1391. He had been using fatwas, declared by Islamic scholars, to justify the expansion into Muslim territories, but this was as far as he would come in Anatolia.

After the peace was negotiated, he turned north with some success but was in the end forced to return west where rumors of an uprising circulated. It was the Hungarian King Sigismund who had cajoled Bulgaria's Ivan Shishman, the king of one of the vassal states, and the Wallachian ruler Mircea the Old, into an anti-Ottoman coalition. News of the alliance reached Bayezid who, true to his nickname, acted swiftly and ruthlessly. The Bulgarian vassal took most of the hit from Bayezid, who recaptured the lands and beheaded Shishman while leaving the distant Hungarian King and Wallachia to be dealt with later. Bayezid had to hurry south to settle disputes and bickering between the Greek lords under his rule.

After a successful meeting in Serre in 1394, he had reinstated his power over his vassal states, and by a series of events also managed to extend his vassalage to include the city of Athens. The same year he also laid siege to the Byzantine capital Constantinople, which called for help from the Hungarian Kingdom. The siege lasted for eight years, and during most of it, Bayezid had to keep fighting on other frontiers of his sultanate.

One of the last major crusades was launched in 1396 by Pope Boniface IX. The timing was perfect for the European kingdoms to unite and form a strong threat to the Turks. The 100-year war between France and England was in a state of truce and King Richard II had just married Princess Isabella of France. Both the Brits and the Franks sent forces to join in the crusade, and so did Hungary, Bulgaria, Venice, Genoa, Croatia, Wallachia, the Holy Roman Empire and the Knights Hospitaller. It is estimated that both the Crusader forces and the Ottoman armies consisted of somewhere between 15,000–20 000 men each, but the sources all tell different stories. Some tell of armies the size of hundreds of thousands of men, and some say that the enemy force was at least twice the size of their own army. The details of the battle are questionable since historians on both sides wrote to please and aggrandize their own leaders. In fact, the actual participation of English soldiers has not been proven, and records of such an army being sent abroad at the time don't exist. Genoa and Venice were probably also more engaged in other areas under their rule, although they surely sent a smaller convoy to backup the crusaders. On the Ottoman side, numbers vary just as much, but the coalition of Serbs and Turkmen could probably be numbered to less than 20,000.

On arriving at Nicopolis on the river Danube, the crusaders laid siege to the Ottoman-controlled city. Their first mistake was not to bring any siege armaments, making any attempt to conquer the city with force futile. The crusader generals changed tactics and decided to block the exits and the port of the city with the intention of starving the citizens, and in such a way make them surrender. During the siege, there wasn't therefore much for the soldiers to do but to play games, drink wine and wait for Nicopolis to give in. When rumors of the approaching Ottoman armies reached Nicopolis the French marshal, Boucicaut threatened to cut off the ears of anyone talking about the Turkmen. He thought the rumors of approaching soldiers would deflate the morals of the troops. Hence, little did they expect that a lightning bolt was rapidly heading their way from Constantinople. When Bayezid and his Serbian ally Lazarevic were six hours away from the camp the crusaders were in the midst of a drunken dinner celebration. In stress and panic, they started executing some 1000 prisoners they had taken in the town of Rachowa, which would later add to the fury of Bayezid.

The French, Hungarian and Wallachian rulers drew a battle plan in all haste, but they couldn't agree on the details. Sending the foot soldiers in first would be an insult to the great French knights having to follow in the lead of peasants, and therefore they had to go first into battle. Sigismund argued that the Turkish vanguard was not worthy of the French knights and that his infantry should take the lead. In the end, the French lords had their will and a couple of hours later the knights rode out to face the Turkish forces. Thanks to a hill hiding the full strength of the Ottoman army, the knights once again underestimated its foes and rode straight into annihilation.

After that initial clash, the rest of the French troops threw themselves to the ground, pleading for their lives. Bayezid knew the value of French nobility, so he took them hostage and later set them free for large ransoms. King Sigismund and the Master of the Hospitallers were the only leaders able to flee, and Sigismund later accused the French of hubris and for putting pride ahead of tactics. The rest of the noblemen were taken prisoners and many of the surviving soldiers were executed as retribution of the 1,000 murdered civilians from Rachowa. After the carnage, the hostages were marched in chains all the way to Gallipoli, where they were kept in prison for two months while waiting for the news to reach Central Europe. The fleeing Sigismund had failed to negotiate the ransom for his allies since Bayezid knew the Hungarian assets were depleted. It took over a year and a half before the last generals and noblemen returned to their homes, and many of them had already died from battle wounds or poor conditions while captured.

While all this took place, Bayezid continued his siege of Constantinople half-heartedly but gave up after striking a compromise with the Emperor Manuel II. It was agreed that Bayezid should have veto in approving and confirming all the future Byzantine emperors. Bayezid left Constantinople, never to return west of Bosphorus again. There was unrest in his annexed territories in Anatolia where the newly arrived Central Asian conqueror Timur was in the midst of establishing a new Mongolian Empire. With Bayezid occupied the Balkans, Timur had managed to form a coalition of the Ottoman vassal states against their sultan. Bayezid rushed to meet him with a strong 85,000 man army consisting of Turks, Serbs, Albanians, Tartars, ghazis and janissaries and even Christians. However, the 140,000 Mongol-Turkish cavalry troops accompanied by 32 war elephants must have put some fear in the defending Ottoman allies.

Heavily outnumbered and tired from the long march, the battle couldn't have started any worse for Bayezid's armies. Two of his allied forces switched sides during the battle, and when a defeat became inevitable the Serbian troops escaped with the Ottoman Treasury and one of Bayezid's sons. Stefan Lazarevic urged Bayezid to flee, but Bayezid kept his position and continued fighting. After the battle had been lost, Bayezid was captured by the Timurids and died in prison a couple of months later. Some historians claim he was being abused while taken hostage and driven to suicide, while others claim the opposite. One of his sons, Mustafa Celebi, was also captured with him but was held in Samarkand until Timur's death in 1405.

Bayezid's death had devastating consequences for the Ottoman Sultanate. Except for Mustafa who was in prison, Bayezid had four more sons, all hungry to rule the sultanate. The youngest, Mehmed Celebi, was confirmed as a sultan by Timur, but his brothers refused to acknowledge his authority. The result would be a civil war known as the Ottoman Interregnum, which lasted for over a decade. During the years of fighting, Mustafa stayed hidden from his brothers, plotting to make his move for when they had defeated each other.

Timur had no intentions of conquering or ruling Anatolia, and after he had won the Battle of Ankara he withdrew from the territory, satisfied with leaving the beyliks divided. The Ottoman family got to keep their lands around Bursa, and no one had made any claim to their acquisitions in the Balkans. The commotion gave a window opportunity for Thessaloniki, Kosovo, and Macedonia to break free from the vassalage, but the other states remained under Ottoman rule, awaiting the next sultan. The only significant losses of the dynasty after the war were pride and the trust of their Muslim neighbors whom they had annexed and ruled.

If Bayezid had not died in prison, the damage done to his sultanate by Timur would have been easy to repair. However, Bayezid had had many sons, and there was no set order of succession within the dynasty. The eldest son had died before the Battle of Ankara, and the next in age, Mustafa, was in prison in Samarkand. Four more sons thus had potential claims to the throne, although the youngest, Mehmed, had been recognized as the new sultan by Timur before he left. Naturally, the three others opposed this appointment of their little brother, and it didn't take long before war was raging between the four of them. The ensuing civil war lasted for 11 violent years.

The sources describing what led up to and finally caused the Interregnum reveal many different storylines about Bayezid and all his sons. He himself is said to have been tortured and compelled to commit suicide in the care of Timur, while one of his wives too was abused. It is said that Mustafa was not taken captive, but mysteriously vanished during the battle and it is also said that Isa and Musa escaped by themselves, while Suleyman and Mehmed were taken care of by Bayezid's allies. Other sources tell of both Musa and Mustafa being captured, with Musa being released after Mehmed's negotiations with Timur and Mustafa when Timur himself died. The order of the brother's ages is also not fully clear, nor is how they were allied with each other during the Interregnum. The general assessment is that three of the brothers each occupied different territories in the former United Ottoman Sultanate. The oldest, Suleyman, moved to the Balkans and established his capital in Erdine. Constantinople was still the capital of the Byzantine Empire, but the lands around it were occupied by Isa, one of the middle brothers. The youngest, Mehmed, took possession of the eastern parts and tried to strike a deal to share the Anatolian territories with Isa, who promptly refused and instead signed a treaty of friendship with the Byzantine emperor. The fourth brother Musa was probably in captivity for one year until Mehmed negotiated his release. Musa then aimed for Bursa, with the aid of Mehmed, and therefore contested the territories already ruled by Isa. It was not hard for Isa to defeat Musa in one of the earliest battles of the civil war, and Musa fled to Germiyanid in Mehmed's kingdom.

Next in line stood Mehmed, with a large army from eastern Anatolia. Mehmed and Isa met in the Battle of Ulubad in 1403. The battle ended in victory for Mehmed, who proclaimed himself King of Anatolia and again united the province under one rule. Isa fled to his allies in Constantinople and later moved even further west to form a coalition with his brother Suleyman. Suleyman took the opportunity to back Isa up and sent him back to Anatolia with a large army. To no avail, Mehmed won once again, and the subsequent fate of Isa is still disputed. Some say he went into hiding, while others say he was spotted in a Turkish bath and killed by Mehmed's agents in 1406. This is usually the year considered as the year of his death.

The belligerent state between the brothers was prodded on by the surrounding entities. Other emirs, the roaming ghazis, the Byzantine Empire, the Italian city-states, and the influential upper class of Bursa all had an interest in keeping the conflict going and weakening the political, economical and geographical stability in the territories. Mehmed gained some support because he was the youngest and hence considered less dangerous than his brothers.

Suleyman, who had been sitting comfortably on his throne in Erdine, together with his Grand Vizier Candali Ali Pashar and the support of Byzantine ruler John VII Palaiologos, started worrying about his brother's accomplishments in Anatolia and decided to take action. He marched on Bursa as well as Ankara and managed to conquer them both. While Suleyman was resting and regrouping in Bursa, Mehmed and Musa formed an alliance. By sending Musa through Wallachia to Suleyman's western borders, the eldest brother suddenly had a war on two fronts on his hands. The eldest brother was overwhelmed and decided to withdraw to fight for his territories in Rumeli. With the support of both Byzantium and also the Serb Stefan Lazarevic, he defended Rumeli and took to ruling his province from Erdine without further involvements in Anatolia.

Suleyman was not an able king though and took no interest in state affairs. After his grand vizier passed away, Rumeli fell into neglect and Suleyman's flamboyant lifestyle caused him to lose support among his allies and subordinates. When the bellicose Musa came for Erdine,

Suleyman had very few supporters left and the capital was easily conquered by the younger brother. Trying to escape to Byzantine lands, Suleyman was killed in 1411.

At this point, Musa and Mehmed co-ruled the Ottoman provinces between them, as had been done during the reign of Murad I. Even so, the brothers had no natural affinity for each other. Musa considered himself the sultan of Rumeli, while Mehmed considered him his vassal. This inevitably caused complications and the peace didn't last long. Musa had laid siege to Constantinople as a retribution for the Byzantine's support of Suleyman, and with the stirring conflict between the two remaining brothers, the emperor turned to Mehmed for help. Mehmed betrayed his brother and formed an alliance with Emperor Manuel II Palaiologos.

Meanwhile, Musa had support from many of his vassal states, along with Stefan Lazarevic, and the initial battles ended in Musa's favor. It wasn't until Lazarevic switched sides and Mehmed gained support from more Turkish emirs that Musa finally could be defeated and killed in the Battle of Camurlu in 1413. This left Mehmed as the sole survivor of the fighting brothers, and he could crown himself Sultan Mehmed I of both Anatolia and Rumeli. That put an end to the Ottoman Interregnum.

Mehmed I

After the fighting was over, Mustafa, the brother in hiding, decided to emerge and play his part in the Ottoman history. Backed up by the Byzantine emperor, whose ever-changing sympathies now had turned against Sultan Mehmed, together with the old Wallachian vassal Mircea, he demanded Mehmed cede half the sultanate to him. Mehmed denied the request and defeated Mustafa quite easily in battle. Mustafa took refuge in Thessaloniki and the Byzantine emperor exiled him by request from Mehmed.

As fate had it, Mehmed's problems didn't end with the death and exile of all his brothers. The ever-conspiring Manuel II Palaiologos cajoled Mehmed's nephew to make a move against his uncle, but the plot was uncovered and the nephew was blinded for his betrayal.

After a few other uprisings and the constant hard work of keeping all his subordinates united peacefully, Mehmed died in 1421, after eight years as a sultan. By this time, it was evident that the empire had become too big for one ruler to govern, and that the threats arising on both frontiers would continue to destabilize the whole sultanate. The empire would need another reorganization to grow further, but the following sultan, Mehmed's son Murad, also was fully occupied with battles for most of his reign. Since Murad was only 16 when he ascended the throne, his uncle thought he would be an easy target to challenge. The Byzantine emperor released Mustafa from his exile under the pretense that he was the rightful heir to the throne. With the emperor's help, Mustafa also managed to conquer Rumeli and become sultan of the province, if only for a couple of years.

Though Murad was young, he was a capable soldier and general, trusted by his troops and allies. After being defeated in battle, Mustafa fled back and took refuge in Gallipoli, with Murat close behind. The sultan laid siege to the city, captured Mustafa, and had him hanged, an undignified way to be executed in the Ottoman tradition but justified by the disloyalty of Mustafa. The hanging was an exceptional act during Murad II's rule since he took great pride in his dynasty's chivalric forefathers. He studied old epic tales of noble caliphs and warriors, always acting in modesty and piety with a strong sense of justice. Murad traced his heritage back to the ghazi kings and modeled his own image on it. This was done to muster support for the reestablishment of a strong, unified empire with aims to expand in the name of Islam.

Murad II

Murad II became known as the Ghazi Sultan and was seen as not only defending Islam against the Christians but also as a defender of other, less powerful Muslim beys. Thus he gained support from Muslims both far and near. He turned his armies towards Venice, the Karamids, Serbia and finally Hungary – all of which he fought successfully. He renounced the throne to his 12-year-old son in 1444, tired of a life of fighting and pleased with his achievements.

The renunciation was, however, seen as a golden opportunity for the Hungarian Empire, together with Venice and the Holy Roman Empire, to again venture into Ottoman lands and reclaim the Balkans. The young Sultan Mehmed II realized his age and inexperience would be a disadvantage and called back his father to lead his armies. Murad II accepted unwillingly, more or less coerced, and took to fighting the Battle of Varna in the same year. Both armies suffered great casualties, and due to the extreme losses, Murad didn't realize he had won until some days after the battle. He continued his reign for seven more years, during which he won the Second Battle of Kosovo, secured the Balkan borders, fought and defeated Timur's son Shah Rokh, and also conquered the Karamanids. His last efforts as a ruler stabilized the region and also deterred the Christian armies from coming to any potential aid for Constantinople when his son would implement one of history's most famous and consequential sieges.

Mehmed II

The Fall of Constantinople

From the moment Mehmed finally succeeded to the Ottoman throne for good in 1451, he took no chance to be vulnerable. For instance, when Murad's widow arrived to congratulate him on his succession, Mehmed received her warmly, but when she returned to her harem she found that her infant son had been drowned in the bath.

That same year, Mehmed moved to secure his borders. He renewed his treaty with Brankovic, leader of Serbia, and created a three-year treaty with Hunyadi, regent of Hungary. He also confirmed a treaty with Venice that his father had made in 1446. All of this would also help further his designs on Constantinople, which the Ottomans had ample reason for coveting. Control of the Bosporus would be extremely advantageous, and control of the Byzantine territory would bring large financial benefits in the form of taxation to the Ottomans. The Ottomans even described the city as their "red apple", an expression for their ultimate aspiration.

Mehmed's attack would be the 13th attempt at conquest against Constantinople, and he intended to do it right. In 1451, he began to build a fortress on the Bosporus at the place where the channel was at its narrowest, opposite Sultan Bayezid's Anadolu Hisar castle. Between the two castles, the Ottomans now had complete control of the Bosporus, which provided them with an ideal base from which to attack Constantinople from the northeast. Emperor Constantine sent embassies to speak with the Ottomans, but they were executed on the spot. Every passing ship was inspected, and when one Venetian ship disobeyed, everyone was killed.

In 1453, Mehmed told his advisors that his empire was not safe as long as Constantinople remained in Christian hands. He began to gather an army in Thrace, and every Ottoman regiment, along with hordes of mercenaries, were recruited; all in all, there were 80,000 regular troops and 20,000 *bashi-bazouks* ("others"), though some historians estimate there were as many as 160,000 troops. Furthermore, the year before, a German engineer called Urban had offered to build the Ottomans a cannon that would blast any walls, so the Ottomans paid for and received the weapon three months later. They then demanded one twice the size and received it in January 1453. It was 27 feet long and 8 inches thick, with a muzzle that was 2.5 feet across, making it capable of shooting a ball some 1,300 pounds a distance of over a mile. 200 men helped the cannon make its journey south to the outside of Constantinople's walls, and their manpower was also needed for smoothing out the road and reinforcing bridges.

Fausto Zorano's painting, *Mehmet II conquering Constantinople*

Orthodox Easter 1453 was on the 1st of April, and on April 5th, Mehmed pitched a tent and sent a message to Constantine - one required under Islamic law - offering to spare all subjects in return for immediate surrender. He received no reply, so the cannon opened fire the next day. The people of Constantinople were not surprised, as they had worked in previous months on their city's defenses, but they were sorely lacking in resources. At their disposal, they had only eight Venetian vessels, five Genoese, and one vessel each from Ancona, Catalonia, and Provence. From the Byzantine Empire's own navy, there were only 10 vessels, meaning they only had 26 ships total. In terms of manpower, there were only 4,983 able-bodied Greeks and 2,000 foreigners, much too few to stand guard along 14 miles of wall, let alone face the 100,000 strong Ottoman army.

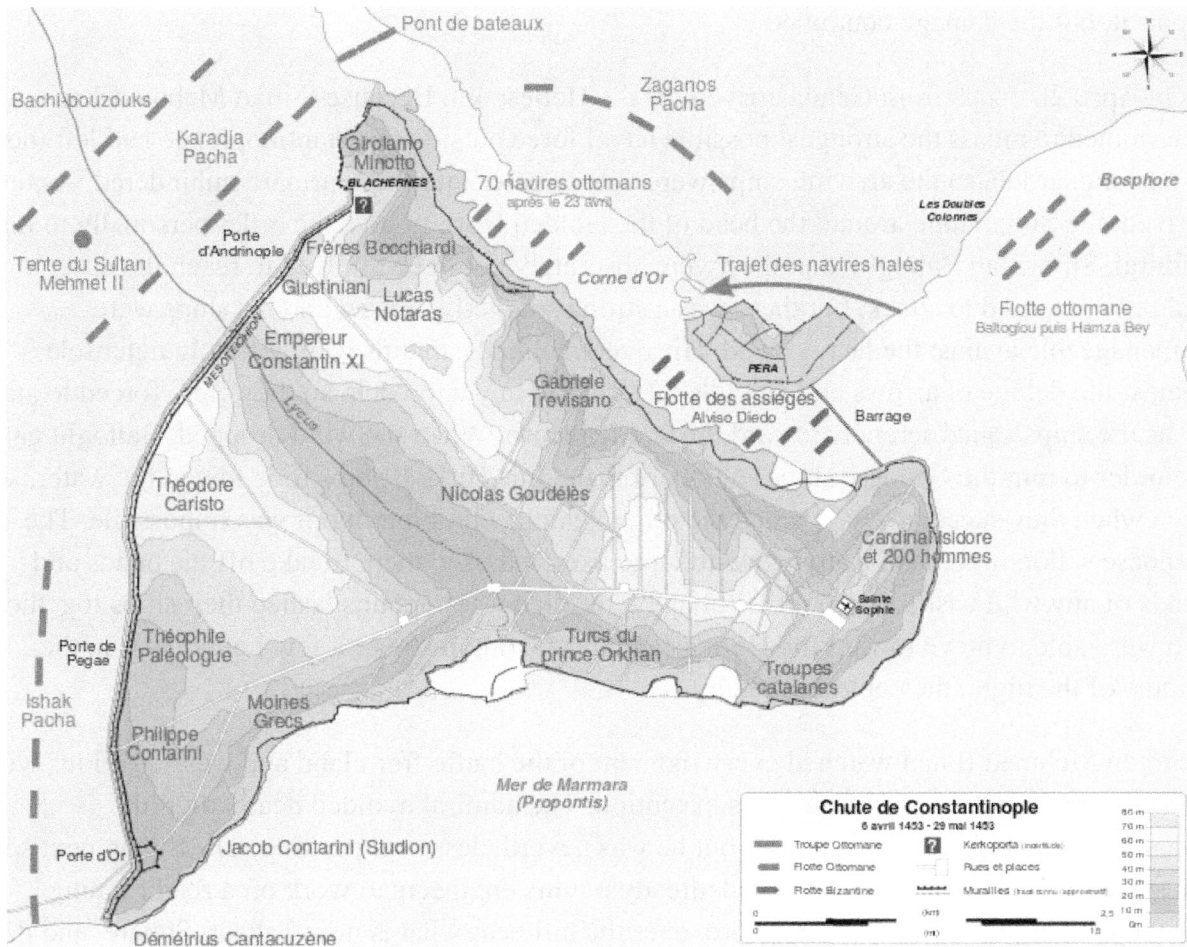

The siege lines, with the Ottomans in green and the Byzantines in red.

Nonetheless, all the defenders were in their places when the firing started. The emperor and Giovanni Giustiniani, the Genoese captain, were in command of the most vulnerable section, the area of the wall that crossed the valley of the little river Lycus about a mile from the northern end. The sea walls were less thoroughly manned than the land walls, but their garrisons also served as lookouts, reporting on the movements of the Turkish ships.

Despite these defenses, the Sultan was subjecting the land walls to a bombardment unprecedented in the history of siege warfare. By the evening of that first day, Mehmed II and the Ottoman troops had pulverized a section near the Charisius Gate, after which his soldiers tried to smash their way through, but it held. They went back to their camp at nightfall, and the Byzantines rebuilt it overnight.

Mehmed decided to hold his fire until he could bring reinforcements, and the bombardment resumed on April 11, continuing 48 more days uninterrupted. The larger cannon could only be fired once every two or three hours, but the damage was enormous, and within a week, the outer wall across the Lycus had collapsed in several places. The Byzantines worked ceaselessly to repair it, but the damage continued.

On April 20, ships from Genoa arrived off the Hellespont. Because Sultan Mehmed was determined to amass the strongest possible naval force outside Constantinople, he had left those straits unguarded, so the arriving ships were able to enter into the Marmara unhindered. As they arrived, the Sultan rode around the head of the Golden Horn to give the order personally to his admiral, Süleyman Baltoglu, that they were absolutely not to be allowed to reach the city. Baltoglu prepared to attack, but there was a strong southerly breeze, and his ships were unmanageable against the heavy swell. His overwhelmed captains were virtually defenseless against the deluge of arrows and javelins that greeted any approach, so they were forced to stand by as the ships sailed serenely toward the Golden Horn. When the wind dropped, Baltoglu gave the order to ram the Genoese ships and board them, but Turkish ships rode low in the water, so even when they successfully rammed the other vehicle, climbing into it was impossible. The Genoese sailors were also equipped with large axes and used them to take off the hands and heads of any who wished to enter. Ultimately, the Genoese captains lashed their ships together and were able to move toward the Horn as a giant floating fortress; a few hours later, in the middle of the night, they entered the city.

Sultan Mehmed II had watched every moment of the battle from land and was so furious with its outcome that he ordered Baltoglu's execution. The admiral avoided death after his subordinates testified to his courage, but he was nevertheless sent packing. The Sultan next set his sights on the Golden Horn. He had already put his engineers to work on a road running behind Galata, from the Marmara shore, over the hill near what is now Taksim Square, and down into the Horn itself. The engineers and laborers had cast iron wheels and metal tracks, and the carpenters were hard at work building wooden cradles that could hold the keels of moderate-sized vessels. It was a remarkable undertaking, and on Sunday, April 22, the Genoese colony in Galata watched with astonishment as 70 Turkish ships were hauled in by teams of oxen over the 200 foot hill and lowered into the Horn.

Fausto Zorano's painting, *Mehmed II at the siege of Constantinople*. This one depicts Ottoman troops transporting their fleet overland to the Golden Horn.

The Byzantines could not believe what was happening, and they no longer had a secure harbor, which also meant that they now had three and a half more miles of sea wall to defend, including the section breached by the Crusaders in 1204. Byzantine attempts to attack the Ottoman navy failed, while initial frontal assaults by the Ottomans also failed. Near the end of April, the defenders ostentatiously beheaded hundreds of Ottomans atop the walls as a sign for the invading army, but they would not be deterred. A Venetian in Constantinople at the time wrote in his diary, "They found the Turks coming right up under the walls and seeking battle, particularly the Janissaries...and when one or two of them were killed, at once more Turks came and took away the dead ones...without caring how near they came to the city walls. Our men shot at them with guns and crossbows, aiming at the Turk who was carrying away his dead countryman, and both of them would fall to the ground dead, and then there came other Turks and took them away, none fearing death, but being willing to let ten of themselves be killed rather than suffer the shame of leaving a single Turkish corpse by the walls."

Medieval depictions of the siege.

By the beginning of May, Constantine knew they would not hold out much longer; they were running out of food, and his troops were taking more and more time off of defending the city in order to find food for their families. His last faint hope was a promised Venetian relief mission, but he did not know whether it was actually on its way, what it held, or how big it was. He also did not know when it would come or how it would get through the Golden Horn, now that the Ottomans controlled it. He felt that his fate lay in the answers to these questions, so before midnight on May 3, a Venetian ship flying the Turkish flag and carrying a crew of 12 dressed in Turkish disguise slipped out.

Meanwhile, the Ottomans had given up on frontal attacks and were trying more traditional siege tactics, including tunneling under the walls to plant mines, not to mention the constant bombardment. The Byzantines dug counter-mines to locate and stop the Turkish tunnels, and they succeeded in destroying several Turkish attempts underground. Growing impatient, Mehmed sent a letter to Constantine on May 21 offering to let the people inside survive if they surrendered, and also letting Constantine head to the Peloponnese, which would be virtually the only remaining Byzantine possession. Constantine was willing to assent to the conditions, but not for the price of Constantinople, replying, "Giving you though the city depends neither on me nor on anyone else among its inhabitants; as we have all decided to die with our own free will and we shall not consider our lives."

However, two days later, when the secret Byzantine ship returned on May 23rd, its captain reported that they had combed the Aegean for weeks but had seen no trace of the promised Venetian relief expedition. Historian John Julius Norwich described the scene: "and so they had returned, knowing full well that they were unlikely to leave the city alive. Constantine thanked each one personally, his voice choked with tears."

There were also omens, or at least so they were interpreted by the Byzantines. On May 22 there was a lunar eclipse, and days later, as the holiest icon of the Virgin was being carried through the streets as an appeal to her intercession, it slipped from its platform. The morning after that, the city was shrouded in fog, which was unheard of at the end of May, and that same night the dome of St. Sophia was suffused with an unearthly red glow from the base to the summit, something that was even disturbing to Mehmed. His astrologers assured him that it was a sign that the building would soon be illuminated by the True Faith, and the Byzantines took it as a sign that the Spirit of God had deserted their city. Constantine's ministers begged him to leave the capital while there was still time and lead the empire from the Morea until he could recover the city. He fainted just as they spoke this suggestion; but when he recovered, he was determined as ever to not leave his people.

Meanwhile, the Sultan held a council of war on May 26, where he declared that the siege had continued long enough and that the time had come for a final assault. He announced that the following day would be filled with preparations, and the one after with rest and prayer, but they would begin the attack the morning of May 29, and they made no effort to conceal their plans from the Byzantines. They prepared for the next 36 hours without interruption, even lighting huge flares at night to help the soldiers with their labors. Then, at dawn on the 28th, they ceased. Mehmed set off on a day-long tour to inspect their preparations, finishing late in the evening and exhausted.

Inside the city, work on the city walls continued, but the people also gathered for one last collective appeal to God. Bells pealed, and the most sacred icons and precious relics were carried out to join a long spontaneous procession passing through the streets and along the whole length of the walls. They paused for special prayers where they expected the Ottoman artillery to concentrate particularly heavily. When the procession finished, the Emperor summoned his commanders and told his Greek subjects that there were four causes worth sacrificing one's life: his faith, his country, his family, and his sovereign. The Emperor told them they must be prepared to give their lives for all four tomorrow, and that he was prepared to sacrifice his own life. Next, he turned to the Italians and thanked them for their service. He told them that they and the Greeks were now one people, and that with God's help they would be victorious.

At dusk on the 28th, people from all over the city made their way to the Church of Holy

Wisdom - St. Sophia, the spiritual center of Byzantium - for the last service of vespers ever to be held in it. Virtually every man, woman and child who was not on duty that evening gathered in the Hagia Sophia to take the Eucharist and pray for deliverance. The Emperor arrived and asked for forgiveness for his sins from every bishop present, both Catholic and Orthodox, and then took communion. Later, after all the candles were out and the church was entirely dark, he spent time in prayer before returning home for a last farewell to his household. Around midnight, he rode the length of the land walls to assure himself that everything was ready.

Picture of the Hagia Sophia taken by Arild Vågen

Mehmed gave his signal at 1:30 in the morning on the 29th, and suddenly the silence was shattered. The Turks made their advance known with blasts of trumpets, hammering of drums, and bloodcurdling war cries. The Byzantine church bells pealed in response. The final battle had begun.

Mehmed knew that to succeed, he could not allow the Byzantines any rest. He first sent forward his mercenary soldiers, the *bashi-bazouks*, who were poorly armed and poorly trained, but they commanded some terrifying initial force. They flung themselves against the walls for two hours. Then, shortly before four in the morning, Mehmed called for the second wave of the attack, made by several regiments of Anatolian Turks who were significantly better trained and disciplined. They nearly forced entry, but the defenders - led by the Emperor himself - closed around them, killed many, and forced them back.

Mehmed determined that victory must be won not by the Anatolians but by his very own elite regiment of Janissaries. He next sent them into battle, offering the Byzantines no time to rest. The Ottoman troops advanced swiftly across the plain, hurling themselves at the stockades and hacking away at the supports. They also put up scaling-ladders to climb the walls. Instead of attempting to use them, however, these Janissaries had the opportunity to alternate with a fourth round of troops and rest while they waited for their next turn. The defenders, short-handed and exhausted, had no opportunity. They could not last much longer, but the walls still hadn't given way.

As if the defenders didn't have enough problems, they were struck with bad luck literally when shortly after dawn, Giovanni Giustiniani, the Genoese general who had been guarding the wall's weakest point with the emperor, was struck by lightning. In excruciating pain, he was carried to a Genoese ship in the harbor, but before the gate could be relocked, Mehmed saw the opening and sent in another wave of Janissaries. They forced the Greeks to retreat to the inner wall, and once they were caught between the two rows of walls, they were trapped and highly vulnerable. Many were slaughtered in place.

A short distance to the north, both sides could see a Turkish flag now flying over a tower. An hour before the slaughter between the fortifications, a group of Turkish mercenaries had found a small door, half-hidden at the foot of a tower, that was unlocked. It was a sally-port through which the Genoese had executed several effective raids on the Turkish camp, but now the *bashi-bazouks* mercenaries managed to force it open and make their way to the top of the tower. They hoisted their flag, left the door open for others to follow, and Turkish regiments poured in through all the open breaches. Emperor Constantine plunged right into the fray and was never seen again.

Theophilos Hatzimihail's depiction of fighting inside Constantinople. Constantine is depicted on the white horse.

By early morning, there were scarcely any living defenders. All the surviving Greeks had raced home to try to protect their families from the Ottomans' raping and pillaging, the Venetians were racing to the harbor, and the Genoese were trusting in the relative security of Galata. The Genoese found the Horn by and large quiet, while the Venetians had no trouble getting out of the harbor, into the Marmara, and out to the open sea.

As was often the custom in the Middle Ages, the Ottomans were ruthless in their ransacking. By noon, the streets were full of running blood, women and children were raped or stabbed, and churches, icons, and books were destroyed. The Empire's holiest icon, the virgin Hodegetria, was hacked into four pieces and destroyed. One writer said that blood flowed in the city "like rainwater in the gutters after a sudden storm", and that the bodies of both Turks and Byzantines floated in the sea "like melons along a canal".

The worst massacre was at the Hagia Sophia, where services were underway when the Turks began attempting to raze the church. The Christians shut the great bronze doors, but the Turks smashed their way in. The congregation was all either massacred on the spot or carted away to a Turkish prison camp. The priests tried to continue with mass until they were killed at the altar. Some Christians believe that a few of them managed to grab the patens and chalices and disappear in to the southern wall of the sanctuary, to wait until the city became a Christian city again, at which time they would resume the service right where it was left off.

Sultan Mehmed had promised his soldiers the traditional three days of looting, but by evening there was nothing left, and he called it off to little protest.

The historian and administrator Tursun Bey provided the sole detailed contemporary account of the siege in the Ottoman language:

> "Once the cloud of smoke of Greek fire and the soul of the Fire-worshipping Prince had descended over the castle 'as though a shadow,' the import was manifest: the devout Sultan of good fortune had, as it were, 'suspended the mountain' over this people of polytheism and destruction like the Lord God himself. Thus, both from within and without, [the shot of] the cannons and muskets and falconets and small arrows and arrows and crossbows spewed and flung out a profusion of drops of Pharaonic-seeming perspiration as in the rains of April - like a messenger of the prayers of the righteous - and a veritable precipitation and downpouring of calamities from the heavens as decreed by God. And, from the furthest reaches below to the top-most parts, and from the upper heights down to ground level, hand-to-hand combat and charging was being joined with a clashing and plunging of arms and hooked pikes and halberds in the breaches amidst the ruin wrought by the cannon.

> > On the outside the Champions of Islam and on the inside the wayward ones,

> > pike to pike in true combat, hand-to-hand;

> > Now advancing now feinting, guns [firing] and arms drawn,

> > Countless heads were severed from their trunks;

> > Expelling the smoke of the Greek fire, a veritable cloud

> > of sparks was rained on the Champions of Islam by the infidels;

> > Ramming into the castle walls, the trenches in this manner,

> > They set off the Greek fire, the enemies;

> > [In turn] they presented to the bastion their hooked pikes,

> > Drawn, they were knocking to the ground the engaged warriors,

> > As if struck in the deepest bedrock by the digging of a tunnel

It seemed that in places the castle had been pierced from below.

By the early part of the forenoon, the frenzy of the fiery tumult and the dust of strife had died away."

Fausto Zorano's painting, *Mehmed II, Entering to Constantinople*

George Sphrantzes, who was in Constantinople when it fell, wrote about the aftermath: "On the third day after the fall of our city, the Sultan celebrated his victory with a great, joyful triumph. He issued a proclamation: the citizens of all ages who had managed to escape detection were to leave their hiding places throughout the city and come out into the open, as they were remain free and no question would be asked. He further declared the restoration of houses and property to those who had abandoned our city before the siege, if they returned home, they would be treated according to their rank and religion, as if nothing had changed."

Perhaps most notably, after the siege was complete, Mehmed, Tursun Bey, the empire's chief ministers, imams, and the Janissaries rode to the Hagia Sophia. Mehmed picked up a handful of earth and sprinkled it over his turban as he entered as a gesture of humility, and as he approached the altar, he stopped one of the soldiers he saw hacking at the building's marble and informed him that looting did not apply to public buildings. He then commanded the senior imam to ascend to the altar and proclaim the name of Allah. With nothing more than the removal of Christian paraphernalia and their replacement with Muslim pulpits and minarets, the legendary Hagia Sophia became a mosque. The simplicity of the transformation was at once delicate and brutal, as evidenced by the way it's referred to among the Western world and the Turks. In the Christian world, the events are known as "the Fall", but for the Ottomans of history and the Turks of today, it was and remains "the Conquest."

For the Byzantine Empire, losing its beloved capital was the final nail in the coffin, and it didn't take long until the last refuge, Morea on the Peloponnese, was annexed and incorporated by Mehmed. The empire had managed to stay alive for over a thousand years, but after the belligerent rise of the Ottoman Empire, the past century had overwhelmed its rulers. Internal and external conflicts brought the empire to its knees, and the strong unification of the Turkish tribes proved to be a worthy successor of the empire. After the last emperor died without any heirs, all of his nephews were taken into palace service at Mehmed's court. As the two families had many intermarriages and alliances during the years, the boys quickly adapted to life under the Ottoman rule, were converted to Islam, and rose in the ranks of the sultanate. The youngest nephew later became the grand vizier to Mehmed's son and heir, Bayezid II.

The rise of the Ottoman Empire was possible thanks to the weakened state of their long-lasting foe, the Byzantine Empire, but also due to the power vacuum left by the Seljuk Empire. The empire was perfectly located, with more or less direct access to both Europe and Asia, yet still far away from the raiding Mongols. The conditions paved the way for determined leaders like Osman and his son Orhan to unite and stabilize the area, while at the same time expand the borders. Whether or not Osman was a Muslim, his successors were, giving incentive to battle and conquer the Christian Balkans, as well as annex other Muslim emirates. The dream of Osman became an important image through the centuries. Like the tree branches in the dream spread all over the world, so would Islam under the Ottoman rule.

Mehmed II

The origins of the Ottoman Empire and the dynasty that founded it are surrounded by legends and mysteries. The mythology around Osman I and his closest family created an image of the dynasty, legitimizing their heritage and right to rule. While some of it surely is true, a lot of it may also be sheer exaggeration. Even the true origin of the Ottoman dynasty is heavily debated by modern historians. The general opinion is that the Ottomans descended from the Kayi tribe, a branch of the Oghuz Turks. This was never mentioned in any records actually written by the time of Osman I's life, but firstly 200 years later, which makes it a highly contested statement. Contemporaneous writers would claim Osman to be a descendant of the Kayi tribe to aggrandize him.

The Kayi Tribe was powerful, prosperous and played an important role in the Caucasus region, both at the time before Osman was born and for hundreds of years to come. To link the Ottoman dynasty with such a tribe would work as an incentive to keep up good relations with the actual Kayi tribe, and also inflate the story about how the Ottoman dynasty descended from power and political influence. It would also support the inherited right of the Ottoman dynasty to rule the area. Though this may never be clearly settled amongst historians today, it is known that Osman's family was one of many Oghuz Turkish people originating from what today is western Kazakhstan, just east of the Caspian Sea.

Osman was the first expansionist chief of what was to be one of the world's greatest empires. After only a few generations, the small *beylik* had grown to include most of Anatolia, the Balkans, and chunks of the Peloponnesus peninsula. By the time of the seventh sultan, Mehmed II, the Ottomans had brought the Byzantine Empire down, formerly the dominant power in the East. This major contestant had been defeated and buried with the conquest of Constantinople in 1453, and the Ottoman Empire had finally displayed its true strength against the Christian alliance in the West. Though Mehmed had already achieved more than many of his predecessors, he did not rest after the conquest. At the end of his reign, he was known all over Europe and Central Asia as the Bloodthirsty, but to his compatriots, he was considered a hero, even to this day. Not only did he annex large portions of territory to his empire, but he also stabilized an area riven by uprisings and political commotion. By developing his militia, the state apparatus, and cultural institutions, he laid the foundation of what would be the apogee of the Ottoman Empire. The inclusion of religious minorities had a positive impact on the prospering empire, and the centuries following are considered a golden age by modern historians.

Mehmed II

After Constantinople had been successfully besieged and conquered, Mehmed claimed the title Caesar—emperor—with the assertion that he was in possession of the former East Roman Empire's capital, as well as having a blood lineage to the former Emperor of the Byzantines by Sultan Orhan I's marriage to a Byzantine princess. The claim was recognised by the Orthodox Church, thanks to the effort made to rebuild and maintain Christian institutions in Constantinople, and the opening of the Ottoman sultanate for both Jewish and Christian minorities.

As an emperor, Mehmed's armies rapidly continued his expeditions to the west. First in line was Serbia, which had long been both a vassal state and an ally of the Ottoman Empire. The two ruling families had intermarried, and the Serbian despot had been by Mehmed and his father's sides in many battles in the previous decades. Mehmed was also married to a family member of the despot, which did not stop the new Serbian king from allying with Hungary, consequently upsetting the Ottoman sultan. It took five years of battles before the Despotate was dissolved, and everything but Belgrade had been ceded to Mehmed. He simultaneously annexed the tip of the Greek peninsula, known as the Despotate of the Morea, to where the Byzantine ex-emperor had fled to live with his brother. Except for a few conclaves belonging to the Venetian Republic, Morea had been dissolved by 1460. It is rumoured that after having conquered the peninsula, upon visiting Troy, Mehmed proudly announced he had avenged the Trojans by ridding the lands of Greek rule.

Mehmed's successes in besieging and annexing new territories seemed perpetual, thanks to his very loyal and competent Grand Vizier Gedik Ahmed Pasha whom, together with governor Turahanoğlu Ömer Bey, led many of the battles on the Balkans and in Greece. While Mehmed was occupied on one front, his officers led fruitful battles all over Eastern Europe, allowing the continuous expansion of Ottoman territory. Leaders of the vassal states tried more than once to rebel against the empire by refusing to pay taxes and forming alliances with Western European kingdoms. Their seditions were more or less futile, and the Ottomans eventually managed to conquer most of the territories they attempted to conquer.

Mehmed led very few losses during his years as a military campaign leader, the most severe of which was in Wallachia, a vassal state of the empire, against the treacherous Vlad III Dracula who, time after time, attacked Turkish forces in the vicinity. After Vlad Dracula had a large number of the Turkish soldiers impaled, Mehmed went to Wallachia to lead a series of battles, eventually ending with an Ottoman victory and a reinstatement of control of the area. At the same time, Mehmed made claims in Moldavia, which turned out to be a costly acquisition to the empire, albeit a victorious one in the end.

Vlad the Impaler

The most serious round of conflicts was the ongoing war against the Republic of Venice. For 16 years, the two powers met in several battles on the Aegean Coast and islands in the Aegean Sea. Venice had dominated the Mediterranean for centuries, and their fleet was outstandingly superior to all other naval powers at the time. During the series of campaigns which became known as the Ottoman-Venetian War, the scales tilted in favor of the Turks. While conquering the island of Lesbos, they also annexed Albania and Negroponte. The war ended with the Treaty of Constantinople in 1479, when the Republic of Venice agreed to cede a few important enclaves on the Dalmatian Coast to the Ottomans in exchange for peace in the ones they were allowed to keep. The treaty also imposed an annual tribute for letting Venice continue to conduct trade in the Black Sea, consequently diminishing their position as a naval trade state in the Levant.

In addition to his focus on the war with the Venetians, Mehmed II also made runs along the Black Sea and sacked the last of the Byzantine successor states, the Empire of Trebizond. Thus, the last vestige of what had been the Roman Empire finally succumbed in 1461. The attack on Trebizond was a pre-emptive strike against a scheming emperor who had been trying to cajole more Christian states to fight the Ottomans and eventually conquer Jerusalem, and these plans gave Mehmed a pretext to erase the last remnants of Byzantium. After the conquest, he allowed the dioceses (administrative areas under the rule of a Christian bishop) to continue administering their services to Christians in the territory.

The Ottoman Empire now had a long stretch of land along the southern coast of the Black Sea, gaining more influence in naval trade. Mehmed took another step toward full dominance when the conditions of the Turkish Tatars living under Genoese rule in the Crimea worsened, and the sultan was called upon for relief. Instead of liberating them, he incorporated the peninsula into the empire, claiming even more of the trade across the Black Sea.

While the war on the Greek Peninsula raged on in irregular bursts, Mehmed was presented with another golden opportunity to conquer an old foe in Anatolia: the Karamanids. After the fall of the Sultanate of Rûm, the Karamanids were the most powerful beylik in Anatolia, but as the Ottoman Empire grew, the Karamanids' influence diminished. At the time of the devastating Battle of Ankara—in which the Central Asian ruler, Timur, crushed the Ottoman armies and killed the sultan—Anatolia fell into disarray. The Karamanids made some effort to re-establish themselves as Anatolia's ruling power, but after the Ottoman Interregnum ended a decade later, the claimed lands were quickly taken back. The antagonism between the Ottoman dynasty and the Karamanids kept rising to the surface over the centuries. When the tables had turned and civil war had broken out amongst Karamanid heirs, Mehmed simply walked in to annex the territory. After another decade, he decided to completely subsume the Karamanid state, abolishing it. In doing so, he also displaced the entire population to the enclaves around his empire to prevent them from uniting and rising against the Ottomans again.

At the end of Mehmed's reign, it was clear that he had been the most important leader of the Ottoman Empire up to that point, except for the founder himself. Apart from the territorial gains, he made significant changes to how the empire was administered. With him, the practice of devshirme was perfected, while the Janissaries gained importance and reliably supported the sultan. To establish complete loyalty and trust between Mehmed and his viziers—whose responsibilities and autonomy steadily grew—Mehmed recruited them via the devshirme rather than from the usual noble families. By elevating poorer families' status and economic stability, he gained the trust of subjects who, by his choosing, would become high-earning officers and members of the government. He also systematically registered his chief officials, created records of their titles, salaries, and responsibilities, and how they were related to each other and the sultan. He broke with the Ghazi tradition of ceremonies and rituals where certain people held a higher rank depending on their heritage. He also gave payment to religious scholars, making them loyal to him and subsequently coming to his defence in religious matters associated with his authoritarian rule. His most important contribution was the institution of a secular code of law in matters where Sharia law couldn't be used. These laws, called kanunnames, dealt mainly with economic and fiscal matters, shedding a pragmatic light on administrative questions arising around the empire. At the same time as Mehmed distributed the power of the empire to more and stronger viziers, he also consolidated his power as the autonomous ruler, excluding himself from the lower officials, so the people had no access to him. His viziers and administrative employees dealt with questions arising on the ground, while he made authoritarian decisions about the structure and build of the empire. Not surprisingly, it was Mehmed who had introduced the word "politics" to the Ottoman Empire.

That said, not everything was politics under Mehmed II's rule. He was apt when it came to cultural and religious matters and entertained scholars, artists, poets, and theologians from the East and West. His court was a multicultural mix of science, religion, and art, where Italian painters, Christian patriarchs, and Persian poets intermingled. He encouraged the translation of the Christian doctrine into Turkish to better understand the minority groups in his empire, and he eventually established the first version of the millets, autonomous courts of laws where Jews, Christians, and Muslims could be tried according to a separate legislature of their religious laws. This let people practice their religion freely within the Ottoman domain, more or less ruling themselves in personal matters without interference from the Ottoman government. The millets came to full practice with the extended and more intricate upgrade of the Kanunnames under the rule of Mehmed's grandson, Suleiman.

Mehmed's final quest was an attempt to conquer Italy. In Rome, the Pope feared suffering the same fate Constantinople did, so he rallied other Christian states to come to his aid. The Republic of Venice was the only one to refuse out of respect for the peace treaty they had signed with the Ottomans in 1479. Hungary, France, and several other of the Italian city-states replied to the appeal, and in the end, the Ottoman expedition in Italy was short-lived. After conquering Otranto in 1480, they negotiated to give it back to Rome in exchange for free passage while withdrawing from Italy.

Mehmed died shortly after this endeavour under mysterious circumstances. Out campaigning, showing no signs of weakness or disease, he suddenly fell seriously ill and died within a few days. Some historians claim Mehmed's son and heir, Bayezid II, had poisoned him, while others say it was due to old age and natural causes. Mehmed was in the midst of planning a possible takeover in Egypt when he died, a dream which did not materialize, much to the joy of the Mamluks ruling the southern Mediterranean coast.

At the news of Mehmed's death, church bells rang throughout Europe, and the Western kings expressed hope of enjoying a respite from Ottoman aggression. Bayezid took the throne, and in accordance with Europe's wishes, the Ottoman Empire changed direction during his reign.

Bayezid II

Mehmed II died in Gebze at the age of 52. After 28 years as a sultan, he had defeated two empires and conquered 14 states and over 200 cities.

Pax Ottomana

Regardless of whether Bayezid poisoned his father, his reign started with the kind of chaos that could be expected after such a sudden takeover. As had more or less become the norm by now, his first battles were against a brother in pursuit of the throne. Cem, his brother, made successful attacks on Bursa, Inegöl, and later, Ankara, Anatolia, and Konya, though he only managed to rule them for a short time. Bayezid defeated his brother with the support of his father's armies, and Cem first fled to the Knights Hospitaller on Rhodes and later to mainland Italy under the Pope's protection. What Cem didn't know was that his brother had bribed the Christian rulers to continue holding him as a prisoner. Cem was not a guest but a hostage in Italy, and he died in prison in Neapel while Bayezid unified and amalgamated the territories his father had annexed.

As a ruler, Bayezid's emphasis was to keep the empire together, to coalesce and strengthen the state apparatus, and integrate minorities with the same incentives as his father. Except for a military campaign that resulted in full control over the Peloponnese and some minor battles with the Shah of Iran in the east, Bayezid did not take to expanding the empire further by conquest. He is most remembered for the evacuation of Jewish and Muslim populations persecuted by the Inquisition in the newly formed Spain. His action bears witness as to the high level of tolerance in the Ottoman Empire, where they not only welcomed refugees but helped them to escape. The cruelty of the Spanish Inquisition stands out in clear contrast to the millet policies which guaranteed a certain level of religious freedom. Bayezid sent his trusted vizier with an Ottoman fleet to ensconce religious minorities in the Ottoman territories. Bayezid is said to have laughed at the stupidity of Ferdinand and Isabella of Spain for "impoverishing their own country and enriching mine!" The Jewish minority was seen as an asset, useful both culturally and economically, and Bayezid encouraged his subjugates to welcome the refugees with open arms. He became known as "Bayezid the Just", and his reign was the beginning of what historians today call the Pax Ottomana—a reference to the Pax Romana, which was a period of peace and prosperity in the earlier Roman Empire. Historians using the term Pax Ottomana refer to the time of Bayezid and the two following emperors, who also shared the goal of developing laws and regulations, giving people freedom and responsibilities as citizens, strengthening the authoritarian rule of the sultan, and building strong relationships of trust between the sultan, viziers, officials, judges, the military, and people. The work had been initiated by Mehmed II, and his successors realized the benefits of building a state based on liberation rather than subjugation, thus gaining respect and dedication in all lines. Apart from the development of political institutions, Bayezid II shared the same interest in culture, religion, science, and education as his father, and the court looked upon other cultures as an opportunity to learn and share.

With the takeover of Crimea and Peloponnesus, the Ottomans also came to dominate trade on the Mediterranean and the Black Sea. In the perfect location to be the only gateway between Europe and Asia, the Ottoman Empire became a natural melting pot, which greatly benefited both the rulers and the people living under the empire.

Bayezid II was also notable for his many children as a result of his eight marriages. Not only did he have 8 sons but also 12 daughters, who were married off in politically convenient arrangements with families all around the empire. As Bayezid grew older, his sons became hungry for power and coveted the throne. Even before he was dead, civil war broke out in 1509 between Ahmet and Selim, two of his sons. Ahmet gathered an unexpected army and succeeded in conquering Karamanid, as well as fighting back a Safavid uproar in Asia Minor. Bolstered by the success, he turned toward Constantinople, where his aging father refused to let him in. In his place, Selim found support among the Janissaries and defeated and killed Ahmet in battle. Selim then, more or less, forced his father to abdicate at the age of 62. Bayezid II withdrew to retire in the territory where he'd been born. Just as mysterious and sudden as his father had, Bayezid died on the road, possibly poisoned by the newly-acclaimed emperor.

Selim I

Selim started his reign by executing his other brothers and chased his nephew, Ahmet's son, into exile. Selim's rule was short but efficient and is generally considered a break in the Pax Ottomana. One cause for Selim's more bellicose persona in comparison to both his father and his future heir was a rising threat in the east; after several decades of relative peace and internal stability, the Sunni Ottoman Muslims discovered a new enemy in the Shiite Persians. Persian Shah Ismail was on a quest to spread Shia Islam all throughout Eurasia, Asia Minor, and across the border into Anatolia. This was the beginning of an ongoing antagonism between Shia and Sunni Islam, thanks to a mutual, personal derision between Selim and Shah Ismail, who sent messages containing insults back and forth while marching into battle with each other. Selim had also put a very strict embargo on Persian silk by shutting Persia's borders, intending to close Ismail off from the rest of the world's trade. While marching on Persia, Selim was treated to scorched earth tactics as Ismail drew further back into his kingdom, trying to starve the Ottoman armies. He was also fighting the Uzbek in the Far East, and his applicable forces were fewer than the large army coming from the west. When they caught up in Chaldiran in August 1514 after only two years of Selim's rule, the Turks were weakened but still outnumbered the Safavids under Ismail's rule.

The battle was swift and acutely executed. What made the victory even more decisive was access to artillery, something the Ottomans had acquired under Mehmed II that the Persian Shah repeatedly had refused to do. Selim gained large amounts of land in northern Iraq, northwestern Iran, and present-day Azerbaijan, while the influence of the Shah diminished. He withdrew to his palace, never to be seen on a battlefield again.

After this success, Selim went on to complete his grandfather's dreams of conquering Egypt, currently under the rule of the Mamluks, where, in Cairo, the last Abbasid Caliph sat on the throne. Again, the Ottomans were faced with a traditionally equipped enemy army, proud to use bow and arrow instead of modernizing their armaments. Against the skilled Janissaries equipped with modern firearms and arquebuses, they didn't stand much of a chance, and Syria was conquered in a single battle. Shortly thereafter, Egypt was defeated after two quick battles, and the Caliph was exiled to Constantinople.

At that time, Selim was in possession of Damascus, Cairo, and Jerusalem, causing the Arabian Peninsula to fear that he was coming for Mecca and Medina. The Sharif of Mecca submitted to Selim without a fight, and with that the holiest cities of Islam had fallen into his hands easier than could have been anticipated. This was a significant conquest, as it shifted the center of the empire from the old Byzantine past toward important, Arabic Islamic strongholds. Selim was graced with the humble title of "The Servant of the Two Holy Cities", and today it is debated whether or not the exiled Caliph transferred his title to Selim, as historians from the 17th century had claimed. Since Selim did not exercise any sacred rights following his possible elevation, modern historians conclude this was not the case.

Selim's reign lasted only eight years, but his legacy was of great importance to what would come with Suleiman, the next ruler. The eight years of conquest expanded the area of the Ottoman Empire by 70%, an expansion made possible thanks to Selim's father and grandfather's interest in science and modernisation. The acquisition of superior armaments and weapons proved pivotal in battles with the traditionally equipped Safavid and Mamluk armies, whereas the modernisation of the Ottoman armies had started since the conquest of Constantinople under the lead of Mehmed II some 60 years earlier. The Janissaries had developed into a very strong and forceful nucleus, which played a major part in Selim's successful conquests. Together with the fiscal and political apparatus improved under Bayezid II, the Ottoman Empire became a world force, ready to take the lead in political, economic, cultural, and military arenas in and outside their territory. All of this paved the way for the real apogee of the Ottoman Empire under the rule of Selim's successor, Suleiman the Magnificent.

Selim I died after only eight years as a sultan, and though his legacy includes great territorial conquests, little is known about him as a ruler. It is also unclear as to how and why he died, though the records suggest a few different possibilities. Some say he died of a plague raging in the area, while other sources state he died of cancer or a skin disease called Sirpence. There are also suspicions his physician might have poisoned him, which is not unlikely considering Selim's somewhat grim reputation. He had a bad habit of executing his viziers, resulting in the coining of the curse popular at the time: "May you be a vizier of Selim's."

However he died, be it an act of revenge or natural causes, his successor ascended the throne surprisingly peacefully. Though his heir, Suleiman, had many brothers, none of them are mentioned in contemporaneous records, suggesting it might have been evident from childhood that the intelligent, eloquent, benevolent, and prudent Suleiman would shoulder his father's responsibilities when the day came. Suleiman was 27 at the time of his father's death, mature enough to revive the Pax Ottomana within his empire.

Suleiman the Magnificent

By the time of Suleiman's ascension, the Ottoman Empire was already in good condition. It was politically stable, culturally flourishing, dominating trade in the area, and in possession of a superior military organisation, which allowed Suleiman I to continue his predecessors' work without much need to change the direction of the empire. Selim's aggressive rule left the Janissaries efficient and strong, the Mamluks defeated, and the holy cities subsumed into the empire. The Republic of Venice in the west, as well as the Safavids in the east, had been weakened, and for the first time, the Ottoman had a fleet able to challenge old trade structures and rise as a new dominant power on the seas. Things were going well, and Suleiman intended to keep it that way.

During his childhood, he studied history, science, literature, theology, and military tactics at the Topkapi Palace in Istanbul. While living in the palace, he became very close friends with Pargali Ibrahim, one of the slave boys who later became vizier and was one of Suleiman's most trusted friends. Suleiman spoke no less than six languages and wrote poetry in three of them. His intellectual capabilities became evident later in life when he rewrote and organised the Kanuni, the laws concerning fiscal and economic issues, and instituted the judicial practices of millets, making ruling the empire more efficient. Suleiman also had a fascination for Alexander the Great, and after reading several biographies on the Macedonian King, he emulated Alexander's military strategies in his various campaigns. Under his father and grandfather's reigns, Suleiman had ruled a province in Crimea in preparation for becoming sultan.

While his somewhat belligerent father had been shaped by his fiery temperament and harsh judgment, Suleiman was more prudent and of a calmer and more pragmatic mind. One of his first actions as sultan was to lift the embargo on the silk trade to and from Persia, which had hurt Turkish traders as much as the Safavids. He then instituted a tax on all citizens, which meant that no matter what a person's ranking or standing was, they would still be subject to taxes. Instead of the whimsical exceptions for people of certain families or descent, the new, transparent tax system would have everyone pay taxes according to their income, a system still largely used today. He later instituted protections for Christians and Jews, freeing them from serfdom and giving the millets authority to rule their subjects according to their religion. Historians called Suleiman "the Magnificent", but to his contemporaries, he became known as "the Lawgiver".

Suleiman had expansionist dreams—not unlike any other Ottoman sultan—and he was immediately thrown into action when an uprising started in Damascus in 1521. Suleiman personally went to fight his first battle as sultan and won quite easily when the treacherous, Ottoman-appointed governor was killed in the same battle. Later that year, Suleiman rode west aiming for Belgrade, one of the last Christian strongholds in Ottoman territory, under the rule of the Hungarian Kingdom at the time. By using both infantry, cavalry, and heavy siege armaments from land as well as a flotilla of ships hindering potential aid arriving via the Danube, Belgrade's futile attempts to defend itself were of little use, and the city fell in less than two months.

The Ottoman expansion continued targeting Christians, as had been the habit for many hundreds of years. Though the founders of the Ottoman Empire—Osman and his first successor, Orhan—had not been strong advocates of the Islamic faith, religion was an integral part of both private and official life in the empire. In the 16th century, it had become such a strong, defining element that most campaigns led by Ottoman sultans were religious in nature, whether against the old Christian enemies or the new Shiite Muslim opponents in the east. Because of this, Suleiman was compelled to march south toward Rhodes to expel the Knight Hospitallers who had resided on the island since the time of the Crusades. The knights had become a nuisance to many groups of surrounding Muslims of late, mostly through acts of piracy. The knights captured ships from the Ottomans and other Muslim states, stealing valuable goods and cargo and enslaving the Muslim crews. They also attacked Muslim ships passing by on their way to perform Hajj, the Muslim pilgrimage, in Mecca. This was something Selim had failed to put to an end during his reign and which Suleiman made his priority.

The residing knights had already anticipated an attack from the Ottomans and had been fortifying their capital using Muslim slaves as laborers. By the time of the siege of Rhodes, the capital of the island had three rings of stone walls as protection and the knights were prepared for the vengeful Ottomans heading their way. Starting with a fleet of 400 ships followed by an army of 100,000 men led by Suleiman himself, the siege started in June 1522. The fortifications resisted the fury of Ottoman bombings and gunpowder mines, and the inhabitants of Rhodes refused to acquiesce to Suleiman. After months of waves of invigorating progress followed by demoralising setbacks, both sides were exhausted. No other Christian allies had come to aid the Knights Hospitallers when the Ottomans had a slight upper-hand in the internecine siege. Through major losses, it was just a matter of time before the walls would eventually give in.

A medieval depiction of Turkish Janissaries laying siege to Rhodes

A truce was negotiated in November, but the population's demands for safety and privileges were too high for Suleiman to accept. The siege continued for another month until the civilians had finally had enough and pressured the knights' Grand Master to negotiate peace. Suleiman showed no acrimony and gave the knights—as well as the civil population—generous terms. The knights were given 12 days to leave and allowed to take weapons, personal belongings, and any religious relics they wanted along with them. The population was given the possibility to live under Ottoman rule for three years and were able to leave whenever they wanted during this trial period. The people who chose to permanently settle on the island would be free of taxes for five years and guaranteed freedom of religion under the promise that no churches would be desecrated and turned into mosques. Most of the population stayed on the island, now a part of the Ottoman Empire. The knights marched from the city in January of the following year onto Suleiman's ships heading for Crete. He had chosen not to annihilate the Knights Hospitaller—something many of his predecessors might have done—after the successful siege. His aim had been to control trade in the Mediterranean, a goal he achieved in the name of Islam. Instead of instigating fear and hatred, his prudent nature and diplomatic solutions earned him respect across Europe and Central Asia, which was uncommon for a conqueror of his measures.

After Rhodes, he resumed his European campaign, which was preceded by some remarkable circumstances. The Habsburg Dynasty had taken over the lead of the Holy Roman Empire, currently under the rule of Charles V, one of the strongest rulers in medieval and Renaissance

Europe. Charles V had chosen to battle the Franks, imprisoning their king after he ceded significant land to the Holy Roman Empire. Now, French King Francis I turned to Suleiman to form an unholy alliance against the Habsburg Empire, an alliance that greatly shocked and offended the Christian world. As it turned out, it was an alliance that would last over three centuries.

Charles V

Francis I

Francis asked Suleiman to wage war on the Habsburgs, residing in Vienna, which coincided with Suleiman's aim to conquer Hungary. Suleiman made Hungary the first stop on the road to Vienna, with the Battle of Mohács taking place just outside of Buda, the capital of the Hungarian kingdom. The Hungarian army suffered from the same shortcomings as many of the Ottomans' other defeated enemies - their army had not acquired modern armaments, but they still invited the enemy to fight in an open field. The Hungarian army had the opportunity to strike the Ottomans in a weakened state after they had marched in the scorching heat for days, but this would not have been considered chivalrous, so the two met in battle after the Ottomans were allowed some rest. Not only did the Ottomans heavily outnumber the Hungarian forces, but they also had about four times as many guns and more than three times as many cannons. The Battle of Mohács could have only ended in one way, and after a few hours, the Hungarians had suffered massive losses, incurring about 20,000 casualties while the Ottomans had lost about 1,500. The king of Hungary, Louis II, escaped at nightfall but fell off his horse and drowned in a river nearby. Most of his army were either annihilated or captured and by the end of the battle,

Suleiman was left shaking his head in disbelief, wondering how the great Hungarian kingdom had only been able to muster a tiny, suicidal force to meet them. As a precaution, the Ottomans waited several days before entering Buda, expecting retribution by a second army. When it didn't appear, they walked into the capital, and the once mighty Hungary saw its last traces of freedom for many centuries to come.

An Ottoman depiction of the battle

Louis II

The losses for the Hungarians include men and territory, but the Battle of Mohács became a watershed in Hungary's history. Over a span of 400 years, old Hungary would be occupied by Ottomans, the Holy Roman Empire, the Austrian Empire, and the Soviet Union, until they finally regained their autonomy in 1989, albeit in an incapacitated state. All this was unknown to Suleiman in 1526 as he recuperated in the capital, initiating a plan to besiege Vienna.

Different chroniclers analyze Suleiman's behavior in different ways. There is a plethora of opinions as to his motives for attempting the takeover of Vienna, a well-guarded city far away from his empire's center. Had he intended to conquer the whole of the Holy Roman Empire? Had he intended to strengthen his borders? Had he acted in accordance with King Francis I's needs in the West? No matter the reason, Suleiman did not halt in his advances, despite the fact circumstances were not favorable for the Ottomans. The summer rains had already begun when he set out for Vienna, making most of the roads inaccessible both for cavalry and moving the heavy pieces of artillery needed for a successful siege. The camels brought from Anatolia proved too sensitive for the cold, constant rain and died in large numbers, and many of the soldiers shared the same fate.

By the time they arrived around Vienna in late September, the Ottoman forces were heavily depleted, and many siege armaments had been left behind when stuck in the mud. The population of Vienna had seen the enemy coming, giving them plenty of time to reinforce, strengthen, and prepare. When they launched the siege, the Ottoman forces lacked conviction, making it easy to fight back during the initial attacks. After making no real progress, the soldiers lost their motivation when the weather took a turn for the worse shortly into the siege. Suleiman's supply of food and water diminished, and the troops were close to mutiny. In a final "all or nothing" attempt, the Ottomans attacked with all the strength they had left, trying to break Vienna's fortifications, which refused to yield. Suleiman accepted defeat, gathered his men, and returned to Anatolia. The hasty departure from Vienna resulted in the loss of heavy armaments, as well as troops and prisoners in the heavy snowfall.

Modern historians speculate as to why Suleiman persisted with the siege even though the Ottoman forces were evidently weaker than the forces in Vienna upon their arrival. As an experienced, strategic warrior, it is most likely he realized his disadvantage and the full scale of his potential losses. It was also probable that the last burst of attacks was merely a means with which to weaken the city walls for a future siege. The second attempt, in 1532, was met with the same mix of bad luck and good defenses, and Vienna marked the limit of Ottoman advances in the West. Suleiman had to turn back to his homeland to face his Shiite antagonist in the east, the new Safavid Shah of Persia Tahmasp.

Shah Tahmasp deposed and executed the Ottoman governor of Baghdad in 1532, and one of the vassal states under Ottoman rule in eastern Anatolia switched sides, swearing allegiance to the shah. In response, Suleiman sent his trusted friend and grand vizier Ibrahim Pasha to initiate the fighting, with the emperor himself showing up the following year. While the Ottomans were marching towards an anticipated battle, Tahmasp employed the same tactics as his predecessor, burning the terrain and withdrawing into his own territories. This pattern repeated itself three times in the coming 20 years, and Suleiman never actually fought Tahmasp in battle. In the wake of an outright war, he annexed the deserted territories in southern Georgia and Azerbaijan, northern and western Iraq, and some of the coastlines of the Persian Gulf. The two parties signed a peace treaty in 1554.

While the landmasses remained stable under Suleiman's rule, real progress was made on the open waters. The Ottoman fleet quickly became a dominating force, and when Suleiman feared a challenge from the Spanish Armada, he employed the notorious Hayreddin Barbarossa Pasha to command his fleet. Under his command, the Ottoman fleet expanded their influence in the Mediterranean, taking the North African coastline where Tunisia, Morocco, and Algeria had become autonomous provinces. He later captured Nice and pillaged the Italian west coast. This affirmed Ottoman dominance in the Eastern Mediterranean. Somalia, Africa's Horn, Yemen, and present-day Oman were also conquered by the Ottomans. They also conducted trade with Mughal India and helped relieve the Sultanate of Aceh from Portuguese raids as far away as

Sumatra.

Hayreddin Barbarossa Pasha

Suleiman had, with help from his capable and trusted officers, expanded the empire to reach farther than ever before, keeping his borders safe and lands in order all the while. His failure to capture Vienna stands out in a long list of successful battles, but he is still remembered more as the "lawgiver" than a warlord.

The Kanun was an earthly code of laws used as a complement to Sharia, the divine law, in matters the Sharia did not entertain. To write the Kanun, Suleiman took to collecting and reading all of the legislative decisions his nine predecessors had taken, analysing and comparing them carefully, before using them as the foundation for the new set of laws. The job took many years, but once it was done, the Kanun and the Sharia were used as the code of laws for the next 300 years in the Ottoman Empire.

Suleiman's most important changes were the inclusion of Christian and Jewish minorities, who were lifted from serfdom. This prompted Christians from other parts of the world to migrate to the Ottoman Empire to live a better life under Suleiman's rule.

He was also known for instituting a great number of schools for younger and older boys. The mosques he built often had a school within the compound, giving Muslim boys the opportunity to learn what he had learned as a young boy. Suleiman was also a patron of the arts and gathered no less than 600 artists of various backgrounds and nationalities in his Ehl-i Hiref Community of the Craftsmen. Many of them were poets—as was Suleiman himself—who wrote some of the most memorable lines in both Persian and Turkish. Many of his verses and proverbs are still frequently quoted.

Another one of his lasting legacies was the remodelling of Constantinople itself. He was, by and large, the main renovator of the city, and together with renowned architect Mimar Sinan, he built bridges, palaces, official buildings, and mosques. He even took to restoring the Dome of the Rock in Jerusalem; the walls surrounding old Jerusalem today are also Mimar Siman's work, paid for by the sultan. The Kaaba in Mecca was renovated by the duo as well.

To successfully succeed as a man of so many talents after a flourishing golden age lasing more than 45 years, it would take more than an ordinary leader. Suleiman had outlived two of his sons but still had four more who claimed to be the right person for the job. Though he had written a full code of laws, there was still no set order of succession. The only mandatory rule concerning the transmission of power was the practice of fratricide instituted by Mehmed II in an effort to prevent any uprisings once the new sultan had been installed, and since the empire was at its height, competition for the throne would be fiercer than before.

Not only did the brothers get involved, but Suleiman's second wife, Hürrem Sultan, played a vital role in conspiring with her sons. Hürrem Sultan was a woman of great influence, simply because Suleiman was head over heels in love with her. His first wife had been put aside, and Hürrem, a slave girl from the harem, rose to become the sultan's favorite and wife, to the astonishment of many. Suleiman had intended his first son by his first wife, Mustafa—a very accomplished warrior and intellectual—to inherit the throne. In contrast, Hürrem, had wanted one of her sons to take the throne to avoid the risk of execution for either of them. Though Mustafa had been favored by Suleiman, the people, the court, and Suleiman's friend, Grand Vizier Ibrahim Pasha, Hürrem managed to convince her husband to have Mustafa executed and Ibrahim Pasha accused treason. The stories about the rounds of executions—among them his first-born son, his grand vizier, his finance secretary Iskender Celebi, his other son Bayezid, and four grandsons—with which Suleiman ended his reign are as many as the victims. Of his two remaining sons, one is said to have died of grief. Suleiman had six sons, yet there was only one left at the time of his death.

The Road to Revolution

The Qajar dynasty was Iran's ruling dynasty from 1794-1925, and it was during this period that the *ulama* developed and strengthened their authority, status, and power, both in the religious and political realms. The rise of these Shi'ite clerics came at the expense of the isolation of other Islamic sects, such as the Sunnis and Sufi orders, and Iran increasingly became closely tied to the Shi'ite branch of Islam.

In essence, while *ulama* were historically religious and legal scholars engaged in the study of Islamic jurisprudence and *sharia* law, it was in Iran that these *ulama* expanded beyond the judicial and religious spheres they had historically occupied, and they ventured into the political arena to wield significant power and authority over state governance – much more so than the *ulama* of other Middle Eastern countries. Much of this was due to the Qajar rulers, who relied on the *ulama* as providers of religious legitimacy to secure the power of the dynasty. The founder of the Qajar dynasty, Aqa Muhammad Khan, and his successor, Fath Ali Shah, both actively engaged the *ulama* and allowed them great freedoms in return for a seal of legitimacy for their rule. Thus, by the end of the Qajar dynasty in 1925, these clerics had gained significant political powers, cementing their position as key components of rulership in Iran.[183]

The *ulama* as a political force only continued to grow, so much so that they became "Iran's first line of defense against colonialism."[184] It was the *ulama* who led the resistance against foreign influence in Iran, and it was the *ulama* who fought for the preservation of Iranian culture, religion, and self-rule in the face of foreign insurgency into the country during the 1800s. In 1890, when a tobacco concession was granted by the Shah of Iran to Great Britain, it was not the merchants or community leaders but the *ulama* who led the mass protests against the concession, as many of them had economic interests in tobacco that was growing on land funded by endowments.[185] Bazaars closed down following the *ulama's* calls for a strike, and many clerics stopped teaching and shut down schools. The protests culminated in a widely-obeyed December 1891 decree issued by Grand Ayatollah Mirza Hassan Shirazi, the highest religious authority in Iran, prohibiting the use of tobacco. By January 1892, the Shah had no choice but to cancel the concession.[186]

The *ulama's* key role during the Tobacco Movement (1891-1892) was only one instance of their influence. Subsequent examples include their role in the Constitutional Revolution of 1905-1911, which has been investigated at length by many scholars and researchers,[187] and naturally,

---

[183] Ahmad Kazemi Moussavi, "The Basis and Nature of Ulama's Authority in Qajar Iran," *Foundation For Iranian Studies,* http://fis-iran.org/en/irannameh/volxv/ulama-authority.

[184] Vali Nasr, *The Shia Revival: How Conflicts within Islam Will Shape the Future* (New York: W. W. Norton & Company, Inc., 2007), 117.

[185] Nikki R. Keddie, *Religion and Rebellion in Iran: The Tobacco Protest of 1891-92* (London: Frank Cass & Co. Ltd, 1966), 65.

[186] Roy Mottahedeh, *The Mantle of the Prophet: Religion and Politics in Iran* (Oxford: Oneworld Publications, 2000), 218.

the political strength and influence the *ulama* possessed played a major role in the Iranian Revolution. To a degree that was unseen in any other Muslim country in the world, these clerics held sway over millions of people, who considered the clerics to be the ultimate source of morality, political legitimacy, and religious authority.

In 1921, a military commander named Reza Khan organized a coup against the ruling regime and ousted the last Qajar Shah. Reza Khan subsequently changed the country's name from Persia to Iran, and in 1925, he adopted the Pahlavi surname and established the Pahlavi dynasty.[188] Mohammad Reza Shah Pahlavi, son of Reza Shah and future ruler of Iran, wistfully wrote in his autobiography that his father's "coup was carried out with such dispatch and so few casualties that the commander of British forces in Persia, General Ironside, is said to have told friends that 'Reza Khan is the only man capable of saving Iran.'"[189]

[187] For example, see: Mohammad H. Faghfoory, "The Ulama-State Relations in Iran: 1921-1941," *International Journal of Middle East Studies* 19, no. 4 (Nov 1987): 413-432.

[188] Marvin E. Gettleman and Stuart Schaar, ed. *The Middle East and Islamic World Reader* (New York: Grove Press, 2003), 107.

[189] Mohammad Reza Pahlavi, *Answer to History* (New York: Stein & Day, 1980), 50-51.

Reza Shah Pahlavi

Reza Shah, whom the people initially had high hopes for, eventually disappointed many. Reform-minded liberals who had hoped for the establishment of an effective and modern parliamentary regime, and the *ulama,* who were expecting the continuation of the powers and high status they enjoyed during the Qajar dynasty, soon found that Reza Shah had no interest in actualizing anyone's visions but his own. He had no intention of upholding the status of the clerics; in fact, Reza Shah undermined the *ulama's* legitimacy by appointing secularists to key government positions and establishing ties with the West, which was considered anathema to both the reformists and the religious clerics.

Moreover, Reza Shah was an ambitious optimist who had great plans for the economic revitalization and modernization of his country, but for his plans to come into fruition, he believed that he needed a strong and centralized government composed of educated and intelligent advisors instead of clerics, who were knowledgeable in religion but not so much in state governance. As a great admirer of Kemal Ataturk, who in 1923 had established a secular modern republic in neighboring Turkey, Reza Shah dreamed of Iran as its own modern republic, free from religious and ethnic divides and united by common patriotism for a secular regime. Reza Shah consequently sent hundreds of Iranians, including his son, to Europe for education and training, and he led the establishment of a modernized national public education system. A new judiciary system modeled on that of France was introduced, and compulsory primary education was mandated across the country.[190] Thus, from the establishment of the new Iran to the 1940s, Reza Shah's development projects led to the urbanization and industrialization of Iran.

Naturally, Reza Shah's efforts to reform Iran into a modern republic were met with great opposition from various interest groups in the country. Reza found difficulties maneuvering between the various powerful political and economic players in his country, including politicians concerned about their future place in a changing government, merchants with various economic interests, and other ethnic groups like the Kurds, Azerbaijanis, and Baluchistanis. However, it was with the *ulama* that he clashed most significantly once the religious clerics were suddenly deprived of their long-held privileges, status, and power. Mohammad Shah wrote that "had my father not curtailed political efforts of certain clerics, the tasks which he had undertaken would have been far more difficult." It was not that Reza Shah was irreligious, or lacked spiritual faith; he quite simply believed that "in the twentieth century, it was impossible for a nation to survive in obscurantism. True spirituality should exist over and above politics and economics."[191] Reza Shah's efforts thus significantly, if not completely, reduced the *ulama's* authority in secular matters of state governance. Gaining strength in the clerics' stead were the newly formed middle and industrial working classes.

Despite the unrest at home, Reza Shah's aspirations ultimately crumbled when World War II swept across the globe. Reza Shah, who had been sympathetic to Nazi Germany[192], was consequently deposed by invading British forces for his pro-Axis sympathies and exiled to South Africa. Upon his abdication, he gave his seat of power to his son, Mohammad Reza Shah Pahlavi. Reza Shah died soon after, on July 26, 1944, in South Africa.

---

[190] Ibid., 51-55.
[191] Ibid., 55.
[192] Mohammad Reza Shah has consistently denied his father's alleged pro-Nazi sympathies. See the Shah's autobiography, *Answer to History,* p. 66 onwards for more details.

Mohammad Reza Shah Pahlav

On September 16, 1941, at the young age of 21, Mohammad Reza Shah ascended to the throne.[193] Unlike his father, or perhaps in fear of being accused of pro-Axis sympathies as his father was, Mohammad Reza Shah was more willing to aid in the Allied war effort. With the Shah's blessing, Iran was used by American and British forces as a shipping conduit for supplies being sent to the Soviet Union during the war.[194] Though the Shah was able to boost his ties with Western powers because of this, in the eyes of much of the Iranian population, Mohammad Reza Shah was largely viewed as a puppet of Western powers, and his legitimacy and ability to rule

---

[193] Spencer C. Tucker, ed. *The Encyclopedia of Middle East Wars: The United States in the Persian Gulf, Afghanistan, and Iraq Conflicts* (Santa Barbara: ABC-CLIO, 2010), 1033.

[194] Tucker, *Encyclopedia of Middle East Wars,* 1033.

increasingly came into question.

The foreign-educated, pampered, yet idealistic young man – passionate about his country but with a mind for the outside world – inherited the governance of a country that was increasingly growing restless with the unprecedented reforms placed upon it. In the post-war liberal climate, a democratically elected Majlis (parliament) appointed an ambitious and aggressive nationalist, Mohammed Mossadegh, as prime minister in 1950. The Mossadegh government was committed to the economic revitalization of Iran and quickly sought to nationalize the Iranian oil industry, which had been controlled by the British company Anglo-Persian Oil Company (AIOC) since a 1933 concession agreement with Reza Shah, a bitter memory for many Iranians. In March 1951, the Majlis unanimously voted to nationalize AIOC and its holdings, which led to a global boycott of Iranian crude, the country's primary export and the main source of state wealth. As the Iranian economy plummeted and national unrest grew, a power struggle between Mossadegh and the Shah led to Mohammad Reza Shah fleeing the country into exile in 1953.

Mossadegh

It was only after a CIA-orchestrated coup effectively ousted Mossadegh and toppled his government that Mohammad Reza Shah was able to return to Tehran and resume his role as absolute monarch, with the blessings of the U.S. and Great Britain. The Majlis was stripped of its powers, and foreign oil companies resumed their work in Iran. That Mohammad Reza so quickly lost his seat of power was an embarrassment for the Shah, and the fact that it required the help of the CIA and Western powers to regain his position would remain as a lasting memory in the minds of his people. It would also come back to haunt him.

Mohammad Reza Shah proved to be not so different from his father in his ways of rule and policies. Mohammad Reza Shah was highly in favor of the U.S., establishing close political ties with the Western country, but he was also restrictive and oppressive in his ways, favoring landowners and the military at the expense of the rest of the population and repressing any opposition to his rule.[195] Through mass arms transfers from his new ally, the U.S., and with the help of American military trainers and advisors, the Shah built one of the most well-equipped, highly trained, and powerful armed forces in the region.

Meanwhile, the secret police that he formed, SAVAK, was given great authority to hunt down dissidents and forcibly prevent the population from voicing opposition. Thus, by the mid-1970s, most of the opposition, including leftist reformists, religious leaders, liberal critics, and nationalists, had been silenced through assassinations, unlawful indefinite detentions, and exile.[196] It was this repression that led to the formation of a more furtive kind of opposition that took root in mosques across the country, and eventually, the Shah's most vociferous critic, Ruhollah Khomeini, was exiled from the country in the mid-1960s.

---

[195] Gettleman and Schaar, *The Middle East and Islamic World Reader,* 108.
[196] Stephen Zunes, "The Iranian Revolution (1977-1979)," *Nonviolent Conflict,* April 2009, http://www.nonviolent-conflict.org/index.php/movements-and-campaigns/movements-and-campaigns-summaries?sobi2Task=sobi2Details&catid=315&sobi2Id=23.

Khomeini

   In 1963, Mohammad Reza Shah launched a national program he called the White Revolution, which had been approved for implementation by a national referendum in January of that year. The five-point program was built upon the purported overarching goal that the five minimum human needs would be met for all citizens of Iran: health, food, clothing, housing, and education.[197] As Mohammad Reza Shah wrote in his autobiography, "If our nation wished to remain in the circle of dynamic, progressive and free nations of the world, it had no alternative but to completely alter the archaic order of society, and to structure its future on a new order compatible with the vision and needs of the day. This required a deep and fundamental revolution which would put an end to injustice, tyranny, exploitation, and reactionary forces which impeded progress. This revolution had to be based on spiritual principles and religious

---

[197] Pahlavi, *Answer to History*, 101.

beliefs, and the preservation of individual and social freedoms."[198]

Western nations, unsurprisingly, applauded the Shah's new program and lauded his efforts. The Shah received a personal note of congratulations from President John F. Kennedy, and in August 1967, U.S. President Lyndon B. Johnson declared that "the changes in Iran represent very genuine progress. Through your White Revolution…Iran has risen to the challenge of new times and new generations…without violence, and without any bloodshed."[199]

Despite the Shah's emphasis on a spiritual and religious basis for this revolutionary program of his, the White Revolution did little to include the *ulama* that both he and his father had ostracized. In fact, the Shah even wrote in his autobiography that "at the inception of our land reforms…I had predicted that the forces of the clergy (the Black reaction)…would attempt to sabotage this program…because they wished the nation to remain submerged in abject poverty and injustice."[200] It is evident from this and from his autobiography, *Answer to History*, that the Shah viewed the clergy and any religious influence on the building of a modernized nation in a negative light. All for the purported goal of modernizing Iran, the Shah disbanded parliament, suspended all future elections, and initiated sweeping reforms in land ownership, education, healthcare, and civil rights.

Though some significant progress came out of the White Revolution, such as women's suffrage, increased literacy, and improved infrastructure and technology, this supposed cultural revolution ultimately proved to be more of an attempt by the power-holding political elite to preempt an actual revolution than anything else. They were wary of an increasingly politically conscious population and hoped to merely maintain the political status quo.

For example, as part of the White Revolution, the Shah created in 1971 what was called the Religion Corps (*Sipah-i Din*) in order to "propagate the ordinances of Islam and place spirituality at an equal level with the desires for material progress under the banner of the White Revolution."[201] This Religion Corps was meant to directly compete with the traditional religious authorities, the *ulama*, and this new brand of Shi'ism came to be called *Din-i Dawlat,* or Government Religion. This new state-sponsored religion had its own mosques and clergy, and the Shah even declared himself the "Representative of the Hidden Imam," according to this new government religion.[202] As expected, this move infuriated the *ulama,* who later became the chief leaders of the protests that eventually led to the revolution.

Mohammad Reza Shah's turbulent reign ultimately demonstrated the distance the Shah had

---

[198] Ibid.

[199] Ibid., 102.

[200] Ibid., 103.

[201] Shahrough Akhavi, *Religion and Politics in Contemporary Iran* (Albany: State University of New York Press, 1980),138-139.

[202] Richard Hooker, "Modern Iran," *World Cultures,* February 27, 1997, http://richard-hooker.com/sites/worldcultures/SHIA/MODERN.HTM.

created between himself and his own people, and thus his own government as well. A lot of this was due to his foreign education, his privileged upbringing, and the special tutelage he received from his father. Mohammad Reza Shah himself wrote in his autobiography, "In 1936, at the age of 17, I returned home to Iran for the first time in five years. It was like I visited a different country. I recognized nothing."[203]

It is difficult to pinpoint a single and direct cause of the Iranian Revolution, as it is with most other revolutions and similar world events. The revolution was highly controversial in both its causes and its consequences, not to mention the surprise it created across the world since it was so unexpected, quick, and impactful.

Few expected the Shah's regime, which had broad international support, a powerful and disciplined military, and state wealth, to struggle so much with popular protests, and even fewer could have even guessed that such a regime would crumble in mere months. As one historian noted, "[The Iranian Revolution was] unique in the annals of modern world history in that it brought to power not a new social group equipped with political parties and secular ideologies, but a traditional clergy armed with mosque pulpits and claiming the divine right to supervise all temporal authorities, even the country's highest elected representatives."[204] Customary causes of revolutions, such as recent defeat in war, a disgruntled military, or a looming financial crisis, were not part of the Iranian Revolution, but there were several political, economic, and social causes that spurred it.

The Shah was popularly viewed as a puppet ruler, and it was a fair assessment because Mohammad Reza Shah largely found himself controlled by others instead of controlling others. First and foremost, the Shah was burdened by the legacy of his father throughout his rule; what his father started, he felt he must complete. There was no other blueprint, no other map that he could follow, and therefore, he dedicated his life to achieving his father's goals and dreams. In his autobiography, the Shah wrote, "When I learned of [my father's] death in Johannesburg in 1944, my grief was immense. I owed it to his memory to continue to the very end the task which he had undertaken."[205]

In addition to being shadowed by his father's legacy, the Shah's strong policy of Westernization and his close alliance and identification with Western powers, particularly the U.S., resulted in a clash between the direction he wanted Iran to take and his country's Shi'a Muslim roots. From his re-ascendancy as ruler in 1953, which was aided and orchestrated by the CIA, Mohammad Reza Shah was very much dependent on his Western allies. He employed many U.S. military and government advisers, frequently invited Western officials to Iran, and granted diplomatic immunity to all of them.[206] The last point was especially controversial, as it

---

[203] Pahlavi, *Answer to History*, 65.
[204] Ervand Abrahamian, *Iran Between Two Revolutions* (Princeton: Princeton University Press, 1982), 430-435.
[205] Pahlavi, *Answer to History*, 69.
[206] Heather Lehr Wagner, *The Iranian Revolution* (New York: Infobase Publishing, 2010), 44-45.

protected all foreigners in Iran from prosecution by law, excusing even severe crimes such as murder.

On the other hand, the Shah was extremely repressive against domestic political interests. He implemented a complete ban on political parties in Iran, and since it is virtually impossible for any regime to be completely lacking in opposition voices, this only forced opposition groups to operate clandestinely. Groups such as the communist Tudeh party, the Marxist Fedaiyan-e Khalq (Devotees of the People), and the Islamic Mojahedin-e Khalq (Fighters for the People) were born in the shadows and flourished underground. These parties, despite the different ideologies they were based on, had one common goal: the overthrow of the Shah and the complete overhaul of the current regime. Their membership also came from varied groups, including the intelligentsia, the *ulama*, some who had been exiled or imprisoned by SAVAK, as well as young students and unemployed youth (whose numbers were growing).[207]

As these groups grew larger, the Shah became even more focused on preventing any political party or influential figure from becoming so empowered that they could challenge his rule. Given what had happened in Russia and China, he placed special attention on dismembering Communist parties like the Tudeh and other ideological parties upholding Marxism, Maoism, and so on. However, because the Shah was so focused on combating different ideologies that could contest his authority, he largely overlooked parties that were based on the same ideology he legitimized his rule with, such as the Islamic party of Mojahedin-e Khalq. His oppression of leftist groups allowed the religious opposition to organize and grow, eventually forming the backbone of the Iranian Revolution.

Furthermore, the Shah antagonized even previously apolitical Iranians, such as those from the merchant class, when he formed the *Rastakhiz* (Resurgence) party in 1975. This was intended to be Iran's new single party, to which all Iranians were mandated to belong. The compulsory membership and dues, the party's aggressively un-Islamic policies, and its intrusion into the political, economic, and religious concerns of the Iranian people's lives angered even those who were previously uninvolved in politics. As a result of the Shah's underestimation of the power of the opposition, later efforts to include them in governance were ultimately "too little too late."[208]

After World War II, Iran was plagued by grave economic problems. The country had an impoverished peasantry (whose numbers continued to rapidly grow), little foreign capital, and an increasing gap between the affluent minority and the destitute majority.

By 1973, Iran had gained full control over its oil industry, and as the price of oil, Iran's major export, continued to rise, Iran's economy grew rapidly. From 1973-1977, Iran's GDP grew by an average annual rate of 8.4 percent.[209] However, the Shah made the grave mistake of making

---

[207] "The Iranian Revolution of 1979," *History in an Hour,* March 26, 2011,
    http://www.historyinanhour.com/2011/03/26/the-iranian-revolution-of-1979/.
[208] Robert Graham, *Iran: The Illusion of Power* (New York: Berg Publishing, 1980), 231.

ambitious promises and delivering far too little; he wasted millions on ambitious yet largely unnecessary industrialization projects and the strengthening of the military, all while inflation lowered standards of living and starved the people. Rapid industrialization became detrimental when the Shah failed to take into consideration the lack of skilled personnel, facilities, and other factors required for such change, and these projects drained the country's treasury. In 1974, Iran's budget had a $2 billion surplus, yet the country had a $7.3 billion deficit by 1978.[210]

The Shah discussing oil in a 1971 press conference

Such badly executed economic policies and industrialization programs led to the country having no option but to depend on imports and foreign trade. This increasing dependence on foreign industries severely weakened the growth and development of Iran's own domestic industries and traditional merchant class, or the Bazaaris. Instead of investing in domestic projects, affluent Iranians chose what they perceived to be a more safe and lucrative route by investing their money abroad. Understandably, these Iranians feared the risks involved in investing in domestic ventures as Iran's economy remained unstable, and even the Iranian Royal Family reportedly invested some $30-$72 billion abroad.[211]

The White Revolution, touted as the key step for the modernization of Iran, brought very little

---

[209] M. Vedat Gurbuz, "The Iranian Revolution," *Ankara Universitesi SBP Dergisi* 58, no.4 (2003): 111-112.
[210] Ibid., 112.
[211] Ibid.

positive economic changes in the eyes of most Iranians. In fact, the land reform laws passed as part of this project had many adverse effects on the livelihood of farmers – a large segment of Iran's population – because they were forced to move to poverty-ridden, overpopulated cities once they were unable to maintain their lands. At the other end of the spectrum, many educated Iranians who were sent to the countryside to aid in modernization efforts suffered greatly because of the lack of infrastructure and eventually returned home without having completed their objectives.

Growing nationwide poverty was only one part of the problem. The other was the unbridled extravagance, unchecked corruption, and privileged elitism (both real and perceived) of the Shah's government. The hostility directed toward the Shah's extravagance amidst nationwide destitution and famine only exacerbated the people's disapproval and resentment for his economic policies.[212] As the royal court continued to amass wealth, unemployment skyrocketed and poverty-stricken cities grew. Thus, some analysts have concluded that it was not the economic modernization and industrialization projects that Iranians gradually began to oppose but the instability and class inequality that they created.

Mohammad Reza Shah's modernization and Westernization projects had severe social impacts as well. The Shah's perceived disregard for Islamic tradition and Iranian culture sparked broad dissent not only from the *ulama,* the traditional protectors of the Islamic tradition of Iran, but also from the general population. For example, the Shah's 1976 decision to change from an Islamic calendar to the Imperial calendar was met with anger among pious Iranians. As historian Ervand Abrahamian wrote, this step "replaced the Muslim calendar with a new royalist calendar allocating 2,500 years for the whole monarchy and 35 years for the present monarch. Thus, Iran jumped overnight from the Muslim year 1355 to the royalist year 2535." Abrahamian further noted, "It should be noted that in the modern era few regimes anywhere have been foolhardy enough to scrap their country's religious calendar."[213]

Those changes were made in addition to various other social and religious policies launched by the Shah that were viewed by many as an assault on the religious traditions and culture of the country. The Shah's party claimed Mohammad Reza Shah to be a spiritual as well as political leader of Iran, and the party denounced the *ulama* – the historical spiritual authority of the country – as "medieval black reactionaries."[214] The Shah's party also discouraged women from wearing traditional Islamic attire, sent government investigators to scrutinize the accounts of *waqfs,* or religious endowments, and placed restrictions on which organizations could publish theology books. Furthermore, the Shah's regime passed a decree raising the age of marriage for girls from 15 to 18, and for boys from 18 to 20. Though the Shah's intentions were to adhere to

---

[212] Sandra Mackey and W. Scott Harrop, *The Iranians: Persia, Islam and the Soul of a Nation* (New York: Dutton, 1996), 236.

[213] Abrahamian, *Iran Between Two Revolutions,* 444.

[214] Ibid.

international human rights standards, this move was in complete disregard of traditional Islamic law and made without discussion or compromise. Furthermore, secular courts were given great jurisdictional authority over matters that were traditionally reserved for religious courts, and secular laws on family, marriage, and inheritance modeled on Western ones were passed, again disregarding the *sharia's* traditional authority over these matters.[215]

Some of these policies may have had genuinely good intentions and may have brought about positive social changes if implemented correctly and with a more conciliatory attitude. For example, under the Shah's reformist policies, women enjoyed significantly more rights, including being given the right to vote, attend universities, adopt Western fashion, and run as electoral candidates. However, the problem was that these changes all came within a short period of time, completely overhauling Iran's centuries-old social and religious systems in the span of mere decades, and the population had no say in them.

As dissent increased, the anger of the population was represented by clerics and religious leaders such as the exiled Ayatollah Khomeini, who declared the Shah's party to be un-Islamic and against the interests of Iran. Khomeini argued that the Shah and his party "not only violated individual rights, constitutional liberties, and international laws, but also intended to destroy Islam, ruin agriculture, waste resources on useless weapons, and plunder the country on behalf of American imperialism."[216] These clerics' voices struck a chord with many Iranians who were increasingly despondent over their poverty, frustrated over the lack of economic opportunities, and angry over the Shah's secular and pro-Western tendencies. This criticism and religiously backed opposition eventually led to the Shah's demise because he failed to cultivate any support among the religious leadership to counter Khomeini's campaign against him.

Thus, the causes of the revolution were numerous and varied, and what was perhaps most unique about this revolution was its novel yet anachronistic nature. In a world dominated by conflicts over politics and economic policies, the Iranian Revolution was shocking in that it called for and eventually established a seemingly antiquated and out-of-date state model: a theocracy.

---

[215] Ibid., 444-445.
[216] Ibid., 445.

Ayatollah Khomeini

A picture of Khomeini returning to Iran in February 1979

Ayatollah Khomeini, the leader of the revolution, slowly got out of a blue and white Chevrolet at the Behesht-e Zahra cemetery in Tehran, home to the shrines of countless martyrs of the revolution,[217] and he addressed the crowd in person for the first time: "I must tell you that Mohammad Reza Pahlavi, that evil traitor, has gone. He fled and plundered everything. He destroyed our country and filled our cemeteries. He ruined our country's economy. Even the projects he carried out in the name of progress pushed the country towards decadence. He

[217] Michael Evans and Jerome R. Corsi, *Showdown with Nuclear Iran: Radical Islam's Messianic Mission to Destroy Israel and Cripple the United States* (Nashville: Nelson Current 2006), 5.

suppressed our culture, annihilated people and destroyed all our manpower resources. We are saying this man, his government, his Majlis are all illegal. If they were to continue to stay in power, we would treat them as criminals and would try them as criminals. I shall appoint my own government. I shall slap this government in the mouth. I shall determine the government with the backing of this nation, because this nation accepts me."[218]

Ayatollah Khomeini's first address to his supporters, delivered to a cheering crowd the day he returned to Tehran from exile in France, is now famous. Khomeini, who was named Man of the Year in 1979 by *Time* and later designated the eternal religious and political leader of Iran, was a highly polemical figure. Without him, the revolution may not have succeeded, and it may not have even transpired in the first place. His life and legacy have played a large impact not only on the revolution but also on Iran's post-revolution politics, economy, and society.

The man who ultimately became the face of the revolution, Ruhollah Khomeini, was born on September 24, 1902. Young Khomeini began his Islamic education by attending a *maktab* (a traditional religious seminary) and spending countless hours of his childhood memorizing the Qur'an. In 1923, Khomeini traveled to the city of Qom and further devoted himself to Islamic education, completing the preliminary stage of *madrasa* (Islamic school) education there.[219]

In his youth, Khomeini did not engage in any political activities, and though he strictly believed that religious authority should remain in the hands of the *ulama,* as it had always been, Khomeini remained quiet even after the rise of Reza Shah and the gradual stripping of power from the *ulama.* Internally, he grew increasingly critical of the regime, but as a still young cleric, he found himself in no position to publicly voice his criticisms. Unable to speak out against an increasingly dictatorial regime that was seemingly departing from its Islamic roots, the frustrated young Khomeini turned to teaching and began to cultivate a loyal group of dedicated students who later became his staunchest and most outspoken supporters during the revolution.

Circumstances began to change in March 1961 when Ayatollah Boroujerdi, the most prominent religious leader in Qom, died. With that, Khomeini suddenly found himself in a position as one of the successors to take up the mantle left by Boroujerdi. Khomeini began publishing his writings on Islamic doctrine and *fiqh* (Islamic law), thereby establishing himself as a knowledgeable and respected religious figure, and he was soon accepted as *Marja-e Taqlid,* or a senior Shi'ite cleric and high-ranking religious authority, by a large majority of Iranians. This was significant because a *marja* is not appointed or elected; he is meant to be the source of emulation and religious knowledge, and his authority is accepted by both the lesser clergy and ordinary believers. Thus, it was incumbent on every believer to make his or her own choice of *marja* by judging who among the clergy is the most learned, the most pious, and the most

---

[218] "The Speeches of Ayatollah Khomeini," *BBC World Service,* http://www.bbc.co.uk/persian/revolution/khomeini.shtml.
[219] Baqer Moin, *Khomeini: Life of the Ayatollah* (New York: I.B. Tauris, 1999), 22-23.

qualified to lead and shape society's morality and spirituality.[220]

Ayatollah Boroujerdi

It was in 1962 that Khomeini began actively protesting the Shah's regime. He engaged in his very first act of rebellion when he organized the *ulama* against a proposed law that would no longer require elected officials to be sworn in on the Qur'an, another part of the Shah's Westernization program. In June 1963, as Mohammad Reza Shah announced the launch of his White Revolution, Khomeini gave a speech critical of the Shah, leading to his arrest and incarceration and sparking a popular protest for his release. Khomeini was eventually released in April 1964 and allowed to return to Qom.[221]

Khomeini continued to deliver inflammatory and critical speeches, leading to his second arrest in November 1964. This time, however, perhaps because his first arrest had sparked such boisterous demonstrations, Khomeini was taken directly to Mehrabad airport in Tehran for immediate exile to Turkey. Once there, due to a Turkish law that forbade the wearing of the cloak and turban, Khomeini quickly left secular Turkey for Najaf in Iraq, where he spent 13 years in exile.

---

[220] Ibid., 33.
[221] "Ayatollah Ruhollah Khomeini," *Biography.com,* 2014, http://www.biography.com/people/ayatollah-ruhollah-khomeini-13680544.

Khomeini in exile in Turkey

Khomeini in Najaf

The Shah's regime genuinely believed that Khomeini's exile would lead to Iranians forgetting about him, but little did the Shah know that Khomeini continued to preach and teach in Iraq. In fact, his lectures were popularly attended, and his work was published and widely distributed across Iraq and then smuggled back to Iran. Demonstrations continued in Iran in his name, and the size of Khomeini's following actually grew.

It was also during his exile that Khomeini explored, developed, and refined his theory on what a truly Islamic state founded on pure Islamic principles and led by a pious *ulama* would look like. Calling such a state *Velayat-e Faqih*, or Government of the Islamic Jurists[222], Khomeini envisioned a state system based on Islamic principles and led by a *faqih,* or a member of the clergy who possesses supreme knowledge of Islamic law and the faculty of justice.[223]

Once Mohammad Reza Shah understood the threat that Khomeini posed even in exile, he

---

[222] Also known as Providence of the Jurists or Guardianship of the Islamic Jurists.

[223] Neil Shevlin, "Velayat-E Faqih in the Constitution of Iran: The Implementation of Theocracy," *University of Pennsylvania Journal of Constitutional Law* 1 (Fall 198): 365-366.

decided to seek the deportation of Khomeini from Iraq. Iraqi and Iranian foreign ministers met and agreed upon the terms in New York, so in September 1978, Khomeini was detained by Iraqi troops and given two options: he could abandon his political activities and continue staying in Najaf, or he could leave the country. Khomeini chose the latter, and the following month, he left Iraq for Kuwait, where he was refused entry. After ruminating over other destinations in the region, Khomeini realized that he would be hunted endlessly by the Shah if he were to remain in the Middle East, so he embarked for France. Once in Paris, he took up residence in the quiet suburb of Neauphle-le-Chateau, which had a substantial Shi'a community. This move to a Western country, where citizens and their rights were protected and media laws were liberal, proved to be a good choice, because from this point on, journalists from across the world made their way to his residence in France, making Ayatollah Khomeini soon became a daily feature in global media.

While in France, Khomeini worked arduously to defend his views and call for the overthrow of the Shah's regime, and mere months after his relocation to Paris, on February 1, 1979, Ayatollah Khomeini made his triumphant return to his home country. By then, students, Bazaaris, and military officers had all taken to the streets in protest against the Shah, and Khomeini was quickly recognized as not only the leader of the revolution but also the new supreme leader of the country. He returned to Tehran, welcomed by a cheering crowd of supporters, and began laying the groundwork for the Islamic state he had long been envisioning.[224]

It would be simplistic to say that the ideology of the Iranian Revolution was based solely on Islam. While the Iranian Revolution took place in the name of Islam, it was what charismatic figures like Ayatollah Khomeini took from Islam that truly drove the revolution. Thus, the ideology of the revolution had multiple roots, an intricate mixture of a desire to preserve and empower the Iranian culture, raw nationalism, political populism, and religious radicalism. The slogan that was chanted by demonstrators across Iran – *Estiqlal, Azadi, Jomhuri-ye Eslami!* (Independence, Freedom, and Islamic Republic!) – demonstrated not only the broad demands of the Iranian people but also the convoluted nature of their goals.[225]

The importance of the Iranian Revolution's ideology has been raised by numerous scholars as a key contributing factor that led to the success of the revolution. Protests had occurred during the Shah's reign before the revolution, most notably in the early 1960s following his reinstatement after the coup, but these early protests fizzled and ultimately surmounted to nothing, whereas the protests that emerged in the late 1970s led to a regime-toppling revolution. The key difference between earlier demonstrations and the protests of the late 1970s can be largely attributed to the emergence of a new revolutionary ideology, which ultimately served as the engine of the revolution.

---

[224] "Ayatollah Ruhollah Khomeini," *Biography.com.*

[225] Asef Bayat, "Iran: A Green Wave for Life and Liberty," *Open Democracy,* July 7, 2009, http://www.opendemocracy.net/democracy-irandemocracy/debate.jsp?page=1.

As initial protests were squashed in the late 1950s and early 1960s, religious political ideology – and specifically, Shi'a political ideology – underwent a deep transformation in subsequent years. During the late 1960s and early1970s, Khomeini introduced a reinterpretation of Shi'a political thought and proposed an altered Islamic theory of state governance that gained popular acceptance among a broad majority of the Iranian *ulama*. The concept of *Velayat-e Faqih,* or Government of the Islamic Jurists, outlined a new state structure in which the *ulama* have absolute authority over the execution of Islamic laws, and this novel vision completely contradicted the current state structure, one led by a religiously illegitimate Shah who was deemed to rule in ways that were inconsistent with Islamic principles. Thus, Khomeini introduced an entirely unprecedented solution to the present woes of Iranian society; there would be no mere reforms or changes in state policy but a complete overhaul of the status quo and the replacement of the monarchy with a truly Islamic state.

This new ideology, or "mutant ideology," as some have called it, gained wide acceptance because it had a key advantage over the Shah's way of rule, which was largely based on secular objectives such as Westernization, industrialization, and modernization. The advantage was that *Velayat-e Faqih* was an Islamic ideology in a dominantly Muslim country, endorsed and led by a group of high-ranking *ulama*. The toppling of the Shah's rule was described as a religious duty, which all pious Muslims were to feel an obligation to participate in. The *ulama's* view that the Shah's regime was illegitimate was nothing new, but "Imam [Khomeini] was the first Shi'a jurist who used the term 'Islamic state' in a book on Islamic jurisprudence."[226] Indeed, the ways of previous clerics and religious leaders were largely "reactive, not initiatory; steps—often steps against some measure of the government—were taken by the great juriconsults [*marjas*] only when the emerging unity of opinion had identified a threat."[227] In contrast, the ideology that Khomeini introduced directly challenged the legitimacy of the Shah's rulership and clearly called for state rule by Islamic jurists. As scholar Mehdi Shadmehr wrote, "Illegitimacy of the state alone does not require action if there is no alternative; nonetheless, if this illegitimacy is combined with a legitimate Islamic alternative and an interpretation of Islam that requires action against injustice, then illegitimacy calls for active opposition, martyrdom, and revolution. The new ideology set a new goal with revolutionary implications: Creating an Islamic state."[228]

Khomeini's argument was fairly straightforward. Like many other Islamic fundamentalists in history, Khomeini believed that Islamic laws were applicable to every aspect of life and society, from the private and personal realms like family and marriage to the public arenas like state governance, economic policy, and judicial system. However, the key point for Khomeini was that those who enforce these laws – the leadership – must have supreme knowledge of them in order to properly and effectively do so. In addition, it was necessary for these leaders to be

---

[226] Mohsen Kadivar, *Hukumat Vilayi* (Tehran: Nashr Niy, 1998), 167-168.

[227] Roy Mottahedeh, *The Mantle of the Prophet: Religion and Politics in Iran* (New York: Simon and Schuster, 1985), 223.

[228] Mehdi Shadmehr, "Ideology and the Iranian Revolution" (University of Miami, January 2012), 7.

completely just and fair, "for otherwise they manipulate the law and lead the country to tyranny."[229] In the eyes of Khomeini, the qualified leaders were the *fuqaha,* or jurists, and therefore, a truly Islamic state was to be controlled and managed by jurists. "It is the jurist who is not influenced by foreigners, and sacrifices his life to defend the people's rights and freedom and independence and the boundaries of the country," Khomeini stated. "The program of the state and administration and its necessary laws are ready…It is our duty to implement and execute Islam's plan for the state."[230]

It is interesting to note that the effect of Khomeini's ideology on the increasingly restless population was also noted by SAVAK. In a report, the Shah's shadowy intelligence agency had noted, "The plan of the Islamic state: Ruhollah Khomeini, parallel to expressing his oppositions to Iran's social reforms and the existing regime in the Iranian society, presented the plan of the so-called Islamic state…the naïve people who always consider the face-value of his statements, employed these ideas as a goal in their propaganda, and some of the religious groups that aim to topple [the regime], too, have made achieving it [,the Islamic state,] a priority. After a few years, it is observed now that religious fanatics, in their books and notes that they publish, compare a hypothetical Islamic state with different social systems and enumerate its characteristics and advantages."[231] Thus, it appears even the Shah's trusted intelligence agency acknowledged the effects Khomeini's ideology was having on the burgeoning protests. The Islamic opposition was emboldened by Khomeini, and this was the key difference between the protests of late 1970s that eventually led to the revolution and previous protest movements. As Ralph Waldo Emerson once said, "Every revolution was first a thought in one man's mind; and when the same thought occurs to another man, it is the key to that era."[232] It may be an exaggeration to say that the Iranian Revolution started with a thought in Khomeini's mind, but the power of Khomeini's ideology cannot be understated.

Key Events

The Iranian Revolution transpired relatively quickly for one that led to such significant changes, and the protest movements that had begun to organize in the mid- to late 1970s flowered into full-fledged demonstrations and riots in a matter of mere months.

The events and causes of the revolution discussed before were building to a crescendo during the later years of the decade. The Shah's White Revolution and policies of modernization, Westernization, and industrialization were underway, but this was also the era of significant steps for democratization and human and civil rights across the world, led by President Jimmy

---

[229] Ibid., 8.
[230] Ruhollah Khomeini, *Gilayat Faqih* (Tehran, Iran, 2007), quoted in Shadmehr, "Ideology and the Iranian Revolution," 8-9.
[231] Akbar Fallahi, *Salha-y Tab'id Imam Khomeini (rah)* (Tehran, Iran: Markaz Asnad Inqilab Islami, Fall 2006), 210-211.
[232] Ralph W. Emerson, *The Essays of Emerson: Volume the First* (London: Arthur M. Humphreys, 1841), 3.

Carter. It was during this decade of global political liberalization that the Shah gradually began to loosen his grip, and even the much-feared SAVAK lessened its degree of surveillance and oppression. In the 1970s, Mohammad Reza Shah invited international human rights organizations to Iran to inspect prisons and observe the trials of his political opponents, and he also announced that parliamentary elections "that would grant the electorate a free choice" would be held in 1978.[233]

The opposition quickly took advantage of the political liberalization by seizing on its chance to organize, and by 1977, the beginnings of protest were already simmering. Over the course of several months, intellectuals and scholars began testing the waters of the Shah's ostensible liberalization process by tentatively beginning to publish their grievances and criticisms in the form of essays, letters, and pamphlets. Organizations and political parties that had long operated underground began to emerge above ground, further testing the limits of liberalization. New student groups and human rights organizations were founded, advocating for President Carter's principles of universal human rights to be implemented in Iran. These groups' "very existence implied an enormous change in the political environment, and they provided important foci for the articulation of grievances and the beginnings of expression of public opinion."[234]

Ironically, it was not religious Islamic groups that first initiated these protests, meaning the prelude to the revolution was largely secular. Leftist groups such as the Iranian Writers Association began demonstrating, denouncing the Shah's rule, and calling for full liberalization, and in the fall of 1977, thousands gathered at the Goethe Institute in Tehran, led by the leftist intellectual Saeed Soltanpour.[235] A sit-in ensued, and the protest eventually turned violent as demonstrators clashed with security forces, leading to several deaths and dozens injured. Though the Iranian Writers Association's contribution to the revolution ended here, it was decisive in that it was the first spark and the biggest sign of things to come; the association "played a crucial role by attacking the government in the initial stage of the conflict when it appeared unassailable."[236]

In October 1977, Mostafa Khomeini, the son of Ayatollah Khomeini, died of a heart attack in Najaf, Iraq. Like his father, Mostafa was a respected cleric in Iraq, and his sudden death and the suspicious circumstances surrounding it brought rise to whispers of foul play and a Shah-sanctioned assassination, which eventually transformed into outright accusations that SAVAK had murdered Mostafa. Khomeini himself, who had initially responded to Mostafa's death calmly and quietly, began shouting anti-Shah slogans at Mostafa's memorial and declaring his son a martyr. In Qom and in Tehran, clerics and Khomeini's supporters gathered to deliver

---

[233] Daniel Philip Ritter, "Why the Iranian Revolution Was Nonviolent: Internationalized Social Change and the Iron Cage of Liberalism" (PhD diss., University of Texas at Austin, 2010), 201-202.

[234] Ritter, "Why the Iranian Revolution Was Nonviolent," 203.

[235] Ibid., 206-207.

[236] Misagh Parsa, *Social Origins of the Iranian Revolution* (New Brunswick, NJ: Rutgers University Press, 1989), 179.

speeches and demonstrations. The police eventually intervened and dispersed the crowd as the protests turned more radical,[237] but demonstrations continued throughout the year, and the number of those arrested continued to grow. Mostafa's death spawned mass political rallies and vociferous demonstrations, and for many Iranians, this was their first exposure to Ayatollah Khomeini and his views. Khomeini would later attribute his son's death to God due to the way it helped forward the cause of revolution.

Mostafa Khomeini

By January 1978, protests were intensifying, with hard-line students, Khomeini supporters, and clerics marching through the streets of Qom. In response, the Shah once again reverted back to repressive measures by shrinking the political space available to the opposition. On January 7, 1978, an article that slandered Khomeini as a British agent and a homosexual of Indian origins was published in the national newspaper *Ittila'at*. Though no author was attributed to the article, the people quickly concluded that the government was undoubtedly involved. Khomeini's supporters reacted vehemently, and the following day, thousands of Islamic teachers, students, clerics, and Khomeini supporters marched the streets of Qom. In conjunction with that, the Bazaari merchants shut down their shops. Security forces clashed with the protestors, and approximately 70 protestors lost their lives, while over 400 were injured. [238]

These deaths and sacrifices again upheld the notion of martyrdom, as it had been when Mostafa Khomeini had died, and this incident marked the beginning of the 40-day cycle of mourning that would become a central element of the opposition's tactics against the regime. On

---

[237] Michael Axworthy, *Revolutionary Iran: A History of the Islamic Republic* (London: Penguin Group, 2013), 101-102.
[238] Ritter, "Why the Iranian Revolution Was Nonviolent," 207-208.

February 18, 1978, mourning processions were organized to commemorate the deaths of those killed in the January demonstrations in 16 cities across Iran. The processions were all peaceful, but in the city of Tabriz in northwestern Iran, demonstrators increasingly grew violent and eventually clashed with security forces. Though it remains unclear which side initiated the violence, activists and protestors died in this incident again, continuing the cycle of protest, martyrdom, and mourning that repeated itself several more times in cities across Iran.[239]

By late March 1978, protests had spread to over 50 cities, and accounts of demonstrations and clashes with security forces were recorded in detail and distributed by the opposition around the country. However, in June 1978, the opposition made the unexpected decision to call for a halt to the 40-day mourning and protest cycle, fearing the regime's increasingly violent means of repression and the growing number of dead.[240] Though this placed a sudden stop on the momentum of the revolution, the protests had already achieved a great goal for Khomeini, who was already recognized as the de facto leader of the opposition movement, with radical Islamists as his most vocal and prominent supporters.

In fact, some believe that it was the government that inadvertently cemented Khomeini's position as leader of the opposition. Before 1978, the opposition had been led by the intelligentsia, leftist groups, and the middle class, less in the form of violent protests and rallies than in the form of written declarations, published letters to the Shah, and pamphlets and brochures. However, the January 1978 publication of the slandering article on Khomeini had sparked the wrath of the Islamists and served as the trigger for the merging of religion and politics. With that, demonstrations were now led by the *ulama* and organized at mosques and around religious days.[241] The opposition was effectively hijacked by Khomeini and his revolutionary Islamists, at the expense of the more moderate, liberal, and reform-minded secular opposition.

The Shah's regime also continued to disadvantage itself by making irreversible blunders that contributed to the revolution instead of preventing it. On August 19, 1978, the Cinema Rex in the oil city of Abadan, in southwestern Iran, was set ablaze. At least 377 people, and possibly more, lost their lives that day, and the government swiftly blamed the opposition without providing justifications. The details surrounding the blaze were suspicious, and the presence of SAVAK agents at the cinema did nothing to stop the rumors that the intelligence agency had orchestrated the fire as a false flag operation.[242] The doors of the cinema had been barred, and remnants of chemical agents were found, indicating that this was an intentional crime. Though later findings concluded that revolutionary students had started the fire, since the circumstances of the tragedy were so murky, the opposition took advantage by carefully crafting the belief that SAVAK was

---

[239] Ritter, "Why the Iranian Revolution Was Nonviolent," 208-210.
[240] Ibid., 211.
[241] Ibid.
[242] Daniel L. Byman, "The Rise of Low-Tech Terrorism," *Brookings,* May 6, 2007, http://www.brookings.edu/research/articles/2007/05/06terrorism-byman.

behind the fire.[243] This was a major blow to the regime, which had failed to come up with an organized and convincing response to the accusations, and the incident sparked protests across the country.

Picture of a protest held in Tehran

Even as the protests widened and intensified, they continued to take Mohammad Reza Shah by surprise, more evidence of the disconnect between the Shah and his people. This created a vicious cycle; since the Shah was "largely baffled by the protests against his rule," he responded to the protests indecisively, at times with placation and concessionary measures but other times with violent suppression.[244] The old Islamic calendar was restored, press restrictions were lifted, and free elections were promised, but clerics continued to be arrested and SAVAK was still beating and detaining activists and protestors. Historian Ryszard Kapuscinski wrote in his book, *Shah of Shahs*, "The Shah was reproached for being irresolute. Politicians, they say, ought to be resolute. But resolute about what? The Shah was resolute about retaining his throne, and to this end he explored every possibility. He tried shooting and he tried democratizing, he locked people up and he released them, he fired some and promoted others, he threatened and then he commended. All in vain."[245] This mixed "carrot and stick" approach had little effect, partly

---

[243] Glenn Eldon Curtis and Eric Hooglund, ed. *Iran: A Country Study* (Washington, DC: Government Printing Office, 2008), 48.

[244] Axworthy, *Revolutionary Iran*, 107.

[245] Ryszard Kapuscinski, *Shah of Shahs* (London: Penguin UK, 2006).

because of the inconsistency of the measures, but mostly because it was too little too late. The Cinema Rex incident further fueled the opposition and sparked an irreversible escalation of anti-regime sentiment.

On September 7, 1978, following another major series of protests, the Shah appointed a general with a ruthless reputation, Gholam-Ali Oveissi, as military governor of Tehran. On midnight of September 8, 1978, General Oveissi declared martial law in Tehran and 11 other restless cities, but either the announcement came too late for those who were planning to continue protesting or they simply didn't care. Regardless, at 8:00 a.m. on September 8, 1978, thousands were gathered at Jaleh Square in Tehran,[246] and the government sent in the security forces, resulting in one of the deadliest clashes of the revolution. Though the official figure of death was 87, many more were likely killed that day as tear gas and bullets filled the square, and further clashes occurred throughout the city for the remainder of the day. Sociologist John Foran described the tragedy of what came to be known as Black Friday: "When ordered to disperse people sat down and bared their chests. Soldiers fired first into the air, then directly into the crowd in a massacre. Shooting continued during the day, including aerial attacks from helicopters on the southern slums. Officially, eighty-six people were killed; bodies in the Tehran morgue were assigned numbers which reached over 3,000. The event came to be known as Black Friday, and it marked the declaration of open war between the government and the population."[247]

---

[246] Axworthy, *Revolutionary Iran,* 112.
[247] John Foran, *Fragile Resistance: Social Transformation in Iran from 1500 to the Revolution* (Boulder, CO: Westview, 1993), 381.

A picture of some killed during Black Friday

The consequences of Black Friday were severe for the Shah. Those who were ambivalent about going against their ruler were now convinced that the Shah had lost his justness and therefore his right to rule. The opposition was now completely radicalized, and compromise with the regime was all but out of the question. That said, evidence has emerged that Mohammad Reza Shah himself was shocked by the incident at Jaleh Square, and one account described a phone call between the Shah and President Carter; "when he spoke to President Carter on the telephone on 10 September he sounded 'stunned and spoke almost by rote, as if going through the motions.'"[248] The full gravity and direness of the situation now fully loomed upon the Shah, as he realized too late that he was witnessing the coming of a revolution.

As summer turned to fall, protests continued in Tehran and elsewhere across Iran. In October 1978, Ayatollah Khomeini, who was expelled from Iraq by urging of the Shah, made his way to France. Yet again, this move by Mohammad Reza Shah to force the relocation of the leader of the opposition to a Western country, where media laws were freer and civil liberties were guaranteed, proved to be detrimental to the regime. Khomeini now had access to the world's media, and he was able to better coordinate the opposition movement from his headquarters at Neauphle-le-Chateau. The pressure against the Shah was now international, and Khomeini began

---

[248] Axworthy, *Revolutionary Iran,* 113.

courting non-Islamist opposition groups to gain their support while unifying his own.

In the fall of 1978, workers in the bazaar, private, and public sectors, including Iran's key oil industry, began striking on an unprecedented and massive scale. The motivation behind these strikes were purported by revolutionaries to be political, but in truth, it was largely economic; workers were hoping to gain some concessions from the regime in these unstable times, such as increased salaries and improved benefits. Though the strikers did call for political changes, many of them were tied to economic ones, such as the expulsion of all foreigners from key industries, the nationalization of the oil industry, and similar measures. By late October, a general strike was declared across Iran, and many major industries came to a halt.

The general strike was absolutely debilitating to the country, paralyzing its economy and severely increasing political and economic instability. Moreover, despite the fact that not all industries went on strike, many other workplaces were still impacted and forced to remain idle because of the impact of the general strike. For example, when custom officials went on strike and "ink could not be delivered to the central bank, the Iranian economy experienced physical shortage of money as no new bills were being printed, resulting in industries closing down since the lack of money meant they could no longer pay their workers."[249] The unfolding power of this non-violent strike has been explored by many, including Amuzegar: "With meticulous and methodical organization and direction, rarely if ever seen in Iran's public administration, the first critical strike began in the oil fields, causing both a drastic drop in oil exports and exchange earnings and a shortage of domestic fuel. Thereafter, one by one, the other strategic centers of the economy – the ministry of water and power, the customs administration, the treasury, the central bank, and Iran Air – joined the antigovernment protesters. While the final cause of the regime's downfall may still be a matter of speculation, there is no doubt that the economic paralysis caused by the public employees' strikes was a most, if not the most, crucial factor."[250]

Mohammad Reza Shah was again shocked by this drastic development. He could not fully confront and suppress the strikers, but he couldn't completely yield to their demands. He could use force to coerce his people off the streets, but he could not use the same tactic to make his people go to work. The Shah therefore continued his vague and ultimately ineffective approach of "carrot and stick," mixing sporadic repression with mild concessions. These ultimately had little effect on quelling the anger, and the number of strikes increased drastically throughout the fall of 1978.[251] On November 5, the Shah dismissed the moderate prime minister and appointed a military government, headed by General Gholam Reza Azhari, commander of the Imperial Guard.[252] Weeks later, Azhari would tell the U.S. Ambassador to Iran, "You must know this and you must tell it to your government. This country is lost because the Shah cannot make up his

---

[249] Ritter, "Why the Iranian Revolution Was Nonviolent," 218.
[250] Amuzegar 1991, 284 in RITTER
[251] Ritter, "Why the Iranian Revolution Was Nonviolent," 216-217.
[252] Curtis and Hooglund, *Iran: A Country Study*, 49.

mind."

Azhari

Though the strikes had not been executed by Khomeini or the revolutionaries, the opposition quickly realized their utility in increasing the already mounting pressure against the Shah and destabilizing the regime. The strikes further made it difficult to repress the opposition without repressing workers, who were key to the restoration of the Iranian economy. As the Shah himself noted, "You can't crack down on one block and make the people on the next block behave."[253] As a result, Khomeini swiftly endorsed the general strike in late November, and he called upon the Iranian people to go on perpetual strike until the Shah abdicated.[254]

The Islamic month of remembrance, Muharram (to Shiites, the month that signifies mourning for the martyrdom of the Prophet Muhammad's grandson Hussein), began on December 2, 1978. Protests were renewed, and the opposition organized massive demonstrations for the days of *Tasu'a* and *Ashura* on December 10 and 11 respectively, which commemorate the death of Hussein. The unprecedented size of these demonstrations was staggering; in Tehran, somewhere between 500,000-1 million people gathered on December 10, and over 1 million people on December 11. Thousands more marched in dozens of cities and towns across Iran. In total, it has been estimated that approximately 6-9 million Iranians participated in the Muharram Protests.[255]

---

[253] Charles Kurzman, *The Unthinkable Revolution in Iran* (Cambridge, MA: Harvard University Press, 2004), 113-114.

[254] Ritter, "Why the Iranian Revolution Was Nonviolent," 219.

[255] Axworthy, *Revolutionary Iran,* 121.

The sheer number of protestors and the non-violent, dignified, yet starkly adamant nature of the protests served as the final wake-up call for the Shah. This was no longer a crazed uprising or a chaotic opposition movement that could be wrestled under control and subdued. The crowds were peaceful, restrained, and determined, and Khomeini's portraits filled the streets. Many Iranians had already taken down their pictures of Mohammad Reza Shah, and foreign advisors and workers were leaving the country, to the extent that by early January 1979, the number of Americans in Iran dropped from 58,000 to just 12,000.[256] Desertions were now rampant in the Iranian army, and soldiers joined the opposition.[257] The message was clear: the Shah must go.

---

[256] Axworthy, *Revolutionary Iran,* 123-124.
[257] Ritter, "Why the Iranian Revolution Was Nonviolent," 234.

Pictures of the protests

In mid-December, the Shah began talks with the moderate opposition and reached out to several of its leaders, including Shapour Bakhtiar. The Shah offered Bakhtiar an opportunity to form a government, and Bakhtiar agreed, provided that the Shah leave the country. On January 3, 1979, Bakhtiar secured a vote of confidence from the Majlis and formed a cabinet. The Shah left Iran on January 16, and the streets of Iran were filled with celebration. Statues of the Shah were pulled down, and processions carrying Khomeini banners and waving Khomeini's pictures filled Tehran.

Bakhtiar

A picture of revolutionaries pulling down a statue of Reza Shah

A picture of protesters pulling down a statue of the Shah

Once confirmed as prime minister, Shapour Bakhtiar swiftly undertook certain liberalizing measures that were designed to appease the opposition. Martial law came to an end, press restrictions were lifted, political prisoners were freed, red light districts were closed down, and the dismantling of SAVAK was promised.[258] Iran withdrew from the Central Treaty Organization (CENTO), a military alliance it helped form in 1955 with Iraq, Pakistan, Turkey, and the U.K., cancelled arms deals worth $7 billion from the U.S., and announced it would no longer sell oil to Israel or South Africa.[259]

---

[258] Axworthy, *Revolutionary Iran,* 129.
[259] Curtis and Hooglund, *Iran: A Country Study*, 50.

Despite these measures, Bakhtiar found difficulties gaining the support of Khomeini and much of the opposition because he was seen as the last prime minister appointed by the Shah, which was true. Bakhtiar was soon expelled from his party, and Khomeini declared his government illegal. Demonstrations and protests continued, largely spurred on by Khomeini and his supporters.

On January 20, 1979, Khomeini announced that he was returning to Tehran. As part of his liberalization efforts, Bakhtiar had initially stated that Khomeini was welcome to return, but he chose to close down Mehrabad airport to prevent Khomeini's homecoming, fearing that the Ayatollah's presence would only further destabilize the country. This proved to be a dire mistake, because between January 26 and 28, as troops worked to shut down the airport, several protestors were killed as they tried to prevent the closure. The deaths were condemned, and Bakhtiar was declared to be just another corrupt leader willing to kill demonstrators at the behest of the Shah. The airport reopened on January 31,[260] and the gates were open for Khomeini's return.

On February 1, 1979, Ayatollah Khomeini landed in Tehran on a chartered Air France plane. Amid a rapturous welcome from millions of Iranians, Khomeini announced that he was appointing Mehdi Bazargan as prime minister of a provisional government – one that competed with that of Shapour Bakhtiar. The army, Western powers, and the people began abandoning Bakhtiar's government en masse.[261]

---

[260] Axworthy, *Revolutionary Iran,* 130.
[261] Ibid., 130.

A picture of Khomeini's return

Mehdi Bazargan

On February 11, 1979, 22 senior military commanders made an announcement declaring the neutrality of the armed forces. The withdrawal of the military was key to the isolation of Bakhtiar's government and its eventual collapse, as it was the only body that had any potential to wrestle power out of the hands of Khomeini. Fearing assassination, by late afternoon on February 11, Shapour Bakhtiar had gone into hiding and was nowhere to be found. The rulership was free for Ayatollah Khomeini to take.

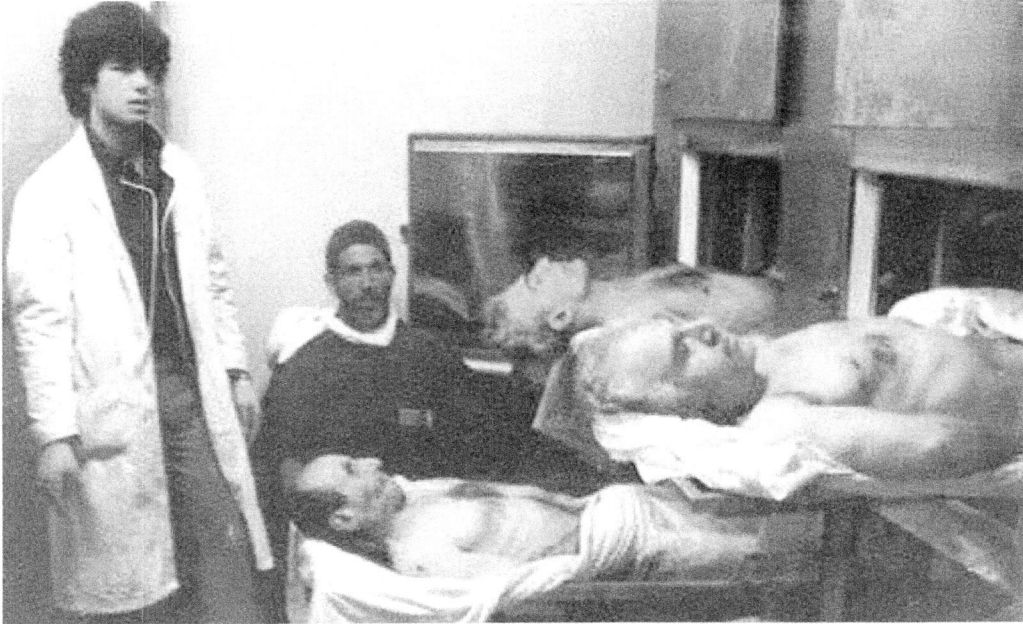

A picture of executed generals in February 1979

The Rise of the Islamic Republic

Khomeini in early 1979

With the fall of Shapour Bakhtiar and his government, Ayatollah Khomeini was free to consolidate his power and build his envisioned state. Within days of the success of the revolution, a flurry of political and journalistic activities arose; political parties were formed, new newspapers and media outlets emerged, and social groups were established. Khomeini recognized the outpouring of activity in this environment of victory and newfound freedom, and he quickly understood that it must be controlled. Nonetheless, he also understood that sudden oppression would be detrimental in such a highly charged environment.

Khomeini's initial caution led to conflicts and power struggles both within the ruling government and between the government and other organizations. Khomeini's subsequent consolidation of power was an arduous process, but one that significantly strengthened his position to an irreversible degree.

Mehdi Bazargan had been selected by Khomeini to head the first post-revolution government of Iran, but in reality, neither Bazargan nor his government had any control. Hundreds of independent revolutionary committees operated in Tehran and across Iran as local administrators, and most of these were not answerable to any central authority. Though many of the functions these committees performed were lawful and well-intentioned, such as policing neighborhoods and guarding government buildings, other were unlawful, such as making unauthorized arrests and conducting de factor tribunals and executions of Shah loyalists.[262] The revolutionary blood still pumped in the veins of the people, and workers, merchants, and students frequently rejected the authority of appointed government officials. New political groups popped up left and right, all professing a wide range of ideologies, from Islamist to Marxist to secular, and Khomeini himself headed the Islamic Republican Party (IRP), created in February of 1979 by his followers only days after his rise to power.[263]

This initial period was chaotic and disorganized, but it was ultimately necessary for the rebuilding of Iran. According to scholar Michael Axworthy, "When initiatives with public consequences were undertaken, ordinary people did not necessarily know who was responsible or why what was done had been done. There were too many independent or semi-independent poles of authority. This was the first phase of the Islamic republic, and in some respects it was the defining phase. To a reduced but still significant degree, that uncertainty, the multi-polar political system and also the occasional application of extra-judicial violence, still persist in Iran today."[264]

Within the provisional government itself, multiple factions and poles of authority emerged. The Revolutionary Council, established by Khomeini in January 1979, was required to share power with the prime minister. The cabinet had supreme executive authority, but the Revolutionary Council held legislative authority. Not surprisingly, the various branches of power quickly began to clash; the cabinet desired to reestablish stability and central authority as quickly as possible, while the clerics of the Revolutionary Council focused on social measures to realign the Iranian population according to Islamic principles. Furthermore, by late February, special tribunals were being conducted by newly established Revolutionary Courts, tasked with trying, sentencing, and executing officials of the pre-revolution government. The activities of these shadowy courts brought about great debate and controversy, as both domestic and international human rights groups and lawyers called for fair trials.[265]

In May 1979, Khomeini authorized the formation of the Islamic Revolutionary Guard Corps, largely made up of leaders of the revolution loyal to Khomeini and the *ulama*, and created as a counterweight to the regular armed forces formed during the Pahlavi dynasty.[266] The Revolutionary Guards were key in the effective curbing of rival political groups and successful suppression of protests and uprisings that emerged throughout 1979. Even while the government fought dissent and rebellion, Mehdi Bazargan and his cabinet found themselves powerless, with

---

[262] Curtis and Hooglund, *Iran: A Country Study*, 52.
[263] Axworthy, *Revolutionary Iran*, 145.
[264] Ibid.
[265] Curtis and Hooglund, *Iran: A Country Study*, 53.
[266] "Profile: Iran's Revolutionary Guards," *BBC News*, last modified October 18, 2009, http://news.bbc.co.uk/2/hi/middle_east/7064353.stm.

authority and power entirely in the hands of Khomeini, the IRP, the Revolutionary Guards, and the Revolutionary Council.

Khomeini and Bazargan

On April 1, 1979, the Iranian people went to the polls to determine what kind of political system would be established, and according to the ruling government, the results of the constitutional referendum were overwhelming: more than 98% had voted for the creation of an Islamic Republic. Of course, opposition groups and critics called for voters to be given a wider choice, since the only option on the ballot was an Islamic Republic.[267] Furthermore, no explanation or description of such a political system was given to the people. Nonetheless, the government declared the will of the people to be the formation of an Islamic republic, and Ayatollah Khomeini subsequently proclaimed the establishment of the Islamic Republic of Iran.

In mid-June, the provisional government revealed a draft constitution that did not differ much from the 1906 constitution, save for the replacement of the monarchy with a president. Khomeini approved the draft and called for its immediate implementation, but there were some calls for changes to be made. A 73-member Assembly of Experts, composed of clerics and IRP supporters, convened in mid-August to review the draft constitution and rewrite certain points, but naturally, the clerical domination of this assembly led to the new draft giving significant power to the *ulama* and "establish[ed] the basis for a state dominated by the Shia clergy."[268] The

---

[267] "Iran after the victory of 1979's Revolution," *Iran Chamber Society,*
    http://www.iranchamber.com/history/islamic_revolution/revolution_and_iran_after1979_2.php.
[268] "Iran after the victory of 1979's Revolution," *Iran Chamber Society.*

Guardian Council, composed of 12 appointed jurists and experts in Islamic law, was also formed and charged with interpreting the constitution and forming Iranian law. This new draft was approved in another national referendum in December, and once again, the government reported that over 98% of the voters had approved.[269]

Meanwhile, Mohammad Reza Shah, who was suffering from cancer, was reported to have gained entry into the U.S. to receive medical treatment. This news sparked protests in Iran, where many feared that the treatment was an excuse for the Shah to amass American support and attempt another coup, much like he had done in 1953. Thousands protested in Tehran to demand the Shah's extradition to face trial in Iran, culminating in the Iran hostage crisis of November 4, 1979, when a group of hardliners occupied the U.S. Embassy in Tehran and took the embassy staff hostage. Days later, on November 6, Bazargan resigned and the Revolutionary Council took his place to perform the prime minister's functions, pending presidential and parliamentary elections. Abdolhassan Bani Sadr, an associate of Ayatollah Khomeini, won the January 1980 elections and became president of the Islamic republic.[270]

The Shah and his wife shortly before their exile

Ayatollah Khomeini utilized political Islam as a means to acquire the necessary position and power to configure the Iranian state, but he did not necessarily allow Islamic principles to directly influence the actual configuration itself. Khomeini legitimized his ascendancy by following the "Doctrine of Mass," the Shi'a belief that the Prophet Muhammed's twelfth *imam* will reemerge at the end of time to reclaim his position as the chosen leader. Khomeini, who

---

[269] Curtis and Hooglund, *Iran: A Country Study*, 56.
[270] "Iran after the victory of 1979's Revolution," *Iran Chamber Society*.

held the title of *marja-e-taqlid*, introduced his new doctrine *Velaya-e-Fiqh* to appoint himself as the de facto twelfth *imam*, consequently legitimizing himself as the ruler while still following Islamic tradition.[271]

Upon rising to power, Khomeini structured the state in such a way that it appeared purely Islamic; Islam became the only source of legitimacy and law, while complete and ultimate sovereignty was held by Allah. However, he was essentially projecting an "Islamic façade" while working hard to solidify his authority as Supreme Leader. The Supreme Leader, in addition to his functions as the most superior religious leader in Iran, also became the commander-in-chief and political leader of the state. The President, nominally the second-in-command, was given limited powers, thus subordinating the executive branch to the Supreme Leader. The Majlis was equally powerless, as it was constantly monitored by the Guardian Council, which was composed of the influential interpreters of all laws passed by the Majlis, accountable only to the Supreme Leader. The Guardian Council, in addition to having veto power over these proposed Majlis laws, was also given the authority to examine and approve or disapprove presidential and parliamentary candidates.[272] According to scholar Mihrangiz Kar's study on Iranian constitutional constraints, "every single reform law that the Majilis has passed over the last two years has been stopped in its tracks by the Guardian Council...and thus, the Iranian Majilis is not a genuine parliament...[it is] completely unable to fulfill its responsibilities."[273]

Such a structuring of the new Iranian Islamic Republic illustrates the point that although political Islam legitimized Khomeini's rise and his reorganization of Iran, it had no direct influence on the state structure that emerged. A clear illustration of this is Iran's alliance with Syria during the Iran-Iraq War of 1980 that immediately followed the revolution. Syria had one of the most extensive networks of political Islamist activists seeking to overthrow the Ba'athist regime and establish an Islamic state, and these Syrian activists looked to Iran for support, but Iran decided to form an alliance with Syria instead of aiding the Syrian activists, thus choosing political cooperation and financial assistance for its war against Iraq over advancing political Islamist ideology and influence.[274] In essence, Islamic principles were found to be lacking in the structure of the state that Khomeini built and in many of his policies, despite the fact that Islam was what he fought for and what he promised to his people.

Over time, the Supreme Leader became less and less inclined to share power as his domination over all aspects of the government grew, and subsequent opposition such as the reformist movement "only set in motion a non-institutional process of accumulation of power by the Supreme Leader...the result [being] the consolidation of a system of personal rule."[275] Political

---

[271] Pauline Jones Luong, "Self-Consciously Islamic States - Saudi Arabia and Iran Compared" (lecture, POLS1430: Roots of Radical Islam, Providence, RI, September 30, 2010).

[272] Ibid.

[273] Mihrangiz Kar, "Constitutional Constraints," *Journal of Democracy* 14, no. 1 (2001): 134.

[274] Shireen T. Hunter, "Iran and the Spread of Revolutionary Islam," *Third World Quarterly* 10, no. 2 (1988): 738.

Islam was thus manipulated to bring a ruler to power, as well as to retain that power and control the state, including any opposition.

With the Cold War raging and a shifting geopolitical order, the world was a turbulent place when the Iranian Revolution occurred. The rise of Ayatollah Khomeini as Supreme Leader and his government's subsequent domestic and foreign policies had great impact on the reconstruction of Iran and the reshaping of the regional and world order.

From the outset, establishing an ideal religious society in Iran, and eventually across the world, was a professed aim of the Iranian Revolution. Since its inception, the revolution operated on a universalistic view of the world, with Khomeini deeming the bipolar system that had emerged as a result of the Cold War flawed. He further declared the two superpowers, the United States and the Soviet Union, to be illegitimate. The revolution was based on the belief that Islam was the solution to all political, social, and economic needs, and thus, once Khomeini gained rulership, he believed that as the only Islamic republic in the world, Iran now had a duty to help implement an alternative political doctrine for all the subjugated populations of the world. In order to accomplish this, Khomeini understood that he first had to consolidate power and strengthen his own rule, and that he and the *ulama* had to institutionalize the clergy's hold over state governance and truly transform Iran from a monarchy into an Islamic republic, with a constitution, laws, political party system, and government structure all based entirely on Islam.

Though the revolution had occurred under the umbrella of Islam, the opposition had not been composed entirely of Islamists. In fact, Iran's revolution had brought together a diverse cross-section of religious, secular, and political groups, as well as guerilla movements and social organizations. Once the revolution was deemed a success and Khomeini went from leader of the Islamic Revolution to leader of the Islamic Republic, many of these various factions realized that they were unaware of the specifics of Khomeini's religious views on the nature of government, politics, and Islam. It could be said that Khomeini intentionally toned down the religious nature of his goals while leading the revolution, and his denunciations of the Shah and calls for a new and just government were kept largely in the political context rather than one that was purely religious. Thus, even though the opposition "had a common enemy (the Shah, Pahlavi despotism, and foreign control) and a common purpose (a more just and egalitarian government), there had been no agreement upon the particular form of government or even its leadership."[276] Aside from his most ardent supporters and followers, few revolutionaries had even heard of Khomeini's novel concept of *Velayat-e Faqih.*

The initial post-revolution months were riddled with frequent clashes between rival revolutionary committees, the forming and breaking of political alliances in government, and

[275] Said Amir Arjomand, "The Rise and Fall of President Khatami and the Reform Movement in Iran," *Constellations* 12, no. 4 (2005).

[276] John L. Esposito, *Islam and Politics* (Syracuse, NY: Syracuse University, 1991), 204.

conflict between members of the IRP. Khomeini set out to consolidate his authority by having his government eliminate political opposition, reorganize and strengthen the Revolutionary Guards, place the revolutionary committees under the management of the Interior Ministry, and incorporate the revolutionary courts into the formal judicial system. Whether the Iranian Revolution brought about a more or less severe political repression has been the topic of an enduring debate. Though SAVAK was dissolved, the Revolutionary Guards was formed in its stead as an equally ruthless and secretive security and intelligence force. Political groups that were seen as a challenge to Khomeini's autonomous rule were swiftly oppressed, much like they were during the Pahlavi dynasty.

In addition to the establishment of a theocracy and the consolidation of power by Khomeini and the *ulama,* the Iranian Revolution resulted in the near complete destruction of the power and influence of the predominantly secular and pro-West political elite who had ruled Iran since the early days of the Pahlavi dynasty. The new political elite was made up of the *ulama,* many from middle and lower classes, instead of Western-educated, English-speaking members of the upper class. Thus, the policies that they implemented were not necessarily progressive but more in line with their stated purpose of the promotion of religious ideals and values. As John L. Esposito noted, religion dominated all aspects of this new Iran: "Overseeing Iran's government was the Ayatollah Khomeini as the guardian. Upon his death, a successor was to be selected by the clerically dominated Council of Experts. The *ulama* controlled the cabinet and the president of the parliament. The Islamic Republican Party held most of the seats in parliament. Most importantly, because Islamic law had been declared state law, the *ulama,* as traditional interpreters and guardians of the *Shariah,* controlled the Supreme Judicial Council, which oversaw the judiciary. They filled political posts or appointed those committed to their theocratic, ideological interpretation. A Ministry of Islamic Guidance oversaw the press and media."[277]

Imagine the shock that the Western world experienced when it saw what came out of this unprecedented Islamic revolution. The Iran of the 1970s had the immense support of Western powers and appeared to be well on its way toward modernization, stabilization, and Westernization, led by an enlightened and progressive Shah. Suddenly, all of that was swept aside, not by a war or financial crisis but merely a series of popular revolts led by clerics calling for a return to the days of the Prophet Muhammad. In a matter of months, all aspects of the government, media, judiciary, and education were managed and controlled by the *ulama,* and politicians and officials who went against Khomeini's doctrines were harassed, exiled, and arrested. History was rewritten to promote Iran's Islamic roots, and the country's pre-Islamic culture and heritage were veiled or destroyed. The Council for Cultural Revolution was established to oversee higher education curricula, and Islamic dress codes were strictly enforced.[278] In the years that followed the revolution that had roused millions and given hope to the entire

---

[277] Ibid., 205-206.
[278] Ibid., 207.

country, the power of the clerics was cemented.

As one of the epochal events of the century, the effects of the Iranian Revolution were not solely constrained within the country's borders. A major foreign policy objective of the new Iranian state that was even written in the new constitution was "to perpetuate the revolution both at home and abroad."[279] As previously mentioned, Iran wished to build and strengthen an ideal Islamic society within its borders first, then replicate this model elsewhere in the world. Thus, the country engaged in persistent attempts to export the revolution to neighboring countries, attempts that still continue in earnest today.

Since Iran is an unmistakably Shi'a country, this caused some tension with certain neighbors and intensified regional rivalries and instability. For starters, the Iranian Revolution inaugurated a period of Islamic fundamentalism and revivalism that had already been underway in other Muslim countries, and Iran's experience resonated with many other countries of the region where Muslims were feeling lost in their quest for identity, frustrated with the lack of economic grievances, and indignant about the degree of foreign influence and intervention in their countries' politics and economy. A cleric whose entire life experience revolved around Islamic studies and theological colleges and who had no measurable knowledge of state governance had ousted a monarch put in place by Western powers and established an Islamic state. In the eyes of those with revolutionary and political Islamist beliefs, the Iranian Revolution was an event that enhanced Islamic fundamentalism as a viable alternative ideology for opposition against and overthrow of a long-established regime, and its success in Iran confirmed the failure of the secular state model and proved the power of Islam. They increasingly believed their religion was capable of overthrowing an entire system that was backed by the West, achieving what secular ideologies like Marxism and Leninism had mostly failed to do.

As a result, Iran became the concrete example of progress and independence as achieved through Islam. From Lebanon to Palestine, Senegal to Malaysia, and even in Muslim communities in Europe, there was an identifiable surge in Islamist enthusiasm inspired by the Iranian experience. However, despite Iranian efforts to export its version of Islamic fundamentalism to other Arab and Muslim countries, and despite some Sunnis' acceptance of the victory attained by the Shi'ite *ulama* in Iran, the Iranian regime's inability to provide sufficient material and economic support prevented the full application of Iran's revolutionary ideology in other countries.[280] The Iranian ideology also found a rival in Saudi Arabia, as the official state religion of Saudi Arabia, Wahhabism, was being propagated and exported by Saudis across the region as well. The wealthy oil kingdom seemingly had an unlimited amount of funds to establish Wahhabi *madrasas* (schools) and send clerics all across the region. Nonetheless, the Iranian experience did inspire and radicalize a large segment of the Middle East, and

---

[279] Ibid., 208.
[280] Emmanuel Sivan, "Sunni Radicalism in the Middle East and the Iranian Revolution," *International Journal of Middle East Studies* 21, no. 1 (February 1989): 22.

traditionally stable Gulf countries like Kuwait and Bahrain were also impacted and experienced unrest.

The Iranian government's goal of exporting its brand of Islam severely impacted its neighboring country, Iraq, due not only to the geographical proximity and Khomeini's work in Najaf but also to the fact that Iraq had a sizable and long-persecuted Shi'a population. The country's majority Shi'a population had been chafing under the oppression of the Sunni-dominated regime of Saddam Hussein. For his part, Saddam decided to take advantage of the instability and chaos that immediately followed the revolution in neighboring Iran. With the pretext of a territorial dispute, on September 22, 1980, Saddam Hussein sent his forces across the border to invade Iran, triggering a grueling eight-year war that devastated both countries and severely destabilized the region. Though Saddam claimed the war was instigated by a dispute over the Shatt al-Arab waterway between the two countries, in truth, Hussein's Sunni regime undoubtedly felt threatened by the Shi'a revolution that had brought down an entire dynasty and installed a Shi'a republic.[281] For his part, Ayatollah Khomeini called on the Iraqi people to revolt and realize their own Islamic revolution, clearly speaking to the oppressed majority Shi'a population.

In the end, the war ended with no Islamic revolution in Iraq, and none of the issues raised between the countries were resolved, but the war sparked fear among the monarchies of the Arabian Peninsula and Persian Gulf, many of which ruled over a sizable and disgruntled Shi'a population. The consequences of the war were dire for Iran as well, not just in terms of casualties but also material and economic costs. Iran acknowledged that nearly 300,000 people died, while an estimated 160,000 to 240,000 Iraqis perished in the war.[282] One journalist wrote, "Few modern conflicts have been so long, so bloody and so futile."[283]

However, the eight-year war did give some time for the Iranian regime to regroup and rethink. The war provided an excuse for some of the economic problems the country was experiencing, and popular support was mobilized for the government and against the enemy. The eventual failure to achieve victory and the immense human and financial toll the war had on the Iranian economy led to public dissent as the war came to an end, but the Iranian government realized it could no longer simply rely on repression and control, so it changed tactics to improve its domestic and international image and regain the support of at least some segments of the population. Post-war Iran engaged in a massive campaign of reconstruction and reestablishing relations with foreign countries, including the West, and as the Iran-Iraq War ended, many were calling for the normalization of relations with the West. Between August 1988 and February 1989, diplomatic contact between Iran and the West increased, and "Iran seemed intent upon

---

[281] Roger Hardy, "The Iran-Iraq War: 25 Years On," *BBC News,* September 22, 2005, http://news.bbc.co.uk/2/hi/middle_east/4260420.stm.

[282] "Iran-Iraq War (1980-1988)," *Global Security,* http://www.globalsecurity.org/military/world/war/iran-iraq.htm.

[283] Hardy, "The Iran-Iraq War: 25 Years On."

improving its international image at the United Nations and in other international contexts."[284]

On June 5, 1989, a decade after the Iranian Revolution, Ayatollah Ruhollah Khomeini died. The people wept, the streets were filled with mourning processions, and for several weeks, the government came to a standstill. A scholar wrote in 1992, "Three years after his departure, Iran's political future remains uncertain. And so does the fate of the Ayatollah Khomeini's vision of an ideal and untied Islamic community."[285] Today, more than three decades since the revolution, this statement remains true; Iran continues to struggle with juggling its Khomeinist roots, its Islamic foundation, and the politics of a modern world.

Due to the unprecedented religious nature of the revolution, Iran is now seen as a model Islamic state by many across the region, and it is a leader in regional and global politics, economy, and security. Its revolutionary past and its political Islamic character still thrive, but its ambitions in the Middle East have also led to the country's practice of realpolitik. Iran has been known to be a significant sponsor of Shi'a militant groups like Hezbollah, but it is also aligned with the Sunni group Hamas, and it is a key supporter of the Alawite regime of Bashar Assad in Syria. Iran has gradually become one of the biggest regional powers in the Middle East, especially in the last decade as it has built up its foreign reserves and advanced its nuclear program. As the scholar Barry Rubin wrote, Iran's growing power is going to become "the most dangerous situation that the world will face in the coming years," a world in which Iran plays an undeniably central political, economic, religious, and ideological role.[286]

Given the influence of Iran today, it could be argued that no other individual or event during the second half of the 20th century changed a nation and the world as significantly as did Khomeini and his revolution. *Time* portrayed Ayatollah Khomeini's victory as a global threat so immense that it may change "the world balance of power more than any political event since Hitler's conquest of Europe."[287] Even decades later, the Iranian Revolution's effects reverberate across the region and the globe and still cause rifts in political alliances and realignments in social and religious orders. All of that ensures the Iranian Revolution continues to be a topic of study and fascination.

Online Resources

Other books about ancient history by Charles River Editors

---

[284] Esposito, *Islam and Politics,* 210.
[285] Shireen T. Hunter, *Iran After Khomeini* (New York: Praeger, 1992), 1.
[286] Barry Rubin, "Iran: The Rise of Regional Power," *Middle East Review of International Affairs* 10, no. 3 (September 2006): 151.
[287] "Man of the Year: The Mystic Who Lit the Fires of Hatred," *TIME,* January 7, 1980, http://content.time.com/time/magazine/article/0,9171,923854,00.html.

Other books about the Persian Empires on Amazon

Other books about the Sassanid Empire on Amazon

Further Reading

The Achaemenid Empire

Briant, Pierre. "Alexander". Encyclopaedia Iranica. vol. 3. Routledge & Kegan Paul.

Kuhrt, Amélie (2013). The Persian Empire: A Corpus of Sources from the Achaemenid Period. Routledge. ISBN 978-1-136-01694-3.

Howe, Timothy; Reames, Jeanne (2008). Macedonian Legacies: Studies in Ancient Macedonian History and Culture in Honor of Eugene N. Borza. Regina Books. ISBN 978-1-930053-56-4.

A. Sh. Shahbazi. ARIARAMNEIA. vol. 2. Encyclopaedia Iranica (Routledge & Kegan Paul).

Schmitt, Rüdiger. "Achaemenid dynasty". Encyclopaedia Iranica. vol. 3. Routledge & Kegan Paul.

Schlerath, Bernfried (1973). Die Indogermanen. Inst. f. Vergl. Sprachwiss. ISBN 3-85124-516-4.

Tavernier, Jan (2007). Iranica in the Achaemenid Period (ca. 550-330 BCE): Linguistic Study of Old Iranian Proper Names and Loanwords, Attested in Non-Iranian Texts. Peeters Publishers. ISBN 90-429-1833-0.

Stronach, David "Darius at Pasargadae: A Neglected Source for the History of Early Persia," Topoi

Stronach, David "Anshan and Parsa: Early Achaemenid History, Art and Architecture on the Iranian Plateau". In: John Curtis, ed., Mesopotamia and Iran in the Persian Period: Conquest and Imperialism 539–331, 35–53. London: British Museum Press 1997.

Wiesehöfer, Josef. "History in pre-Islamic period". Encyclopaedia Iranica.

Wiesehöfer, Josef (2001). Ancient Persia. Translated by Azizeh Azodi. London, New York: I.B. Tauris. ISBN 1-86064-675-1. There have been a number of editions since 1996.

Curtis; Nigel Tallis, eds. (2005). Forgotten Empire: The World of Ancient Persia. Berkeley and Los Angeles: University of California Press. ISBN 0-520-24731-0. |first1= missing |last1= in Authors list (help) A collection of articles by different authors.

Pierre Briant (January 2002). From Cyrus to Alexander: a history of the Persian Empire. ISBN 978-1-57506-031-6.

The Greco-Persian Wars, Peter Green

Philip Souza (2003-01-25). The Greek and Persian Wars 499-386 BC. Osprey Publishing. ISBN 978-1-84176-358-3.

The Heritage of Persia, Richard N. Frye

History of the Persian Empire, A.T. Olmstead

The Persian Empire, Lindsay Allen

The Persian Empire, J.M. Cook

Persian Fire: The First World Empire and the Battle for the West, Tom Holland

Pictorial History of Iran: Ancient Persia Before Islam 15000 BCE–625 A.D., Amini Sam

Timelife Persians: Masters of the Empire (Lost Civilizations)

M. A. Dandamaev (1989). A Political History of the Achaemenid Empire. Brill Academic Pub. ISBN 978-90-04-09172-6.

Hallock, R., Persepolis Fortification Tablets

Chopra, R.M., an article on "A Brief Review of Pre-Islamic Splendour of Iran", INDO-IRANICA, Vol.56 (1–4), 2003.

Sideris, A. "Achaemenid Toreutics in the Greek Periphery", in Darabandi S. M. R. and A. Zournantzi (eds.), Ancient Greece and Ancient Iran. Cross-Cultural Encounters, Athens 2008, pp. 339–353.

Wilber, Donald Newton. (1989). Persepolis: The Archaeology of Parsa, Seat of the Persian Kings. Darwin Press. Revised edition ISBN 0-87850-062-6.

The Parthian Empire

Bleeck, Arthur Henry. 2005. *Avesta: The Religious Books of the Parsees from Professor Speigel's German Translation of the Original Manuscripts*. Lexington, Kentucky: Eilbron Classics.

Boyce, Mary. 2001. *Zoroastrians: Their Religious Beliefs and Practices*. London: Routledge.

———, ed. and trans. 1990. *Textual Sources for the Study of Zoroastrianism*. Chicago: University of Chicago Press.

Brosius, Maria. 2010. *The Persians: An Introduction*. London: Routledge.

Cassius Dio. 1954. *Roman History*. Translated by Earnest Cary. Cambridge, Massachusetts: Harvard University Press.

Clark, Peter. 2001. *Zoroastrianism: An Introduction to an Ancient Faith*. Brighton, United Kingdom: Sussex Academic Press.

Colledge, Malcolm A.R. 1967. *The Parthians*. London: Thames and Hudson.

Herodotus. 2003. *The Histories*. Translated by Aubrey de Sélincourt. London: Penguin Books.

Lightfoot, C.S. 1990. "Trajan's Parthian War and the Fourth-Century Perspective." *Journal of Roman Studies* 80: 115-126.

Plutarch. 1968. *Lives*. Edited and translated by Bernadotte Perrin. Cambridge, Massachusetts: Harvard University Press.

Rostovtzeff, M. 1943. "The Parthian Shot." *American Journal of Archaeology* 47: 174-187.

Strabo. 2001. *Geography*. Translated by Horace Leonard Jones. Cambridge, Massachusetts: Harvard University Press.

Suetonius. 2007. *The Twelve Caesars*. Translated by Robert Graves. London: Penguin Books.

Tacitus. 1962. *The Annals*. Translated by John Jackson. Cambridge, Massachusetts: Harvard University Press.

Thorley, J. 1971. "The Silk Trade between China and the Roman Empire at Its Heights." *Greece and Rome* 18: 71-80.

Temin, Peter. "The Economy of the Early Roman Empire." *Journal of Economic Perspectives* 20 (2006): 133-151.

Wenke, Robert J. 1981. "Elymeans, Parthians, and the Evolution of Empires in Southwestern Iran." *Journal of the American Oriental Society* 101: 303-315.

The Sassanid Empire

Bleeck, Arthur Henry. 2005. *Avesta: The Religious Books of the Parsees from Professor Speigel's German Translation of the Original Manuscripts*. Lexington, Kentucky:

Eilbron Classics.

Boyce, Mary. 2001. *Zoroastrians: Their Religious Beliefs and Practices*. London: Routledge.

————, ed. and trans. 1990. *Textual Sources for the Study of Zoroastrianism*. Chicago: University of Chicago Press.

Brosius, Maria. 2010. *The Persians: An Introduction*. London: Routledge.

Cassius Dio. 1954. *Roman History*. Translated by Earnest Cary. Cambridge, Massachusetts: Harvard University Press.

Charles, R. H., trans. 2007. *The Chronicle of John, Bishop of Nikiu: Translated from Zotenberg's Ethiopic Text*. Merchantville, New Jersey: Evolution Publishing.

Clark, Peter. 2001. *Zoroastrianism: An Introduction to an Ancient Faith*. Brighton, United Kingdom: Sussex Academic Press.

Frendo, David. 2008. "Religious Minorities and Religious Dissent in the Byzantine and Sasanian   Empire." *Bulletin of the Asia Institute* 22: 223-237.

Herodotus. 2003. *The Histories*. Translated by Aubrey de Sélincourt. London: Penguin Books.

Julian. 1913. *The Works of the Emperor Julian*. Translated by Wilmer Cave Wright. Cambridge,   Massachusetts: Harvard University Press.

Lee, A. D. 1991. "The Role of Hostages in Roman Diplomacy with Sasanian Persia." *Historia: Zeitschrift für Alte Geschichte* 40: 366-374.

Malandra, William W. 1983. *An Introduction to Ancient Iranian Religion: Readings from the Avesta and the Achaemenid Inscriptions*. Minneapolis: University of Minnesota Press.

Procopius of Caesarea. 1916. *History of the Wars*. Translated by H.B. Dewing. London: William   Heinemann.

Sprengling, M. 1940. "Kartīr, Founder of Sasanian Zoroastrianism." *American Journal of SemiticLanguages and Literatures* 57: 197-228.

Made in the USA
Las Vegas, NV
15 February 2025

18212565R00181